THE COMPLETE BOOK OF
Fly Fishing

SECOND EDITION

THE COMPLETE BOOK OF
Fly Fishing

SECOND EDITION

Tom McNally

with illustrations by Tom Beecham

Ragged Mountain Press
Camden, Maine

The McGraw·Hill Companies

1 2 13 14 15 16 17 18 19 20 DOC DOC 0 9 8 7 6 5 4

Questions regarding the content of this book should be
addressed to:
Ragged Mountain Press
P.O. Box 220
Camden, Maine 04843

Questions regarding the ordering of this book should
be addressed to:
The McGraw-Hill Companies
Customer Service Department
P.O. Box 547
Blacklick, OH 43004
Retail Customers: 1-800-262-4729
Bookstores: 1-800-722-4726

For every book sold, Ragged Mountain Press will
make a contribution to an environmental cause.

The Complete Book of Fly Fishing is printed on 60-
pound Renew Opaque Vellum, which con-
tains 50 percent waste paper (preconsumer)
and 10 percent postconsumer waste paper.

Library of Congress Cataloging-in-Publication Data
McNally, Tom.
    The complete book of fly fishing / Tom
        McNally. -- 2nd ed.
        p.   cm.
    Rev. ed. of: Fly fishing. 1978.
    ISBN 0-07-045638-0 (alk. paper)
    1. Fly fishing. I. McNally, Tom. Fly fishing.
II. Title. III. Title: Fly Fishing.
SH456. M36   1993b
799. 1' 2--dc20   93-9152
                                                         CIP

Printed by R.R. Donnelley, Crawfordsville, IN
Typeset by Farrar Associates, White Horse Beach, MA
Designed by Joyce C. Weston
Production by Janet Robbins
Edited by J.R. Babb, Pamela Benner,
    Dorathy Chocensky
Photo processing by Joe Grobarek
Unless otherwise noted, all photographs were taken
    by Tom McNally and Bob McNally.

To Phyllis
. . . and to Bob, the late A. J. McClane,
and the late Joe Brooks—four
who contributed the most
to the enjoyment of my fly-fishing years.

Contents

Foreword

Late one afternoon when the tide was ebbing at Chub Cay, Tom McNally hooked a tailing bonefish that I would have given a hundred-to-one odds he'd never bring to net. It was not only a big fish, but we were in a small mangrove-studded "lake" containing more roots than water. That bonefish ran into, through, and around one bush after another with such speed that Tom's fly line literally ripped across the surface. There's not much anybody can do to stop that awesome first run into the backing. The maestro didn't panic, however; he simply followed the fish, untangling his line from each obstacle until finally he was "out of the woods" and in open water, where he subdued the 10-pounder. A bonefish of that size on the fly is not an everyday event, even without running an obstacle course. Maybe there was an element of luck involved, but the performance was pure McNally—making the impossible look like something he did all his life.

If there's one word that describes Tom McNally, it's Izaak Walton's term "compleat." He has mastered many skills, including billiards, shooting, fly casting, boxing, golf, and archery. That Tom would face Minnesota Fats across a pool table, hunt Africa's big game with a bow and arrow, or turn pro boxer barely scratches the surface of his multifaceted career. Above all, he is a skilled journalist who follows outdoor sports in all seasons and in all parts of the world. His syndicated columns command a wide and devoted audience, and his previous books, annuals, and magazine articles have been nationally acclaimed.

Since this is a book on fly fishing, let me tell you about Tom McNally's skill with a fly rod. Without doubt, he is one of the most talented fly fishermen I have seen at work—from Bahamian bonefish flats to the cold rivers of the Arctic.

Fly fishing is ordinarily done in an erect position; the higher you are over the water, the easier it is to cast. Yet, there are times when an angler must kneel, squat, crawl, sit, or lean chest-deep in a roaring river.

These off-balance postures require absolute line control, and laying out a full length of line from any one of them is the hallmark of a master. Some years ago, this kind of handicap casting was even incorporated into international competition in what was known as the Little River Event; it defeated some of the world's great platform artists.

Once on a mirror-calm lake I watched Tom McNally sit in a seatless aluminum pram about the size of a washtub and shoot a fly at cruising trout. I don't know of any tougher test for the classic caster than being immobilized from coccyx to toes in a buttocks-on-deck, legs-out position. It's like playing Wimbledon in a pair of swim fins. The entire burden of maintaining line speed is now between rod hand and elbow. From where I was lunching on the bank, Tom's casting could be described as a mere flick of the rod, which sent his taper rolling high in a tight loop before it sailed forward—dead on target. The fact that McNally caught fish was less impressive than his throwing line a country mile without creating tidal waves in that tippy boat. Only an expert can make it look easy.

I doubt if there are many places Tom McNally hasn't fished, nor many species of game fish he hasn't caught on-fly, yet after more than forty years of angling, his enthusiasm has not flagged but accelerated.

There will always be room for another book on fly fishing. This one will not clutter your mind with peripheral information. McNally is not a peripheral writer; he goes right to the heart of a subject. Whether it be choosing the right rod, fishing the dry fly, or casting for tarpon, he speaks with the authority of an expert who has honed and polished his skills to a fine edge.

A. J. McClane
Palm Beach, Florida

AUTHOR'S NOTE: A. J. (Al) McClane died of cancer at his home in Palm Beach, Florida, on December 20, 1991. He was sixty-nine.

For thirty-five years McClane was angling editor of *Field & Stream* magazine. He authored more than twenty-five books on fishing and on fish and game cookery, including the all-time classic, *McClane's New Standard Fishing Encyclopedia*. He was the most talented all-around angler and angling writer I ever knew.

Preface
to Second Edition

BEGIN at the beginning" is a truism whose origin is lost in time, but for those swept away on fly fishing's newest wave of popularity it's a truism worthy of contemplation, so I'll say it again: "Begin at the beginning."

Piscator non solum piscatur—there is more to fishing than catching fish. Dame Juliana Berners wrote those words five hundred years ago, and she was talking about fly fishing. Its beauty, complexity, and elegance make fly fishing unmatched as a restorative nostrum for those afflicted by the pressure and mundanity of Modern Life. Small wonder the world's streams and rivers, lakes and ponds, bays and estuaries are newly dotted with false-casting anglers, freshly attired in and equipped with the Best and Latest. Too bad so many catch so few fish. Perhaps it's because they didn't. . . .

Begin at the beginning.

For me, Beginning was a fly-rod-waving family and a book called, in the gender-exclusive idiom of the middle Eisenhower era, *Fishing for Boys*, by a gentleman named Tom McNally.

Tom McNally is a gentleman of the old school—a consummate fisherman, an outdoor writer of rare ability, unequalled in the breadth and depth of his knowledge and his ability to communicate The Beginning—and for that matter the middle and the end—to the uninitiated. He was so recognized by his peers, among them perhaps the greatest outdoor writers ever assembled between two covers: A. J. McClane, Ted Trueblood, Warren Page, Robert Ruark, Corey Ford, H. G. Tapply, Ed Zern.

In his years as midwestern editor of *Field & Stream*, and as outdoor editor of the *Chicago Tribune*, Tom McNally wrote more than 4,500 articles, 10,000 newspaper columns, and 26 books, including a number that were literally and figuratively bibles. The first edition of this book, *Fly Fishing*, was published in a valley in the sine wave of fly-fishing history, falling between a generation on the wane and one in ascendancy. When *Fly Fishing* was published, only one struggling magazine devoted exclusively to fly fishing existed. Imagine that.

Now there are *eight* fly-fishing magazines, and McNally is back with *The Complete Book of Fly Fishing*, Second Edition. It covers every aspect of fly fishing—from trout to tarpon, bonefish to bluegills, marlin to mackerel. And it contains those rarest of qualities in today's technological fishing literature: simplicity and wisdom.

I had the rare privilege of editing this edition in Tom McNally's family room—a short walk from Montana's Madison River and an even shorter walk from Tom's pool table. About halfway through it suddenly dawned on me just how little I actually knew about the whole subject of fly fishing, despite nearly 40 years' experience. Right on cue, McNally turned to me and said, "I didn't know I *knew* this much about fly fishing." He does, though, and it's all here—nearly fifty years of fly-fishing experience distilled to fit between two covers.

For those of you in the beginning, middle, or end of your fishing career, who love the elegance and rich complexity of the long rod and its unequalled ability to catch fish of whatever species, and who aspire to fish *well* with the fly, this book is your friend and companion.

James R. Babb
Ragged Mountain Press
Camden, Maine

Introduction

IN 1653 Izaak Walton took pen in hand and, on parched paper, suggested that all of us "Be quiet, and go a-Angling." Surely when Walton scratched out that simple line, he had fly angling in mind. No matter where practiced, when, or by whom, no other form of fishing offers the challenge, frustration, provocation, stimulation, intoxication, fascination, excitation, tranquility—and base rewards—of fly fishing.

Fly fishing is the world's most captivating form of angling. It is the *only* fishing that totally captures the souls and *brains* of intelligent people, and imprisons them for their lifetimes. A fly fisherman is a fly fisherman is *always* a fly fisherman. I propose that the serious fisherman who goes through life without taking up fly fishing—in whichever of its varied forms—denies himself the really meaningful pleasures of angling.

Fly fishing is difficult. That is not to say that fly fishing is not for everyone, because it assuredly is. But compared to most forms of fishing, fly fishing isn't something you just go out and do. To become a skilled, all-round fly angler takes time. It requires dedication, effort, and experience. There is little of the element of "fisherman's luck" in the continuing successes of a fly fisherman.

Fly-fishing tackle is far more complicated than most fishing gear. The rod must be right for the fishing or casting job at hand; the line must properly match the rod; the leader must be correctly designed; and the fly or bug used should as nearly as possible represent the natural fish food that is present.

Becoming an accomplished *fly caster* isn't easy, either. With just a few minutes of instructions a novice may cast reasonably well with a spincast outfit, but few people—no matter how dexterous or quick to learn—can master the niceties of fly casting in a short practice and instructional session. True, with professional direction and practice, a beginner may quickly learn to cast a fly 40 to 60 feet, and to execute some of the simpler casts. But most fly fishermen spend their lives attempting to master all the intricacies of truly skillful fly casting.

To be consistently successful in his pursuit of the various gamefishes, the all-round fly angler must be at least an amateur entomologist, ichthyologist, and meteorologist. In other words, after he has learned the rights and wrongs of tackle selection, and how to cast, the fly fisherman must then know about insects and other natural life forms that fish feed upon; he must have a full understanding of fish and their habits; and he needs to know something about weather and how its extremes can affect the aquatic environment.

In addition to the challenges already mentioned that face the all-round fly fisherman, and the varied skills he must attain, the fly-rod angler by choice elects to pursue fishing methods that provide the highest possible sporting qualities. Like the bowhunter who disdains the high-powered rifle, the fly fisherman often deliberately underarms himself.

The trout fisherman, for example, at times will take hefty fish on leaders whose tips will snap at a pull of less than a pound, and on diminutive flies that may be no larger than a match head. The salmon angler may choose a wispy rod 6 feet long, weighing a mere 1½ ounces, to subdue Atlantics of 20 pounds or more. And the saltwater fly angler will face the awesome runs of bonefish, in which 300 feet of line may burn off the reel; the spectacular leaps of tarpon, in which rough gill plates and heavy scales abrade the leader; or the shocking strength and unstoppable drive of sailfish, in which his tackle and prowess at playing fish—plus plain damn good luck—are tested to their extremes.

The fly fisherman, with his long, light rod, gossamer leaders, and delicate flies, is the epitome of sports fishing. His skill represents the pinnacle of the angler's art.

Fly fishing, however, has a practical purpose and can be deadly efficient.

Fly fishing is practical because it is generally the best means of presenting to fish small artificials that represent a large portion of the smaller food forms upon which fish feed. Nymphs, which are the larval stage of aquatic insects, are best imitated by artificial flies, as are all other natural insects. Streamer flies are readily mistaken by all game fish as real minnows, and fly-rod surface bugs do a good job of representing frogs, wounded minnows, grasshoppers, locusts, and the like. In salt water, no other lure better fools wily bonefish and permit into striking than an artificial fly-rod shrimp, and certainly small streamers with tinsel or Mylar tied in do a good job of representing glass minnows, which many saltwater fish relish.

Under many circumstances, no other form of fishing will be as efficient as fly fishing. When there is a hatch of natural insects over a trout stream, for example, and the trout are rising, only the fly angler will do a workmanlike job of taking fish. Much of the time a fly fisherman is more capable of presenting his lures well, and fishing them more tantalizingly or realistically, than are anglers using bait-casting, spinning, or spin-cast gear.

In situations where the water is shallow and clear, and the fish spooky, fly fishing often can be the most successful method. A skilled fly fisherman who approaches cautiously and casts delicately can deliver his fly or bug with far less disturbance than can the angler casting heavier artificials.

Nowadays the opportunities for good fly fishing are almost endless. Countless trout streams, for instance, are set aside by state conservation departments for "Fly Fishing Only." Modern hatchery methods are improving the numbers and quality of fish to be stocked in fly-fishing areas, and there are even fishing camps now catering only to fly fishermen.

Saltwater fly fishing has come of age. I remember years ago boarding Chesapeake Bay charter boats for striped bass fishing and being laughed into a corner for bringing aboard fly rods; now, fly fishing in the bay for stripers is routine. I also remember a day years ago off Ocean City, Maryland, with Captain Jim Whaley, bringing up the first white marlin ever hooked on a fly; now, taking billfish on flies is nothing unusual.

Fly fishing is accepted now, and guides, boat captains, and fishing camp operators *in all areas* assist and cooperate with fly anglers—almost regardless of the species of fish sought.

And, of course, fly fishing is not restricted to one type of water, or to a specific part of the country, or the world. The fly fisherman practices his art in brook, stream, and river; in pond and lake; in tidal estuary, salty bay, and ocean blue. The whole world of fish-filled water is the fly angler's beat.

It should be pointed out here that no single volume can present all there is to fly fishing. The sport is too great, the average printed text far too small. It is my hope, however, that *The Complete Book of Fly Fishing* will interest and reward the novice and experienced fly fisherman alike. If it shortens the time between rises and brings more violent strikes, I'll consider this modest effort partially successful. If, however, it instills in the reader a greater love for fly fishing, then no better reward is possible for the time spent in writing it.

Tom McNally
Ennis, Montana

1
About Fly Fishing

A S MIGHT be expected, the exact origins of fly fishing are clouded in the mists of time, but it is known to be one of the oldest, if not *the* oldest, forms of sport fishing. In the third century A.D., the writer Aelian described a "Macedonian way of catching fish," which probably were trout, on artificial flies fashioned of wool and feathers. In the late 1400s, fly fishing was discussed in the essay "The Treatise of Fishing with an Angle," which most historians credit to Dame Juliana Berners. Izaak Walton wrote of fly fishing in his *The Compleat Angler*, first published in 1653.

The initial writers on fly fishing were concerned almost exclusively with trout, but gave some attention to "the graylings and salmons." Among the early authors who contributed importantly to fly fishing's progress were Charles Cotton (1676), Alfred Ronald (1836), Frederick Halford (1844), Frank Forrester (1850), Theodore Gordon (1903), G. E. M. Skues (1910), George LaBranche (1914), and Ray Bergman (1938).

It is amazing what knowledge, angling skill, and intense interest were possessed by our fly-fishing pioneers. One of my treasures is a copy of Frank Forrester's *Fish and Fishing* (revised, 1866), which includes a section on fly fishing. Forrester wrote:

Fly fishing may well be considered the most beautiful of all rural sports. For, in addition to the great nicety required to become proficient in the art, it is also absolutely requisite, for its successful attainment, to study much and long—how to adapt and blend the various materials used in the construction of a fly; how to construct the fly on certain defined rules; and, lastly, how to select your flies, thus carefully and correctly constructed, in accordance with the state of the sky, the color of the water, and the peculiar habits of the fish in different rivers.

Ernest H. Peckinpaugh, of Chattanooga, Tennessee, who died in 1947, is credited with fashioning the first bass bug sometime in the early 1900s. Peckinpaugh took bass, and panfish too, on his fly-rod

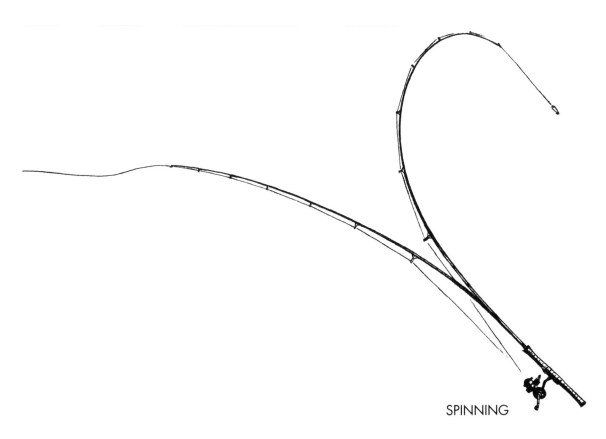

SPINNING

popping bugs, and that kind of freshwater action is probably what got fly fishing really on its way.

After World War II saltwater fly fishing started to grow tremendously in popularity; but there were hundreds of fishermen prior to that who were stripping their flies through salt water with good results. American (white) shad were being taken by fly fishermen in the Maryland portion of the Susquehanna River in the late 1800s. One of my first mentors in saltwater fly fishing, Tom Loving, of Pasadena, Maryland, who died in the 1950s, caught Chesapeake Bay striped bass on bucktail streamers as early as 1923.

The most recent innovation in saltwater fly fishing is the taking of billfish on flies and bugs. Dr. Webster Robinson, of Key West, Florida, who died in 1966, reportedly was the first to catch a billfish on regulation fly tackle in a regulation manner—that is, casting to the fish, retrieving the fly, landing the fish without improper assistance, and so on. Robinson's catch, a 74½-pound Pacific sailfish, was made off Panama in 1961. (I lost a white marlin, on-fly, off the Maryland coast during gaffing in September 1954. But lost fish are just that—*lost fish*.) Lee Cuddy of Miami caught the first on-fly Atlantic sailfish of record in 1964, a fine 47-pounder.

Since the early catches of billfish, dozens of fly-rodders have registered legiti-

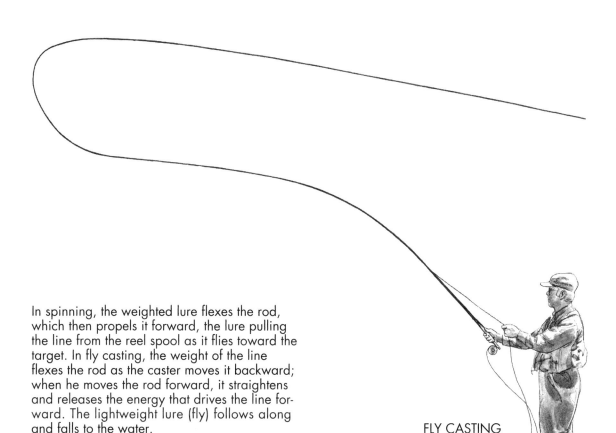

In spinning, the weighted lure flexes the rod, which then propels it forward, the lure pulling the line from the reel spool as it flies toward the target. In fly casting, the weight of the line flexes the rod as the caster moves it backward; when he moves the rod forward, it straightens and releases the energy that drives the line forward. The lightweight lure (fly) follows along and falls to the water.

FLY CASTING

mate takes of Pacific sailfish, and other billfish species as well.

WHAT'S DIFFERENT ABOUT FLY FISHING?

Fly-fishing tackle differs considerably from other tackle. In all other forms of casting—spinning, spin casting, bait casting—the weight of the propelled lure pulls the line after it. In fly casting the weight of the line furnishes the momentum to carry the lure, or fly. The lure merely rides along, attached to a nylon leader that is tied to the end of the fly line. In fly casting it is the *line* that is cast. The heavy line "works" the rod as the caster moves the rod back and forth.

The line is sized and designed to work the rod. On the backcast the line extends straight behind the caster, bending and "loading" the rod. When the rod straightens and flexes forward, with an assist from the caster, it releases the energy that drives the line forward to the target. The lure follows along and lights on the water.

Fly rods are generally long and whippy compared to other kinds of rods, and there's a big difference in reels, too. In other casting methods, when the rod is flexed and the lure flies out, the lure pulls line from the reel. In fly casting, however, the reel contributes nothing to the cast. It merely furnishes storage space for the bulky fly line and usually some backing

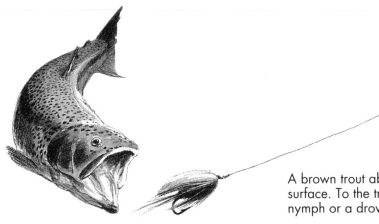

A brown trout about to hit a wet fly beneath the surface. To the trout, the fly may resemble a nymph or a drowned insect.

A trout rising to hit a dry fly it mistakes for an aquatic insect on the surface of the water.

line. Except for some of the expensive, heavy-duty reels, most fly reels are simple little mechanisms compared to bait-casting and spinning reels, which are complicated miniature winches that contribute not only to every cast but also to the playing, or fighting, of hooked fish. Nevertheless, it pays to pick a reel carefully, for reasons we'll discuss in Chapter 3.

FLIES AND BUGS

The "lures" used in fly fishing, which more properly are called flies or bugs, in most respects are far more natural, more lifelike, more genuine representatives of real insects or minnows than are the plugs, spoons, and jigs commonly used in other kinds of fishing.

The streamer, another type of underwater fly, is tied to resemble various types of minnows found in lakes and streams.

A popping bug attracts a bass to the surface. Bugs are made of cork or light wood and can be cast with a fly rod. They are effective on many freshwater and salt-water fish.

In strict terminology, all "lures" used in fly fishing are either artificial flies of one kind or another, or bugs. (Metal spinners, spoons, and similar hardware, in the minds of most fly anglers, are not a part of true fly fishing, even if used with a fly rod, fly line, and fly reel.)

Since there are tens of thousands of artificial flies and bugs used in all of the various forms of fly fishing (for trout, bass, saltwater species, etc.), it is no simple task to attempt to classify flies and bugs, and it is virtually impossible to identify all of them.

Strictly speaking, in my opinion *all* artificial flies fall into one of two categories: *wet* or *dry*. *Bugs* should be a third and distinct category, because they are totally different from flies. By way of definition, a wet fly is *any* fly that sinks beneath the surface. A dry fly is *any* fly that floats. A bug is *any* surface floater (usually of comparatively large size), often made of cork or light wood, and meant to suggest a frog, locust, or mouse, rather than a small fly that has fallen to the surface.

Bugs, which so often are called, incorrectly, "bass bugs" (they can be used effectively on northern pike, muskies, ladyfish, or tarpon), may be of various types: popping, sliding, or skipping, floating-diving, or a hair bug type.

To the basic categories of wet flies, dry flies, and bugs, we might add *steelhead flies*, *salmon flies*, and *saltwater flies*. These are specialized flies intended for specific kinds of fly fishing. Salmon flies include wet and dry patterns, while saltwater flies include wet (underwater) patterns and floating bugs.

As the name implies, steelhead flies are made primarily for West Coast sea-run rainbow trout, or steelhead. Most steelhead flies are brightly colored, and since steelhead usually hug river bottoms, steelhead flies are generally tied on heavy, short-shank hooks.

Salmon flies are designed chiefly for fishing Atlantic salmon. Like steelhead patterns, the majority of the salmon patterns are gaudy, made of brilliantly colored materials, and they're the most expensive flies you can buy because they are difficult to make.

There is quite a variety of saltwater flies, and new types are being made all the time, some with special purposes. Bonefish flies, for example, are smallish—seldom tied on hooks larger than 1/0—while tarpon flies are considerably larger, rarely tied on hooks smaller than 1/0. All saltwater flies are tied on heavy, strong hooks. Saltwater flies are meant to imitate a variety of marine life. They may represent minnows, shrimp, crabs, small eels, squid—anything that may be important in the gamefish's diet.

Streamer flies are a kind of wet fly that is used for all kinds of fish—from panfish to sailfish. These underwater flies are long and narrow, tied on long-shank hooks, and generally meant to imitate a live minnow or small baitfish. The upper part of a streamer fly, called the *winging*, may be made of hair (such as bucktail, impala, etc.), feathers (the saddle hackles from chickens), or marabou (silky plumes from domestic turkeys). Streamers also are made with combinations of those materials.

The greatest complication in classifying flies is among trout flies. More than any other flies, most trout flies are designed to represent real insects as closely as possible in the various forms of their life cycles. The entomology involved will be discussed in Chapter 10.

GOOD FLY-FISHING SPECIES

Some of the beauty of fly fishing lies in the fact that just about any gamefish can be taken by the fly-rodder. Any fish that feeds on other fish, or on small life forms, will strike a properly presented and worked fly or bug. The only gamefishes really off-limits to the practical fly fisherman are

AMERICAN GRAYLING

BLUEGILL

some of the salty giants (black marlin, for example), and species that habitually hang in very deep water and cannot be reached by standard fly-fishing methods.

Certain species of fish are perfect for the fly fisherman and, in fact, seem to have been created solely for the pleasure of fly anglers. Most notable, of course, are the trouts, whose diet consists chiefly of insect forms readily imitated by the fly fisherman's artificial flies. The Arctic grayling—more correctly known now as the American grayling—is a superior fly-rod fish. Grayling rise so readily to flies that no

NORTHERN PIKE

SHAD

other method of angling will catch more of them.

In my opinion nothing will take largemouth and smallmouth bass—when they are in shallow water—faster than fly-rod popping bugs. I'm also convinced that because of delicate presentation and the "naturalness" of his flies, the fly-rodder will catch more bonefish than anglers spinning or bait casting with other artificial lures.

Lake (common) and Rocky Mountain whitefish feed almost exclusively on minute insects, and again, no one can catch more of them, more quickly, than the fly fisherman. I think a northern pike or muskie, and a tarpon as well, will hit a large streamer fly in preference to any other lure.

TARPON

In addition to the species already named, the list of gamefish that are ideal for fly fishing includes bluegills, crappies, white bass, perch, Arctic char, landlocked and Atlantic salmon, walleyes, chain pickerel, and American and hickory shad in fresh water; and in salt water, amberjack, barracuda, striped bass, bluefish, cobia, dolphin, mackerel, permit, sailfish, snook, sea trout, sharks, and blackfin tuna; and silver (coho) and Chinook (king) salmon in salt or fresh water.

And those are only some of the species that are waiting . . . and willing . . . to hit your flies.

2

Fly Rods

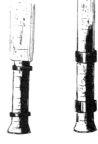

IN AN unsigned column titled "Out-Of-Doors," printed in the April 16, 1910 issue of the *Saturday Evening Post*, the author observed: "There are tastes in fly-rods—indeed, fashions in fly-rods—and stubborn theories regarding them, and into all of these matters intrudes the personal equation, that most mysterious thing in sport. Some men like a whippy rod, some a stiffish one. Some like a soft middle action, while others like all action far out toward the tip, with a lot of backbone, as it is called."

I suspect that the modern angler's likes and dislikes in fly rods are as distinct as were his predecessors' in 1910. One thing that has changed drastically, however, is the choice of rod materials.

ROD MATERIALS

The first fly rods were made of wood—hickory, willow, ash, fir, lancewood, Osage orange, and greenheart. Bamboo became the major rodmaking material after 1850, and the first split-cane fly rod was turned

out by a Pennsylvania craftsman, Sam Phillippe, who built a six-strip rod in 1846.

In the early 1900s some manufacturers turned out rods of solid and tubular steel. The solid-steel rods were heavy, with generally bad actions, and the hollow ones, while lighter and with better actions, were easily broken.

I well remember the appearance of beryllium copper rods in the early 1940s. They had a brief surge of popularity, but beryllium fly rods were heavy, with very slow or "soft" actions, and they were generally considered second-rate by experienced casters, who still preferred quality bamboo rods.

Tastes in rod materials changed drastically, however, following the introduction of glass rods in 1948. The first glass rods were rather poorly designed; they were very limber—the rod's tip could be bent to its butt without breaking—but casting quality was inferior.

Most of the early glass rods were made of solid glass, and some had such soft, whippy actions that anglers referred to them as "wet noodle" rods. Manufacturers kept improving their hollow fiberglass rods, though, and by the mid-1950s, a hundred hollow fiberglass rods were sold for every bamboo stick. The Shakespeare Tackle Company, with its Howald-process hollow fiberglass rods, became an industry leader; the distinctive white glass rods were seen on fly-fishing waters worldwide.

Wood rods, or ones of copper or other metal alloys, generally are no longer made, but many premium-grade rods of bamboo are still available. A lot of fishermen still prefer rods of bamboo for certain fly-fishing situations, and some select bamboo rods for *all* of their fly fishing.

In 1974 another innovation in rod materials was introduced—high-modulus carbon graphite. In 1977, Shakespeare introduced the Ugly Stik—a rod made of a unique blending of graphite and fiberglass. So today we have fly rods of four basic types: bamboo, hollow glass, graphite, and graphite-glass combinations. (For a short time recently some rodmakers offered rods made of boron, but they were expensive and fragile.)

Bamboo

Rods made of split bamboo have exquisite actions—*action* being the manner in which a rod flexes, or bends. Bamboo rods are heavier than hollow glass rods, and most makes can take "sets," or permanent curves. The Orvis Company of Manchester, Vermont, produces high-quality bamboo rods that are impregnated with Bakelite resin or plastic material, greatly reducing the bamboo's tendency to set. I have some thirty-year-old Orvis rods that are as straight today as the day they were made.

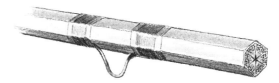

Bamboo rods are made of triangular strips glued together to form a hexagon-shaped blank. Craftsmen once planed the strips by hand, but commercial rodmakers use milling machines.

Impregnated bamboo rods withstand the normally damaging effects of heat and sunlight, extreme cold, and salt water reasonably well, but untreated bamboo rods (only varnished) should be given special care. Varnished bamboo rods must be refinished periodically, while impregnated rods never require refinishing, though with extensive use they will need new guides, wrappings, ferrules, tip-tops, and other fittings.

Hollow Glass

For the budget-minded angler, hollow glass rods are a good buy. They are resilient; can have excellent action; do not take a set; are practically impervious to sun, heat, cold, or salt water; withstand hard use; and, compared to rods of some other materials, are inexpensive.

Most hollow glass fly rods are made by weaving glass fibers into cloth. The fine cloth is cut into patterns, then rolled around a calibrated steel template or tapered wooden dowel. Then it is placed in an oven and receives heat treatment, under pressure, that forms the permanent hollow glass shaft, and the steel mandrel or dowel is removed.

Fly rods of hollow glass are very light,

yet very strong. They can be broken through carelessness (slamming one in a car door), but seldom will one snap under the stresses of casting or playing hooked fish. In general it would be difficult to find a better buy than a hollow glass fly rod, regardless of the manufacturer. Any hollow glass fly rod—from the least to the most expensive—will certainly be well worth its selling price.

Graphite

Carbon graphite has been called the space-age rod material, and graphite fly rods, while expensive, have become very popular. I own a couple dozen graphite fly rods (by Orvis, Heddon, Sage, Shakespeare, Pflueger, and Fenwick) in weights ranging from $1\frac{3}{8}$ to $4\frac{1}{4}$ ounces, and lengths of $6\frac{1}{2}$ to 9 feet. I'm very fond of graphite fly rods, and there is no denying that graphite sticks have characteristics uncommon to bamboo or fiberglass.

Rods made of carbon-graphite fibers are fifty percent lighter than comparable bamboo rods, and at least twenty-five per-

cent lighter than comparable glass rods. Rods of graphite are very strong, too—though they can be broken, like glass or bamboo—and they have actions that make it possible to use a variety of fly-line sizes satisfactorily on a single rod. In other words, the action of a graphite rod usually is not so critical that it must be used with *exactly* the correct size of line.

Without getting too technical here, graphite fly rods have less vibration and quicker recovery during the casting stroke, and therefore they cast tighter line loops than rods of other materials, and the cast line is freer of waves or humps. Stated more simply, an average caster usually can cast better with a graphite rod. His line loops will be smaller, he will probably cast farther with more accuracy, and he will suffer less casting fatigue.

Incidentally, it should be understood here that no tackle company manufactures sheets of graphite, the material that is rolled onto tapered dowels, heated under extreme pressure, and turned into rod blanks. At first, only one firm made

Orvis 8½-foot HLS Adams rod for 4-weight fly line.

graphite sheets; today there are at least three or four, and more are always getting into the game. Different graphite manufacturers supply their graphite sheets to different rodmaking companies, and the competition between rod companies to convince buyers that their graphite rods are the best is pretty keen.

In studying catalogs and reviewing the conflicting claims of graphite-rod manufacturers, it is easy to be confused. For example, the G. Loomis Company markets IMX graphite rods as well as IM6 graphite rods. Loomis claims both types are superior to most graphite rods, yet the IMX class sells for nearly $100 more than the IM6 group. Why? Because the IMX is eighteen percent lighter than the IM6, and is up to thirty percent lighter than standard graphite rods.

Moreover, there's considerable difference in the tensile strength of graphite rods, and where the Loomis IMX and IM6 are concerned, there is increased stiffness-to-weight ratio in the IMX, which makes a lighter, stronger rod.

When it comes to purchasing a graphite rod (or any other) you can't go far wrong by watching the price. If a graphite rod has a $300 price tag, be sure it is better quality than the rod with a $75 to $100 tag.

If the prices of graphite rods seem a bit out of reach, why not make your own? Nearly all graphite-rod manufacturers, including Loomis, Winston, and Thomas & Thomas, sell assortments of graphite blanks with which about any kind of fly rod can be made. Most such companies also sell the fittings, which include cork handles, reel seats, guides, and wrappings, but there are also many tackle outlets (including regular tackle shops) selling rod-

making supplies. It's possible to make a quality graphite fly rod for a fraction of the cost of a factory model. One firm selling an exhaustive selection of rodmaking supplies, by mail, is the Madison River Fishing Company, P.O. Box 627, Ennis, Montana 59729.

Graphite-Glass Combinations

Shakespeare's Ugly Stik fly rods are made mostly of graphite-carbon filaments, but the tip sections are of fiberglass. Shakespeare claims they are the strongest rods ever made and markets them with pretty firm guarantees against ordinary breakage "while fishing."

The Ugly Stik fly rod feels very much like a 100 percent graphite rod in casting, and despite its power it's a comparatively light rod with fine action. The two-piece 9-foot model would be an excellent choice for heavy saltwater fly fishing—on tarpon, for example.

HARDWARE AND GRIPS

All fly rods have the same components—guides, ferrules, reel seats, grips, etc. The tips, guides, and ferrules are very important on any fly rod. If a rod's tip-top and guides are not of quality material or are badly designed, they will wear quickly and then can ruin a fly line, or perhaps nick your leader and cause you to lose a good fish.

Fly-rod tip-tops and guides are made of various materials, and the better the material, the more expensive the rod. The tip-top on a fly rod receives the most wear, so it should be made of the hardest material, such as aluminum oxide or carboloy. The lowest guide, called the stripping guide, receives almost as much wear as the tip-top. On the better rods the lowest of the two lower guides as well as the tip-top are generally made of very hard material. Occasionally you'll see an older fly rod with a tip-top and/or lower guide lined with agate, which is very hard and glass-like, but seldom used in rod construction today. Agate can take years of ordinary wear, but is too easily cracked or broken.

Some new, very hard manmade materials are being used as guide linings on some fly rods. Aluminum oxide is one example; it is hard, smooth, and durable, as is silicon carbide, such as the Fuji S.I.C guides and tip-tops. Each manufacturer seems to have come up with his own special trade name for such guides.

A fly rod's snake guides, which run between the lower guides and the tip-top, normally are made of hardened wire, either stainless steel, plated black, or chromed. They don't take the same punishment the tip-top and stripping guide do, but they do need to be durable and rustproof. Saltwater rods require guides and tip-tops that are especially corrosion-resistant.

Some fly rods, even some of the better ones, are mounted with guides that are far too small. Not only should all of a rod's guides be made of good material, but they must be sufficiently large to allow easy passage of the fly line. Guides that are too small create excessive friction while casting, reduce casting distance, and can cause problems when knots must pass through them.

The ferrules—the sockets that join fly-rod sections together—must be made of good materials and be well designed or they will not last long. Nothing is more annoying to the fly caster than a loose ferrule.

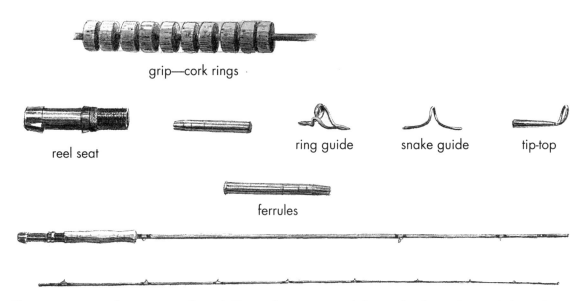

grip—cork rings

reel seat

ring guide

snake guide

tip-top

ferrules

The components of a two-piece fly rod. The cork rings at top left are glued together and shaped into a grip.

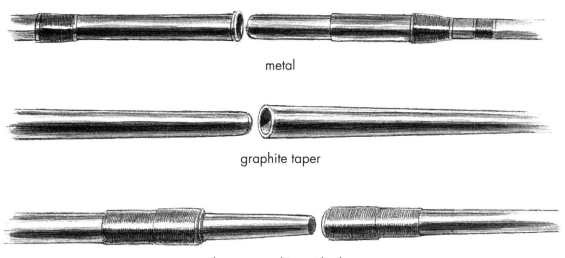

metal

graphite taper

glass or graphite with plug

Three types of ferrules used on fly rods.

The best rod ferrules are made of nickel silver or, as a second choice, brass. Both metals are strong, long-lasting, lightweight, and corrosion-resistant. Some newer hollow glass rods and graphite rods do not have real ferrules; one rod section merely slips into a larger section. Such connections are perfectly adequate, and, in fact, they make for a lighter rod and a more continuous, smoother action when casting.

Quality ferrules fit tightly when a rod is new, so much so that it is difficult to join the rod sections totally without considerable effort and perhaps some lubricating. A new rod whose ferrules fit quickly and loosely should be avoided.

Reel seats of the screw-locking type are best. They will hold a fly reel firmly in place even after hours of casting. An improvement over the ordinary screw-locking reel seat is the double screw-locking reel seat, which is just what the name implies: there are two threaded washers, which are screwed down to lock the fly reel in place.

If you want the lightest possible fly rod—say, for small-stream trout fishing—buy one with a skeleton reel seat. Such a rod has a cork reel seat, with a simple sliding band to secure the reel, rather than the typical heavier metal reel seat. Regardless of the type of reel seat on the rod you buy, be sure it will accommodate any fly reel you will use with that rod. The reel seats on some fly rods will not hold some fly reels.

It should be possible to mount a fly reel quickly and easily on the reel seat. There should be no need for pushing or forcing to get the reel-seat hood over the reel foot, or the rear reel foot into the rear hood of the seat. Once in place, a reel should not be

ROD JOINTS NEED LUBRICATION

The ferrules or joints of a quality fishing rod always fit snugly—sometimes so tightly it's difficult to separate them.

Before joining the ferrules, lubricate the male ferrule by running it through your hair or beside your nose; disassembly will be easy.

Keep rod ferrules clean and free of rust and dirt, and occasionally apply a high-quality, lightweight lubricant to the male ferrule, then wipe dry.

loose and wiggly in the reel seat. Reel seats of anodized aluminum are popular, because they are long-lasting, resist corrosion and rust, stand up to hard wear, and are very light yet strong.

Fly-rod handles, or grips, are uncomplicated. The cork grip can be one of many different shapes—cigar (the most popular), half Wells, fishtail, full Wells, and so on. All that is really important about the fly-rod grip is that it be comfortable and well made.

Fly rods may be one-piece, two-piece (the most popular), or three-piece. Some are available with extra tip sections, some with only one (an extra tip is desirable to replace one that may be broken or lost, but second tips add to the price of a rod).

HEAVY FLY RODS

Some of the larger heavy-duty fly rods have extension butts, most of which are removable. An extension butt is fixed to the bottom of the rod, going into a socket at the bottom of the rod handle. An extension butt adds about 4 inches to the handle length, and it can be used as a second hand grip or pressed against the angler's belly to provide leverage when fighting a husky fish. Extension butts are generally unnecessary unless the angler hooks large, strong fish that take a long time to play out, such as salmon or saltwater species. Even then, many experienced fly fishermen never use extension butts, feeling they add weight to the rod and are not really necessary.

There are two-handed fly rods, too—the second handle usually being a long extension butt, which may or may not be removable. Two-handed rods are used chiefly for Atlantic salmon, though some are used in saltwater fly fishing.

A few fishermen who chase tarpon of 100 pounds and more use a rod with a

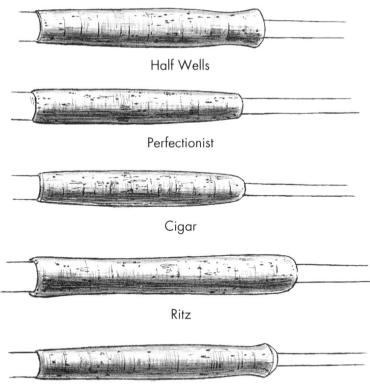

Half Wells

Perfectionist

Cigar

Ritz

Fishtail

Some of the popular styles of grips.

second handgrip mounted about halfway up the butt section of the rod. This gives the angler an "up-the-rod" hold and permits him to exert greater lifting force on a fish when it is at the boat. I suppose such rods are perfectly legal so far as tournaments and contests go, but I won't use one—not even on arm-wearing tarpon or husky amberjacks. I think a fly rod is meant to be held by a standard handle, and not by some special grip mounted up by the first ferrule. In my opinion the legitimate fly fisherman fights his fish, no matter what size, with a fly rod of standard design—otherwise he is not fly fishing.

Still another innovation in "heavy" fly-rodding is a husky rod with a separate section that can be slipped into the rod's lower, or butt, section after a big fish has been hooked. The glass insert greatly beefs up the rod and makes it much easier to handle the fish. In my opinion that isn't fly fishing, and, in fact, altering tackle after a fish has been hooked is illegal under the rules of most fishing tourneys.

ULTRALIGHT FLY RODS

One of the latest innovations in the fly-rod world is the introduction of what I would

The purpose of these ultralights, of course, is to give fishermen fly-casting gear that will make a hooked 8-inch brook trout feel like a gamester and, more importantly, make for more fishing success when fishing for extremely difficult fish in exceptionally shallow or gin-clear water. Any stream trout fisherman who has fished much has experienced conditions when he could see trout in low, clear water, but when he cast they dove for bedrock. That's because his fly line, though maybe only a No. 5 or 6 line (line sizes are covered in Chapter 4), hit the water hard and spooked the fish.

These spanking new, incredibly light fly rods taking only 1-, 2- or 3-weight lines, however, pretty much solve that problem, making it possible for an angler to drop his fly right on the nose of a spooky fish (whatever species) and draw a walloping strike.

The new extra-light fly rods I have tried have been, in my mind, too "soft," too whippy, and with many of them I've had trouble hooking fish. But by using them with their very light lines I've also been able to catch some fish I never would have with heavier conventional fly tackle.

Most of the new graphite, extra-light fly rods are incredibly efficient casting machines. One needn't think that because we are casting a mere 1-weight fly line we can't toss a fly more than 15 or 20 feet. True, we can't throw it out there 80 or 90 feet, but casts of 50 and 60 feet are more than possible with 1-, 2-, and 3-weight lines, and under most fishing situations casts of that length are more than adequate.

The Orvis Company has been a leader in the development of the ultralight rod,

call ultralight fly rods. These are featherweight wands that take 1-, 2-, or 3-weight lines. (Keep in mind that as recently as ten years ago there was no such thing as a 1-, 2-, 3-, or 4-weight fly line.)

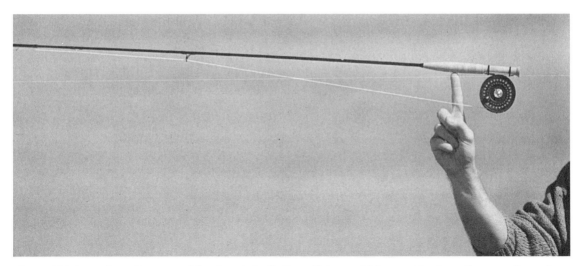

Orvis 6½-foot, One Ounce rod for 2-weight fly line. This would be an ideal small-stream fly rod.

making graphite fly rods as light as *1 ounce*, for *1-weight* lines. Orvis promotes itself as maker of "the world's lightest fly rod"—a 6½-foot graphite, weighing all of 1 ounce and taking a 2-weight fly line. If that's impressive, Orvis also is marketing a 7½-foot graphite fly rod, weighing 1³⁄₈ ounces, that takes a 1-weight line. The only way you can get lighter than this is to build a fly rod that takes a *0-weight* line.

The Cortland Line Company, Cortland, New York, markets a 7-foot, 1½-ounce graphite fly rod that takes a 2- or 3-weight fly line. The Thomas & Thomas Company, of Turners Falls, Massachusetts, markets a 7-foot graphite fly rod that weighs 1³⁄₈ ounces and matches a DT2 line (double-tapered, 2-weight).

And would you believe that the Fenwick Company is offering a 9-foot graphite rod "with helical-based construction" (whatever that is) that takes a mere 2-weight fly line?

FLY-ROD ACTION

Fly rods are available in various actions and lengths. *Action* means the amount of flex in a rod under certain stress, and generally it is the material of which a rod is made, and the taper of that material from butt to tip, that determines a rod's action. A rod's length also can affect its action—as can the number of sections (whether one, two, or three) and the size, quantity, and distribution of guides.

In loose terms, we generally describe rod actions as very light (ultralight), light, medium, heavy, and very heavy. And we have fly rods with actions that are "slow" or "soft," and ones with "fast" or "stiff" actions. Unfortunately, what one angler calls a soft rod another might consider to be stiff. There also are rods with so-called "parabolic" actions, and "wet-fly," "dry-fly," "steelhead," "salmon," and "bass" actions—about any action you might want.

What should be understood is that fly rods are, indeed, different. Much of the action problem can be solved simply by thinking of fly rods, regardless of their material or length, as being light, medium, or heavy. So you then select a rod to match the fishing for which it will most often be used.

The best way to determine what a fly rod's action is like is to press its butt against your belly, then wiggle it briskly from side to side, holding the rod with two hands. The amount of force it takes to flex the rod into a reasonable bend will give you a pretty good idea of the rod's action, or *power*.

In a sense, fly rods are "sized," and must be selected for length, weight, action, weight of line they will use, and the fishing purpose they will serve. Remember that it is the fly line that is cast, so no fly rod—regardless of its quality or high cost, and regardless of how expert the caster is—can perform properly if it is not matched with

SPARE THAT FISHING ROD

It's sad but true: Careless fishermen annually smash thousands of fishing rods—many of them expensive models.

There's only one correct way to walk with a fishing rod, and it doesn't matter if it's a fly rod, spinning rod, or bait-casting rod. Grip the rod by its handle, tip pointed up and backward, rod butt toward the ground. It's easier to snake one's way through heavy brush this way, and, more important, should you trip and fall you'll go down rod butt first. When a rod is carried tip forward, invariably the tip hits the ground, bends, and breaks.

Cars are hard on rods, too. Don't rest a rod against a car; it could slip inside and be smashed by a hastily closed door. Don't lay rods on the ground, where they're sure to be stepped on or driven over. The safest spot is the car's roof (but don't forget it's there; the author lost a 6-foot Orvis Superfine that way). If fishing's over, disjoint it and put it in a rod case.

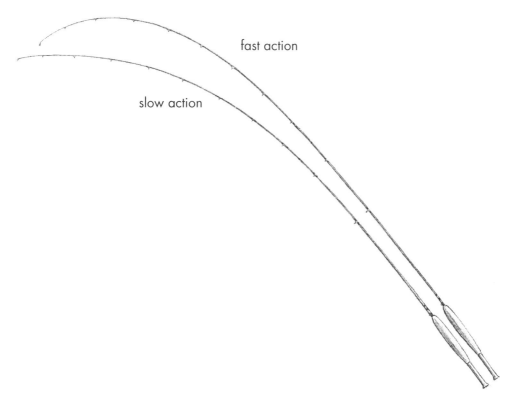

fast action

slow action

A fast-action fly rod flexes mostly in the tip section. A slow-action rod flexes throughout its entire length.

the proper weight line. (Most fly rods today are marked by the manufacturer to indicate the size fly line suited to the rod, and buyers should adhere to the manufacturer's line recommendations.)

The fisherman who uses one fly rod for all of his angling—which may be bluegill fishing one day, trout or bass fishing the next, and walleye or northern pike fishing another day—would probably be happiest with a rod 8 or $8\frac{1}{2}$ feet long, weighing 4 to 5 ounces, and taking a No. 7 or No. 8

line (fly lines are discussed in Chapter 4). For very light fly fishing—panfish in lakes, small stream trout—most anglers would prefer a rod weighing 2 to $3\frac{1}{2}$ ounces, ranging in length from 6 to $7\frac{1}{2}$ feet, and taking No. 4, 5, or 6 line.

In heavy fly fishing—bass-bug fishing and salmon, steelhead, or saltwater fishing—a rod $8\frac{1}{2}$ to $9\frac{1}{2}$ feet long and weighing $4\frac{1}{2}$ to $5\frac{1}{2}$ ounces is about right. Such a rod should have a slow action and should take a No. 8, 9, 10, or 11 line.

THE RIGHT ROD

Having exactly the right rod, matched with exactly the right line, for the exact fishing at hand isn't always easy. But it's something we strive for. As the *Saturday Evening Post* writer I mentioned earlier once said:

"When, at last, you run across the right rod you know it as clearly as you do when you are bitten by a rattlesnake. It is precisely like the time you saw your real best girl for the first time. A great, surging soul-impulse comes over you which, in articulate vernacular, interprets itself somewhat as 'Me for this.'"

3
Fly Reels

For years, fly-fishing experts have been conning beginners and one another over the relative unimportance of fly reels. They often claim that the fly reel is nothing more than a line holder, and that actually the pinnacle of fly fishing would be to fish with no reel at all, since the angler then would be spared that much extra weight and would enjoy the added thrill of having a direct connection with the fish he hooked.

Many fly fishermen claim further that the fly reel contributes nothing to the cast, and contributes little to the playing of average fish.

All that, of course, is at least partly true. But the notion that a fisherman should spend his next mortgage payment on a fine rod, then try to repair the family budget by purchasing a reel at the nearest dime store, is a fishing fallacy. Just about every fly-rodder today knows he must use judgment in selecting a fly reel for saltwater fishing, since so many saltwater species are strong, fast fighters, but too

many fishermen still cut corners when choosing a reel for freshwater fly fishing.

Regardless of the kind of fishing involved, equip yourself with a good reel, the best you can afford. Some saltwater fly reels are very expensive, but even the very best freshwater reels are not so costly that the average fly fisherman has to go in hock to buy one.

The performance of a good fly reel may go unnoticed season after season, but a poorly constructed reel sooner or later can cause the loss of a prized fish, or make for other difficulties. Those points were brought home to me one June on a trip to northern Saskatchewan.

All of my fly-fishing equipment, except rods, was lost in transit from La Ronge to Careen Lake. I had to borrow a Canadian-made reel to fish the nearby Clearwater River for American grayling. The reel had no drag whatever, and when I'd strip line from it swiftly to make a quick cast to a rising fish, the spool would overspin and I'd end up with a tangle of line on the reel.

Orvis CFO fly reels are machined from solid aluminum bars, as are most high-quality fly reels. Drags are smooth and dependable.

("Drag" on a fly reel is braking pressure applied to the revolving reel spool by a mechanical device built into the reel. Usually the amount of drag pressure can be varied by knob adjustment.) One grayling I hooked bolted into swift water and caromed downstream. I couldn't stop him, and line payed out from the reel until it reached a snarl—which I didn't know was there—that had been caused by overspin. The line snapped taut, the leader went *pop!* and the grayling continued downstream.

A few days later I flew into Middle Lake to fish for big northern pike with Walt Schaeffer, who then ran Camp Grayling. Again, because I'd lost my reels, I had to borrow one—a well-constructed English model, filled with a WF-9-F line, but with a line capacity so slight it had no backing line.

The first morning out I hooked a northern we guessed at about 25 pounds. The fish bore doggedly toward a clump of flooded alders. The pike was running so fast I couldn't slow him by pressuring the fly line as it whizzed through my fingers; when I tried that, I received a line burn an inch long. The pike ran out all the fly line, and when the jolt hit the reel and the rod tip bowed 'way down, the leader snapped like cotton thread. *That reel didn't have enough line capacity to handle a good-size bluegill!*

I received another lesson on fly reels fishing Deep Water Cay, in the Bahamas, for bonefish. As Gil Drake, Jr. ran the boat and we headed for distant flats, I started rigging a 9-foot fly rod. I put a large English-made "salmon" reel on the rod. The reel bore a famous name, but it had a pretty inferior drag for bonefishing.

"Why are you using that reel?" Gil asked. "It doesn't have a drag suitable for bonefish."

"Maybe not," I replied, "but it has a beautiful-sounding click. I want to hear this reel scream when I hook a bonefish and he goes off on those line-burning runs."

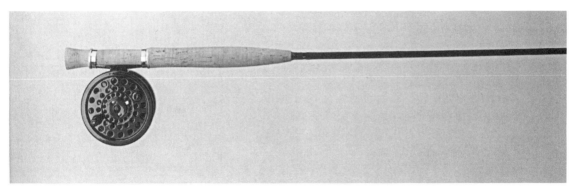

The Browning company's Waterton Series of fly reels are being acclaimed by many fishermen as among the best. They are top-quality reels, available in many different sizes, from light panfishing models to heavy deep-sea types.

Before long I cast to a good bonefish. He took, was hooked, and went rocketing away as only a bonefish in foot-deep water can. I had the fly reel's modest drag screwed down as tight as it would go, but the bonefish ran as though he were swimming free. The reel's click, or "brake," whined—and that's a sound I love to hear. Lots of fishermen dislike noisy fly reels, but I still get a kick out of hearing a reel go "*bwwiiizzzzzzzzzzzzzhhh!*" when I've hooked a fish.

The bonefish's first and only run burned the drag out. I heard little broken parts rattling around in the reel frame, and the reel's handle was a blur with the reel spool spinning so wildly. The bonefish quickly broke off.

Gil and I both laughed over the incident, and a few weeks later, back home, I received in the mail a large envelope from Gil. Gil is a top photographer, and unknown to me he had photographed me trying to control that bonefish with that totally inadequate "salmon" reel. The photo showed the reel handle whirling crazily and me wearing a pained expression. On the photo Gil had penned: "Yep! Sure like to hear a fly reel scream!"

So the fly reel, while it serves primarily as a storage unit for the fly line and its backing line, still must be well made and of practical design for the kind of fishing for which it will be used.

TYPES OF FLY REELS

There are three general types of fly reels: automatic, multiplying, and single-action. Few veteran fly fishermen use automatics. An automatic fly reel has a spring tension device which, when wound tight, can be triggered by depressing a lever so that the reel's spool revolves quickly and respools loose fly line. Put another way, an automatic reel has no handle or crank; extended line is respooled automatically via the built-in tension-spring mechanism.

Automatic fly reels have been greatly improved in recent years, but in the minds

EXTRA SPOOLS MEAN VERSATILITY

All fly fishermen should use single-action reels that have easily removable spools. Dry-fly and bass-bug fishermen both want their lines to float high and dry all day long. By having two spools loaded with identical lines, the fly fisherman can snap in the extra spool with fresh, dry line when one line starts to sink.

Carry an array of extra spools, one mounted with a floating double-tapered line, one with a torpedo-tapered line, one with a sink-tip line, one with a full-sinking line, and one with a shooting-head line. Thus equipped, you'll be prepared for almost any angling situation.

of most fishermen their disadvantages still far outweigh any possible advantages. Most automatics are very heavy and bulky, have too many parts, and therefore can be unreliable, and have minimal line capacity. Moreover, it is not possible to control a good fish with an automatic fly reel. Any fish apt to run out much line can become a nightmare when played from an automatic reel.

In saltwater fly fishing an automatic reel is an absolute no-no. Taking an automatic fly reel to the salt would be like going after elephants with a .22. Most saltwater fish would quickly tear up the usual automatic fly reel.

A multiplying fly reel has a spool that turns two or two and a half times for each revolution of the handle. An advantage of the multiplying reel is that line can be recovered, or respooled, more quickly than with a conventional single-action reel. Not too many multiplying reels are made, and they are, in fact, considered to be illegal gear in many fishing tournaments. Some anglers believe multiplying reels give one an unfair advantage over the fish.

With a single-action fly reel the angler must turn the reel handle to retrieve line, and the reel's spool revolves once with each turn of the handle. The single-action reel is normally the choice of the experts, and for many good reasons.

Single-action reels are lighter than most other fly reels, and they have few moving parts, so not much can go wrong with them. They have great line capacity, interchangeable spools can be obtained for most models, and the better single-action reels have reliable drags.

The Scientific Anglers Co. calls its System 3 reel the "ultimate fly reel." It's designed especially for heavy fly fishing, with a powerful drag and capacity for line weights 10 to 12.

Single-action reels are made in a wide range of sizes and prices. The simplest single-action fly reel is merely a spool within a frame connected by posts. It may not have a drag, or at best it might have an inferior one, but it likely will have a light brake or "click" that prevents the reel spool from revolving freely. A click mechanism is not necessary on a reel with a good drag.

The size of the fly reel is important. Small fly reels with small line capacity match very light fly rods taking light lines—outfits that would be used, for example, in small-stream trout fishing or for panfish. For heavier fly fishing with longer, stouter rods and heavier lines, larger fly reels are needed.

The size of a fly reel, incidentally, has nothing to do with its quality. A small reel can be very expensive, a large one inexpensive. While an expensive reel may not

always be necessary, a quality reel will seldom jam, lose screws, loosen, or otherwise perform badly. Moreover, a good fly reel will last indefinitely if cared for properly.

Sometimes you need a fly reel with great line capacity. This is especially true in saltwater fly fishing, but even in some trout fishing a fish may take out all the fly line when it races downriver with the current. If there is no backing line behind the fly line, the fish will break off. I have a home on the Madison River in Montana, and there's a lake nearby full of large rainbows and browns. Fully eighty percent of the fish we hook there take out all the fly line and get into the backing. Some trout I've hooked in that lake took off like bonefish!

Single-action reels with quickly interchangeable spools are desirable because with them fly lines can be switched readily. You may want to change from a double-

A HOMEMADE CASE TO PROTECT FLY REELS

Dick McGuire of Ennis, Montana, is one of the West's best-known and most popular trout-fishing and hunting guides. His specialty is float trips on big rivers such as the Madison, Jefferson, Yellowstone, and Missouri.

On a typical one-day trip, McGuire's McKenzie River boat will carry two fishermen plus McGuire, three pairs of chest-high waders, assorted fishing tackle, an ice chest, rain gear and cold-weather gear, photo equipment, oars, a charcoal grill, a grub box, and other equipment. While some fishing is done from the boat, more often anglers leave the boat to wade. With people climbing in and out of the boat all day, it's not unusual for equipment to be damaged.

To protect his fly reels from loss or damage, and to conveniently carry a number of reels with extra spools, McGuire designed and built an excellent wooden reel case. Shaped like a thin suitcase, it has two hinges, it's lockable, and it will hold eight reels, or four reels and an extra spool for each. Foam plastic lines the case, and each reel or spool's shape is cut into the foam.

McGuire's case is ideal for protecting reels on river float trips, or when traveling by air, and is easy to make, as you can see from the photo.

tapered to a weight-forward line, or from a floating to a sinking line. (Line types are discussed in Chapter 4.)

SELECTING A REEL

Ideally, a fly reel should be light yet sturdy, with a minimum of parts, no exposed screws that can loosen and fall out, an adequate drag, and ample line capacity. The first thing to look for in any fly reel is sturdy construction. The best practical design would be a one-piece frame and reel shoe, coupled with a one-piece die-cast spool. Reels of this type are available, but they are expensive—$150 and up.

Reels built with a lot of nuts, bolts, and screws can be trouble. These parts can become rusty, and they may need constant tightening and checking to prevent them from being lost. One of the most popular American-made single-action fly reels— available in various line capacities and sizes—has a number of very good features. It is lightweight and nicely balanced, and the smaller models have adequate drags and fine clicks. But a total of twelve screws are used to connect the side frames to the crossbars, and the screws are forever loosening or falling out. You must constantly tighten the screws on these reels, or "glue" them into place with a drop of lacquer or Loctite.

The tail plate and head plate of a good fly reel are rigid enough to support the reel's spool properly. Be sure the crossbars connecting a reel's side plates are sufficient in number, and strong enough to keep the reel case aligned, regardless of stresses encountered while fishing. Most quality reels have solid metal bars connecting the head and tail plates.

The shoe, or foot, of a fly reel must be strong and fastened to the frame solidly to prevent loosening, twisting, or breaking. Most good reels have the shoes lock-screwed into place, or they are riveted. The shoes of many reels, even expensive ones, are too short, too long, too narrow, too wide, or too thick. There are a lot of rods with reel seats that will not accommodate many kinds of reels, even popular makes. It is impossible to mount some fly reels on some rods, or at least it is difficult to get a secure and proper fit. When buying a new fly reel be certain it will fit firmly into your rod's reel seat.

Reel spools must be extremely strong. Nylon backing line wound onto a spool under tension causes stress on the side plates. This may warp a spool so that it won't revolve smoothly or may cause the reel to jam. It may even make the reel explode right under your nose.

I prefer a fly reel with a rigid, hard, metal line guard. One fairly expensive English-made reel has heavy-gauge steel wire around the reel frame. The wire is twisted back in two places, forming curves meant to serve as line guards. But the wire guard tends to shift, and at times closes against a pillar. This can prevent the line from being respooled properly, and also can keep the line from flowing freely off the reel.

We don't see many fly reels with agate rings for line guards anymore, but there are still a few of those around. Most of the agate rings put on fly reels as line guards are too small and, more important, they break easily. My favorite single-action reels have hard metal plates that cover the entire aperture through which the line passes. This is an efficient line guard because most

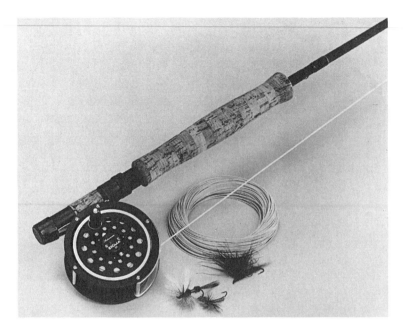

The Shakespeare Company has been in the tackle business for generations, and their new Sigma Series of fly reels are among the best moderately priced fly reels.

of the reel spool is open, and that makes it possible to spool the fly line evenly without difficulty.

Drags of fly reels work in several different ways. Some are remarkably simple, others complicated. Most important is that the drag works smoothly, with no hesitation or binding. For heavy fly fishing I like a reel with a drag handy enough that I can alter its pressure even as a fish is running line. My favorite heavy-duty fly reel has an extremely smooth, strong drag, which I can control by twisting a big, easy-to-turn knob mounted on the reel's left faceplate. With this reel I'm able to increase or decrease the drag pressure on a fish almost instantly. Another model of that same reel has the drag adjustment on the right side of the reel, as do many high-priced, top-quality fly reels.

Except for the very smallest fly reels,

you should attach backing line to the rear end of your fly line. Backing is used not only because a hooked fish might run out all the fly line, but to fill the reel spool and to bring the fly line properly up to near the spool edge. Dacron or nylon squidding line can be used for backing, and it should be attached to the fly line with as small and sturdy a connection as possible. Some anglers make elaborate splicing connections, but a loop connection or a well-tied nail knot (see Chapter 6) will do to fix backing to fly line. Just be sure the splice or knot is smooth so that it will not catch when going through the rod guides.

A reel for saltwater fly fishing must be selected with special care. There are fewer than a dozen top-grade, heavy-duty saltwater fly reels made today. All are expensive, but worth it.

A good saltwater fly reel has great line

capacity, taking a full-length three-diameter fly line, up to size No. 11, plus 200 to 250 yards or more of 20- to 30-pound-test Dacron or nylon squidding line. The reel's drag must be faultless, and spring drags that operate against carboloy ball-bearing washers and cork composition rings are generally preferred. Most good saltwater reels are made of anodized aluminum (which is not affected by salt), with working parts of carboloy. The frames of such reels, incidentally, are fitted so snugly that few particles of sand ever get into the works. The spools of the best saltwater reels are cut from solid bar-stock aluminum, all-one-piece construction.

While most fly reels are made of anodized aluminum or aluminum alloys, some new materials have crept into reel manufacturing. These include graphite, magnesium, and magnesium alloys, all of which make strong, light reels.

No matter what the make, material, or cost of a fly reel, good ones are of simple design, with instant takedown—preferably without the use of tools. Such a reel can be cleaned and oiled easily so that it can be kept in tip-top condition, ready to serve properly when the need arises.

The fly reels available today are vastly superior to the reels that were being made ten or fifteen years ago. Not only do we now have superior materials, we also have better design in both fresh- and saltwater reels. Fly reels today are stronger, more functional, more corrosion-resistant, sturdier, longer lasting, have greater line capacity, and are more resistant to wear. Not only that, but they are far lighter than the reels we were strapped with years ago— and they are better looking, too.

Some companies turning out fly reels nowadays deserve special attention. A leader in this department is the Orvis Company. Easily one of Orvis's most popular fly reels is the CFO, called by many anglers "the world's finest freshwater fly reel." They are cast from aluminum alloy, and the design includes a one-sided frame, which permits quick and easy spool changes. These reels, which are made in England, have adjustable drag systems and can easily be converted from right-hand to left-hand wind.

The latest CFO reel is an anniversary edition, "machined from aerospace-grade bar-stock aluminum, for the ultimate in precision, durability, and long-lasting quality."

Thomas & Thomas has introduced some unusual high-quality fly reels. One is the classic "limited edition Kosmic commemorative reel," a beauty and a collector's item if ever I saw one. It has excellent line capacity; a smooth, sturdy drag; and it's built to last at least a couple of lifetimes.

Another unusual and classic reel by Thomas is called the Individualist Reel. These reels, made exclusively for T&T by famed reel-maker Joe Saracione, are machined from aluminum, bronze, and stainless steel, and are polished, fitted, and hand-assembled. Spools are easily interchanged without tools, and the reels have excellent adjustable drag systems and nicely balanced serpentine handles.

Thomas also markets several other high-quality but much less expensive fly reels, including their T&T Classic reels, Trophy reels, Tournament reels, and a series of lightweight fly reels by Hardy Bros., England.

It's no news that saltwater fly fishing is extremely popular nowadays. But not too many years ago there were almost no fly reels designed and built for the rigors of saltwater fly fishing. Today, there are too many to discuss in limited space.

Probably the first fly reels designed specifically for saltwater fly fishing were the Tycoon/Fin-Nor reels (Miami), especially the Fin-Nor Model 3 tarpon reel.

Fin-Nor is still producing an outstanding line of big-game saltwater fly reels, and other manufacturers have joined the game. One big-game fly-fishing reel well worthy of mention is the Billy Pate Reel, designed by tarpon and billfish angling great Bill Pate and manufactured by T. Juracsik Tibor Reel Corporation, Oakland Park, Florida. Like most quality heavy-duty saltwater fly reels, the Pate is machined from solid bar-stock aluminum and has a very strong, smooth drag.

Another reel that ought to be included in any discussion of saltwater fly reels is the so-called "Bogdan salmon reel." Originally designed by S. E. Bogdan (Nashua, New Hampshire) for Atlantic salmon fishing, many of the big Bogdan reels have migrated, very successfully, to the saltwater fronts.

Bogdan reels are crafted from bar-stock, anodized aluminum and have great line capacity and an easily adjusted, smooth, strong drag.

The Browning Company (Morgan, Utah) is marketing a heavy-duty Waterton Series fly reel—along with smaller models—that takes a generous supply of backing line along with a size 8, 9, or 10 fly line. These reels also are machined from solid, bar-stock aluminum, and according to Browning no other reel has a more "consistent, reliable drag system."

4

Fly Lines

Y EARS ago fly lines were braided of silk and were finished with "enamel" or "oiled." They were heavy, and while they cast well, they were hard to keep afloat. A dry-fly fisherman using a silk line had to dress it—that is, rub it down frequently throughout the day with a flotant, such as Mucilin paste. The finishes of silk lines never seemed to last long, and they had to be carefully dried and kept uncoiled after use or they would rot and develop kinks.

The biggest trouble with silk lines, though, was their tendency to sink. Anglers and manufacturers were fighting that problem all the time. I had a silk line that was braided hollow, and it was the hottest thing around when it first came out in the early 1940s. The one I had was a size GBF, as lines were measured then, and I figured it would be great for bass-bugging the ponds on Maryland's Eastern Shore, because a floating line is important in bugging. The line cast well and floated very high, but only for a short time. It was hollow, all right, but the line sprung leaks, with microscopic pinholes showing up here and there.

It took on water and then would start down like a rock. I don't remember the name of the line or the manufacturer, but I do recall that it cost $40—a terribly high price, in those days, to pay for a fly line. The hollow silk lines didn't stay on the market long, however—not so much because of the price but because they just didn't float.

The first silk fly lines were *level,* meaning they had one constant diameter (more or less) from end to end. Next came *double-taper* and *torpedo-taper* lines. The double-taper lines tapered from a heavy middle or "belly" section to the two ends, and torpedo tapers were three-diameter lines—having a small-diameter running or "shooting" section first, then a short, thick belly, and finally a forward section tapering down to the line end. (More on line tapers and designs later.)

Since it is the weight (size) of a fly line that works a fly rod and makes casting possible, manufacturers identified the weights, or sizes, of their respective lines alphabetically, generally from the heaviest, or largest

One of the most innovative new fly lines is the Monocore, a nearly translucent line developed by Scientific Anglers.

size, A, to the lightest, or smallest size, I. The letters indicated the line diameters, A being .060 inch, and I being .020 inch. So the heaviest, largest (in diameter) level line would be an A line, while a double-taper line, one suitable for, say, an 8-foot rod weighing about 4 ounces, would be an HDH line. Those letters would indicate that the line had two ends tapered down to size H, while its belly, or heaviest section, was a D. A three-diameter line, or torpedo line, such as my old hollow silk GBF line, had a long, fine-diameter running line, size G; a very heavy belly section, size B; and then a lighter forward taper, or end section, size F.

Thus in the days of the silk fly line, a fisherman could buy a line of a certain size and be reasonably assured the line—regardless of make—would be of sufficient weight to work his rod properly. In that era a line of specific size made by one tackle company pretty well matched in weight the line of similar size produced by another tackle company.

In the mid-1940s, nylon, plastic, and other manmade materials became available, and line manufacturers quickly switched from silk to synthetic materials for their fly lines. The synthetics were better than silk; they didn't rot, and most floated far better and were stronger than silk.

But the introduction of synthetic fly lines brought some special problems. The synthetic lines did not match in weight the old braided silk lines, and a line sized by one manufacturer did not weigh the same as a similarly sized line turned out by another.

The result was chaos for many fishermen. For example, a fly fisherman who had been using a size HEH silk line with excellent results would buy a new synthetic line in, naturally, size HEH. The plastic line, much lighter than the silk line, wouldn't work properly on his rod. The fisherman would be out several dollars and have a new fly line that was useless to him. And even once he did find a synthetic line that was right for his rod, if he replaced it later with the same size line from another manufacturer, chances were he was out of luck again.

MODERN STANDARD CODING

Finally, in 1961, the American Fishing Tackle Manufacturers Association (AFTMA), following the suggestions of an excellent West Coast fisherman and fly caster named Myron Gregory, standardized fly-line coding. Line sizes or weights now are identified by number rather than letter. Rather than describing lines as sizes A through I, they are designated from, generally, No. 3 through No. 12 (smaller and larger sizes can be obtained specially). In addition to numerically sizing fly lines, manufacturers now also use letters to identify the *kind* of fly line—whether it is a floater or a sinker, level or tapered.

The sizing and design of fly lines is so important, to experienced fly-rodders as well as to beginners, that I'd like to repeat some things from the beginning.

Since fly rods come in different weights, lengths, and, more importantly, actions, they necessarily use lines of different weights. A line that is too light simply will not "work," or bend, a heavy rod; a line that is too heavy cannot be supported in the air by a light rod, and might even break the rod. A line must match or "balance" a rod. If it doesn't, good casting will be difficult if not impossible. Even a champion fly caster will not be able to cast *well* with a

STRINGING-UP A FLY ROD

It's surprising how many anglers don't know the proper (and easy) way to string fly line through rod guides and tip-top. Most simply grab the end of a fly line or the leader-point and thread the line or leader slowly through the rod guides, one guide at a time. This takes time, and often the angler loses his grip on the line or leader and the line slips back down through the guides.

The easiest and surest way to string a fly rod is to double the line over on itself, which in effect makes the line thicker and easier to handle, and resistant to slippage.

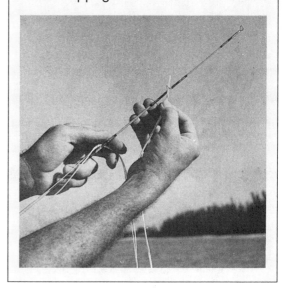

poorly balanced fly rod and line, and an inexperienced caster probably will not be able to handle it at all.

Now back to the tapers of fly lines. The three basic types are level, double-taper, and *three-diameter*. Three-diameter lines are commonly called weight-forward lines. A level fly line, as the name implies, has no taper. It is evenly sized, of a single diameter, from end to end. Level lines designed to float usually float very well (as compared to some other types), but they do not cast as well as some other kinds of lines and, moreover, tend to hit the water harder than finely tapered lines. Level lines are the least expensive.

The double-taper line tapers gradually from a heavy center section to both ends. Double-tapers are considered two-diameter lines. They are good floaters (if designed to float), they cast very well, and because they settle to the water gently with their finely tapered front sections, they are the lines most used by trout fishermen. Double-tapers also execute certain kinds of casts better than other types of lines do—roll

casts, for example, and curve and S casts. (Basic casts are described in Chapter 7; advanced casting in Chapter 8.) Double-tapers are more expensive than level lines.

Incidentally, some fishermen can get *two* lines out of a single double-taper. Most double-tapers are about 90 feet long. Fishermen who seldom cast more than 45 feet, such as small-stream trout anglers, often cut their double-tapers in the middle. Since the double-taper line tapers off from the mid-portion to both ends the same way, cutting gives two identical lines, each 45 feet long. When one line wears out, the angler can replace it with the other half.

Weight-forward lines are tapered from a long, thin tail-end or "running" section to a very thick, heavy belly section, then finally to a quickly tapered, fine forward tip. Weight-forward lines, with their heavy

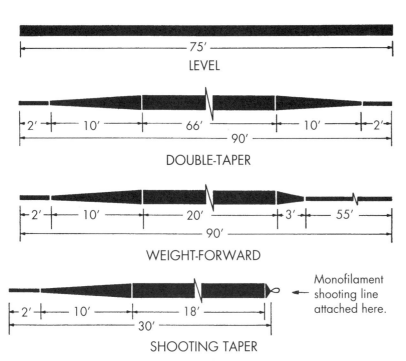

Four types of fly lines.

belly sections, are primarily designed for distance casting and for heavy fly fishing. They are the best lines for handling large popping bugs and streamer flies, for saltwater fly fishing, and for any conditions where powerful casts are needed, such as when using wind-resistant flies and bugs and when casting in strong wind. Casts of 100 feet and more are possible with weight-forward lines.

Since weight-forward lines generally cast better than other types, these are good lines for beginners. Moreover, a lot of expert fishermen are using light weight-forwards for all-around fishing. Some line manufacturers now are making weight-forwards with long, finely tapered front ends, and these lines cast farther than standard double-tapers and perform about as well in all other respects as double-tapers. Last year in Montana I used, almost exclusively, a graphite fly rod 9 feet, 3 inches long, with a matching but very light (No. 5) weight-forward line. The outfit was a dream to fish with.

Weight-forward tapers have all sorts of names: torpedo tapers, bug tapers, forward tapers, rocket tapers, teardrop tapers, saltwater tapers, salmon tapers, and even long-belly tapers. But no matter what they're called, all are three-diameter lines, and they're the most expensive of all fly lines.

Under the new AFTMA system of standard fly-line coding, the various tapers now are identified by symbols. For example, L denotes level line; DT means double taper; WF means weight-forward taper; and ST means single taper. (The ST lines, with only one end tapered, often are called *shooting tapers*.)

In addition to the basic differences in taper of fly lines, there are also many different *types* of fly lines. Most fly lines are of either floating or sinking type. But some newer kinds of fly lines are half sinking and half floating. And some float through most of their length, but their forward tips sink. In the AFTMA code, F means floating, S means sinking, and I (for "intermediate") means floating-sinking.

Now to the sizing, or weighting, of fly lines. The unit of weight in the fly-line standard is the grain. In general the line numbers are assigned to the standard grain weights, ranging from a fairly light line—say a No. 4—to a rather heavy line—about a No. 12. Where these weight numbers are concerned, a line's diameter, material, finish, and other characteristics are unimportant—all that is being identified is the line's weight, in grains.

Only the first 30 feet of the "working" section of a fly line, excluding any tapered tip, is weighed to determine the line's weight classification number. So if an old HCH line weighed 160 grains in its first 30 feet (excluding the taper), it would be designated a No. 6 line. If the old HCH line was a floater, under the AFTMA's sizing and identifying system the line would be marked DT-6-F—meaning double-taper, No. 6 weight, and floating.

An HCF three-diameter or torpedo-tapered line and a level C line, if the first 30 feet of each of their working sections weighed 160 grains, would both be No. 6 lines. The present coding for the HCF would be WF-6-F, indicating the line has a weight-forward taper, is No. 6 weight, and is a floating line. The level C line would be L-6-F—a level line, in No. 6 weight, that floats.

The table below lists the *common* fly-line sizes in use, and the comparative weights, in grains, for each line, in accordance with American Fishing Tackle Manufacturers Association standards.

Line No.	Weight
1	60
2	80
3	100
4	120
5	140
6	160
7	185
8	210
9	240
10	280
11	330
12	380
13	420

The best way to tell what weight line, in grains, works best on a particular fly rod is to try several lines until you find the one that casts best. If you do not own several different kinds of rods, and therefore do not have many lines in various sizes, perhaps you can borrow lines in differing sizes from friends, and cast with those, too. Almost all fly rods made today, happily, are marked by the manufacturer to indicate the best line size for a particular rod. While not always perfect, the recommendations usually are pretty accurate.

Trying different lines on a rod is still the best way to determine what line or lines cast best, simply because there still are manufacturing differences in line making and design, despite attempts to more or less standardize things. A double-taper line by one company, for instance, may have only a 10- or 12-foot front taper, while a double-taper line in the same weight from another firm may have a very long forward taper. And the belly sections of three-diameter lines are not identical lengths from manufacturer to manufacturer; a few companies, in fact, even make three-diameter lines of the same weights with bellies of different lengths.

It is difficult, on paper, to match line sizes to rods, since the size line a specific rod handles best will depend upon the rod's action, which in turn is basically determined by the rod's length, weight, and taper. But here is a general guide loosely matching rods, by length, to line weights:

Rod length (feet)	Line No.
5–5½	4
6–7	5
8	6
8½	7
9–9½	8, 9

There are a number of special-purpose fly lines on the market, including various sinkers and shooting-head lines, and all have practical purpose and application in the vast world of fly fishing.

SINKING LINES

There are sinking lines available that go down for their entire length, and others that sink slowly, ones that sink moderately fast, and some that go down like lead. Then there are sinking lines in which only the first several feet go down. Some have about 10 feet of line that sink (from the tip back); others have 20 feet that will sink; and again these sinkers are available in

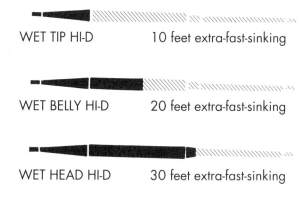

WET TIP HI-D   10 feet extra-fast-sinking

WET BELLY HI-D   20 feet extra-fast-sinking

WET HEAD HI-D   30 feet extra-fast-sinking

Three types of sinking lines.

designs that take them down slowly to modest depths, or faster to still deeper depths, or like cement blocks so that the angler can drag his fly across bottom in 20 or 25 feet or more of water, depending upon current and/or boat movement.

I personally dislike using sinking lines, and shooting heads too, but sometimes they really make all the difference between catching and not catching fish. Any sinking line, whether it is full-length sinking or just tip style, is more difficult to use, and takes some of the fun out of fly fishing, compared with high-floating lines. Some sinking lines must be retrieved right to the rod tip before they can be sensibly picked up for the backcast, and some must be rolled up into the air, in front of the caster, before they can be thrown on back for the backcast. The full-length, high-density sinking lines that go way down are the most difficult to handle. They must be fished out to the very end of the retrieve, then lifted slowly and carefully from the water.

Lines that float most of their length but have sinking forward sections of 10, 20, or sometimes 30 feet are easier to use than full-length sinkers. And it follows, of course, that the line with only a 10-foot sinking tip section will cast and otherwise handle better than one with a 30-foot sinking forward section. The more line that floats between the rod tip and the part of the forward section that goes down, the easier it is for the fisherman to handle his line. He doesn't have to bring in all of such a line before picking up for another cast; he can execute a long roll cast with a line that has a comparatively short sinking tip; and he can "mend" line (throw curves upstream in the floating portion) so that current won't pull his line, create drag, and cause his fly to drift unnaturally.

But sinking lines, in all their various forms, fill a much-needed gap in the fly fisherman's armament. When fish are really deep in lakes, it's the sinking line that puts the fly-rodder's offering down where the fish will see it and hit. When rivers are high and roiled, a sinking line sometimes is the only way to take fish. In very heavy current, flows that would buoy up an ordinary floating line and keep even a weighted fly right on top, it's the sinking line or one of the sinking tip lines that does the job.

Then there are certain other fishing situations, peculiar to some species of fish, in which sinking lines work best. Compared to other areas, bonefishing the Bermuda flats is *deep* bonefishing, with the fly-rodder frequently casting to fish cruising bottom in 4 to 6 feet of water. Thus a sinking-tip or sinking line often will get more bonefish for the fly caster in Bermuda waters.

I've taken largemouth bass in 20 feet of water by fishing a full-length, high-density sinking line with a *floating* bass bug. The

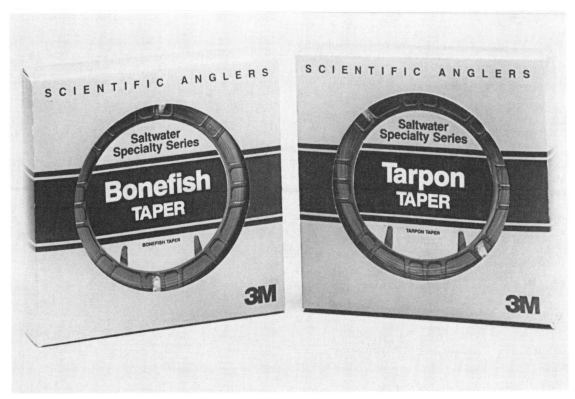

Nowadays many fly-line manufacturers are designing and producing "specialty" lines, ones with specific and different tapers meant for particular kinds of fishing.

line went right to the bottom, very quickly, dragging the cork-bodied bug after it. But the bug's buoyancy kept it off the bottom by 3 feet. I'd snake the line along in foot-long hauls, which gave good action to the bug, a minnow type. I suspect the bass hit it thinking it was a scared minnow trying to dive into the cover of bottom rocks.

Steelhead are notorious for hanging their noses against bottom rocks and boulders, and if you don't get your fly bumping the bottom, you're usually wasting your time. Big tarpon dislike rising too far for a fly, too, and usually you'll get more tarpon using a sinking-tip line.

For extremely deep fishing in either fresh or salt water, some fly-rodders make lead-core shooting-head lines. Not many line companies make lead-core fly lines, so most fishermen make their own by purchasing 100-yard spools of nylon-braided lead-core line (normally used for deep trolling), cutting out a section about 25 feet long, then attaching around 100 feet of monofilament shooting line to the back end of the lead-core line. The monofilament shooting line should test, as a rule, no less than 20 pounds and no more than 40. It isn't critical. What test is best depends on the kind of fishing for which the line will be used. Most fishermen like 20- and 25-pound test, but some use 30. A 30-pound shooting line would be a good choice if, for example, the lead-core line will be used for fishing amberjacks around a deep reef. Enough backing line (such as Dacron) is attached to the shooting line to fill the reel spool, and, of course, a leader goes on the front end of the lead-core line.

Years ago I never, never used sinking lines of any kind. For one thing, they weren't all that available, and not many good ones were around. Today, however, I never make an important fishing trip without taking several types of sinking lines along to match the rods I'll have. While I still dislike using sinking lines, I've now been in enough fishing situations where sinking lines were necessary that I won't travel without them.

SHOOTING-HEAD LINES

Single-taper or shooting-head fly lines are made by almost all line manufacturers, and for some fishing they are essential. A shooting-head line consists of a short forward section of tapered line (normally in the heavier weights, such as No. 8, 9, 10, or 11), and the "head" length most commonly is 30 feet, though some are shorter and a few a bit longer. To the back of the head is tied monofilament "shooting line" or special small-diameter level fly line. A leader, of whatever type suits the fishing, is attached to the forward tip of the head.

Shooting heads are used for super-distance casting, with casts of 125 feet and more executed easily. They're fine for much saltwater fly fishing, for deep fishing, for conditions that require a quick, short false cast and then a long cast, and when fishing along high banks or wooded shores which do not permit long backcasts.

The shooting-head line is cast by first getting all of the head out of the rod guides and laying it on the water out in front. Then yards of shooting line are stripped from the reel, and as carefully as possible spread loosely on the ground or boat bottom. Now the shooting head is picked up on a backcast, a short forward false cast is made, another backcast, then the final forward cast. On the final forward toss the caster releases the shooting line from his left hand, and the heavy shooting-head flies off, pulling yards and yards of the running or shooting line along behind it. The simple physics involved in casting shooting-head lines is that the short, very heavy fly line swiftly pulls the fine-diameter shooting line behind it, just as a rock tied to a string and thrown would haul the string a long way. Shooting heads are used in all tournament distance-casting events, and, in fact, it was in the tournaments that these lines were developed.

A good caster need not even make a false cast to get a long throw with a shooting-head line. With 30, 40, or 50 feet of line out in front, he can pick up the head on a backcast, then go right into the forward cast, releasing the shooting line at the proper moment so that the cast extends to 125 or more feet.

One winter evening, on behalf of the Johnson Tackle Company, I gave a casting demonstration before 8,000 people at a Sportsmen's Night in the St. Paul Stadium. Minnesota Vikings pro footballers did some canoe tilting, there was log rolling, water retrieving by gun dogs, and a pair of

Berkley's unusual Specialist fly line is only 82 feet long, instead of the usual 90 feet.

casters from a local casting club demonstrated accuracy dry-fly casting. They did a fine job of dropping their dries into target rings set at 25 to 40 feet. I followed them up to the casting platform and, while Rollie Johnson of WCMO-TV explained the various casts, I went into an ordinary casting routine, using an 8-foot rod with a WF-8-F line. I made casts 80 to 90 feet, with 90 feet the length of the tank. A lot of people *ooohed* at the 90-foot throws. Then, by prearrangement, Rollie observed over the microphone that he'd now like to see a long cast. I picked up a 9-foot rod rigged with a No. 9 shooting head with monofilament shooting line. I stripped yards of line off the reel, spread it carefully around the casting deck, flipped the head out on the water, then picked it up and let it go without a single false cast. The crowd went bananas as the line flew far beyond the tank, over some display boats, and fell

short of the far wall. We measured the cast later at 152 feet. Considering that the shooting line was dry (there's less friction through the rod guides with a dry line), and that the shooting line had been perfectly set on the casting deck, the cast wasn't all that unusual. Many casters can do that, and a whole lot more can do it with a shooting head. But to people who had never seen a shooting head in use, the cast was something special.

Some exhibition fly casters use shooting-head lines for maximum long-distance casting but fail to explain to their greatly impressed audiences that the line is not an ordinary, typical fly line; but rather, one especially designed for distance casting, and with which any accomplished caster can make very long throws.

The two casting-club members who had done the accuracy act at the St. Paul show came up to me afterward, and one said they weren't interested in shooting-head lines and never used them because they weren't needed in regular fishing. Certainly shooting heads are not needed in "regular" fly fishing, but they're just the thing for some kinds of fishing.

One June afternoon I was fishing around the piers of the Chesapeake Bay bridge, near Annapolis, Maryland, with Chuck Besche and my son, Bob. We were drifting live eels on plug-casting tackle for the big striped bass (many over 20 pounds) that were hanging around the bridge structure. Bob got the first one that day, a chunky 22-pounder, then Chuck followed with one an even 20 pounds. We'd run the Mako uptide from the huge bridge supports, then cast our eels, with 1/2-ounce lead sinkers on the line, toward the rock, cement, and steel piers where the stripers were hanging out. The lead and the tide would swing the eels deep, and we had fairly consistent action.

Finally I decided to try a fly rod. I rigged a 9-foot Heddon graphite and a big single-action reel holding a No. 9 sinking shooting-head line and backing. I knew I'd have to get my fly down deep, and figured a sinking head would do the job. Chuck would run the Mako uptide from a pier, and as we'd drift by I'd make a long cast about 100 feet up-current from the pier. That gave the line plenty of time to sink before my 5-inch-long McNally Magnum streamer fly reached the pier. I could tell by the boat position and the end of the line about when my fly was close to a pier, and was down about 20 feet. When I figured the fly was in the right position I'd strip line in with foot-long hauls, working the big streamer slowly but with lively action. We made six drifts past different bridge supports, during which a 12-pound striper picked up Chuck's eel, but I didn't get a hit. But on the seventh drift-by I had a strike so solid the rod almost jumped out of my hand. I held on and tightened up hard to keep the fish away from the bridge structure. Chuck kicked the Mako into gear and slowly backed away, getting us out into open water. The striper took off on a run, and now I just let it go, knowing the fish had the entire bay to run around in. It bore deep, and went far into the backing line. I'd work it close, then out it would go again. We seesawed back and forth like that for perhaps twenty minutes, until at last the fish rolled up on its side at the boat and Chuck gaffed it in the lip—a fine, silver-bright, black-barred Chesapeake

With so many fly fishermen these days pursuing billfish in the oceans, some fly-line manufacturers are making very heavy lines to match actions of heavy fly rods. Lines of 13, 14, and 15 weight are available.

Bay striped bass that went an even 17 pounds. It was a fish I could not possibly have taken on a fly rod, under the existing conditions, without using a sinking shooting-head line.

Steelhead fishermen habitually use shooting-head lines, not only for the longer casts but also because in sinking types they will get down faster than other sinking lines; the specific gravity of a short sinking head is great, taking the line right down, and the fine running or shooting line causes little drag even in strong current.

Many fishermen use shooting heads

even in dry-fly fishing, for trout or salmon. First of all, the head makes long casts easier, thus they can fish water they otherwise could not reach. Second, there are many spots in most large rivers where currents of unequal speed prevent floating a dry fly without drag unless the angler is able to keep part of his line off the water. You can hold more monofilament up off the water with your rod than you can standard fly line. Also, because of the greater distance it gives him, the trout fisherman using a shooting head often is able to fish water that most anglers can't reach. So the caster at times gets to work on fish that haven't been spooked every day of the season.

Some fishermen feel roll casts (see Chapter 7) can't be done with shooting heads, but nothing could be more wrong. A good caster, in fact, can lay out extremely long roll casts with a shooting head, because the head permits him to shoot many yards of additional line as it lifts off the water, rolls over, unfolds, straightens, and pulls shooting line after it. Roll casts of 60 and 70 feet are possible with well-designed shooting heads.

Today most line manufacturers make shooting-head lines of several types. You can get them with loops at the back end so that they can be attached or detached quickly from the shooting line, thus making rapid line changes possible. Heads are also available that are permanently spliced to the shooting line. There are ones with flat, oval, and round monofilament shooting line (in various diameters or tests), or with small-size level fly line. And you can get shooting heads that float, sink slowly, or sink fast.

You can make your own shooting heads from either double-tapered or three-diameter lines. Using a double-tapered line, you'll get two heads—one from each end. In my opinion, heads made from three-diameter lines cast far better than those made from double-tapers. I once made an 18-foot shooting head from an old Cortland GAF (No. 9) line. In those days the line tapers were braided in, and the line was then lightly coated with plastic. That line cast a mile. I eventually lost it when a bush plane's door opened while in flight over Canadian wilderness, and my tackle bag rolled out.

If you make your own heads you'll want to experiment with double-taper and three-diameter lines, with the lengths, and with the kind (mono or fly line) of shooting line used, and with the diameter or test of the shooting line.

If you'd like to make a typical shooting-head line, one you could use for heavy-water trout fishing, bass and pike fishing, or saltwater fishing, get a No. 9 weight-forward line, either floating or sinking. Cut the line 30 feet back from the forward taper. Attach monofilament shooting line to the back end of the fly line, using a loop knot and clinch knot, nail knot or variation, or Albright Special knot (see Chapter 6). Coating the finished knot with Pliobond or similar rubber cement smooths it and makes it easier for the knot to slip through the rod guides. The monofilament shooting line should test 20 to 30 pounds. The lighter the line, the less friction and the longer the casts; but heavier line kinks less and is generally easier to handle. Twisting, knotting, and kinking always have been problems with mono shooting heads, but at this writing at least one line manufacturer

Tabs of medical adhesive tape, marked with special codes to identify fly-line types and sizes and the amount and test of backing line, can be put on fly reels to show the kind of fly line and backing on the reel. The reel in this photo holds a weight-forward No. 9 floating fly line, and 100 yards of 18-pound-test Newton backing line.

(Sunset) markets an exceptional "memory-free" monofilament shooting line it calls "Amnesia." It spirals the first time it comes off the reel spool following storage, but when pulled taut it remains straight. It is truly excellent for shooting-head lines.

LINE COLORS

Fly lines are available in many different colors and hues, and what color the angler selects is chiefly a matter of preference or availability. I like a line I can see, which means I prefer cream, ivory, or white. When white lines first came out (all earlier fly lines were in dark colors, such as mahogany) many fishermen refused to buy them, feeling they were easier for fish to see. Actually, under normal circumstances

light-colored lines should be more difficult for fish to see, since usually the fish is looking up at the line against a clear, bright sky. Under those conditions a dark line would be more clearly visible to wary fish.

Also, the fly leader makes a nearly invisible connection between lure and fly line, and to my mind it is the leader construction (its length and fineness) that counts in taking fish. When the leader is right and a cast is properly delivered, a fish shouldn't be aware of the fly line. (Leader design is covered in Chapter 5.)

Using a line you can see well will improve your casting. You are more accurate, you can better judge distance on the false casts, you can adjust casting motions, timing, and application of power better for tighter or wider loops, and it is much easier to correct any casting error—any slip in timing—that might creep into a particular cast. You can fish a fly better with a line you can see well, because you always have a pretty good idea where the fly is and what it's doing. In some forms of fishing (nymphing, for example), a white line helps you to determine strikes. It's easier to throw left and right curve casts and S casts when you have a highly visible line.

The sinking lines turned out by most manufacturers are dark-colored, usually gray or dark green. Here again, I suppose the feeling is that fish will see a light-colored line that is swinging along down deep more quickly than a darker one, but I seriously doubt that anglers would catch fewer fish using light-colored sinking lines. For the reasons mentioned earlier, I certainly wish light-colored lines in the various sinking types were more readily available.

Trout suck in nymphs washing along in stream current so gently and slowly that only an alert fisherman watching the extreme tip of his line for the slightest pause or twitch will consistently hook a large percentage of them. So here it is vitally important that the angler have a highly visible line. To that end, many manufacturers today are making white and ivory lines—ones easily seen under almost all fishing conditions—and then coloring the tips or points of the lines bright red, orange, or yellow. The idea is that those colors, which may run from a couple to several feet up from the line tip, are easier to see than white, and therefore are just right for nymphing. This may not be all that necessary, but when you buy a line specifically for nymph fishing, be sure it's

one you can see well away out there, *at the very tip of the line.*

NEW DEVELOPMENTS IN LINES

As new materials become available and new manufacturing techniques are developed, it is certain that different kinds of fly lines will be marketed. At this writing, for example, the Scientific Anglers Company is marketing an unusual fly line it calls the "Monocore." The line has a clear, single-strand monofilament core and a clear coating that makes it almost invisible, like ordinary monofilament line. This is a great line to use on the ultraclear bonefish flats, or in extremely clear lakes and streams. The Monocore is available in weights 6 through 13. These lines are among my favorites for castability.

Other unusual developments in modern fly lines are ultralight lines in weights of 1, 2, and 3 and ultra-heavy lines in weights of 13 to 15, designed for ocean fishing for billfish. Most of the ultra-heavy lines are comparatively short, meant for short, quick casts with heavy fly rods. These special ocean-fishing fly lines are the result of increased angler interest in taking billfish, of all species, on standard fly-fishing gear.

As an example, though, of how lines may change in the future, consider that in the 1940s Myron Gregory, an ingenious West Coast angler and caster, made a three-diameter heavy fly line out of pure nylon monofilament line. Myron hit on the idea of taking very heavy, large-diameter mono line and tapering it by sanding with fine sandpaper. It worked—the line cast well, and, in effect, gave Myron a full-length fly

GETTING THE KINKS OUT

Kinky or twisted nylon leaders mean trouble for fly fishermen. A kinked leader makes accurate casting difficult, ruins the presentation of a fly, and makes the correct drift or float of a fly unlikely.

There are several ways to get the kinks and twists out of a leader, but one quick and easy method is to draw the leader repeatedly through a folded leather wallet, so that the leather rubs the leader on all sides. A few quick swipes should straighten the leader perfectly.

Other ways to get the kinks out: draw the leader across the rubber sole of a hip-boot, wader, or sneaker, or use a small square of rubber purchased at a tackle shop or cut from a discarded automobile innertube.

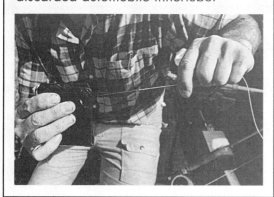

line as nearly invisible as his regular fishing monofilament leaders. It was painstaking work to make one, though, and I believe the first was the last Myron ever turned out. At the time I was doing consulting work for the DuPont company, the leading manufacturer of monofilaments, and I tried

to convince them of the practicality of nearly translucent, nearly invisible, full-length monofilament fly lines. But it was no go.

Most experienced fly fishermen cut the tips back some from the forward tapers of their lines, both double-tapers and three-diameters. No matter what the make or the taper (and regardless of advice to the contrary by some line manufacturers), today's lines usually handle and cast better if a foot or more is cut from the front end. Too many line manufacturers design their lines with front tapers that are too "slow," or gradual, and as a result the lines do not cast as well as they should—they do not give tight enough loops on the cast, or do not turn the fly over soon enough or properly—and so they must be cut back. Years ago the front tapers of lines were so long, even those of three-diameter type, that a knowledgeable caster would cut off 6 or 8 feet of line from the front end. Lines are better designed today, though, so it's seldom necessary to take off more than 2 or 3 feet from the front end, and some anglers may not even want to do that.

CARE OF LINE

Fly lines are expensive, so it is important not only to get the right ones for your fishing and your rods, but also to take good care of them. Some fishermen will wear out a couple lines of the same type in a single season, but the average fisherman ought to get at least three or four seasons of use out of a line if he cares for it properly.

Most mosquito repellents and suntan lotions break down the chemicals in the coatings used on modern fly lines, so don't get them on your line. Gasoline and oil will ruin a line, as will dirt, sand, and grit. Standing on a line does it no good. Nor does pinching a line between floorboards on a boat, or pinching it between the spool and frame of a reel.

You'll get the longest wear and best performance out of a line if you wipe it occasionally with the manufacturer's fly-line cleaner or line dressing. In the course of a hard day's fishing, strip the line from the reel, if you can, and lay it out in large, loose coils. This will help keep any tough kinks from forming, and also dry the line a bit.

Using a line in salt water will make it gummy, so rinsing afterward in fresh water is a good idea. Follow that with drying, and then lightly rubbing in a good dressing. Fly lines made of modern synthetics can be damaged if left exposed to hot sun too long.

5

Leader Design and Construction

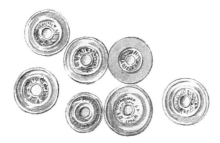

THE leader used in fly fishing serves as a nearly invisible connection between your fly or bug and the thick, fish-scaring fly line. The leader is, in effect, an extension of the fly line, transmitting the energy of the cast all the way down to the fly or bug, making the lure turn over at the end of the cast and drop properly to the water. It is not possible to cast skillfully without a well-designed leader, and a correctly made leader is essential to the accurate and gentle presentation of a fly.

Early fly fishermen made leaders of horsehair and, later, of silkworm gut. Modern anglers prefer leaders of nylon or similar synthetic materials.

Some fishermen have used strange materials for leaders. Al McClane at one time used dental floss for leaders when fishing Catskill trout streams. (In fact, using dental floss for trout leaders was the subject of McClane's first magazine story, which he wrote at age 16 for *Outdoor Life*.) The floss, Al said, was strong and fine and took some wily fish, though it lacked the castability of good-grade silkworm gut or nylon.

One windy afternoon I came upon a trout fisherman in the canyon section of Maryland's Big Hunting Creek who was fishing with a 15-foot leader of size 00 black silk thread. The thread had been waxed with beeswax to give it firmness and body and to help make it waterproof.

The fisherman's hat was covered with Pennsylvania angling licenses, and knowing that Pennsylvania spawns some of our finest trout fishermen, I watched as he fished. Using a long but light 9-foot rod, he'd roll his line into the air, then lower the rod as the wind kept his light line and gossamer thread "leader" just off the water. The fly was big, a wind-catching bivisible, and as the fisherman raised and lowered his rod tip the wind—holding the leader and line up—would cause the fly to touch the water, bounce up, touch again, and so on. The action was like that of a real insect dipping to the surface and laying eggs. Up and down went the fly—*dap . . . dap . . . daaapp . . . skim . . . dap*—like that. I watched dumbfounded as a 10-inch brown socked the fly hard, was hooked, played out, and gently released. That fish was one of many the Pennsylvania angler had taken that day, using the gusting wind and his black thread "leader" in dapping dry flies to the surface of slick pools.

Nowadays there is hardly any logical reason to use leaders other than ones made of nylon monofilament. Nylon leaders provide the angler with about everything he could want in a connection from fly line to fly—reasonable invisibility, good casting characteristics, strength, and uniformity of diameter according to pound test.

LEADER LENGTH AND TAPER

Basically, there are two kinds of leaders—*level leaders* and *tapered leaders*. The level leader is simply a continuous length of nylon monofilament of the same diameter and pound test. It is used chiefly in fishing bait, or in fishing hardware such as spinners or fly-rod spoons, in which delicate presentation and casting exactness are relatively unimportant. The level leader has no place in serious fly fishing, since the tapered leader does a far superior job of presenting the fly and of casting well.

Leaders vary considerably in design depending upon the kind of fishing being done. Some leaders must be very fine and very long, to present a small fly delicately to scary fish in clear water. Others must be comparatively short and heavy, in order for the angler to cast heavy, bulky, wind-resistant flies or bugs.

As a general rule, I use leaders as fine and as long as possible. The lighter or finer the leader "point" or tippet—that is, the smaller its diameter—the less visible it is to fish. By the same token, the longer a leader

is the less likely spooky fish are to see or detect the heavy, bulky fly line.

I am a nut about long, fine leaders. I'd rather get a strike from a tough fish and have him break off because I had such a light tippet than to cast to the fish and not get a rise because the fish was scared off by a heavy leader.

Most fishermen seldom use leaders shorter than $7\frac{1}{2}$ feet or longer than $9\frac{1}{2}$ feet, but *if I can* I use a leader generally half again as long as the rod I'm using. In other words, if I'm fishing a rod 6 feet long, I'll use a leader 9 feet in length; if I'm using a 9-foot rod, I'll likely fish a leader about 13 feet long. To me leaders of those lengths (and much longer), on the rods I described, are quite easy to cast, provided I have room enough to put sufficient fly line in the air to carry the leader.

"Sufficient fly line in the air" is the crux of the matter. You cannot very well cast a 14-foot leader with only 2 feet of fly line out of the rod tip. We must remember that in fly fishing we cast the *line*, and that the leader and fly simply follow along. In fishing small, brushy trout streams one of my favorite rods is a 6-foot Orvis Superfine. Since the average cast will be 15 feet or less, I use a 6- or 7-foot leader with that rod. Thus, on a normal short cast I'll have the leader in the air along with 7 to 8 feet of fly line—more than enough line to work the rod and carry out the leader and fly. With that same small rod I can easily cast to 70 feet, and when I'm on a larger river allowing casts to such distances, I will often use leaders 9 or 10 feet long. The greater length of fly line *in the air* takes care of the longer leader.

In bass-bug fishing, with a 9-foot rod I

seldom use a leader shorter than 9 feet, and more often I use one of 10 to 12 feet. Bonefish in shallow, bright water are readily spooked by a fly line, or even the shadow of a fly line, so in bonefishing I *rarely* fish a leader under 13 to 15 feet. Most of the casts to bonefish are quite long—60, 70 feet or more—so it's easy to handle a long leader. As stated earlier, though, I'm enthusiastic about long leaders and have no difficulty casting them. The average fisherman, however, prefers comparatively short leaders, and even expert fly fishermen employ short leaders and offer good arguments for their use. They'll tell you that in trout fishing, for example, they cast in such a way that they do not allow the leader to fall over the fish—so whether the leader is long or short doesn't matter. Same thing in bass fishing—they don't put the line by the stump or log where they think a bass is, just the bug, so leader length is unimportant. In fishing underwater with heavy streamer flies, too, many fishermen favor shorter leaders; they feel that a long leader will buoy up the fly. And saltwater fly-rodders also generally use leaders on the short side, believing that most saltwater species are not particularly shy, but rather tend to be aggressive and quick to strike.

Perhaps leader length is a matter of personal preference. But certainly a wise rule to follow, when fish are present but not hitting, is to go long and fine with your leaders.

DESIGNING YOUR LEADERS

I am constantly amazed at the numbers of fly fishermen I encounter who have no idea of what is, and what is not, correct leader design. A lot of fishermen, even some who've been fly fishing for years, buy commercially made leaders that are wispy, poorly designed things without sufficient body to hold a little size 18 dry fly in the air. I've seen fishermen trying to cast big popping bugs with well-chosen 9-foot rods and matching WF-9-F lines, but with hairy little leaders meant for dry-fly trout fishing. If a leader is not right for the casting job to be done, not even a fly-casting champion will cast well with it.

If you use a leader designed for light bluegill or trout fishing, then try to cast heavy flies or bugs with it, the heavy lure will surely fail to roll out with the line and will fall back on the leader. Anytime your fly line is straight and hump-free on the backcast and equally proper on the forward cast, but the leader falls back or drops in snarls and coils—and in general behaves as though it were not connected to the fly line—you have a serious leader-design problem.

Most fly fishermen know that for a particular fly rod to work and cast right it needs a matching fly line. (Thus a light trout rod might take a light DT-5 line, while a heavier bass-weight rod would need a heavier WF-9 line.) Yet those same fly fishermen will wrongly use practically the same leader whether fishing a bass-weight rod or a trout rod; the only change they make to the leader might be altering the tippet from, say, 3-pound test to 10-pound test. Otherwise, the leaders are the same.

Always use a tapered leader, but be sure it is of the *correct* taper and design. A proper leader has two major features: *castability* and *fishability*. Castability is the leader's capacity for turning over smoothly, and correctly delivering the fly to the target, even under conditions of unfavorable wind. Fishability is the combination of leader length, pound test (diameter), and proper stiffness or suppleness that encourages strikes by permitting the fly to work freely and in lifelike fashion in the water.

I cannot stress enough that a well-designed leader keeps the fly from falling back on the leader or line when the forward cast is made. A well-designed leader rolls over as the forward cast ends, and a well-designed leader lays out straight on the water.

How long a leader should be, and what strength or diameter the tippet should be, depend upon fishing conditions. Clear water and spooky fish call for long leaders and light tippets; in dingy or heavy water, perhaps with streamer flies, you might use shorter, heavier leaders.

Armstrong Spring Creek, near Livingston, Montana, is a vodka-clear stream with wall-to-wall trout and heavy insect hatches that come off daily. The late Dan Bailey and I were both fishing size 18 Light Cahill dries, but Dan was taking three fish to every one I hooked. I checked with him and learned the difference was in our tippets; Dan had gone down to a 3-foot-long 6X (1.8-pound test) tippet, while I'd been fishing a 15-inch 4X (3½-pound test) tippet. When I switched to 6X, I started matching Dan almost fish for fish.

The next day we were on the big, brawling Yellowstone River, fishing 3-inch-long bucktail streamers on 1/0 hooks for big brown trout. Under those conditions of heavy water, heavy flies, and heavy fish, we found 7½-foot leaders tapered down to 2X (7-pound test) just right.

All leaders—whether for small trout or big tarpon—should have long and heavy butts, the butt being the first and heaviest section of the leader, that part that is knotted to the fly line.

The first two-thirds of a leader (from the butt end) should be of comparatively hard, heavy, stiff nylon. This is the part of the leader that transfers the force of your cast, the forward momentum of the fly line, to the fly or bug and lays your cast out properly. The final one-third of your leader may be of short, graduating strands leading to as long and fine a tippet as desired.

Each of your fly lines should have a *permanent leader butt* (PLB) of heavy nylon attached to it with a nail knot or some variation (see Chapter 6). The PLB is a vitally important component of all your leader systems. It is actually a part of the leader, and, being the first section tied to the fly line, it contributes the most to progressively transferring the force of the cast on down the leader to the fly. (Some fishermen who do not know about the PLB system and its benefits, or who simply prefer to have a standard, old-time leader-to-line setup, tie their leaders directly to the fly-line end, using a nail knot or tucked sheet bend knot.)

The PLB should be about 3 feet long, of a diameter slightly smaller than that of the fly-line end, or *point*. Nylon testing 30 to 50 pounds (.022 to .028 inch in diameter) usually will make proper-size PLBs for fly lines from sizes 5 through 10. All leaders are knotted to the PLB, and while most leader alterations will involve changing the tapers of strands making up the final one-third of the leader, enough complete changes of leader are sometimes made that the PLB may be severely cut back—reduced in length each time a new knot is tied to connect it to a fresh leader. Thus the PLB is not actually permanent—it will not last forever—but since complete leader changes are normally rare, a PLB will serve through many seasons.

Some fishermen prefer tying a loop into the end of the PLB and either clinch-knotting the leader to the loop, or attaching the leader with another loop—that is, a loop-to-loop connection. This is a fast and easy way to join a made-up leader to the PLB, but I dislike loop-to-loop connections in a leader, except in the case of heavy salt-water leaders when doubled sections of leader are used and fast changes with ready-made leaders are so often necessary.

In ordinary freshwater fishing, particularly for trout, I'd rather not have a loop-to-loop PLB-to-leader connection because I feel it can interfere with the cast and presentation, and with the "natural" movements of the leader in the water. Actually, if a basic leader were loop-connected to a still larger loop in the PLB, this cumbersome joint would act like a hinge and would pretty much negate all the reasons for a PLB.

The best system is to blood-knot the butt end of the regular leader to the PLB. All the remaining strands in a leader also are joined by blood knots, which are small enough to pass readily through rod guides, lie flat in the finished leader, are strong, and are quick and easy to tie. Leader strands also can be connected with the wolf knot.

The leader tippet, or final strand, is another vitally important part of your leader. The tippet length, pound test (diam-eter), and hardness or softness of the nylon depend upon the size and kind of fly used, water conditions, and the species and size of fish sought.

For most fly fishing a tippet 12 or 15 inches long may be adequate; other times a tippet may be 2 or 4 feet long. A long tippet, and probably one of fine diameter, would be desirable when fishing very small dry flies, or nymphs, in clear water. A long, fine, supple tippet would permit the tiny dry fly to float more naturally, with little hindrance from tippet drag, and the nymph, too, would drift more freely in the tricky subsurface currents.

A heavier, shorter tippet, perhaps of stiff nylon, would be a good choice in fishing fan-wing dry flies or spiders, which tend to spin on the cast and twist a leader. A short, strong tippet would be desirable also in fishing heavy-hook flies or bugs—as when using streamers or popping bugs. Stout tippets are needed to turn such lures over at the end of the cast, as well as to set their large hooks into striking fish.

In turbulent water, where fish often strike fast and hard, strong tippets are needed, and the stronger tippet is necessary, too, to hold a good fish in the heavy current. Naturally if the fish you are after is one of the toothy varieties or is of better than average size, your tippet will have to be strong, and perhaps of hard rather than soft nylon.

Use "shock" tippets when fishing for needle-mouthed fish such as northern pike or barracuda (some fly fishermen use wire tippets on 'cudas and other saltwater toughs), or for fish like tarpon and snook. Fish that battle long and hard can wear through tippets; some, like snook, have

LEADERS FOR FRESHWATER FISHING

TROUT (dry fly and nymph leader) 8½ ft., tapered from 30 lb. to 3 lb.

3 ft.	1½ ft.	1½ ft.	1 ft.	6 in.	1 ft.
30 lb.	20 lb.	15 lb.	10 lb.	6 lb.	3 lb.

TROUT (streamer and bucktail leader) 7½ ft., tapered from 30 lb. to 6 lb.

3 ft.	1½ ft.	1 ft.	1 ft.	1 ft.
30 lb.	20 lb.	15 lb.	10 lb.	6 lb.

TROUT (for spooky fish in clear water) 12 ft., tapered from 30 lb. to 3 lb.

4 ft.	2½ ft.	2 ft.	1½ ft.	1 ft.	1 ft.
30 lb.	20 lb.	15 lb.	10 lb.	6 lb.	3 lb.

TROUT (very wary fish, clear water, small flies) 14 ft., tapered from 30 lb. to 6X (1.8 lb.)

5 ft.	3 ft.	2 ft.	1½ ft.	1 ft.	1½ ft.
30 lb.	20 lb.	15 lb.	10 lb.	6 lb.	1.8 lb.

PANFISH 7½ ft., tapered from 30 lb. to 4 lb.

3 ft.	2 ft.	1 ft.	1 ft.	6 in.
30 lb.	20 lb.	15 lb.	10 lb.	4 lb.

BASS 9 ft., tapered from 50 lb. to 10 lb.

3 ft.	2½ ft.	2 ft.	1½ ft.
50 lb.	25 lb.	15 lb.	10 lb.

NORTHERN PIKE 9 ft., tapered from 50 lb. to 12 lb. with 30-lb. shock tippet

3 ft.	2 ft.	2 ft.	1 ft.	1 ft.
50 lb.	25 lb.	15 lb.	12 lb.	30 lb.

LEADERS FOR SALTWATER FISHING

LIGHT (shad, bonefish, ladyfish, etc.) 9½ ft., tapered from 50 lb. to 12 lb.

LIGHT, LONG (spooky bonefish, etc.) 13½ ft., tapered from 50 lb. to 6 lb.

MEDIUM (small tarpon, channel bass, striped bass, etc.) 9½ ft., tapered from 50 lb. to 12 lb.

HEAVY (large tarpon, snook, barracuda, etc.) 9½ ft., tapered from 50 lb. to 12 lb. with 30-lb. to 100-lb. shock tippet.

SPECIAL HEAVY (large tarpon, sailfish, sharks, giant barracuda, etc.) 9 ft., tapered from 50 lb. to shock tippet of wire or 80–100 lb. monofilament.

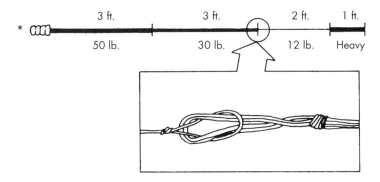

*Permanent leader butt nail-knotted to fly line.

sharp, razor-edged gill plates; and abuse from a fish's slapping tail or even its scales can cut and fray light leader tips. Use shock tippets 12 inches long of hard leader material testing 30 to 100 pounds, depending on the fish you're after. A 30-pound tippet will be okay for most northern pike fishing, although I've been into big ones that cut 60-pound tippets. If you want 100-pound-class tarpon you'll likely need 80- to 100-pound-test tippets. Attach a shock tippet to the leader with a surgeon's knot, improved blood knot, nail knot or variation, loop-to-loop knot, shocker knot, or Albright Special knot.

The preceeding illustrations show some basic leader designs for fresh and salt water. These are intended only to be a general guide, something to work from, as fishing conditions as well as individual skills will dictate, on a day-to-day basis, what is a proper leader.

Regarding the special heavy saltwater leader: Some fly fishermen make them up with continuous butt sections 6 feet long, of monofilament testing 30, 40, or 50 pounds, then a section of mono of 12- or 15-pound test (or less) measuring no less than 1 foot.

The rules for various fly-fishing tournaments usually stipulate that the weakest part of the leader can be no less than 12 inches in length. This is the section of the leader tied in for qualifying purposes in the various pound-test divisions of tournaments, and it might test 6, 10, 12, or 15 pounds. For most tournaments, 15-pound test is the maximum allowed.

There are many different ways to build a special heavy saltwater leader, and many

varied knots that can be used, but the majority of fly-rodders prefer to tie loops in both ends of the lighter monofilament, and in the heavy butt end. Loops facilitate quick changing of the weaker strand, as well as of shock tippets. Light qualifying strands are pre-tied to, say, 80- and 100-pound monofilament shock tippets, or to wire. Any loop knot can be used to put a serviceable loop into the heavy leader butt, but the Bimini twist or spider hitch are preferred to put loops in the lighter leader section, because those knots double the line.

One of the doubled ends of the lighter monofilament should be folded back and doubled again by tying in a surgeon's or a double surgeon's knot. This gives a doubly strengthened loop to be interlocked with the loop in the heavy butt strand.

The other end of the light mono is tied to a heavy monofilament shock tippet either with a surgeon's knot or an Albright Special knot. If the shock tippet is braided wire (cable), however, connect it to the lighter mono with a surgeon's knot. If it is single-strand wire it's best to make a loop in the wire using a haywire twist, then attach the light mono to it with an Albright Special knot. Whatever the test or material, for most tournament purposes shock tippets may not be longer than 12 inches.

Flies or bugs can be tied to very heavy monofilament shock tippets with a two-wrap hangman's knot, Homer Rhode loop knot, or a $3\frac{1}{2}$-turn clinch knot. If the tippet is single-strand wire, attach flies or bugs with the haywire twist or the overhand wire wrap; if it is cable or braided wire, use the figure-8 knot or Homer Rhode loop knot.

A final leader type to consider is the multiple-fly leader, applicable almost exclusively in freshwater fishing, especially trout fishing. The multiple-fly leader can be of any length, test, or overall design. Its only variation from the norm is that it has additional strands (called "dropper" strands) from the base leader at points above the tippet to which extra flies are tied. In general, dropper strands should be somewhat weaker than the strands making up the basic leader. This way if one fly should snag, only it will be lost and none of the flies or other parts of the leader. A good rule is to have the dropper strands test the same as the leader tippet. And another idea for dropper strands is to use stiffer nylon in the droppers than in the basic leader. Stiff nylon helps keep the dropper flies well away from the main leader to avoid fouling.

The multiple-fly leader is used chiefly in fishing wet flies for trout. While fishing two or more wet flies is a technique seldom used by modern anglers, at one time it was a common method. Most fishermen trying multiple-fly setups seldom use more than two flies, or perhaps three, but leaders rigged with four flies (of varying patterns and sizes, to determine which the fish prefer) can be very effective.

On a Green River, Wyoming, trip a friend fished almost daily with a leader having ten different nymphs tied on dropper strands. He did very well with it, too.

One spring day on Wisconsin's upper Wolf River, at the height of the white bass spawning run, I rigged a leader with three size 1/0 bonefish flies—one on the point or tippet, and two on dropper strands on either side farther up the leader. There were so many white bass that I'd make a cast and twitch the flies until a fish hit one and was hooked. Then that fish would pull the other flies around, darting here, then there, and soon a second white bass would strike one of the flies, and then finally a third. I'd play three white bass at a time, and by fishing that way I literally filled our ice chest with the tasty panfish.

Following is a basic diagram for the construction of a typical multiple-fly leader.

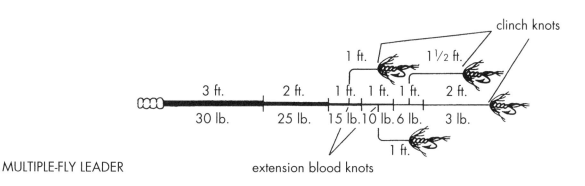

MULTIPLE-FLY LEADER

Something else to clarify regarding leaders is the X and /5 classifications. A couple of centuries ago European watchmakers, attempting to standardize their draw-plate holes, marked or sized the holes with the symbols X or /5. (A draw plate is a metal plate with a gradation of conical holes through which wires are drawn to get the desired thickness). The watchmaker's diameter symbols carried over to the practice of drawing silkworm gut to be used in leader construction. Although now our important leader materials are synthetic, the classification system is still with us, and almost all ready-made leaders are sized and marked according to those symbols, and much nylon leader material is similarly coded.

Following is a table to serve as a guide to classifications, diameters, and tests of leaders and leader materials. While there are variations in synthetics according to manufacturer, the table is basically accurate.

LEADER MATERIAL

Classification	Diameter (inch)	Pound test
1/5	.021	32.5
2/5	.020	29.0
3/5	.019	26.3
4/5	.018	23.6
5/5	.017	20.5
6/5	.016	18.5
7/5	.015	16.8
8/5	.014	14.0
9/5	.013	12.1
10/5	.012	11.0
0X	.011	9.0
1X	.010	7.8
2X	.009	7.0
3X	.008	5.3
4X	.007	3.5
5X	.006	2.5
6X	.005	1.8
7X	.004	1.0

While many kinds of ready-made leaders are on the market, and some are of good quality and design, in my opinion you are better off making your own. First of all, most factory-made leaders are no good. They are, in fact, abominable. The reason for this is not that tackle firms cannot make good leaders, but that the people designing them do not know enough about fly fishing to understand the features needed in a good leader. Moreover, even if you buy ready-made leaders, you will be knotting on flies, cutting tippets back, adding tippets, and so on, so you might as well learn to fashion your own leaders from the beginning. You'll save money, too, since for a few bucks you can buy enough monofilament leader material to make leaders for several seasons.

Many years ago I designed the first "leader-tie" kit ever made, for the DuPont company, one of our largest monofilament producers. The kit consisted of various tests of monofilament on handy spools; a pamphlet giving leader designs, knots, and instructions on how to make up leaders; a plastic tube for tying nail knots; and a square of rubber to use in straightening leaders.

That particular kit is no longer available, but a few companies imitated it and, in fact, made leader-tie kits far superior to the original. I recommend that you purchase a leader-tie kit, at least to get started in making your own leaders.

Knotless-tapered leaders are being turned out by many companies, and slick advertising cons a lot of fly fishermen into thinking knotless-tapers are the last word in fly fishing—giving faultless casting, perfect presentation, and none of the weaknesses or bad characteristics of knotted leaders. Most knotless-tapered leaders are extruded in a continuous taper, and many of them will *not* turn over on the cast except for a fly-casting expert. In recent years, however, at least a few manufacturers have redesigned their knotless leaders, stiffening and enlarging the butt sections and generally tapering them better so that some indeed cast very well. The thing to consider, though, is that a knotless leader is only knotless until you need to attach a fresh tippet to it, and then it is, like every other leader, one with knots. I think the so-called advantages of knotless leaders are far overdone. To repeat, I feel we are better off designing and building our own leaders.

No matter how well designed a leader, it will tend to kink or, if reeled onto a fly reel and left there for long, it will come off in loopy spirals and need straightening. You can straighten a leader by drawing it back and forth through a square of rubber (automobile innertube rubber is fine, if you can find an innertube to cut), or a soft piece of chamois will do, or as a last resort you can pull a kinky leader under the sole of a tennis shoe or around the rubber bottom of a pair of hip boots or waders.

Many fly fishermen want their leaders to sink, especially trout fishermen using dry flies. They feel the leader that doesn't sink will make "dents" on the surface, and otherwise will be noticeable to trout and the fish will shy away. So those fishermen employ various kinds of "leader sink" to get their leaders under the surface. There are commercial preparations of leader sink, and spittle will take a leader under for a while, as will fish slime, or a little mud or clay applied to the leader. Trouble is, all

Many tackle companies market knotless-tapered leaders, which are preferred by some fly fishermen. Other anglers prefer to design and make their own leaders, using nylon monofilament of various sizes that is packaged by manufacturers on handy spools.

such applications to a leader do not last long, and after a few casts they wash off and the leader again is floating in the surface film.

I long ago quit using any kind of leader sink, not only because it doesn't last, but because it has doubtful value. I have not noticed that I catch more fish when my leader sinks. As a matter of fact, I do not know a skilled fly angler who any longer uses any kind of leader sink.

A final point on leaders: While fishing, check your leader periodically for nicks and abrasions throughout its length. This is especially important when angling for the big, tough guys—tarpon, snook, large northern pike—because they might nick a leader and, if it goes unnoticed, the next fish you hook may be lost. And it just could be the trophy of your fly-fishing lifetime.

This brings us to the choices of *brands* of monofilament in tying our own leaders. Excepting the point or tippet section of leaders I tie, I want my leader to be reasonably stiff so that it turns over at completion of the cast. To have a wispy leader that doesn't follow through with the forward momentum of the cast is a serious mistake.

Today there are a zillion different kinds of monofilament leader-tying material on the market, all of it different. All of us need to try the different monos available and determine which suits our needs best. For what it's worth, my favorite leader-tie monofilament is Maxima, made in West Germany. It has a stiffness I like, fine enough diameter (for test), and is strong enough (for test). Other kinds of monofilament for leaders I like are Ande, Berkley's Performa, and Feather Merchants Umpqua. I feel that DuPont's monofilament is far too soft, too supple, to make for good fly leader material.

For serious fly fishermen who may be interested, Al McClane used the following leader for almost all of his trout fishing, anywhere in the world: 40 inches of .018 nylon monofilament, 36 inches of .017, 7 inches of .016, 7 inches of .014, 7 inches of .013, 7 inches of .012, and, finally, 28 inches of .010.

All that leader was good for was catching fish.

6

Popular Fly-Fishing Knots

IT COULD be said that a fly fisherman is no better than his knots. Certainly it is no good to own the best tackle, have plenty of fly-fishing knowledge, and be a skilled caster if, when fish are hooked, leaders snap or knots pull out. Fly fishermen, perhaps more so than other anglers, must look to their knots.

A fly fisherman cannot expect to successfully turn on enough rod power to keep a husky bass out of brush if his leader knots are poor. The angler who hooks a nice trout in heavy current is sure to lose it if the fly is not properly tied to the leader tippet. And the husky saltwater fish—tarpon, sailfish, king mackerel, striped bass—are a supreme test of the fly fisherman's knots. The fly angler who does not take the time to learn to tie correctly at least a representative and practical assortment of knots might as well hang up his rod. His fishing will only be one defeat, one frustration atop another.

The leader is the weakest part of the fly fisherman's equipment. And, commonly,

the knots in a leader are its weakest parts, as is the knot connecting the leader tippet to the fly or bug. The skillful knotting of the leader butt to the fly line, of the various sections making up a tapered leader, of shock tippets, and, finally, of the leader point to the fly—all this means the difference between simply hooking fish or *hooking fish and landing them.*

The average fly fisherman, under most conditions, needs to know how to tie only a few knots. For example, if you can tie a nail knot, blood knot, clinch knot, surgeon's knot, and, say, a Homer Rhode loop knot, you will be able to handle almost any knot-tying situation that comes up while fly fishing. But all-around fly fishing, for various species of gamefish under varying conditions, calls for a working knowledge of many different kinds of knots. Certain circumstances arise in diversified fly fishing that make specific knots especially valuable. So the skilled fly fisherman is capable of tying many different knots; he is able to tie them quickly and to tie them well.

Just about every knot known reduces the strength of the line or leader it is tied into, but how much the line/leader test is diminished depends upon the knot tied and how well it is tied. For example, nylon monofilament in a leader tippet, when tied to a fly with a clinch knot, loses 10 to 15 percent of its strength. If the clinch knot is tied badly, the tippet strength is reduced even more.

The best knots, however, when tied right, usually will provide close to 95 percent of the stated line strength, and other knots when tied correctly should reduce line strength by no more than 85 percent.

When monofilament line is turned over on itself at certain angles, it is *self-cutting*. Thus certain knots that bend over themselves are *cutting knots* and shouldn't be used unless absolutely necessary. Such knots include the half-hitch, double half-hitch, and figure-eight.

To learn to tie a knot, practice with heavy cord, light rope, or a discarded fly line (which is perfect), rather than with slick, fine, nylon monofilament. Practicing with heavy, easy-to-handle material will help you see how a knot is shaped and formed.

Fly fishermen tying monofilament nylon to another material must be very careful to tie knots properly. In knots where the friction is against material other than nylon monofilament, the knot will likely slip. In knots where the friction is chiefly on the mono itself, there is less likelihood that the knot will slip, break, or untie.

The first step in tying any knot—forming, or shaping—is important. A knot that is not formed correctly will not draw up properly; neither will it tighten as it should.

Every knot should be formed slowly, carefully, being sure that each turn is as it should be, each loop in its proper place. When the knot has been correctly formed it should then be drawn up slowly. Never yank—always pull evenly, gently, deliberately, so that all components of the knot remain in their proper places and fit together snugly.

Wet a knot to be drawn up with saliva, which will serve as a lubricant and aid in fitting the knot turns tightly together. And use your thumb and the nail of the first finger to force knot turns tightly together. In tightening a knot, pull firmly and steadily on its standing parts, as well as on all ends. Apply as much pressure in tightening as the material will take without breaking. You cannot tighten a knot too much. Remember that a knot that isn't tightened correctly is going to slip under pressure, and once the knot slips it is almost sure to break or to pull free.

Some of the most painful cuts a fisherman can get come from tightening nylon monofilament knots. Fine mono, especially, can slice through a finger as easily as a razor. Use pliers, wear gloves, or wrap a handkerchief or boat rag around your fingers when pulling knots tight. When I'm on a boat and have to pull up a knot tied to a fly in very heavy monofilament, I hang the hook bend in a screw eye, or to a metal ring that is well seated somewhere on the boat, and then I pull on the standing line and the knot's tag end to tighten it securely. Jimmy Albright, the famed bonefish-tarpon guide at Islamorada in the Florida Keys, always goes barefoot, and his feet are so tough he can wrap 100-pound-test mono around a big toe and, with gloved hands, pull a knot tight. I need to wrap heavy mono around a sneaker to tighten a knot.

The final step in tying a knot is checking to see that it is perfect. If it is less than perfect, a knot should be redone. No experienced angler ever simply ties a knot and then starts fishing; the skilled fisherman *always* checks a new knot carefully before making his first cast.

In checking a knot, first take a good look at it to see if it appears right. Many improperly tied knots look just that way— like improperly tied knots. If you see that a turn hasn't pulled into place exactly right, that there is perhaps an unwanted hump in the knot, or some other deficiency, cut the knot off and tie another.

If the knot is one that joins lines—for example, fly line to backing—pull on both ends as hard as the lines will bear. If the knot connects to a fly or bug, pull on it to see that it holds.

Never test a knot by yanking on it. A sudden yank against even a perfectly tied knot can pop it or the line/leader/backing. Neither backing lines nor fly lines nor leaders are made to withstand that sort of abuse.

The tag ends of knots (overhang) should always be trimmed as close as possible. Many fisherman do not trim excess tag ends because they fear the knot may pull out. A knot that has been tied correctly can be trimmed very close, and it will not pull out. Always cut or clip tag ends, never burn them with a cigarette or a match. Burning may weaken the knot or the line. The best tool for trimming knots closely is a pair of so-called nail clippers, and the best are those made especially for fishermen. Heavy-duty clippers are available that will easily cut the heaviest nylon, and the better ones have files, cutting edges, hook-disgorgers, and other tools.

When tying a knot, always allow yourself plenty of material with which to work. Probably half the trouble beginners have in learning to tie knots is never taking enough material. You should have at least 8 to 10 inches of line to work with when tying a knot, and some knots require more than that if they are to be formed readily. By working with plenty of monofilament or line, you'll be able to best form and tighten a knot, and, moreover, you'll tie the knot more quickly.

An attempt has been made to present the fly-fishing knots that follow in useful order. For instance, since the first thing the fly fisherman does is attach line to his fly reel (either backing line or fly line), we show this connection first. Next for most fly anglers is attaching backing to the fly line, then attaching a leader butt to the fly line, then tapering a leader, and finally building shock tippets and/or tying on a fly.

FASTENING BACKING LINE (OR FLY LINE) TO A FLY REEL

Wrap the backing or fly line around the reel spool. Tie an overhand knot around the standing part of the line. Tie a smaller overhand knot at the line end, tighten both knots, and "jam" them against the spool.

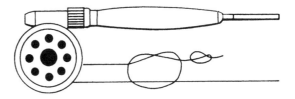

KNOTTING BACKING LINE TO FLY LINE

1. Form a square knot in the fly line and backing line.

backing line

2. Draw the fly line straight, and tug the backing line downward. Pull the square knot tight, and tie 6 half-hitches around the fly line with the short end of the backing.

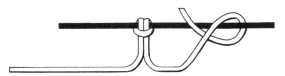

3. Tighten the half-hitches, and trim the short end of the backing line. Wrap the knot with nylon thread, and continue over the knot, wrapping the short end of the fly line to the backing.

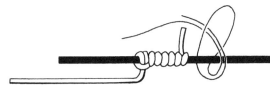

4. After wrapping with nylon thread, coat the entire knot with Pliobond cement or lacquer.

MAKING A FLY-LINE LOOP

Most fly fishermen no longer use fly line loops for attaching leaders to fly lines, or for joining backing to a fly line, but some anglers still prefer fly-line loops. When properly made the following loop is very strong, yet small enough to pass through rod guides easily.

1. Soak about 3 inches of the fly line's end in nail-polish remover to loosen its finish. Scrape off the loosened coating.

2. Bend the cleaned fly line back to form a loop.

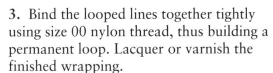

3. Bind the looped lines together tightly using size 00 nylon thread, thus building a permanent loop. Lacquer or varnish the finished wrapping.

TYING A PERMANENT LOOP IN MONOFILAMENT FLY LINE

This loop can be made in any type of fly line, but it is used most often in looping monofilament fly lines. Double back the fly line to make the desired-size loop. Then, with lengths of light monofilament, tie two fast nail knots (see below), about ¼ inch apart, around both fly-line strands. This loop is exceptionally strong and passes readily through rod guides.

NAIL KNOT

To the fly fisherman, this is one of the most important of all knots. Every angler should master it. There are many variations of this well-known tie, but the basic nail knot remains the one most commonly used.

The nail knot is perfect for joining backing line to a fly line, and for connecting leader butts to a fly-line point.

A small tube or air-pump needle, rather than a nail, can be used in tying a nail knot. It's easier to pass line back under the knot's wraps by using a tube or hollow needle.

1. Lay out the fly line and leader with the nail between.

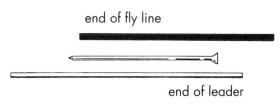

end of fly line

end of leader

2. Wrap the leader toward the end of the fly line, making 5 tight turns, then pass its free end back through the center of the loops.

end of fly line

end of leader

3. This is how the knot should now look, with the nail still in place.

4. Pull on both ends of the leader and fly line, and slowly withdraw the nail. Once the nail is removed, pull tightly on all four strands of line protruding from the knot.

pull again

pull again

5. This is how the finished nail knot looks, with the two short ends trimmed close.

FAST NAIL KNOT

The fast nail knot is the best of the nail knots for attaching a leader butt to a fly line. It can be tied in seconds. The fast nail knot, however, is of no use in attaching backing line to a fly line, since it is necessary to loop the line over itself, and that can't be done when tying to backing line.

The fast nail knot can be made with a straightened paper clip (as illustrated), a nail, a toothpick, a sliver of wood, a needle—anything straight and rigid.

1. Hold a paper clip (or similar rigid item) parallel to the fly line. Form a loop with the nylon filament and lay it over the fly line and paper clip. A is the leader butt, B is the leader butt end. All components are held at point X with the thumb and forefinger of the left hand.

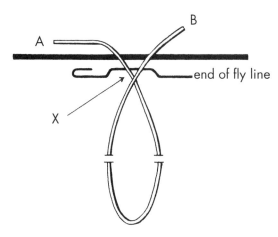

2. Continue holding all components at X, and with the right hand holding the mono leader at about D, begin rolling the monofilament line over itself at C. The mono is looped over itself, the fly line, and the paper clip.

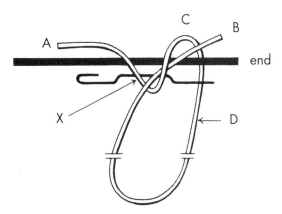

3. Still holding at X with thumb and forefinger, wrap the mono around itself, the fly line, and the clip about 6 to 9 times.

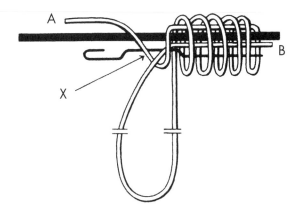

4. Holding firmly at X, pull the mono end B through on the right side of the knot until the knot tightens. End B will lengthen as the mono is pulled through the nail knot.

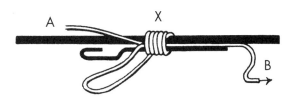

5. Now the paper clip is withdrawn from the knot, and the knot is tightened by pulling on both A and B ends of the monofilament.

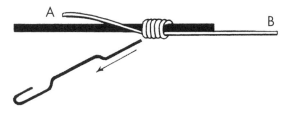

6. The completed fast nail knot looks like this after it has been trimmed and tightened.

VARIATION OF THE NAIL KNOT

As with the other nail knots, this one is most useful in fastening heavy leader butts to fly lines. Since this knot has only a few turns, some anglers find it easier to tie than other types of nail knots.

1. No tying is done with the fly line. Hold the nail parallel to the fly line and form a loop with the leader butt.

2. Hold the loop below the fly line and wrap the leader's butt end twice around the fly line and standing part of the leader.

3. Put the butt end through the last wrap and the first loop, as shown.

4. Push all the wraps tightly together with your thumb nail, and withdraw the nail slowly.

5. Pull on both ends of the leader, then trim the tag ends of leader and line.

NEEDLE NAIL KNOT

This is an excellent knot for joining leader to fly line, It takes a little time to tie, but it permits the leader to lay out very straight, because the leader is drawn through the center of the fly line.

1. Push the needle through the end of the fly line and out again about 1/4 inch from the end. Put the end of the leader through the needle eye, and pull the needle through the fly line, which will bring the nylon leader after it.

leader   needle   fly line

2. Now tie a conventional nail knot, but use the needle instead of a nail. Make 4 to 6 wraps around the needle, then put the end of the leader through the needle eye.

3. Now pull the needle through the knot, and the leader will follow.

4. After the short leader end is trimmed, the finished knot looks like this.

VARIATION OF THE NEEDLE KNOT

This is a good line-leader connection for light freshwater fishing. Some fly-rodders prefer this knot because it comes straight out the center of the fly line.

1. Thread the leader butt through the eye of the needle. Push the needle through the center of the fly line, then out about ½ inch from the line end.

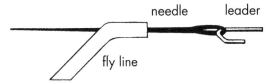

needle leader

fly line

2. This is how the knot should look thus far.

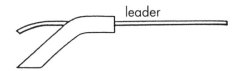

leader

3. Push the needle completely through the fly line a second time, 1 inch above the point where the needle passed through the line initially. Then insert the needle a third time—into and out of the fly line—as illustrated.

4. At this stage the knot should look like this.

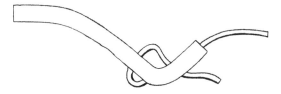

5. Tie a figure-eight knot in the end of the leader butt.

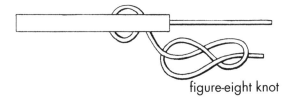

figure-eight knot

6. Pull on the standing part of the leader to draw the knot tight.

SINGLE OVERHAND LOOP KNOT

This is the easiest knot for making a loop in the end of a length of line. Simply double the line and make an overhand knot.

This is not the strongest knot to use in making a line loop. For most light fresh-water angling, this is an adequate tie. However, its strength can be substantially enhanced by passing the loop through a second time to create a *surgeon's loop*.

LEADER LOOP KNOT

This is a strong knot, quickly tied, for forming a loop in a line to which a leader may be attached. This loop is best when used with stiff monofilament or a fly line, rather than with braided lines.

1. Tie a loose overhand knot about 6 inches from the end of the line. Pass the end of the line through the center of the overhand knot.

2. The end of the line is then brought around the overhand knot and passed through the two openings of the knot.

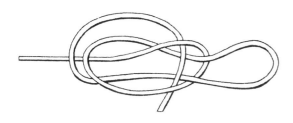

3. The finished leader loop knot after the tag end has been trimmed.

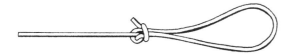

JOINING TWO LOOPS

This is a very popular method for joining a fly line to a leader, but it's not the best way.

A nail knot is superior. This loop-to-loop connection is also used to join monofilament line to braided line.

1. Pass one loop through the other loop. Then pull the remaining line through the loop, as shown.

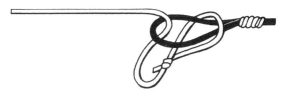

2. The knot when the two loops are drawn tight.

JAM KNOT

Jam knots are used chiefly for joining fly lines to leaders. They're practical for connecting almost any kinds of lines, but the overhand knot must be tied well before pulling the jam knot tight.

overhand knot

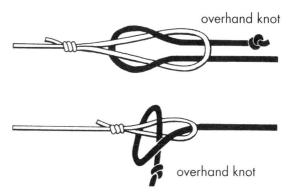

overhand knot

TUCKED SHEET BEND

This is a fairly popular knot for connecting a leader to a fly line. It's quick to tie.

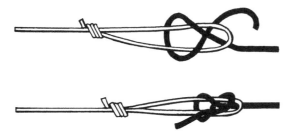

BLOOD KNOT

This is the knot commonly used by veteran fly fishermen for connecting mono strands when building tapered leaders. The knot is easy to tie, and it's very strong when formed properly. It's a small knot and runs through rod guides easily. Only monofilament of nearly equal diameters should be joined with the blood knot to assure maximum knot strength.

1. Cross two sections of monofilament and wrap one section 3 or 4 times around the other. Now place the wrapped end through the loop formed by the two mono sections.

2. Turn the other line around the standing part of the first line 3 or 4 times and put its free end through the loop from the opposite side.

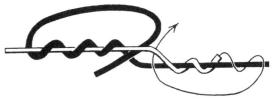

3. At this stage the turns should look this way. Now slowly pull on both ends of the line.

4. The finished knot, with ends trimmed closely.

IMPROVED BLOOD KNOT

This is an excellent knot for connecting lines of different diameters, such as 12- to 60-pound monofilament.

1. Double the smaller-diameter line. Wrap it 5 times around the larger, and bring it back between the two strands.

2. Twist the larger diameter line around the doubled line 3 times, and place its free end back through the loop in the opposite direction.

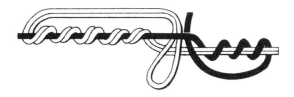

3. Pull the knot slowly to tighten it. Use your fingernails to push the loops of the knot together. Trim all loose ends ½ inch from the knot.

WOLF KNOT

A fine knot for connecting monofilament of about equal diameters; used most often in tying leaders.

EXTENSION BLOOD KNOT

This is the best way to form dropper strands in a leader for fishing two or more flies. Other knots are better, though, if the leader is already "made up," since with a completed leader it would be necessary to cut it, then to rejoin with the extension blood knot.

If the angler knows, however, while making up his leader, that he will use a dropper fly or two, then this *always* is the knot to use.

1. Wind one leader strand 3 times around the standing part of the second leader strand, and bring the end back behind the first turn. Do the same with the other leader end.

2. Pull on the standing part of both leader strands to draw the knot tight. Trim only one of the tag ends of the knot. The other lengthy tag end becomes the dropper line for attaching a fly.

DROPPER SNELL KNOT

This is the quickest way to fasten a snelled fly to a leader. It's an adequate tie for light fishing.

ANOTHER DROPPER KNOT

A good knot to use for tying a dropper strand to a leader when an extension blood knot is impractical. Jam the dropper knot against a knot in the leader and it will be a small connection.

1. Lay the leader and dropper side by side. Wrap the dropper around the leader 3 times, then push its end back through the first loop.

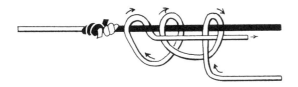

2. Pull the knot tight and trim all ends except the long dropper strand.

IMPROVED DROPPER LOOP

This loop can be tied quickly in a standing leader. Once the loop is tied, another strand of monofilament is tied to the loop, and a fly is knotted to the other end of the dropper strand.

1. Form a 3-inch loop in the line. Pinch the two lines that cross to make the loop and twist the loop 5 times around the two crossed lines. When this is done correctly, the loop appears as illustrated.

2. Open the center of the twisted lines and pass the loop through. Now draw the two ends tight. A finger or pencil placed in the loop will prevent the loop from pulling out while tightening.

3. The finished loop.

SPIDER HITCH KNOT

To double a line, most fishermen now use this knot rather than the Bimini twist. The spider hitch is faster to tie and has good strength—double the strength of a single line.

1. Double the line, then put a small reverse loop in it.

2. Hold the reverse loop with thumb and forefinger.

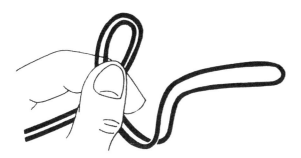

3. Wrap the doubled line 5 times around the thumb and the reverse loop. Then pass the large loop through the small loop.

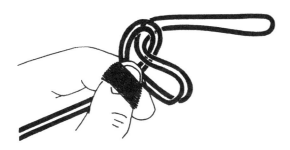

4. Slowly pull the large loop so that the line unwinds off the thumb, pulling until the knot tightens.

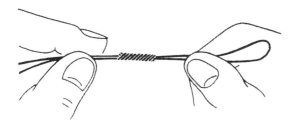

BIMINI TWIST

Though some knots serve as well or better than the Bimini twist, and are easier to tie (the spider hitch, for example), many fishermen still prefer the Bimini for making a doubled line. The Bimini has 100 percent knot strength. It is used in making up heavy saltwater leaders or shock tippets.

1. Double the end of the line along the standing part of the line for about 4 feet. Then twist the line 20 times, creating a loop, as shown.

2. Pull all four ends apart so that the 20 twists will be forced tightly together, leaving a wide loop.

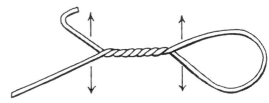

3. Keep the twists tightly together, and begin winding the end of the line back over the twists.

4. Continue winding the end of the line over the twists until the line reaches the loop.

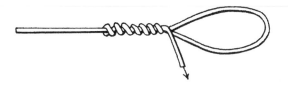

5. Hold the end of the twists with one hand, and make an overhand knot around one side of the loop.

6. Make an overhand knot around the other side of the loop. (Some anglers make this overhand knot around the two lines of the loop rather than around just one side and then the other.)

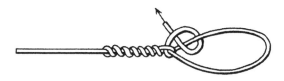

7. Wind the line end 3 times around the two lines of the large loop, and push the end back through the small loop just made.

8. Slowly pull on the standing line and the large loop to draw the Bimini twist tight.

ALBRIGHT SPECIAL KNOT

This is a preferred knot for connecting light monofilament to heavy, or for tying mono to wire cable, nylon-coated wire, or to small-diameter single-strand wire. A most useful, important, and strong knot.

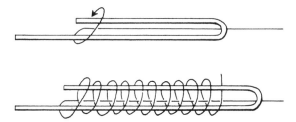

SURGEON'S KNOT

Many highly skilled fly-rodders consider this the best knot for joining two strands of monofilament of greatly varying diameters. It's used primarily to attach heavy shock tippets to lighter leader tips, usually 12-pound-test mono.

This can be a difficult knot to tighten. It should be moistened after forming, then drawn tight by pulling slowly and evenly on all four loose ends.

shock leader

leader tippet

SHOCKER KNOT

Another good knot for tying together mono of different diameters. It's easy and fast to tie, but strong and secure.

1. Make an overhand knot in the light mono. Form a loose overhand knot in the heavy mono and pass the end of the light mono through the knot.

2. Make 3 wraps with the light mono around the heavy, and thread the end back through the first loop.

CLINCH KNOT

The favored knot among fly fishermen for tying flies to leader tippets. It can be untied by grasping the mono between the thumbnail and first fingernail, at the hook-eye, and pulling slowly away. The improved clinch knot cannot be untied.

1. Thread the end of the leader through the hook-eye. Put about 6 inches of mono through the eye so there will be ample line with which to tie the knot.

2. Bring the end of the mono back toward the standing part and wrap the end 5 times around the standing leader. Next pass the mono end back through the first loop.

3. Slowly pull on the standing part of the leader, and the leader end, until the turns in the knot draw tightly against the hook-eye.

4. To increase the strength of the clinch knot, pass the end through the large loop before tightening. The result is called the *improved clinch knot*.

DOUBLE IMPROVED CLINCH KNOT

1. Double the leader, bringing the end back parallel to the standing mono so there is about 8 inches of double line. Take the end of the doubled leader and push it through the hook-eye. Wrap the doubled mono end 5 times around the doubled standing part, and pass the line end back through the loop formed near the hook-eye.

2. Thread the doubled leader end through the loop in front of the hook-eye, then put the end through the large loop, as shown.

TURLE KNOT

The Turle is a desirable knot when tying flies with turned-up or turned-down eyes to leaders, because this knot causes the leader to pull away from the hook-eye in a straight line—important in getting decent action or float from the fly, and in striking fish.

1. Pass the leader end through the hook-eye, tie a simple overhand knot around the standing part, and form a loop in the leader.

2. Pass the fly through the loop.

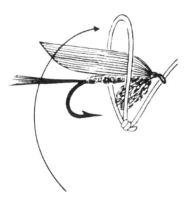

3. With the loop snug behind the hook-eye, pull the knot tight against the fly's neck.

HOMER RHODE LOOP KNOT

This knot, named after the famous Keys guide who developed it, is used for attaching a heavy shock monofilament leader tip to a fly or bug. Very heavy mono will not pull up with some knots, but it will with the Rhode Loop.

1. Tie an overhand knot about 4 inches from the end of the leader. Push the end of the leader through the hook-eye, then back through the center of the overhand knot.

2. Next, with the end of the leader, make another overhand knot around the standing part of the leader. Slowly pull the two knots tight, at the same time sliding them together so they "jam" or lock one against the other.

PORTLAND CREEK HITCH

An important knot in fly fishing. It is used most often by Atlantic salmon anglers, and by trout fishermen who wish to skim a fly over the surface. The knot causes the leader tippet to pull the fly at about a forty-five-degree angle, which keeps the fly head up and makes the fly form a wake on the surface.

The Portland Creek hitch is just that—a hitch, or loop, thrown over the head of the fly. So another knot, preferably a Turle knot, is first tied to the fly's eye; then the Portland Creek hitch. The hitch slips off the fly's head when a fish strikes and the leader draws taut. It does not leave an unwanted knot in the leader.

END-LOOP KNOT

A good knot for attaching flies or bugs to heavy monofilament shock tippets. The knot forms a large loop through the hook-eye, allowing the lure to have good action in the water.

1. Tie an overhand knot about 6 inches from the end of the leader, then pass the leader through the hook-eye.

2. Put the leader through the open overhand knot and tie a half-hitch with the leader end onto the standing part of the leader.

3. Slide the overhand knot either up or down the standing part of the leader. This will determine the size of the loop that the knot will form. Slowly pull the leader end and its standing part to tighten the knot.

4. Trim the knot, leaving a tag end about ⅛ inch long.

NAIL LOOP KNOT

By far the best and most reliable knot for tying a loop to a fly so that it will have the best free-swimming action in the water. This is a strong, recommended knot.

1. Put the line end through the hook-eye, leaving about 8 inches with which to tie the knot. Lay the line end parallel to the standing part and place a nail, tube, or toothpick between the two strands. Then make 3½ wraps with the end of the line back toward the hook-eye.

2. Next slip the line end forward through the loops made by turning the line over the two parallel strands.

3. When this knot is tied carefully, and the loops are pulled tight, the knot should look like this.

TWO-WRAP HANGMAN'S KNOT

This is an especially valuable knot for fly fishermen because with it, a loop of any size can be tied in a leader tippet—even a heavy shock tippet—and the loop will permit a fly to swim in a lifelike manner. This is a sliding loop knot. When a fish strikes and is hooked, the knot slides down the leader and tightens against the hook-eye.

1. Thread the leader tippet through the hook-eye, then make 2 wraps around the standing leader back toward the hook-eye. Keep the loops loose, holding them open with your fingers.

2. Push the leader back through the two loops, away from the hook-eye.

3. Next pull slowly on the standing part and tag ends of the knot. When the knot is almost tight, it can be slid up or down the leader, forming whatever size loop is desired. Then the knot should be pulled completely tight.

WIRE CONNECTIONS

Wire is needed for shock tippets in leaders for much fly fishing, particularly for certain saltwater species such as sharks, barracuda, king mackerel, and bluefish. Some fishermen use wire shock tippets in fishing for northern pike and muskies in fresh water, but I feel heavy nylon monofilament makes much better pike–muskie tippets.

In any case, wire tippets are occasionally needed, and tying them to flies or bugs presents special problems. Wire is stiff and it kinks, so the practical knots that can be used in connecting wire to fly-rod lures are limited. The following are the knots preferred by most fly fishermen.

OVERHAND WIRE WRAP

Pass wire through the hook-eye, wrap around standing part of wire 5 times, then break off.

HAYWIRE TWIST

Thread about 5 inches of wire through the hook-eye. Bend the end of the wire back over its standing part, forming a small loop. Wrap the end of the wire over the standing part 6 or 7 times. Then hold the standing part straight out from the hook-eye and wrap the wire end tightly around it 6 times. Bend the tag end of the wire until it breaks.

FIGURE-EIGHT KNOT

This is a fast knot to tie, and it is reasonably secure when working with braided wire.

Pass the wire through the hook-eye. Bring the end back and wind it once around the standing part of the wire, then insert the end through the loop formed in front of the hook-eye.

7

Fly-Casting Basics

MANY an expert fly fisherman professes that fly casting is the simplest kind of casting, much less difficult than bait casting or spinning. And many a fisherman who does no fly fishing, only bait casting and/or spinning, will hurriedly agree that fly casting is "the easiest casting of all."

Baloney. Pure baloney.

Certainly, *ordinary* fly casting is easy; I can teach a five-year-old child to cast a fly 25 feet in a half-hour or less of instruction. But that is a long way from *skillful* fly casting—the kind of casting that will enable an angler to cast all day long, in all kinds of weather and wind conditions, with big flies or bugs, and do it efficiently, effortlessly, and with little if any fatigue.

One of my dearest friends was the late Leo Pachner, once a tackle manufacturer and editor–publisher of *Farm Pond Harvest Magazine*, Momence, Illinois. Leo was a nut for bluegill and bass, in that order, and to him a long cast with a fly rod is 40 feet. Leo insisted that anyone (including me) who advocates that a fly fisherman learn to cast farther than 40 feet, or that he

learn things such as the double haul and shooting line, is merely complicating things and scaring people away from fly fishing.

As I told Leo face-to-face (many times) . . . *baloney!* Leo's problem was limited fly-fishing experience, and I'm sure he would have readily admitted it. Leo had never fished for bonefish on a windswept flat, where casts of 60 to 80 feet are absolutely essential to hook many fish. He had never fly-fished for tarpon, where it is usually necessary to throw a popping bug or streamer fly big enough to handle on a spinning outfit, and he has never been on a broad western trout stream where trout were rising in a back eddy, 70 feet cross-river, where it became necessary to throw 80 feet of line, with an S cast, to take the rising fish.

Many of those who say fly casting is easy are talking about *rudimentary* fly casting. They are not familiar with the casting problems, and the skills required, in all-around fly fishing.

Becoming a good all-around fly caster isn't easy. On the other hand, an awful lot of junk has been written on fly-casting techniques within the last ten years—some of it enough to scare away an old-time fly-casting champion reading the stuff today.

In summary we might say that anyone can become a *fair* fly caster (I'm not talking about fly *fishing*), many may become *good* fly casters, some can become *expert* fly casters, and a few (comparatively speaking) can become *great* fly casters.

How good a fly caster (and, in a sense, how good an all-around fly fisherman) any of us becomes depends on physical and intellectual abilities, and dedication, practice, and experience. Timing, for example, is a basic key to good fly casting, but there are some people, unfortunately, who *never* can acquire the timing required to squirt a fly to 80, 90, or 100 feet.

None of what I've said is meant to scare anyone off. Actually, the opposite is true. My intent is to present fly casting as something *anyone* can do, and do damn well if they apply themselves, attacking casting problems seriously and with an attitude of challenge until they master them. And if the individual has some natural athletic abilities, more than usual dedication, and time for much fly fishing under varied conditions, he can easily become not only expert, but perhaps even one of the greats of the game.

Skilled fly casters often explain away their skills. They think it's easy because they've been at it for so long and they've forgotten the years of experience behind them. Most non–fly casters who claim fly casting is easy simply are misinformed, or they deliberately knock fly casting because they themselves are inept at it. A man who once was the angling editor of one of the "big three" outdoor magazines called the double-line haul a "show-off" kind of casting. Frequently he wrote that the double haul and distance casting were *never* necessary. Not true.

It does not, of course, require much talent to toss a fly 30 or 40 feet. And it is not difficult to make ordinary short casts with small flies under good weather conditions, in an open area, for a brief time. But how many fly fishermen do you know who can cast large, wind-resistant flies or bugs in bad wind, maybe from a small, bouncy boat—and do it all day without fatigue?

A good fly caster is capable of much more than merely putting out an ordinary overhead wide-bow cast to 70 or 80 feet. With typical light trout tackle, a skilled fly caster is able to execute all the practical casts—such as the overhead wide bow, the wind-cheating tight bow, left and right side casts, backhand cast, roll casts both left and right, and curve casts both left and right.

None of those are "trick" casts for display. They are useful and often necessary casts to present the fly, in a demanding situation, so that a fish will take it.

A good caster can make a roll-cast pickup of his line, as well as a snap pickup. He can "mend" line, send out a perfect lazy S cast, and put a dry fly down on a slick pool so lightly that it settles like goose down. He can put his flies accurately to within inches of close targets, to within feet of distant targets. He can cast under almost any wind condition, and seldom is there a wind so strong as to force him to bait casting or spinning tackle.

A good fly caster is a master of the double-line haul. He can shoot 20 or 30 feet of line, can shoot line on both the forward cast and the backcast, and he can execute a long cast—100 feet or more with a heavy outfit—with a minimum of false casts, and sometimes none at all. Most important, his casting is effortless, does not tire him, is done automatically, gracefully, almost unconsciously. He is able to concentrate not on his casting, but on his fishing.

Being a good caster isn't "show-off" stuff. Casting ability is the skilled fly fisherman's ace in the hole; it's some of the edge he has over the ordinary guy, and it's what consistently puts fish in the pan for him. Anyone who takes his angling seriously— whether it be fly fishing, spinning, or bait casting—will enjoy his sport much more by working on his casting until he becomes expert at it.

Some people believe that strength is an important factor in fly casting. In an overall sense, strength has no bearing on fly-casting results. In light fly casting, strength does not even enter the picture. In *heavy* fly casting, or in tournament distance events, strength (coupled with perfect timing) can matter.

For a parallel, let's consider golf. If we have two pro golfers and one is a slight man, the other heavy, tall, and very strong—and their swings are equal—certainly the stronger golfer is going to hit the ball farther. The same applies to heavy fly casting.

In my own experience I know that if I have not been fishing or doing any fly casting for a couple of weeks or more, I need four or five days of fishing before my casting gets anywhere near right. That's not just a matter of getting proper timing back, but of tuning muscles. Bear in mind, I'm speaking of *heavy* fly casting, throwing large bugs and very large streamer flies with big hooks.

Joan Salvato Wulff has the tiniest wrist and forearm of any accomplished fly caster I know. Joan was world women's professional casting champion for years, and could shame most fly fishermen in distance casting. Joan frequently pointed out, however, that rarely could she match the men champions (such as the late Jon Tarantino) because of their superior strength. Another world professional casting champion, and a superb distance performer, was John Dieckman, who unfortunately died in an airplane accident some years ago. John was tall and wiry, so slightly built that I doubt that he weighed 140 pounds, yet he could cast a big fly out of sight. I think the records show, though, that Tarantino did the distance work better because he had an edge in strength. Not only was Jon's timing perfect, but he was a handsome brute of a young man—barrel-chested, with forearms like a wrestler's.

Thus strength—or being in shape for heavy casting—can be a factor in performance even for you and me, but there's no need to be King Kong.

Years ago many fishing writers advised beginning fly casters to hold a handkerchief at the side with the elbow while casting. This was bad advice, for no casting technique is more ridiculous. Actually, a good caster can throw line with his hand and arm in almost any position, but best form is with the rod hand high. This way, all the body and not just the wrist is put into the cast.

Naturally, you can't become a skilled fly caster if your gear isn't right. The rod should be a quality one with proper action, and the line or lines you get for it must be of the correct weight to work the rod. Any experienced fly fisherman can check your tackle for you, or the fishing expert in the local sporting-goods store may be able to help.

THE GRIP

A proper grip on the fly-rod handle is perhaps the first step toward decent casting.

There's much room for hair splitting here because there are many excellent fly casters with different rod holds. Some casters use different grips at different times, and I frequently find myself rolling a thumb around the cork, while at other times the thumb is straight on top.

Many casters—especially Europeans—like to lay the index finger straight down the rod handle. They believe this aids in accuracy as well as in stopping the rod in

THE SHOOTING BASKET

Fly fishermen who do much angling on large rivers or who wade the bonefish flats might be interested in trying a casting aid used by many steelhead fishermen in the West, called the "shooting basket."

A shooting basket is a vinyl or plastic tray, usually about 5 or 6 inches deep, that is strapped around the angler's waist to hold the backing, or "shooting," line, and part of the fly line.

Long casts are the rule in steelhead fishing, and anglers usually are forced to wade very deep, in heavy water. Line retrieved following a cast is either dropped loose to the water—where it's invariably grabbed and pulled away by the current—or held in loose coils; some fishermen hold coils of line in the mouth. All of these methods add to the difficulty of casting the necessary 90 or 100 feet or more.

With a shooting basket strapped to his waist, the deep-wading fisherman merely strips loose line into the basket, then shoots it on the forward cast. The fly line and backing literally zoom out of the bas-

ket, and casts of 100 feet become simple routine. Homemade shooting baskets can be constructed from heavy cardboard boxes or plastic dishpans. Make two slits in the back of the box or pan and slip a heavy belt through. (Commercially made shooting baskets are available from firms such as Orvis and Eddie Bauer.)

Tom McNally (left) models a shooting basket made from a cardboard box, while son Bob wears a commercially made vinyl basket.

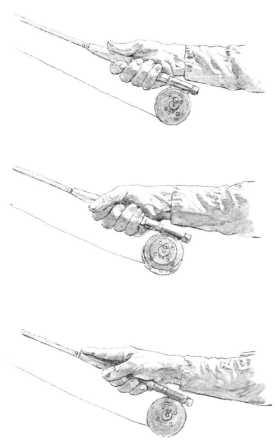

Three basic grips. The thumb-on-top grip is preferred by most casters, but you can vary your grip at different times.

the proper position as the backcast extends. A lot of fine casters tend to roll the wrist over, so that the knuckles of the casting hand face backward—toward the backcast—rather than having the thumb aligned with the backcast.

The majority of skilled casters use the thumb-on-top grip, for two reasons. For one, the thumb-on-top aids in halting a rod at about the one-o'clock position on the backcast, while still allowing the necessary

drift of rod from one o'clock to about two o'clock as the backcast straightens. Second, the top grip permits considerable application of power on the forward cast. The heel of the thumb pushes against the cork, giving power that a lot of top casters insist cannot be obtained with a thumb-on-the-side hold. John Dieckman, who I believe was one of the world's best all-around tournament and *fishing* fly casters, strongly advocated the thumb-on-top grip.

(All that follows in this chapter and the next is written with the assumption that the caster is right-handed.)

THE LINE HAND

In all fly casting, the left hand is vitally important. It serves as the line controller, keeping the fly line taut at all times so that the full weight of the line is transmitted to the rod during casting. The left hand is needed to prevent line slack, and to provide extra line speed when wanted (the double haul, discussed in Chapter 8), and the power for distance casting.

Take a good grip on the fly line with your left hand and maintain a firm grip on the line throughout your casting. Don't take a mere pinching hold on the line with your thumb and index finger; instead, secure the line across the four fingers of your left hand, and under the thumb, with the hand nearly clenched.

THE OVERHEAD CAST

To execute a *normal forward cast*, after leader and line have been strung through the rod guides, strip (pull) a few yards of line from the reel and drop it at your feet.

You want to get that line extended out in front of you, say, 20 or 30 feet. It's easy to get that much line out simply by waving the rod back and forth in a kind of buggy-whip fashion. The line will sail forward, then back, as you let the loose line slide out of your left hand and through the rod guides. The forward-and-back motion of the rod, with the fly line moving in cadence in front and then behind you, will be enough to extend a working length of line—the 20 to 30 feet of line you originally stripped from the reel.

Now that you have sufficient working line out in front of you ("working" line being an amount adequate to flex the fly rod), strip more line from the reel and drop it loosely on the water, the ground, or on the bottom of the boat, whatever the case may be, taking care that the line doesn't tangle. With 15 to 20 feet of loose line at your feet, reach out with the rod tip, keeping the tip low. Grip the free line in your left hand near the bottom guide on the fly rod. Pick up the extended line for the initial backcast by making a quick upward movement with the rod, at the same time tugging back sharply with the left hand (Figure 1). (All slack is taken out of the line by slowly raising the rod tip before making the quick upward movement with the rod.) As the fly line goes back, an attempt should be made to stop the rod in the perpendicular, or twelve-o'clock, position (Figure 2). It will be almost impossible to stop the rod there, and it will drift on back to the one or two o'clock position—which will be correct. (Skilled casters delivering long throws will take a fly rod back much farther—reaching high up with the casting arm, and way back, so that the rod is at the three-o'clock

position—but that is not short-line casting, nor is it for beginners.)

As the line goes up and back, turn your head and watch the line unfold, roll over, and straighten out behind you. Notice how the rod tip bends under the weight of the

Figure 2

line as the line straightens. At the completion of a perfect backcast, the fly line will be as straight as a needle.

As I mentioned previously, in picking up line and tossing it back, the rod positions will range from twelve to one to two o'clock (on the face of an imaginary clock, of course). Between twelve and one o'clock, the rod *pauses* and slows measurably, giving time for the line to unfurl and for its weight to flex the rod. Under the weight or "load" of the line, the rod now will *drift* to the two-o'clock position—and it is at this point that the backcast should be needle-straight (Figure 3A).

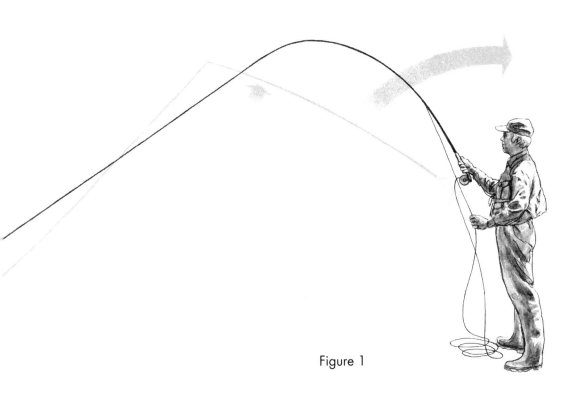

Figure 1

All this time, from the pickup of the extended fly line to the absolute leveling of the backcast, the left hand should have been keeping the line tight. As the backcast rolls out, you should feel the weight of the line pulling against your left hand.

When the backcast has straightened, begin the forward cast by slowly *nudging* the rod forward. It is most important that changing the direction of the moving fly line, from going backward to forward, be done very slowly. Time must be allowed for the fly line to unfold on the backcast and to straighten, and for the rod to pause, then drift, then bend and flex under the weight of the straightened line—*before* the forward cast is begun.

With the rod tip bending nicely and moving slowly forward, gradually speed up the forward movement of the rod, and add *pushing* power to your casting stroke as the full weight of the line bends the rod (Figure 3B). The rod at this point should be in full bend, with a good curve in it from the tip down through the middle section and right into the butt. This is the point at which the line's weight has loaded the rod, forcing the rod into a natural arc, and as the rod is moved forward another foot or so, it will be under *full load*—the point at which the rod is at maximum casting flex. This is the critical moment of power application in the forward cast.

Now that the rod is under full load, it is a simple matter to continue the forward movement with the casting arm, forcing the rod to "turn over," pulling the line after, and making it fly ahead on the forward cast (Figure 4). Under full load the rod was bending somewhere between the one-o'clock and eleven-o'clock positions, and

now it straightens somewhere around ten o'clock, as the line straightens in front and drops to the water surface in a completion of the forward cast. If a longer cast were to be made, the fly line would not be released at completion of the first forward throw; instead, a second backcast would be made, and a second forward cast, with extra yards of line (previously stripped from the reel) added to lengthen the second forward

Figure 3

cast. Additional false casting would be done as necessary until the desired amount of line was in the air, or until the caster had as much line extended as he could handle. (False casting is executing both back and forward casts, keeping the line in the air, and not delivering the forward cast. False casting always should be kept at an absolute minimum.)

Turning around to observe the backcast is a quick way to improve and perfect your timing, to learn to throw a high backcast, and to develop a proper sense and feel of the casting cadence needed in skillful fly casting. To watch the backcast, don't stand with your toes pointed at the target and then twist your torso around and crane your neck like an Olympic gymnast. The easy way is to stand at a right angle to the target—with toes pointing east rather than

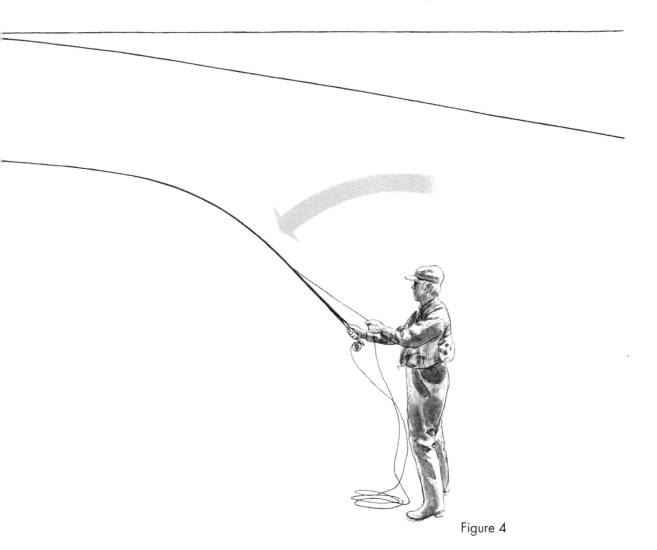

Figure 4

north, so to speak. In this sideways position, it is easy to observe both the backcast and the forward cast as they roll out. In these "study periods," repetitive false casting is helpful.

The straight overhead cast can be either a *wide-bow cast* or a *tight-bow* cast. A wide-bow cast is a forward cast with a very open, or wide, loop (Figure 5). A tight-bow cast, of course, is just the opposite—a forward cast with a very narrow, or tight, loop (Figure 6).

The Wide-Bow Cast

A wide-bow cast can get you extra distance when the wind is behind you, or quartering from behind and one side. Use the wind by throwing the fly line high into the air, releasing the line or letting it go when the rod is in about the eleven-o'clock position. The higher the line is thrown, the longer the wind will give added momentum to the line and lengthen the cast.

In delivering a normal wide-bow cast, the line is released when the rod is between ten and eleven o'clock. The power stroke with the rod must be reduced, or shortened, in effecting the wide-bow cast, since normal application of power will tighten or close the line loop. More power in the delivery, in fact, is the casting technique used in sending out a tight-bow cast.

The Tight-Bow Cast

A tight-bow cast is one with the narrowest possible loop, with the line shooting out close to the water. This is the cast to use to get a fly or bug under overhanging tree limbs or beneath a boat dock, and when casting into wind (Figure 6).

To get a good, tight loop into your forward cast, accelerate the line speed, and exaggerate the line speed by overpowering the forward cast. When the rod is under full load, make the top third of the rod turn over more quickly than normal, getting as

tight bow

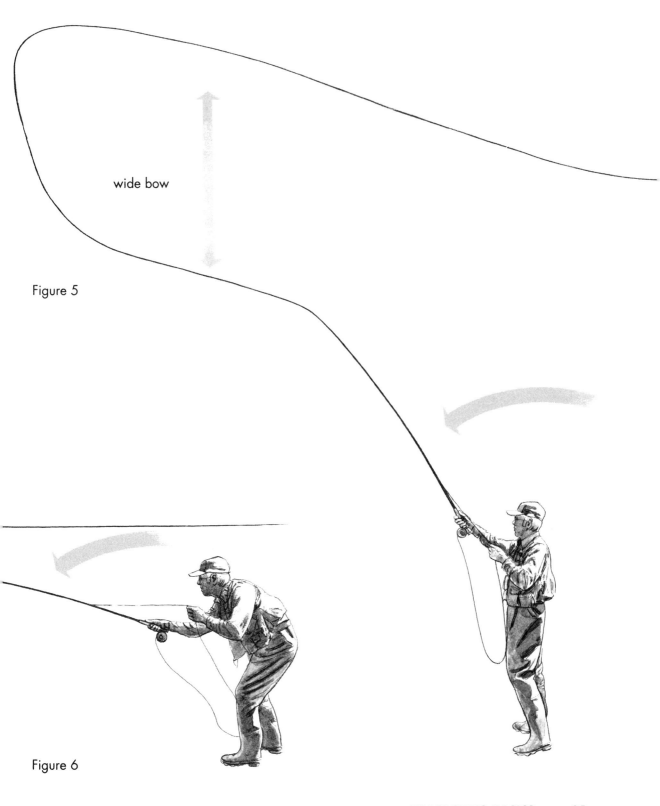

wide bow

Figure 5

Figure 6

much "tip" into the cast as you can. To help keep the line as low as possible, and to keep the tip action of the rod into the cast longer, I find it is very helpful to bend low at the waist as final power is put into the cast.

One of the things that makes a successful trout fisherman is the ability to present his flies lightly, with no fish-scaring slap of line. The best way to deliver a delicate cast, usually most needed in dry-fly fishing, is to be an *up* caster as opposed to a *down* caster. A down caster throws his cast low over the water so that the forward part of the line hits the water hard just as the cast loses steam. An up caster throws his line high so that it straightens like a spike, then falls flat and lightly to the water. In up casting you can help the fly and line to drop gently by lifting back slightly on the rod just as the line begins to fall after losing its forward momentum.

Many excellent fly casters throw very low backcasts, and a low backcast is necessary in distance casting because only through a low backcast can a longer rod "stroke" be achieved on the forward cast. A long power stroke is needed to throw a long cast. In tournament casting, backcasts are so low that the fly often "ticks" the water at completion of the backcast.

For most fly casting and fishing, how-ever, a high backcast is recommended. That the forward cast can be only as good as the backcast is a well-known, overworked, but very true fly-rodding maxim. A high back-cast is most likely to straighten well, and the caster has greater opportunity to load the rod properly for the forward cast.

ROLL CAST

A roll cast is one that has no backcast. It is accomplished by rolling the line out in front instead of casting back and then for-ward. Since there's no backcast, this is the cast to use when there is brush, a high bank, or other obstacles behind the caster. Small-stream fishermen often use the roll cast almost exclusively.

To do a roll cast, get about 20 feet of line on the water in front of you. Reach up with your casting arm, get the rod past the vertical position, and cant the rod some-what out from your right side. The rod tip should be at about one o'clock, with the line hanging loosely down from the tip (Figure 7). Now slowly, smoothly start the rod tip forward, then increase speed and power as the rod tip reaches the eleven-o'clock position. From eleven to ten o'clock the rod tip should be thrown hard and fast into the cast. A proper blending of all these movements will cause a large loop to pick up and roll down the line, turning the forward part of the fly line over and carrying it out and onward to the target (Figure 8).

It is easy to make a roll cast of 40 to 50 feet with a comparatively light outfit and a double-taper line. Some casters claim it is not possible to roll-cast with a three-diameter line, but it is, and in fact even shooting line is possible by roll-casting a three-diameter line, a shooting-head line, and a double-taper line, though the last gives a much shorter shoot.

Left and right roll casts are identical, the only difference being the side of the body on which the cast is executed. The left roll cast often is as valuable as the standard or right-side roll cast, since there will be times when, in brush, a fisherman cannot station himself for a roll cast anywhere but from his left side.

Figure 7

BACKHAND CAST

For right-handed casters, the backhand cast is a cast in which the line is tossed back over the caster's left shoulder, then the forward cast is done by rolling the casting hand over, in a backhand style (figures 9 and 10). Turning some at the waist and looking back while making the backcast, then swiveling forward on the backhand cast, is helpful. This cast is the one to use when it's desirable to put the backcast into an opening in trees behind you, or when the wind is coming from your right side so strongly that it would throw an ordinary backcast, executed on the right side of your body, into your scalp when you brought the line and fly forward.

SIDE CASTS

Left and right side casts can be very helpful in certain wind situations, or when trees or overhanging foliage make a normal overhead cast difficult or impossible.

To make either cast, the rod is held par-

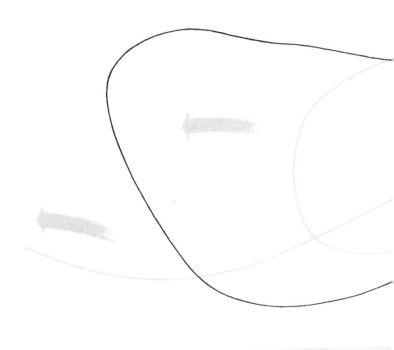

allel to the water or the ground, and then line is extended as in an ordinary overhead cast.

PRACTICING YOUR CASTING

In all areas of fly fishing, casting accuracy is most desirable, if not entirely essential. Having a properly designed leader (Chapter 5) is the first step toward accuracy; casting experience and practice are the next steps.

Nothing matches actual fishing time to enhance your casting accuracy, but half-hour sessions on the back lawn, casting the fly line between two chairs, or dropping the fly into an old automobile tire, can do wonders for your casting precision. To practice the tight-bow cast, and to simulate a situation in which you want to throw a bass bug under a boat dock or a dry fly beneath a distant overhanging tree limb, place a board across the top of two chairs. Start with the chairs 4 to 5 feet apart, the board high up on the chair backs. As your casting improves, you can reduce the size of

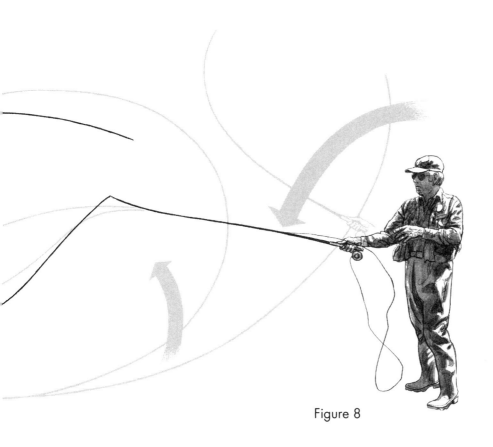

Figure 8

Figure 9

the target opening by lowering the board and moving the chairs closer together.

Some common casting problems, and their causes, follow:

Sloppy pickup. Trying to lift line off the water with rod held too far back, perhaps at twelve o'clock or farther; not removing all slack from line; striving to lift too much line off the water; failure to lower rod tip close to the water and to reach forward with the line hand, securing the fly line in the fingers of the left hand close to the rod's butt guide; failure to reach out with the rod, while slowly raising the rod tip to lift most of the line off the water, then accelerating into the complete line pickup.

Sagging backcast. Putting insufficient power and speed into the backcast; allowing too much time for the backcast to straighten; bringing the rod too far back with no left-hand line control; starting the backcast too soon.

Sagging forward cast. Too little power; starting the cast while backcast is incomplete; beginning cast with fly rod not "loaded" due to rod starting from too far back, coupled with poor line-hand control.

Waves in the line. Bad timing and rhythm on the forward cast or backcast, or both; applying too much power to the cast, or too little.

Snapping off the fly or having line "crack the whip." Hurrying the backcast, and bringing line forward while leader is still uncurling on backcast; starting forward cast too forcefully and too soon.

Fly catching on leader or line. Making the back and forward casts in identical planes; starting the forward cast too soon.

Fly or line striking rod or caster. Casting in identical planes; delivering forward cast too soon and too hard; lack of coordination; improper timing; jerky movements.

Line not laying out straight. Too little or too much power in delivering the forward cast; starting the forward cast too soon or too late.

Slapping the water. Overpowering the forward cast and casting down instead of up; throwing the rod tip down and hard toward the water, forcing the line to follow and slap the surface.

Wind knots. Casting in the wrong planes; line speed too great, at the wrong times.

Figure 10

8

Advanced Fly Casting

NOW THAT we have been over the fundamentals of fly casting, we can consider some more advanced, more technical aspects. Right here we must make it clear that while there are definite rules for skillful casting, there also are many different *styles*.

In recent years one fishing writer has advocated taking the fly rod far back on the backcast to the three-o'clock or horizontal position before starting the forward cast. He has presented that technique as something novel and "new." It's about as new as the Pyramids. Tourney casters have been starting forward casts from that position ever since we've had distance-casting events.

The thing to be concerned about as you progress into advanced fly casting is the development of *your own style*. So long as you develop timing, muscular coordination, a feel for the application of power, and good left-hand line work, you won't have to worry much about rod positions.

THE DOUBLE HAUL

It is not possible to become a polished fly fisherman without knowing how to execute the double-line haul. You will never be able to cast far without the double haul. You will not be able to fish all day long without fatigue if you cannot do the double haul. You will not be able to cast in strong wind well without the double haul. You will not be able to cast heavy, wind-resistant flies and bugs without the double haul. You will not be able to deliver a fly to a target quickly without the double haul. And you will not be able to reduce false casting to a minimum without the double haul.

In essence, the double haul increases line speed and takes much of the load off the rod, and it is the *one* thing that makes exceptionally long casts possible. Distance casting is a physical impossibility without proper application of the double haul. This concerted use of your left hand, however, does much more for your casting than merely lengthen line.

By using the double-line haul, the author is able to cast completely across river.

Hauling takes all the drudgery out of fly casting. Even on short casts a properly executed haul is beneficial. It can improve your accuracy, for example, and help you throw a tight loop that will put your fly beneath an overhanging bush or, with very light tackle, successfully cast oversize dry flies into the teeth of a strong wind.

A fly rod can support only so much line in the air. To get more line up, the left hand (or line hand) must tug or haul on the line at the start of the back and for-ward casts. This use of the left hand to tug on the line on *both* the forward cast and the backcast, thereby increasing line speed, is the double haul. If line pulls are per-formed only on the forward cast or only on the backcast, then we have a single haul. A single haul, of course, is only half as good as a double haul, but it is better than no haul at all.

To do the double-line haul, start by extending a working length of line (with a 9-foot rod and WF-9 line this should be about 50 feet), and pull about 30 feet of line from the reel and drop it loosely at your feet. Take a *firm* grip on the line with your left hand. (If the line slips from your fingers while casting, you'll lose control.)

To pick up the extended line, reach out and down with your rod. Reach up near the bottom guide on the rod and grasp the line in your left hand (Figure 1A). Now raise the tip slowly, gradually lifting the line from the water. At the same time tug on the

line slightly with your left hand (Figure 1B). When most of the line is off the water, make a quick upward sweep with the rod and tug sharply on the line. This combination of rod lift and line tug will toss the line up and back, producing a fast, neat, tight-loop backcast.

As the fly line goes back (Figure 2), raise your left hand along with your rod hand. Both hands should be working together. When your hands are about head-

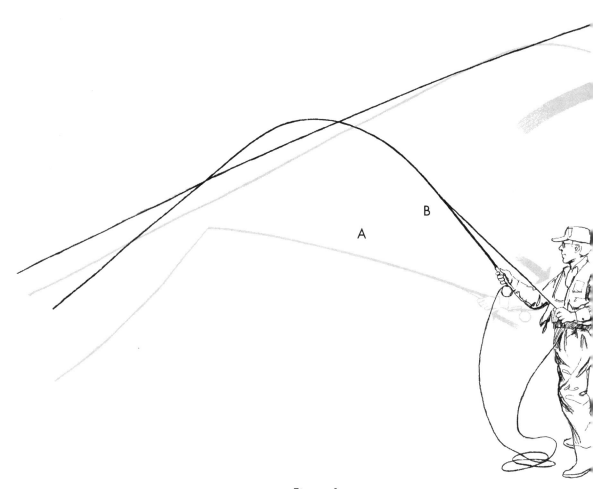

Figure 1

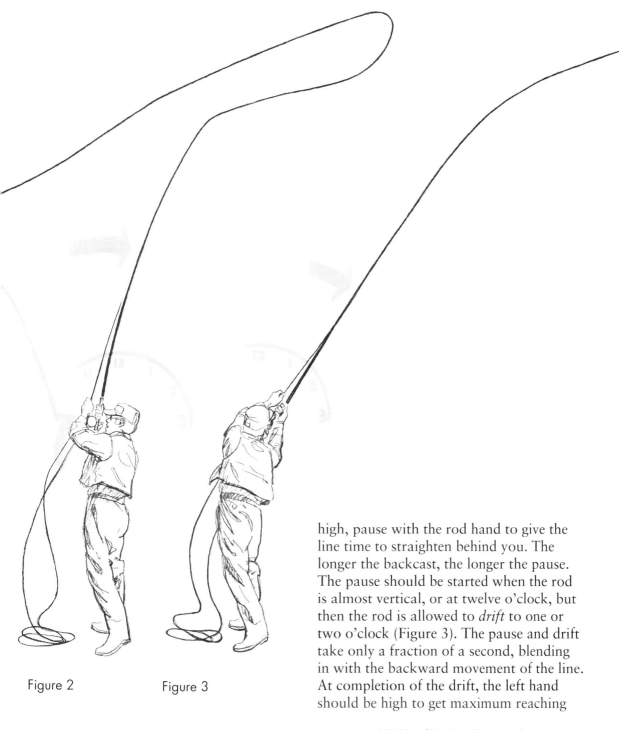

Figure 2   Figure 3

high, pause with the rod hand to give the line time to straighten behind you. The longer the backcast, the longer the pause. The pause should be started when the rod is almost vertical, or at twelve o'clock, but then the rod is allowed to *drift* to one or two o'clock (Figure 3). The pause and drift take only a fraction of a second, blending in with the backward movement of the line. At completion of the drift, the left hand should be high to get maximum reaching distance for the next left-hand tug on the line.

The first movement in starting the forward cast is a nursing forward of the rod as the line straightens behind you (the longer the backcast, the sooner the rod must be started forward). When the rod has been brought forward to twelve o'clock it should be under full load of the line (Figure 4A). No real power has yet been put into the forward cast. But as the full weight of the line is felt, start driving the rod ahead forcefully, at the same time tugging downward on the line with the left hand. This final yank with the line hand should be a long one, the hand ending well below your waist (Figure 4B). This is the last push that you give the cast. It is the punch that kicks the line, giving it a jolt of speed and power that couldn't be obtained if just the rod were doing all the work. During the various stages of the final haul, the rod hand naturally moves forward, coordinating with the left—slowly at first, then faster and stronger until the rod finally turns over and the line starts flying forward in a fast,

tight loop. At this point the cast and the double-line haul are complete, with all left-hand and rod power having been transferred to the line—which now is flying away. All that remains is to extend the rod, point it toward the target, and let the loose line that was on the ground shoot through the rod guides (Figure 5).

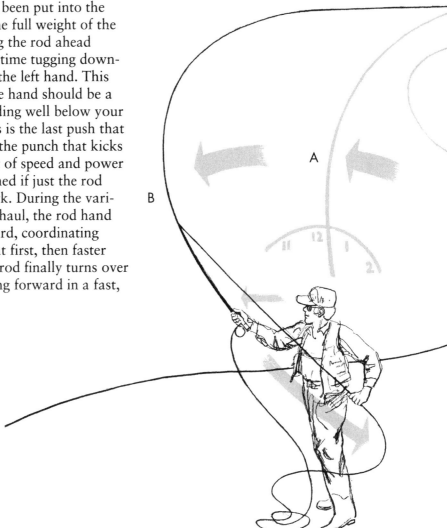

Figure 4

Double hauling is the best way to eliminate excessive false casting. The left-hand work increases line speed so much that a comparatively short length of line will adequately load the rod and make a final cast and shoot of line possible.

Shooting line—lengthening your cast to considerably more than the amount of line you hold in the air while false casting—is, along with the double haul, the way to distance, and it is the only way to reduce false casting and get line out in a hurry. To shoot line, strip several yards of line from the reel and let it rest on the ground or boat bottom. Make a high forward cast, use the double haul, and just before the cast loses its forward speed . . . *zipp!* . . . release the line held in your left hand. The slack line at your feet will shoot out and extend the cast.

Shooting line on the backcast also is done to accomplish a long cast quickly. It's executed in the same way as shooting line on the forward cast, except that much less line is shot and the cast is not released.

To shoot line on the backcast, wait until the backcast unfolds properly and you feel the weight of the line pulling against your left hand. As your left or line hand comes up, following along with the rod hand, ease your grip on the fly line when you feel the line pulling in your hand. This will allow several feet of line to shoot into the backcast. As the backcast slows and starts to drop, tighten your grip on the line again, and start into the forward cast as usual.

The double-line haul is a step-by-step operation. There are distinct, separate movements of both the line hand and the

Figure 5

rod hand, yet all these motions are related. Each motion must be connected to the others, without jerks or vibrations, so that they are a coordinated series of timed, graceful motions.

Besides being your tool for executing the double haul, you'll learn that there are other uses for a talented left hand. Throughout the casting routine, your line hand can compensate for errors in timing. It will increase or decrease the distance of your cast if you tug sharply when more distance is desired, or not so sharply, if at all, when you decide to shorten a cast. If you should be false casting with considerable line toward a target and then realize—just as you shoot—that you have fired too much line, you can pull the cast up short by tugging with your line hand and braking the cast in midair. You can use your left hand to achieve greater casting accuracy, too. A tug on the line with the left hand just before your fly drops to the water will straighten the leader and give teacup accuracy.

Because the double haul is made up of a series of casting steps, you may master it quickest by learning one step at a time. First learn to pick up line properly, using the left hand to speed the line up and back. Keep practicing pickups until you do them right. Then turn around and watch your backcast roll out, and practice sliding your hand up toward the rod's first guide. Next practice tugging on the line at the start of the forward cast. With each step of the haul gradually perfected, you then can meld the single movements into a whole— and refine the whole until you're throwing fly line a country mile.

Probably the best way to learn the dou-ble haul is to practice it with just a fly-rod tip section, because long casts with a fly-rod tip are not possible without hauling. Using a tip literally forces you to develop line haul.

One afternoon at a national casting tournament being held in Warren, Michigan, John Dieckman and I were fooling around with a 9-foot two-piece glass rod. Casting with the assembled rod seemed a bit too easy, so John took it apart and we started casting with just the tip section. By holding the 54-inch tip section just above the ferrule, it was possible to cast about 50 feet without using the double haul. However, the rod tip could not support more than that amount of line in the air.

When we'd get 35 or so feet of line in the air, though, we could feel the little tip bending and the line pulling hard in our fingers. So we would naturally tend to tug with the line hand, increasing the line's speed, holding it up, and then letting go with a hard, hauling shoot. By double-hauling and shooting line, we'd get an extra 20 to 40 feet in the cast (the added distance depending upon whether John was casting or me) for completed throws of 70 to 90 feet.

An authoritative double haul makes it possible for you to cast into a headwind that drives other fly fishermen to cover. Under such circumstances you will want to haul harder on the forward stroke than usual, and strive to throw as tight a line loop as possible. The tighter the loop, the less air resistance and the better the fly line will bore into the wind. What we try to do here is execute a very tight cast, getting as much line speed as possible and throwing the line low and close to the water, *under the wind.*

BEATING THE CURRENT

When wading in strong current, loose line from the reel will be washed downstream, and picking up that line to extend a cast is very difficult because of the pull of the current against the line. Most fishermen, in retrieving line after a cast, form large loops of loose line in their left hand and pay it out on the next cast—thus defeating any pull of current on the line. But West Coast steelhead fishermen developed another way to defeat current pull on fly line. They coil the line during the retrieve, then hold the coils loosely in the mouth. A few coils are released on a false cast when the next cast is made, and then all the line coils are dropped when the final shoot is delivered. This method pretty well eliminates any current drag on loose fly line when wading deep.

There's also a way to beat current when you're casting across a heavy flow and you want your dry fly, for example, to float naturally and slowly in slower water on the far side of the fast water. It's called *mending line.* It's advantageous to mend line whenever strong current will sweep your fly line and cause the fly to drag unnaturally.

Mend line by canting the rod to one side (either left or right), then sweeping the rod across your chest in the opposite direction. That will cause a large loop to form in the line, to be thrown out in the direction that is upcurrent. (If current is coming from your right, you must mend line, or throw a loop, to the right, upstream. The opposite is true if the flow is from your

Figure 6

left.) Before the current washes out the large loop you've put into your line by mending, your fly will get a natural float—at the same speed as the current—for several feet (Figure 7).

Another way to beat the pull of current against the fly line, when casting across fast water, is to make a *lazy S cast*. A lazy S is a cast in which the line does not go out straight on the water but instead falls in a continuing series of waves, with the line ending up snakelike on the water. A lazy S cast has so many curves in it that by the time the current has washed out all the curves and started to bow the line and then pull or drag the fly unnaturally, the fly

current

mend

Figure 7

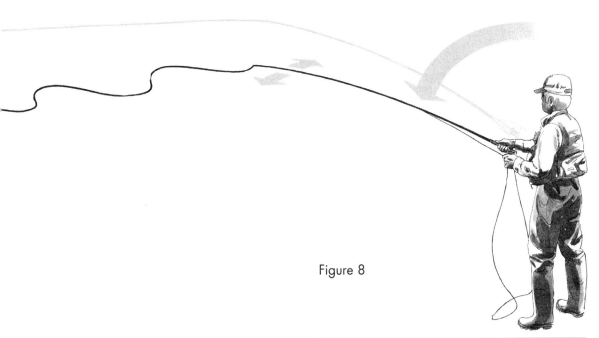

Figure 8

already has floated several feet in a natural, drag-free manner (Figure 8).

There are two ways to deliver a lazy S cast. One is to overpower an ordinary forward cast so that the line jumps against the reel at the end of the cast, kicks backward, and falls slack to the water with some curves or S-shapes in it. A much better way, in my opinion, and the method I use most of the time, is to make a typical forward cast and, just as the line straightens and begins to fall, waggle the rod tip from side to side while the rod is held horizontal. This method puts a perfect and lengthy series of S-shapes into the line as it settles to the water.

SPECIAL CASTS FOR SPECIAL SITUATIONS

Curve casts often make the difference between a trout and no trout to the stream fisherman who finds himself in a situation where a fish is otherwise unreachable (perhaps rising behind a rock). Curves left or right can be delivered by canting the rod almost to the horizontal position, left side or right, and then sending out a weaker-than-normal forward cast. A better way to throw a curve into the leader and line is by tilting the rod slightly right or left (depending on the curve wanted), then delivering a normal cast but to the proper side of the target, and finally lifting up and back with the rod just before the forward cast unfurls and is completed (Figure 9).

Very few fly fishermen, even skilled casters, are really familiar with the proper method of making a *bow-and-arrow cast* with the fly rod. Most simply grasp the fly at the bend of the hook on a tight line, then pull back to put a bend in the rod, and let go. The fly naturally leaps ahead, in following the line and leader, as the fly rod snaps back into a normal straight position. There's nothing wrong with that kind of bow-and-arrow cast, except that it doesn't

A PERFECT CASTING DECK

A common sight among southern fishermen, and one rarely seen in the North, are fishing boats rigged with casting decks. A casting deck elevates the angler so he can better spot fish, underwater logs, brush piles, and weed lines.

So much fly fishing is done in the Florida Keys that nearly all skiffs are fitted with casting decks. Fly casting is effortless when standing in the elevated bow. Northern anglers, whether fishing for bass, pike, or trout, should be similarly rigged.

If you don't have a casting deck, and can't rig one, lay a 6-foot square of nylon, cloth, canvas, or plastic sheeting over the gunnels and floor of the boat before casting. Yards of fly line stripped from the fly reel and kept ready for long casts will not catch on bothersome items when the line is dropped on this deck cover.

Figure 9

put the fly anywhere. The only length to such a bow-and-arrow cast is, roughly speaking, the length of the rod.

The proper way to make a bow-and-arrow cast—which can be a cast of many feet—is to draw several feet of fly line through the rod tip. Drop the fly and leader to the water, along with 3 to 4 feet of fly line, and grasp the fly line between the thumb and index finger about 4 feet up from the line-leader connection. Now pull back on the line to flex the rod as much as necessary (putting a bow in the rod) so that when you release the line the snapping forward of the rod will propel the line-leader forward.

By executing a bow-and-arrow cast this way, you get the rod to cast many more feet of line than if you merely drew line back and bowed the rod by holding a fly at its hook bend. Depending on leader length and the amount of line pulled past the rod tip, bow-and-arrow casts of 20 to 30 feet or more are possible.

The *roll-cast pickup* is used frequently by stream fishermen, especially trout fishermen using dry flies, when the fly has drifted too close for a normal pickup of the line-leader-fly to be practical. A roll-cast pickup is just an incomplete roll cast. Make the usual moves necessary to make a roll cast, but as the line lifts off the water and rolls forward, raise your rod *sharply*, start a backcast move with the rod, and at the same time tug down on the line with your left hand. These moves will keep the forward-rolling line from dropping onto the water as it would in an ordinary, completed roll cast and instead will send it backward into a normal backcast (Figure 10).

The *Galway cast*, sometimes called the reverse cast, is an important throw for stream and river fishermen, and sometimes too for those who wade lake shallows. The Galway is one of the casts that get you out of trouble when there is heavy foliage directly behind you, a standard backcast can't be made, and a roll cast won't produce a long enough cast.

When you find yourself in such a predicament, turn around and take a good look at the trees or high brush behind you. Chances are good that somewhere in all the forest you'll spot an opening big enough to cast into. You couldn't do it with an ordinary backcast, but by turning and half facing the opening, you now can cast the fly and line directly into the hole. That done, turn back to face the water and bring the line forward on a normal forward cast.

Like the Galway cast, the *steeple cast* can help you get a fly out on the water even though very high trees or a high bank are directly behind you. As its name suggests, the steeple cast is a nearly vertical cast, with the line being thrown straight up and then allowed to float back a few yards to about the one-o'clock position—but staying short of the obstructions behind you.

To make a steeple cast, get the length of line you want to cast extended on the water in front of you, perhaps by rolling the line out or swishing it out through the rod guides. Reach straight out with the rod, holding it horizontally at about eye level. Take any slack out of the line by raising the rod horizontally; then, without stopping the rod movement, lift quickly and firmly, using a lot of rod-tip action, to throw the fly line straight up toward twelve o'clock. The rod now should be straight up too, and you should be reaching straight up as far as you can with your rod hand. As much force as possible should be put into the cast to drive the line upward.

The forward cast must be started before the line begins to sag and fall. The forward stroke is made mostly with the rod tip, and with the rod still held straight up, spearing the sky. When the forward stroke is properly timed and the right amount of power put into the cast, the line will turn over, start down, and then curl out over the water.

Casting in crosswinds is something every fly fisherman has to do sooner or later. The accomplished fly fisherman

doesn't quit just because the wind blows, or go to spinning or bait-casting tackle.

When the wind is coming from the left, the right-handed caster has no trouble. Such a wind blows the line, leader, and fly *away* from the caster, so in a sense such a wind is more of a help than a hindrance. With wind from the left it is wise to cant the fly rod a bit more to the right than you

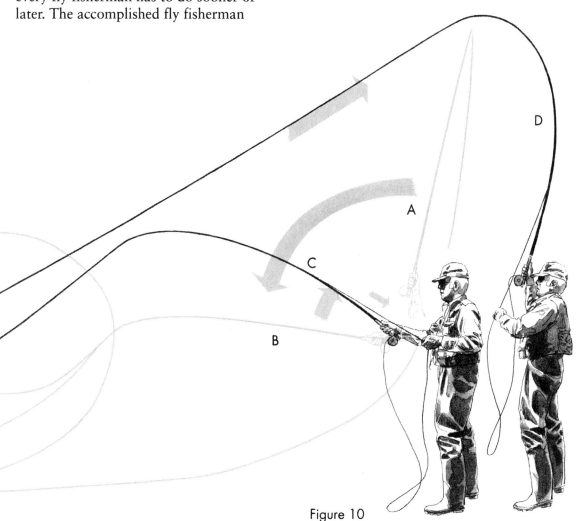

Figure 10

With trees obstructing a normal backcast, the fisherman turns and casts into a "hole" in the foliage . . .

would normally, cast as low as possible with a very tight line loop, put plenty of zip into the cast, and aim a little left of target, allowing for the wind to blow the line toward the target.

When there is a good wind coming from the right, a right-handed caster cannot throw a standard overhead cast, or the wind will move his backcast out of its usual plane and into a line directly behind him. If a normal forward cast is then made, the line, leader, or fly is almost sure to strike him in the back or the back of the head. Many a fly hook has been driven into many a caster's right ear by casting that way when plagued by wind from the right.

To beat wind from the right you can do two things: make a right side (horizontal) cast, or deliver the backcast over the left shoulder.

If you make a right side cast, keep the rod tip as low as practical, do not try to

. . . then turns again and executes the backcast to the target.

handle too much line, use the double haul to get line speed and power into the cast, and shoot the line hard and low to the right of target. The wind will move the line toward the target.

More line can be cast, with a strong right wind, by turning to your left—as though you were going to make a Galway cast into a hole in trees—looking back, and then making an ordinary forward cast behind you. When the line straightens behind you, deliver the forward cast by using the backhand method, being sure to assist the rod by tugging on the line with the left hand. Long shoots, and therefore long casts, can be made with this method almost regardless of how strong the wind is coming from the right.

When wading parallel to streamside obstructions—a high bank or trees, for example—the *change-of-direction cast* can be employed. It is not difficult.

A right-handed caster wading along a high bank at his left side can get a cast out across the stream by false-casting straight upstream until he has extended the desired length of line. Then, making a final false cast rearward—and pausing longer than usual to give the line plenty of time to straighten and to flex the rod—he starts the line forward, at the same time slowly turning his wrist to the right. This move throws a slow curve into the line, which follows the path of the rod (controlled by the caster's wrist), and the line then comes around almost in a circle, and drops to the water at an oblique angle to the caster.

A snap pickup of fly, leader, and line is made by lifting the rod straight up in front of you to about the eleven-o'clock position. From that position the rod tip is snapped quickly downward, with only the tip action of the rod allowed to influence the cast. This will put a large hump in the line which will continue down the line to the leader, at which moment you lift the rod straight up quickly. The leader and fly will then pop off the water vertically, to a height of 3 or 4 feet, and all you need to do then is execute a normal backcast.

9

Gear for the Fly Fisherman

MANY an angler has a bad time instead of a good time when fly fishing simply because he is poorly outfitted. Not even an expert angler, for example, will do his best work if, on a given day, he's equipped with a light midging outfit when conditions dictate the use of a big rod and large flies. And no one fishes well when he is too cold or too hot, when wet and miserable, or when being chewed by mosquitoes.

There is certain equipment needed by *all* fly fishermen—rain parkas and polarized glasses, for instance. But the angler who habitually fishes the same areas—say a small trout stream and a bass lake—usually will not need the varied equipment used by the fisherman who fishes many different streams and rivers, lakes, and saltwater areas both inshore and offshore.

Considering the gear needed for stream trout-fishing, an eastern angler, usually working small streams, may require only hip boots and a light 6- to 7½-foot rod. A western trout fisherman, however, generally fishing large rivers, will need chest-high waders and an 8- to 9½-foot rod.

Then the well-traveled angler—who today fishes Wisconsin's Pine River, tomorrow Montana's Yellowstone, and next winter Argentina's Traful—will require quite an assortment of tackle and gear. Most serious trout fishermen do, in fact, fish various rivers and streams in the course of a season. Yet even the well-traveled angler need not own a tackle shop full of gear; all that's really necessary to be properly equipped for almost any trout-fishing situation is three outfits—one light, one medium, and another heavy. The general accessories that go with one usually go with the other, so naturally that simplifies the problem of correctly selecting gear.

BOOTS AND WADERS

As to the trout fisherman's boots or waders, one of the first considerations is whether to have the ankle-tight kind or the loose type. Both have advantages and disadvantages. Ankle-fitting hip boots or chest-high waders are most comfortable. They provide support while wading that

Chest-high waders for deep streams and hip boots for shallower waters. Felt soles are recommended for safe wading on slippery rocks.

A belt should always be worn with waders to prevent water from rushing into the legs in the event of a spill.

looser boots do not. However, ankle-fitting boots are difficult to get in and out of. Loose boots are just the opposite—they're easy to get in and out of, but they offer almost no ankle support.

The trout angler also has to decide if he wants felt soles, cleats or hobnail strapping, or ordinary soles. Felt soles are best on all streams, and are absolutely necessary on many. It costs $15 to $25 extra for felt-soled boots, but they're worth it. Felts grip the stream floor and provide walking ease and surefootedness unattainable with ordinary boot soles. Felts are particularly important for older anglers who have lost some of their agility. Quality felted boots can spare you many a wicked fall that may result only in a scraped shin but could mean a broken leg.

Special kits are available at most tackle shops with which you can cement felt soles on boots yourself. Many fishermen cut up discarded household wool or nylon carpeting to make soles for their boots.

Hobnails or cleats must be removed from boots and waders when leaving a creek and hiking down a road for any distance, and most trout fishermen think they're noisy in the stream. Thus hobnails and cleats, generally speaking, aren't too popular.

Pure gum-rubber boots usually wear best. Some of the ultrathin, stretchy boots and waders now available, although light and comfortable, tear easily. The same is generally true of nylon or plastic boots. Even twigs, branches, and briars can puncture them. And a puncture usually develops into a tear. The light nylon-plastic boots also can be very cold when wading frigid streams, but the fact that they are cool can be a plus feature when fishing in hot weather. These boots also can be rolled or folded into compact little bundles (of real help when traveling), and most such boots and waders are comparatively inexpensive.

One kind of felt-soled, loose-ankle hip boot is made of heavy, pure rubber from the boot foot to just below the knee. Above that point the material is rubberized canvas. This isn't as durable or as warm as pure rubber; but these boots are good in warm weather, are considerably lighter than all-rubber boots, and they fold into a small pack.

Many fishermen prefer waders and hip boots of neoprene. Neoprene is very light, reasonably tough (if you avoid barbed-wire fences), folds up nicely, and on average is less expensive than rubber waders and boots.

You can spend well over $200 for a pair of neoprene chest-high waders

TURN WADERS INTO BOOTS

Most sportsmen use chest-high waders for one outdoor activity or another. No matter how good they are, or how well cared for, none last forever. And when a pair of chest-highs wears out, most sportsmen simply throw them in the trash.

The tops go first. After enough abuse (and use) the rubberized canvas cracks, dries out, tears, and gets pinholes. They can be patched and repaired for a while, but eventually even patching won't save wader tops.

The boot-feet of chest-high waders seldom wear out, however. So when your next pair of chest-highs are ready for the rubbish, cut the wader tops away from the boot-feet with a sharp knife or a heavy pair of scissors for an excellent pair of boat boots or light hunting boots in wet weather. You can even use them around the house when washing the car or watering the lawn.

(Streamline's pro neoprene waders cost $244.95) but Hodgman's Lakestream neoprene waders are available for under $100.

Hip boots or waders? Most trout

A BELT WITH WADERS ADDS SAFETY AND COMFORT

Fishermen who use chest-high waders should always wear a heavy-duty belt around the waist outside the waders. Wearing a belt with waders adds comfort and, more important, a degree of safety when wading in rough water or through strong currents.

If a wading angler loses his footing and takes a spill, water-filled waders will make swimming almost impossible, even for a strong swimmer. This is trouble of the first order. But a tight belt keeps out most water and traps air in the legs, which helps support someone taking an unscheduled plunge.

A belt tightens baggy waders and makes wearing them for long hours much more comfortable. It also seems to provide additional back support, reducing fatigue when you've been wading and casting all day.

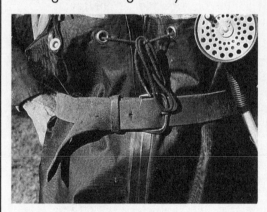

anglers who do much fishing need both—hip boots for small, shallow streams and chest-high waders for big water. If you operate on a really tight budget and must choose between one or the other, your selection should depend on the kinds of streams you fish most. Waders are more expensive, so if the bulk of your fishing is on small streams, get hip boots; otherwise, buy chest-high waders. In any case, purchase the best you can afford. Trying to save a buck on boots or waders is false economy. Cheap ones won't serve you well and won't last long.

JACKETS AND VESTS

A good jacket for cold weather and a vest for warm days are essential gear to the stream fisherman. The trout angler carries so many fly wallets and plastic boxes of flies, spools of leader material, dry-fly oil,

A fishing jacket is useful in cool weather. It should have ample pockets for carrying the many items a fly fisherman needs on the water.

This is a typical fishing vest designed to meet the fly angler's needs. It contains numerous pockets, a wool pad for holding flies, and other small conveniences.

back pocket, as well as a folded rain parka. (Never be on the stream without the parka.)

Be sure, too, that the jacket and vest you buy are of lightweight water-repellent material. If you kill trout now and then you'll want a zip-in, zip-out type of "creel" zippered into your garment. Be certain, however, to get one with a thoroughly waterproof fish bag or it won't last much beyond opening day. Such creels or fish pockets should be washed after use, so it's important that the pocket be removable.

Buy a fishing jacket for its overall utility, not warmth. You want the jacket for wear in cold weather, of course, but what you really want is a jacket to hold your gear on those days when it is too chilly to wear a trouter's vest. Then, if you're fishing in really cold weather, for warmth you can

and the like that he needs suitably designed garments with ample pockets.

The important thing to look for in a jacket or vest is the right number and size of pockets. Some have far too many small pockets. Look for a couple of large billows-type pockets to take large fly wallets and big plastic boxes of dry flies. And only buy jackets and vests with full-size billows-type pockets on the back. When on the stream for a long day you can put a few sandwiches and a small thermos of coffee in the

This vest is designed to keep fly boxes high and dry while wading even in the deepest pools. It's called a "shortie."

Among the newer fly-fishing items are mesh fishing vests. They're designed to keep the angler cool in the hottest weather.

As a classic example, the Patagonia Company (Bozeman, Montana) has designed the SST (salmon-steelhead-trout) jacket, made in three layers to "keep the elements at bay while you do your fishing."

Patagonia also sells a shortie fishing vest that is made of webbed material for coolness and is ultrashort so that you can wade very deep without getting the vest's pockets and whatever is in them wet.

Stream Designs (New York, New York) has introduced the Imperial, a 28-pocket vest for fishermen who need plenty of carrying capacity. It's made of high-tech polyester/cotton waterproofed poplin.

The Simms company (Jackson Hole, Wyoming) is selling fly-fishing vests made of DuPont's new fabric, Supplex. Besides being tough, fast drying, stain and odor resistant, and washable, it's more comfortable than cotton or other clothing material.

SOCKS AND UNDERWEAR

Unless it's extremely cold the trout fisherman should be comfortable in his boots or waders, wearing a thin pair of nylon or silk dress socks under a pair of good woolen socks. The thin socks are extra insulation, but mostly they allow a kind of foot freedom inside the woolen socks. The woolens provide the real warmth and should be about knee-high. Get them a half size or a full size large so your feet will be comfortable. Too many socks, or socks that are too heavy, make boots fit so tight there's no air space. Air space is necessary in a boot if your feet are to stay warm. If you fish where there's still snow and ice on opening day you may want

slip on a sweater or a goosedown or nylon-insulated vest under the jacket. Most quality fisherman's jackets protect from the wind very well, so when an insulated vest is worn underneath they provide comfort in the coldest weather.

In recent years the tackle industry has introduced some remarkable outdoor garments made of high-tech materials far superior to what we've been using for years.

insulated rubber or nylon booties, or the older type of fleece-lined booties, inside your boots. To accommodate booties, boots and waders have to be at least one size larger than usual.

In the warmer states ordinary cotton underwear may be adequate even in early spring. But in many areas the weather and water are cold enough in spring and again in fall to make heavy underwear necessary. Ordinarily a light suit of long-john woollies will do, but if you wade cold streams— wearing chest-high waders—heavy woolen underwear may be necessary. However, with many kinds of warm, lightweight pile underwear suits of the "thermal" type now available, a lot of fly fishermen have discarded their long johns. The new insulated underwear takes little space in a duffel bag and is comfortable and warm in the coldest weather. Many fishermen wear just the insulated underpants (under regular trousers) when fishing, but then slip matching insulated jackets over their fishing shirts if it becomes really cold—as toward evening when the warm sun drops below the trees.

OTHER CLOTHING

Fishing shirts and trousers are no problem. Early in the season most anglers wear a woolen outdoors shirt and old woolen trousers. Those specially designed fishing shirts are nice but not really necessary. If you'll be wearing boots or waders you may want a pair of knit-cuff pants, or the kind that fold over and snap at the cuff for an ankle-tight fit. Socks pull over these trousers easily, and such pants generally are more comfortable under boots or waders.

A lightweight water-repellent hat with a visor will shield your eyes from the sun. This is important, because in many forms of fly fishing we strive constantly to see *through* the water to locate fish. Without a visored cap, the sun and surface glare can prevent you from spotting fish. Being able to see fish is important, since we do a better job of presenting a fly to fish we can see.

Something else about a visored cap: If you wear glasses and it should rain, the visor will keep raindrops from your specs. One bad thing about most visored caps, though, is that they do not have a brim all around. Rain can run off the back of such caps and pour down your neck. Of course if it rains hard you can pull out a rain parka, and the parka's hood will cover your head—cap and all.

RAIN GEAR

All fly fishermen need rain parkas, and all parkas should have tight-fitting hoods and elastic cuffs so that rain will not roll up the sleeves. The trout fisherman wearing hip boots or waders will do nicely with a half-length parka, and he'll want one that can be folded small to fit into a vest or jacket pocket. Other fly fishermen, especially when working from boats, will want a full-length parka, and they may select ones of heavier material than would trout fishermen. Rain parkas, incidentally, do more than just keep you dry. They can help keep you warm if the temperature plunges, and when you're running in a fast boat they protect you from the wind.

The fly fisherman who does much boat fishing ought to include a pair of light plastic or rubber booties in his gear. If you're caught out there in a real downpour, in addition to the full-length rain parka, you'll need waterproof booties to slip on to keep completely dry. They can be pulled on over sneakers, too, for added warmth.

MISCELLANEOUS ACCESSORIES

Polarized glasses are a must in the fly-rodder's gear, especially when trout fishing or fishing for bonefish, tarpon, and such on the flats. Polarized glasses help us to see *through* the water, eliminating surface glare, and in clear water make it possible to see fish even at considerable depth.

I use a couple of large plastic boxes to carry popping bugs and big streamer flies. These unbreakable plastic boxes are compartmented and are about 12 inches long, 6 inches wide, and 2½ inches deep. They'll

accommodate plenty of flies and bugs for bass, northern pike, and all saltwater species. I have special boxes with just bugs for freshwater angling, another with streamers for freshwater fishing, and then two more for salt water—one with bugs, the other with streamers, shrimp imitations, etc. for tarpon, bonefish, and so on.

The bug and fly boxes are carried, with other small accessories, in a canvas shoulder bag originally called a salmon bag. Such bags are especially designed for the fly fisherman, with inside compartments and outside end pockets. The bags have shoulder straps, as well as carrying handles, and straps and buckles for closing the pockets and main bag. Canvas kit bags are available at the better sporting-goods stores and from the Charles Orvis Company and the Eddie Bauer Company (Redmond, Washington).

wicker

hook-on

shoulder

Three types of creels for holding the catch.

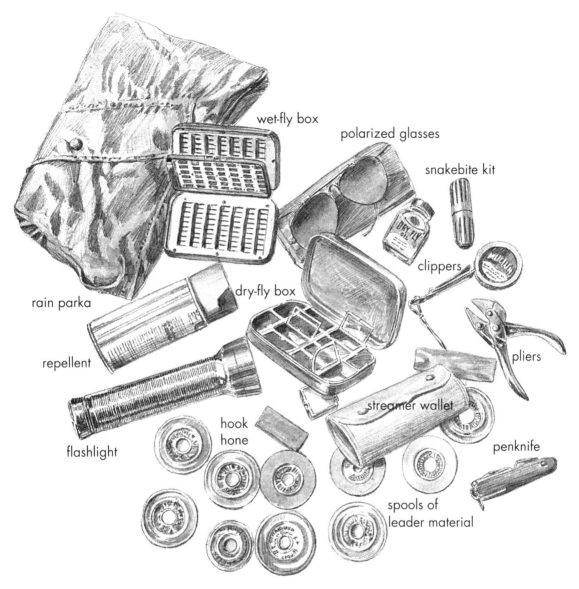

Here are some of the items a trout angler should carry with him on the stream. That's why he needs so many pockets.

A flashlight, even a small one, may be something of a bother to tote around, but it's worth the trouble when you tramp out from some river after dark, or are caught out in a boat past sundown.

Mucilin or cleaner is a dressing for fly

lines which helps float them, makes them soft and supple, and serves to lubricate the line a little and cut some friction between line and guides when casting. Modern fly lines float extremely well, so there's no need to grease them frequently to keep them floating. Some fly fishermen, in fact, never grease the synthetic lines available today.

It's a good idea to use a reel of a type that permits quick changing of spools. Then you should have two or three extra spools (with lines) for each reel stored in your kit bag. For each reel in my bag I usually have two spools mounted with floating lines and a third spool with a sinking line. If you're fishing one of the floating lines and it should start to sink after hours of hard fishing, it's easy to remove that spool and line and snap in another spool with a fresh, dry line. And the spool with the sinking line, of course, is ready for use anytime.

Removable fish bags, mentioned earlier, are excellent, yet some fishermen still use regular trout creels, those wicker baskets woven of willow or bamboo. Others carry special ventilated canvas bags. Creels and bags also are useful for toting lunches or other gear.

Some other basic items used by all fly fishermen include a knife; hook hone or small file; insect repellent; snakebite kit; spools of assorted tests of nylon monofilament leader material; extra fly lines (including sinking lines); nail clippers or a special angler's tool for snipping monofilament when making up leaders; fly books and fly wallets; wader or boot repair kit; dry-fly flotant; split-shot sinkers; and pliers.

GEAR FOR TRIPS

Something else traveling fly-rodders need, especially anglers who travel by air frequently, is a quality rod roll or case. Airline baggage handlers are notorious for throwing tackle around, and unless rods are well protected you can expect damage.

Rod rolls are canvas carriers with special tubelike pockets that accommodate a fly rod in its aluminum case. Such carriers usually take six or eight rods, which, when rolled up in the carrier, are bound together by leather straps. These carriers can be torn, they wear in time, and they are not lockable.

Strong, lockable plastic rod cases are available. But the case I now use is all-aluminum, with quality foam-plastic padding inside. It takes a dozen rods easily, is very strong yet lightweight, and can be locked.

A fair-size duffel bag with extra clothing should be taken on most fishing trips, even if it's only a one-day trip. A leather-trimmed, sturdy canvas bag about 3 feet long and 1½ feet wide will hold extra trousers and shirts, a fishing jacket and vest, several pairs of socks, extra cap, loafers or sneakers, camera and film, and perhaps spare leaders, flies, and such.

It's a good idea to have extra trousers, shirts, and socks of different weights—some heavy, some light. Quite often the weather will throw you a curve, and if you leave home dressed for cold weather the day is sure to turn hot. It won't matter, however, if you can change into light clothing.

Something I'm never without, no matter what the kind of fishing, is what I affectionately call my survival bag. If I'm wading somewhere, the bag stays back in the car; but if I'm fishing from a boat, I'll have it aboard.

The survival bag can be any sort of bag, even an ordinary, old-style canvas boat bag. The one I use is made of heavy, tough, water-repellent nylon, and it measures about 24 by 12 by 12 inches—not too large, not too small. It has a heavy-duty, two-way nylon zipper, plus Velcro. Two heavy canvas straps give support to the bag and serve as handles.

This type bag is available at most quality outfitters, and sells for around $25. I've given one extremely tough use now for about seven years, and while it's spotted and stained it otherwise is in perfect condition and will probably last another seven years.

Depending upon the season, I carry somewhat different items in my survival bag. But some items are always there: two cameras, film, flashlight, rain parka, goose-down vest or jacket, extra eyeglasses, sunglasses (polarized), matches, thin rubber booties (described earlier), Band-Aids, aspirin, and so on.

The bag always goes with me in a boat, or if I'm traveling in someone else's car. At certain times I'll add to my survival bag a 6-foot-square plastic sheet (to lay over junk in a boat bottom so my fly line can't be caught up), a couple tins of sardines, chocolate bars, a can of peanuts, and a can of beef bouillon.

What items are carried in such a bag naturally will vary with the whims of the fly fisherman, but there's no better way to be sure you are never without your rain gear, sunglasses, and other essentials.

10

Trout-Fishing Flies

THE flies needed by trout fishermen are many and varied. There are hundreds of thousands of fly patterns, and every trout fisherman accumulates scores of flies as one season follows another. A fly pattern, incidentally, is the manner in which a fly hook is dressed and the kinds of fly-tying materials used. Perhaps the most famous fly pattern of all time is the Royal Coachman. This pattern calls for a tail of golden pheasant tippets, peacock herl wound Palmer-style fore and aft on the fly, a body of red silk floss, hackling of brown saddle hackles, and wings of white duck-quill feathers. Specific fly patterns always are identifiable by name, and many, such as the Royal Coachman, are world-famous.

Generally speaking, the eastern trout fisherman will acquire a stock of small flies—since as a rule they take more fish for him than larger flies—while the western angler, fishing big rivers, tends to use patterns tied on larger hooks.

However, all trout fishermen, no matter where the bulk of their angling is done, need a representative assortment of streamers, dry flies, and nymphs. Some fishermen will add trout wet flies, and some other special flies such as tiny midges, and perhaps some "terrestrials"—that is, imitations of ants and other nonaquatic insects that occasionally fall in the water and become trout food. All these fly types and some other special ones will be described in detail farther on.

THE NATURALS

Since most of the flies used in trout fishing are meant to imitate some form of real insect (except streamers, which represent minnows), we should here consider a little basic stream entomology. Entomology, which is the study of insects, is of major importance to the trout fisherman, because he continually attempts to imitate with his artificial flies real insect forms—naturals—on which trout may be feeding. The dedicated trout angler always tries to select flies of a type that represent genuine insects in their various stages of development.

The life cycle of most aquatic insects

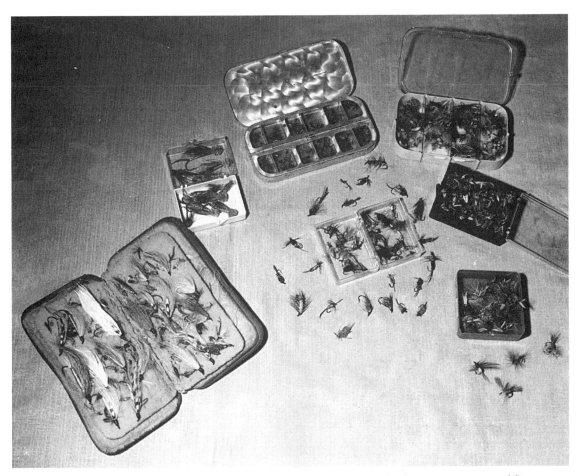

Trout fishermen—perhaps more than any other fly fishermen—need a large assortment of flies: streamers, nymphs, dry flies, wet flies, etc.

begins when the female deposits her eggs on the water. She is a full adult then, known to entomologists as an imago, and to anglers as a *spinner*. If the female fly dies after laying her eggs and falls to the stream surface, wings outspread, she is called a spent spinner, and in this stage is imitated by dry flies known as spent-wing patterns.

The female fly's eggs settle to the stream bed and eventually hatch into *nymphs*, which are the larval or immature stage of the adult flying insect. The angler imitates the various forms of real nymphs with any of a multitude of artificial nymph fly patterns.

In time the nymph is ready to transform from its larval stage to the adult insect. It will leave the stream bed, usually to float in the surface film as it undergoes its meta-

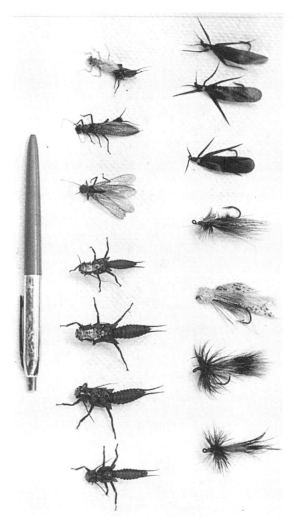

terms. This is the time when insects literally fill the air and constitute a true hatch.

With a hatch underway, trout normally go on a feeding orgy, rising greedily to suck in the floating insects. Any of thousands of dry-fly patterns may then be used, but normally the dry fly selected will be one having upright wings, or divided wings.

The mature flies that escape hungry trout leave the stream but eventually return to mate and, in the case of the females, deposit their eggs to resume the life cycle for their species.

TYPES OF FLIES

In Chapter 1, I divided flies into only two types—dry and wet—and identified any fly that is fished underwater as a wet fly. That's accurate, but there is a category of trout flies known specifically as wet flies. Nymphs and streamers are also fished wet but are usually considered separate categories.

All this categorization is useful to some degree, but the fish didn't invent the categories. For example, trout probably hit wet flies in mistaking them for nymphs, but wet flies generally do not look anything like regular nymph fly patterns. Artificial wet flies come closer to representing drowned insects.

There are various other categorizing terms. *Midge* is a general term for a large group of minute mosquito-like insects, and for their artificial counterparts. Midges are important trout food. Flies representing midges are usually tied on hooks no larger than size 16, and often on hooks size 22 or smaller. *Terrestrial* is another general classification, covering various land insects

From top left, a live western stonefly nymph (salmon fly) starts emerging from its nymphal case. The two insect photos below it show the adult salmon fly as it dries its wings. The four bottom photos, column 1, are of live salmon-fly nymphs. The right-hand column is of various fly patterns representing stonefly nymphs.

morphosis. As the nymph grows into a full-blown winged insect it becomes a subimago, in scientific terms, or a *dun*, in angler's

which may be blown or fall into the water, such as grasshoppers, ladybugs, bees, ants, and beetles. And there are other classifications which we'll discuss later.

FLY PATTERNS

Many trout fishermen burden themselves with detailed study of entomology, then strive to duplicate real insects perfectly with their artificial flies. There is no denying that trout can be very selective at times—totally ignoring one pattern of dry fly, for example, while quickly sucking in another similar pattern—but there really is no need for the trout fisherman to be a walking fly shop, toting hundreds of patterns.

One evening I stood near the tail of a flat pool on Michigan's Boardman River and watched my white marabou streamer wiggling along the bottom. I had pinched a BB split-shot sinker on at the hook-eye, so the fly played hopscotch over the bottom as I retrieved. With each twitch of the rod the fly rose a couple of inches, then nosed down and bumped bottom. Each bump sent up a tiny puff of sand, which I could see clearly in the 6-inch-deep water. The marabou had danced beside a brush pile before it slid into the shallows, and so it drew a nice brown trout from the shade. The fish followed the undulating, sensuous marabou, and when it started that bump-and-grind routine over the gravel bottom the trout nosed down and inhaled the fly the way a bonefish sucks up a crab.

Another time I worked a bend of Wisconsin's Oconto River first with dry flies, then wet flies, then streamers, but couldn't raise a fish. I switched to nymphs—casting a short line upstream and allowing the fly to drift down naturally with the current—and suddenly the place erupted trout. I guided several nymph patterns through the current and the trout hit every one.

On Big Hunting Creek, in Maryland, John Daley and I fished a spot called the Swimming Pool. The water was clear and cool as a martini. We could see three small rainbows positioned to pick drifting mayflies from the surface. John floated a size 10 Irresistible to the nearest trout, which clobbered it. He withdrew the fish quickly and released it. Then I sent a size 14 Royal Coachman to the second trout—which took it unhesitatingly. When I released that one, John cast another dry fly, a Badger Spider, to the farthest rainbow—which rose to it with abandon.

Those experiences help point up that it is not so much the fly *pattern* you use as it is the fly *type*, and the method employed in fishing it.

We must never become overly concerned with trout fly patterns. While "matching the hatch" sometimes is not only desirable but critical if many fish are to be creeled, more often exact duplication of the natural insect with an artificial is relatively unimportant.

Once, on New York's Chichester, I met a gent who insisted the only fly he could catch trout with that day was the Lady Beaverkill, dry. He tried "every fly in the box," including the Beaverkill pattern, but nothing else worked—this despite the fact that the major difference between the two patterns is a tiny yellow "egg sac" decorating the rear of the Lady Beaverkill. I'm sure that guy was relating fiction, because it's a rare day when trout take or refuse a dry fly

Mayflies are the most common insects on most trout streams. Their life cycle begins when the female deposits her eggs onto the water. The eggs hatch into nymphs, which eventually hatch into winged duns that emerge and float on the surface of the stream before taking to the air. Hungry trout feed on the surface insects. The escaping duns soon return to the stream and mate, and the cycle is repeated.

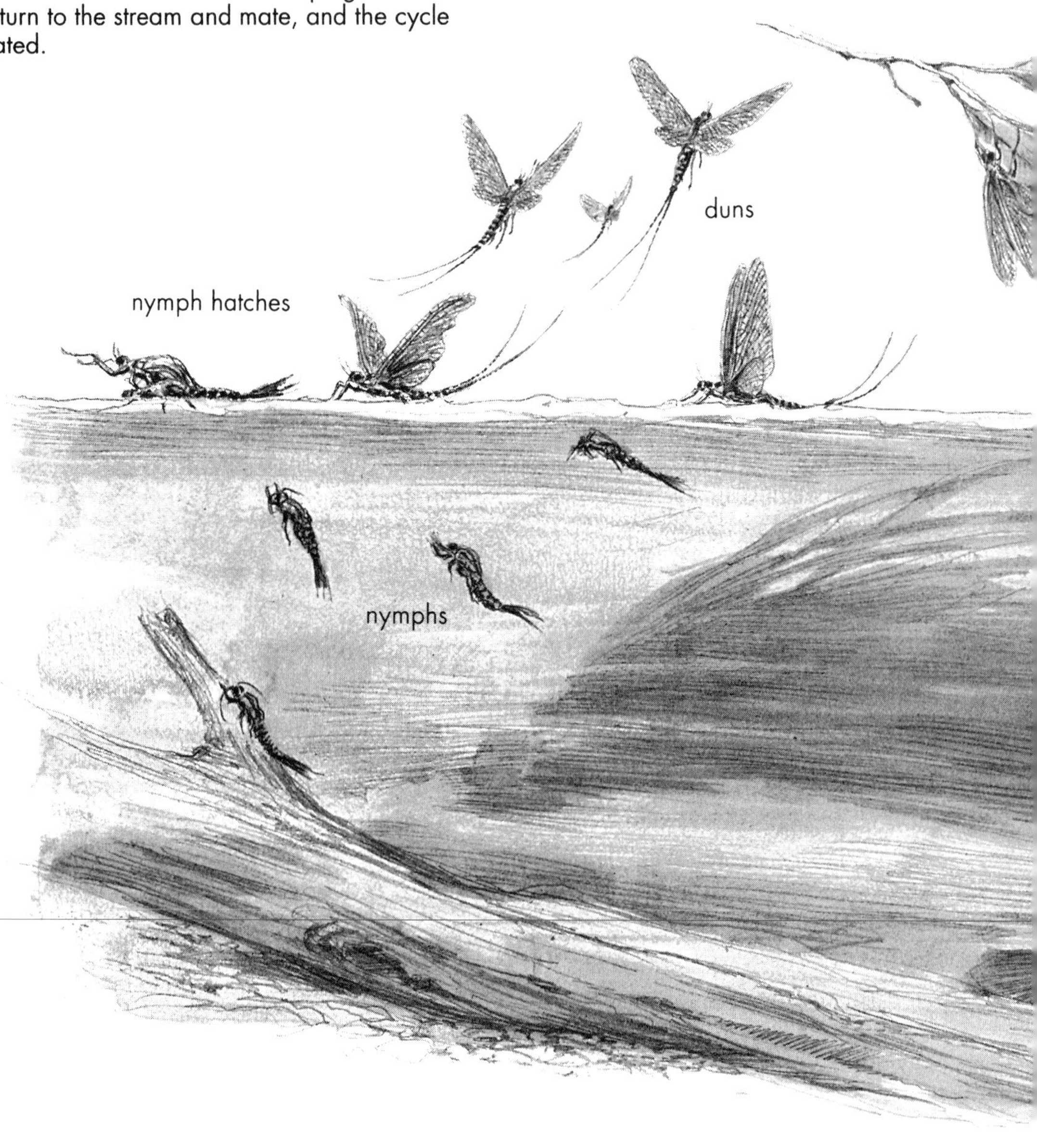

duns

nymph hatches

nymphs

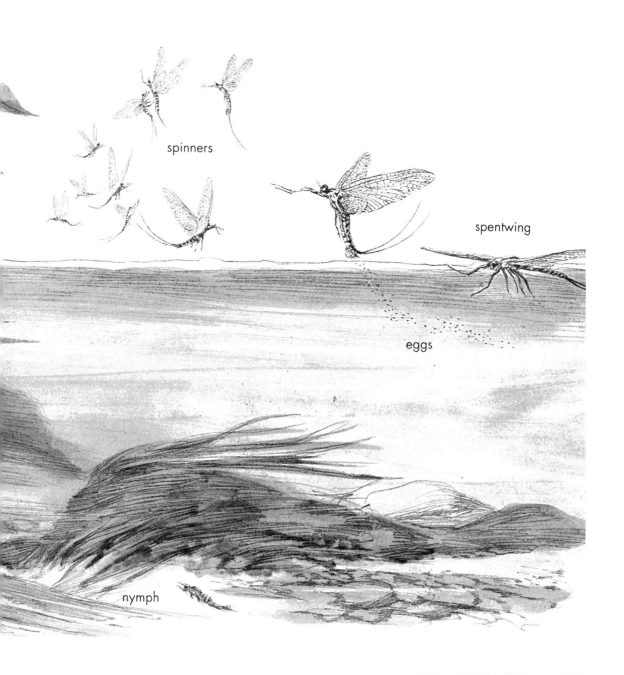

spinners

spentwing

eggs

nymph

depending solely upon the presence or absence of a yellow chenille tag not much larger than a pinhead.

Most trout experts agree that, at best, they hope only to *suggest* a real insect or live minnow or nymph with their phony flies. Even the most perfectly modeled artificial fly cannot compare favorably with the real-life insect, or minnow, it is supposed to duplicate.

None of this is to say, however, that a bivisible dry fly (one with hackles wound Palmer-style the length of the hook shank) will take trout as well as an artificial mayfly on a day when genuine Green Drake mayflies are filling the air like snowflakes. The same is true when trout are feeding selectively on midge pupa floating in the surface film. Under those conditions you'd probably strike out fishing a size 10 Black Gnat dry fly, but score repeatedly using any of a variety of midge nymph patterns. Along

these lines, we should note that at a given time on the stream a representative imitation of the genuine insects that are momentarily available to trout is of more importance to the dry-fly fisherman than to the angler using wet flies, streamers, or nymphs.

To put it another way, if trout are picking midges from the surface, surely we should fish a midge fly. But whether the artificial is black or dusty brown most often will matter little to the trout. And if trout are feasting on the corpses of spent flies, wings outspread on the surface, then we'll do better with a representative spent-wing dry fly than with, say, a Hairwing Coachman, which looks nothing at all like a spent-spinner fly.

DRY FLIES

The size of a dry fly can be very important, as can its profile or its type. These factors

A good assortment of dry flies. Author favors dry flies of deer hair for their flotation.

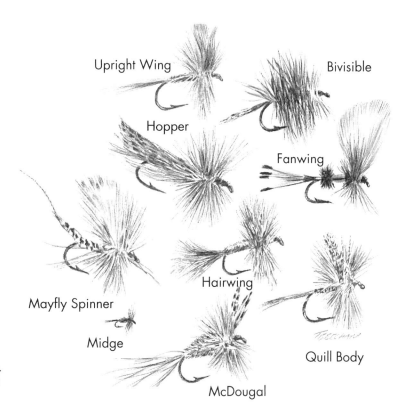

Upright Wing

Bivisible

Hopper

Fanwing

Mayfly Spinner

Hairwing

Midge

Quill Body

McDougal

These are the basic types of dry flies. Most types can be tied with materials of different colors to produce a variety of patterns.

are far more vital than the specific pattern of fly.

The best dry flies, the ones that will float high for some time, are tied on light wire hooks, and they have quality hackling, usually a little oversized for the hook. Dry flies with chenille material in the bodies will soak up water and not float well, and wool isn't a particularly good body material either.

As a rule, a dry fly should be sparsely tied, made with good, stiff hackles, and it ought to come downcurrent sitting jauntily upright on its tail and hackles. Never use dry flies tied on heavy wire hooks; heavy wire is for wet flies and nymphs.

A properly stocked dry-fly box should

hold standard upright-wing dry flies, bivisibles, a few fan-wings (these are like regular dry flies except the wings usually are made of duck breast feathers and flare broadly outward, like miniature fans), some quill-body patterns, high-floating deer hairs (such as the Irresistible and Rat-Faced McDougal), midges, several mayfly types, grasshopper imitations (like Joe's Hopper, the Michigan Hopper, or Muddler Minnow), and some hair-wing patterns.

Except during those short periods when large mayflies are present, small dry flies usually score best on eastern and midwestern streams. From opening of the trout seasons until about mid-July, dry flies in sizes 10, 12, and 14 seem to score most consistently on trout waters east of the Mississippi. From late July to late fall, dries in sizes 14, 16, 18, 20, and even 22 often are best. There are exceptions, of course, and a hatch of large mayflies becomes a major exception, but as a rule small dries produce best during low, clear-water periods in the eastern half of the United States.

In the far west, large dry flies have become standard, just as westerners have come to dote on oversize streamers, wet flies, and nymphs. A bushy, heavily winged size 6 or 8 dry fly is a popular tool on western rivers, and rare is the Montana angler, for example, who will often drop down to dry flies smaller than size 10. The tendency in the west toward using big dry flies is partly due to the large size of the rivers—and of the fish.

Although I've stressed that trout fishermen should be concerned chiefly with acquiring a representative assortment of flies, following are some dry-fly patterns that produce well on most trout streams: Irresistible, Adams, Hendrickson, Quill Gordon, Mosquito, Light Cahill, Dark Cahill, Blue Dun, Joe's Hopper, Muddler Minnow (greased to fish dry), Brown Bivisible, Dark Brown Cranefly, Gordon Spinner, Green Drake, Multi-colored Variant, Badger Spider, Olive Spent-Wing, Gray Wulff, and Brown and Black Midges.

WET FLIES

The old-time wet-fly fisherman is fading from the American angling scene, but we still have plenty of addicted wet-fly anglers,

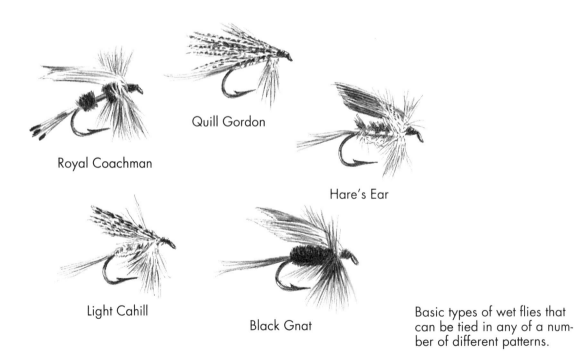

Royal Coachman

Quill Gordon

Hare's Ear

Light Cahill

Black Gnat

Basic types of wet flies that can be tied in any of a number of different patterns.

especially on our western and northeastern rivers and lakes. These fishermen are chiefly dedicated to the *system* of fishing wet flies, however, and not so much to the wet fly itself. It's fun to fish wet flies, though, if only for practice, to experiment, or as a change of pace.

Wet flies normally are tied on short-shank hooks. They may or may not have a tail, usually have a body of tinsel or water-absorbing material (such as chenille), wings that lie back over the body, and some hackling at the head.

Wet flies should be tied on extra-heavy hooks so that they will sink readily, and as a rule the sparser ties are best. If you tie your own, make some weighted patterns by wrapping fine lead wire over the hook shank before tying in the body material.

Brightly colored wet-fly patterns are used by New England and Canadian fishermen for brook trout—the Parmachene Belle, for instance—but in general, drab wet-fly patterns are preferred by most anglers. Popular wet dressings include the Black Gnat, Hare's Ear, March Brown, Hendrickson, Dark and Light Cahill, Brown Hackle, Coachman, Adams, Royal Coachman, Greenwell's Glory, Quill Gordon (in nature this insect matures underwater), Alexandria, Blue Dun, Cowdung, Gray Hackle (Peacock), and Western Bee.

Regarding the sizes of wet flies, I think that on most streams under most conditions the best all-around size is No. 12. But 10s are very useful, too, along with 14s, and a wallet complete with wet flies should have them additionally in sizes 18, 16, 8, and 6.

NYMPHS

There are literally thousands of real nymph forms, but all live for a time in the stream in the larval stage, either clinging for a while to rocks or sticks or holding down in the mud, gravel, or sand—and then, on maturing, rising to the surface and transforming into an adult winged insect.

There are basically three types of nymphs: mayfly nymphs, or Ephemerida; caddis-fly nymphs, or Trichoptera; and stonefly nymphs, or Plecoptera. Any trout stream worth the name will have a bottom literally coated with nymphs. I've been on eastern streams, particularly in western Pennsylvania, where caddis larvae were so thick on rocks that you slipped when stepping on them. And along the banks of the better western streams, you will see the shucks of stonefly nymphs covering streamside stones. I once was camped on the Big Hole River, near Twin Bridges, Montana, when a huge stonefly hatch came off. The big, $1\frac{1}{4}$-inch-long insects crawled into the tent, onto bunks, up tent poles—everywhere. We were glad to see them because they were trout food, but there were so many they were a nuisance in camp.

In choosing artificial nymphs it is best to concentrate on "attractor" types—ones that reasonably suggest a multitude of genuine nymphs but which do not perfectly represent any specific natural insect larvae.

The dull, drab, dark colors almost always produce the most hits with nymphs, and the fur-bodied types easily outfish other nymphs. Synthetic seal fur today is a top nymph-body material, as are gray muskrat, fox underbelly, otter, and mink.

Mayfly nymph (top) and artificials that mimic it.

Fur-bodied nymphs have a marked difference in appearance underwater, the fly edges filtering light and making the nymph appear partially translucent. The most productive nymphs commonly have a thorax—that is, some material tied in to form a hump at the shoulders representing the real nymph's undeveloped cased wings. Hackles of a soft, webby type under the chin simulate legs in a good nymph tie, and duckwing quill over the fly's back, hardened with an application of glue or lacquer, give a phony nymph a graphic silhouette underwater. Nymphs that are weighted by the tier usually have copper or lead wire wound on the hook shank, then the body material laid over.

The size of the nymph fished often is as important in taking fish consistently in a given situation as is the size of dry flies when trout are rising selectively during a hatch. The smaller nymphs are generally more effective on eastern streams, larger ones in the west. Eastern anglers use chiefly sizes 10, 12, and 14 nymphs, and occasionally 16 and 18. Western anglers strive to simulate the big stoneflies, so the most commonly used western nymph is a No. 6 on a long-shank hook. However, one season I had good success fishing a giant black nymph on western rivers. It was so large and heavily weighted I could hardly cast it; it was fully 3 inches long, tied on a long-shank No. 1 hook, and it looked like a bastard hellgrammite.

Be sure to have plenty of Gray Nymphs (a pattern calling for gray muskrat underbelly fur in the body), because rainbow trout in particular relish them. Other important nymph patterns are the Caddis,

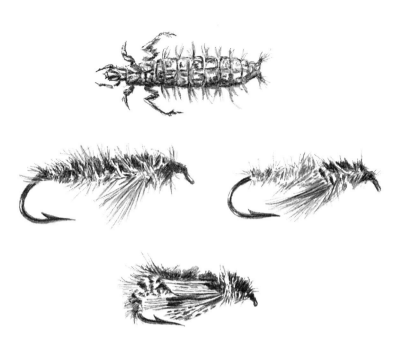

Caddis larva (top) and artificials that mimic it. A Caddis pupa imitation is shown at bottom.

Stonefly nymph (top) and artificials that mimic it.

Some of the many types of streamers that are tied to imitate minnows and other baitfish.

March Brown, Stonefly, Hendrickson, Strawman Nymph (a fuzzy, clipped deer-hair nymph), Squash Bug, Leadwing Coachman, Quill Gordon, Whitlock's Black Stone Nymph, Ginger Quill, Michigan Nymph, Light Cahill, Zug Bug, Montana Nymph, Hare's Ear Nymph, Stonefly Creeper, and Shellback Nymph.

STREAMERS

Any streamer, regardless of pattern, does a good job of imitating the dace minnows, shiners, silversides, chubs, darters, and sculpins on which trout feed. Quite likely streamers are sometimes mistaken by trout for other forms of stream life besides minnows, but not often.

A well-stocked streamer fly wallet will contain several streamers of each type—that is, ones with saddle-hackle winging, bucktail, impala, squirrel tail, or marabou, and ones made of combinations of those materials. Streamers should be selected according to size, too, and for basic color.

Thousands of saddle-hackle streamers are available, and the same is true of bucktail patterns. So remember that it is primarily the fly winging, the streamer's size, and its overall silhouette that is important. All trout fishermen should have some standard hackle-wing streamers in their fly wallets, some with "breather-style" winging, and plenty with silver or gold tinsel bodies. Some streamers with Mylar bodies, or with Mylar stripping tied in the wings, ought to be included, too.

Brown and white bucktails with "optic" heads (a big-eyed, pea-size head) are deadly at times. So is the Black-Nosed Dace pattern. And Muddler Minnows must be in the trout fisherman's fly book in good numbers, types, and sizes.

Keep plenty of brown and black bucktail streamers on hand, plus white, yellow, brown-and-white, and black-and-white. Many streamer patterns are meaningless to my mind, but a lot are not. Most patterns look nothing at all like minnows or other true life forms, but some streamers have nice bright bellies, bright silver stripes, or dark side-bars—just as do a lot of real minnows—and they catch trout.

In most situations a Black Ghost Marabou (which has a white wing) probably is no more effective than a plain White Marabou, but a Yellow Marabou might work wonders under certain light and water conditions in which a Black Ghost Marabou or White Marabou fails.

The plain White Marabou is an excellent streamer. I make them by wrapping lead wire over a 3X-long hook shank, and then just add the marabou. The fly really is simply a hook with lead wire and marabou. No fancy trimmings, yet it is surprisingly effective.

Yellow, Yellow-and-Red, White-and-Red, and Black Marabou all are good streamers. Marabou has such rippling, waving action in the water that these flies will draw trout out of hiding, so they are superb "attractor" flies.

Trout sometimes hit short in striking

Streamer flies are a good choice early in the season, or when streams are high and discolored.

marabou streamers and so miss the hook. If this happens too often it may be profitable to shorten the winging material. Do this by chewing or tearing the marabou fibers, not by snipping or clipping. Marabou loses much of its natural action when it is trimmed or clipped with scissors or a nail clipper.

Some other streamer patterns you might find useful are the Black Ghost (saddle-hackle winging), Gray Ghost, Mickey Finn, Edson Tiger, Black Ghost (bucktail), Warden's Worry, Silver Doctor, Brown Trude, and Nine-Three.

For most trout fishing, streamers on long-shank (3X) hooks are best since they are more apt to connect on short-striking fish. The trouter who works a variety of streams and rivers holding fish of differing sizes will want streamers tied on 1/0 and 1 hooks, and in sizes 4 through 12. Size 12 is very small, and 10, too, but you'll employ them often in fishing small eastern mountain brooks, or some western spring creeks.

The streamer sizes most commonly used in fishing average streams for modest-size trout are 6 and 8. In the west, larger flies are common and streamers on 1/0 hooks are fished by many anglers. In the fall, on larger western rivers such as the Yellowstone, where a 5-pound brown trout is no news, I often fish streamers on 1/0 and 2/0 hooks. These are big flies, but they take big fish.

OTHER TROUT FLIES

Some of the other flies all trout fishermen ought to be familiar with include variants, spiders, and skaters; hair-wing dry flies; spent-wing dries; no-hackle flies; Wooly Worms and Wooly Buggers; midges; and terrestrials. Some are fished dry, some wet, some both.

Variants, spiders, and skaters are much alike. Each is a big, broad-hackled job, looking not unlike a real spider. A variant (like spiders and skaters available in various patterns) has wings, a body, and a tail. A spider may be wet or dry (variants and skaters are dry only) and has a body and tail but no wings. The typical skater has a short body. Variants, spiders, and skaters should be tied on the best-quality short-shank light-wire hooks.

These unusual flies are designed primarily to be skimmed over the surface. In fact, variants and skaters shouldn't be fished any other way, and Edward Hewitt developed his spider on New York's Neversink River for just that sort of retrieve.

The variant flies *must* be tied on very light hooks, nothing larger than size 16. A variant-type fly is not supposed to rest horizontally on the water; it should stand vertically on its spindly legs, and only a fly tied on a very small hook, with good stiff hackles, will float that way.

Badger Variants, Badger Spiders, and Badger Skaters are especially effective, as are ones of furnace hackles, and ones that are all black, brown, Coachman red, grizzly, and white.

Hair-wing dry flies can be any pattern, but the wings usually are of fuzzy impala. Typical hair-wings are the Wulff series, the Hair-Wing Royal Coachman, and the Royal Trude, a terrific fish-getter.

A spent-wing dry fly, or spent spinner, is a dry fly with its wings tied in so that they lie flat on the surface of the water, rather than standing stiffly upright from the float-

Variant

Spider

Inch Worm

Letort Cricket

Midge

Black Ant

Beetle

Skater

Jassid

Wooly Worm

Slate/Tan
No Hackle

Hairwing

Spentwing

An assortment of unusual
trout flies.

ing fly. For the most part, spent-wings, which may conform to any standard or bastard pattern, are meant to suggest dead mayflies.

No-hackle flies are dries which, as the name suggests, have no hackling to support them on the water. Their bodies are of dubbed fur, which gives them adequate flotation.

The Wooly Worm is a well-known fly, used primarily in the west, and it has accounted for some huge trout. There are variations, but it is generally a large fly, meant to represent a drowned caterpillar, and it is tied with thick body chenille, over-wrapped with webby hackling tied in Palmer style to suggest the many legs of a caterpillar.

Wooly Buggers, a comparatively recent introduction, basically are Wooly Worms with a marabou tail, and are extremely popular in the far west—and increasingly so in the east. Wooly Buggers can imitate various swimming nymphs, minnows, or even small leeches.

Midges are tied as dry flies or nymphs. Real midge larvae are like tiny worms, usually hanging tail-down from the surface. Many are no more than $1/32$ inch long, so they are difficult to duplicate with hair and feathers tied on a hook.

The best midge nymphs are sizes 16 to 22. Perhaps the size most often fished is a size 18. Midges are tied on short-shank hooks.

The majority of midge imitations have quill bodies and tiny hackling around the head, or bodies of fine silk and then hackling—but all are very simple ties, sometimes with the body material curving around the hook bend to give the fly a wormlike appearance.

Nymph midge patterns are very plain. The Mosquito Midge is good. The Quill Gordon and March Brown, and some fur-bodied midge nymphs in green, black, red, olive, cream, and brown, will fill out a midge nymph selection nicely.

There are times when trout go on a midge surface-feeding spree, and if the angler does not come up with a reasonable representation of the natural, he might as well leave the stream.

Quality midge dry flies are tied on the lightest, best-grade wire hooks, because the fly's hackling is rightly sparse to better suggest the natural insect. If heavy hooks are used the fly will float briefly or not float well. Best sizes for midge dries are the same as for midge nymphs—16 to 22.

Patterns for midge dry flies should match those suggested for midge nymphs, but add the Black Gnat, Gray Midge, Wetzel's Green Midge, Henryville Special, Ginger Midge, and Dun Midge.

Most of the flies imitating terrestrials (the land insects) are dry flies, but some are wets. Terrestrial patterns often catch great numbers of trout, so they should be well represented in every trout fisherman's kit. Terrestrials include grasshoppers, crickets, bees, ants, beetles, and a vast family of little bugs classified as Jassidae or Cicadellidae, but more commonly known as leaf hoppers.

Flies representing crickets and ants have their periods of providing exceptional fishing, so I would recommend that you have black cricket imitations tied of deer hair, and an assortment of ants made with bodies of black deer hair or closed-cell foam, and some with cinnamon-red foam or floss. There are trouting veterans who stake their reputations on ants fished dry, usually in sizes 14 through 22.

The Jassid is a minute artificial terrestrial no trout fisherman should be without. This fly was developed by Pennsylvanian Vince Marinaro. Vince discovered Letort River trout selectively feeding on leaf hoppers, and he could not catch those trout in any conventional way with any conventional fly. So he built the Jassid, a wisp of a fly in sizes 18 to 24, which floats high in the surface film. Its back is made of the eye of the jungle cock feather, black and yellow-white, which makes the tiny fly easier to see.

The Jassid must be used with a long, fine leader, often to 7X, and it is allowed to fish awash on the surface with no action imparted by the angler. At the end of a normal float, a slow skimming of the fly, with the resulting miniature wake, can bring up hard-to-get summer fish.

I've covered the basic fly types and listed some of the more important patterns. They should form the nucleus for a stock of good trout flies. However, with experience the angler will be able to add and deduct patterns according to seasonal conditions and the various streams fished. But we must constantly remind ourselves that it isn't the fly pattern that counts so much as it is presentation, fly type, and the method of fishing.

11
Special Flies and Bugs

THERE are literally tens of thousands of flies and bugs available to fly fishermen. Many are standard and proven patterns; some are not. That good selections of such flies and bugs ought to be in every flyrodder's kit isn't disputed, but over the years I've come across certain streamer flies and bugs that are *special*, and no well-rounded fly fisherman should be without them. Some of the lures I designed myself to fill an unusual fly-fishing need, and for decades they have proved to be lastingly successful.

The flies that I suggest are unique are the Muddler Minnow, Marsh Hare, McNally Magnum, McNally Smelt, and Bill Catherwood's saltwater streamers. Special bugs are the McNally Frog, and three others I designed—the Bullet Bug, Bluegill Bug, and Powder Puff. The Marm Minnow, a bug developed on Florida's St. Johns River, must be included as *very* special.

THE MUDDLER MINNOW

By now most experienced fly fishermen are familiar with the Muddler Minnow. It's been getting good press since 1949. I first used the Muddler that year, and in subsequent seasons found it devastating on everything from trout to bonefish, and in just about every place from West Virginia's Blackwater River to the flats at Grand Cayman.

One spring, Baltimoreans Willy Weaver, Simeon Yaruta, Lloyd Gerber, and I toured West Virginia trout streams. As I recall we didn't hurt the trout population much, but one hot, bright afternoon I looked upstream on the Blackwater and there sat Willy Weaver on a small boulder in midstream. His rod lay beside him, next to his boots, and his bare feet dangled in the cool water. Half dozing, Willy didn't notice my approach. I'd just started fishing a Muddler, and when I was 60 feet below Willy I dropped it right next to the boulder and between Willy's feet. A 1-pound brown trout nailed the fly the instant it touched the water—and may He strike me down if that is not the absolute, sworn, God-fearing truth. The trout jumped immediately, rising upward in foamy spray between Willy's knees, and I suspect I'll go to my grave never forgetting the sudden look of astonishment on Willy's face.

I have fished with most of America's best-known fly fishermen, and with many of international note, but the best small-stream trout fisherman I know is John Daley of Baltimore, a machinist in an aircraft factory. Since about age four John's every free hour, in season, has been spent on the trout streams of Maryland and Pennsylvania. He is a deadly nymph fisherman and, in fact, taught me fully ninety percent of what I know about nymph fishing. When John is using nymphs, fishing behind him on a trout stream is like fishing behind a net. He misses nothing.

We were on Pennsylvania's Dwarfskill River one afternoon, in a cool, hemlock-shrouded stretch then leased by the Fifty Club. The Dwarfskill was stiff with wild, bright brook trout and colorful, gold-spotted browns, most in the 6- to 12-inch range—as is typical of small eastern mountain streams.

I sidled up to John as he started fishing the Home Pool, the one below the swimming-pool dam at the clubhouse. John was kneeling on the shoulder of the pool, so as not to be seen by the trout, and was fixedly dredging a weighted nymph over the gravel bottom as I slipped to my knees beside him.

"Do any good?" he asked, never taking his eyes from the end of the fly line.

"Okay," I said. "All small stuff."

"Same here," John replied, continuing his fishing. Nothing interferes with John Daley's concentration when he is drifting a nymph.

Out would go the nymph on a short roll cast, then down it would come with the current—the white fly-line tip marking its path—the nymph swimming deep by this rock, searching along that current edge, bumping the gravel over there. John put the nymph carefully into every pocket, along each crevice, beneath every rocky ledge, anywhere a trout might lie. No way could a trout be in that pool that did not see John's nymph. John saw to that. And no way could there be a trout that, seeing John Daley's nymph, wouldn't take it.

"Hmpf!" said John. "Hard to believe there's no fish there. Whatcha' using?"

"Gotta Muddler on."

"Try it."

I flipped the Muddler up and across stream to a rock-ledge pocket, and twitched it once. Twice. The trout that came out, with the Muddler drooping like a squished grasshopper from its lower jaw, was the loveliest, biggest 14-inch brown trout I'd ever seen.

John's mouth fell open in undisguised astonishment. Never, but never, does one fish behind John and catch trout that John's nymph missed. I wanted to yell, but instead put on the detached expression of a man to whom such things happened all the time. The "Dwarfskill incident" (as I've come to remember it) was just one more event endearing the Muddler Minnow to me.

With Muddlers I have caught every species of freshwater North American gamefish—except inconnu, for which I have not yet fished. In addition, I've taken a large number of saltwater gamefish on heavy-hooked Muddlers. Quite probably no other fly pattern devastates more species of fish than the Muddler.

Freshwater trout can mistake a Mudd-

Author Tom McNally demonstrates various moves necessary to execute the double-line haul, an advanced casting technique that greatly increases casting distance, even when using oversize flies and bugs. The double haul is an essential casting method when fishing large, wind-resistant bugs, and when saltwater fly fishing, where high winds are the rule.

When double hauling, the caster uses both hands (and arms) to extend a reasonable length of line forward (initial false cast) and starts the first backcast by gradually changing the direction of the moving rod. When the rod comes under load, the caster tugs sharply on the taut fly line, which takes some of the strain off the rod and increases line speed. These movements are repeated in reverse when starting the next forward cast: on the backcast the line goes back; on the forward cast it goes forward. Each time the rod changes direction, a sharp tug, or haul, with the line hand increases line speed dramatically.

To execute the double haul you shouldn't need to make more than one or two false casts. Once you've made the final cast, loose (excess) line on the boat bottom or at your feet is "shot" through the rod guides. The ability to shoot a great deal of line is another advantage of the double haul.

The photo on the left shows the moves necessary to execute a double haul on a backcast, while the photo on the right shows the double haul on a forward cast. Shooting slack line through the rod guides on the forward cast, in conjunction with the double haul, makes day-long distance casting—even in bad weather—a pleasure.

THE COMPLETE BOOK OF FLY FISHING

Even lake trout, notorious for hanging deep-down much of the time, are readily taken on flies when they are in shallow water, usually in early spring and again in fall.

Generally speaking, streamer flies are the most productive for lake trout, but other flies take them as well. At Great Bear Lake in the Northwest Territories, quite a few anglers, fishing after midnight, have taken large lake trout on small dry caddis imitations.

Professional fly tyer of Hot Springs Village, Arkansas, Jim Poulas plays a feisty rainbow trout on Montana's Beaverhead River. Note that the hooked trout has jumped a distance almost five times its own length.

This trout was one of several in the 3-pound class taken on midge dry flies. Because upstream and cross-stream casts were ruled out due to fickle currents, casts were made upstream of the fish-holding area by casting directly downstream then lifting the rod and pulling back before the line and fly fell into the water. This technique gave the midge flies a perfect 10- to 12-foot float to the readily visible trout.

The late A. J. McClane shows a fine 6-pound brown trout taken below Toston Dam on Montana's Missouri River. This trout hit a Muddler Minnow that was greased to work across the top like a struggling grasshopper.

The Missouri is one of the West's best-known big-trout rivers. Late fall—September through October—is the prime time for trophy trout.

At one time the grayling was quite a controversial fish. Biologists believed that different species inhabited different areas of the continent. Many anglers swore that the fish had the odor of thyme (perhaps this is why the species' Latin name is *Thymallus arcticus*). An equal number of anglers swear that the grayling has no special odor—if anything, it smells like fish. I've sniffed grayling from Athabasca to Hudson Bay and never detected an odor of thyme.

In any case, fisheries biologists today agree that the grayling is just one fish—to be known as the "American grayling"—no more Montana, Wyoming, or Arctic grayling.

This 2½-pound grayling, photographed and carefully released, was taken on a fly at far-northern Saskatchewan's Fon-du-Lac River, one of the better areas for large grayling. Note the extremely large dorsal fin on this cock grayling. Hen grayling have much smaller dorsal fins.

A smallish Arctic char, dressed in its brilliant spawning colors, is readied for release. This one succumbed to a bright streamer fly in the Coppermine River on the Arctic Ocean coast in far-northern Canada's Northwest Territories. This char undoubtedly traveled hundreds of miles from the Arctic Ocean through the Beaufort Sea to the Coppermine River to spawn.

In full spawning colors an Arctic char is hard to distinguish from our native brook trout, which, incidentally, is also a char.

Many fly fishermen, particularly in the Northeast, cherish the brook trout for its excellent table qualities, among other things. Arctic char, even large ones, are just as delectable.

Yes, Junior, muskies definitely will hit flies, and bugs as well. The muskie in this photograph was hooked one crisp October day at a lake in northern Wisconsin. It weighed 24 pounds and fell for a 6-inch-long McNally Magnum streamer.

This largemouth bass took a Standard Yellow popper in Florida's St. Johns River, while the chunky and colorful smallmouth (bottom left) rose to a deer-hair bug in Manitoba's Winnipeg River.

While stealth, finesse, know-how, proper presentation of a fly, and knowledge of insect life may be paramount to the trout fisherman's success, few of those factors are crucial in fly fishing for muskies and bass. Fly fishing for muskies, bass, and other warm-water species can be a refreshing change from the perfectionistic techniques required by many forms of trout fishing.

More than any other species, *Albula vulpes*—the lightning fast bonefish—is most responsible for the unbelievable surge in the popularity of saltwater fly fishing.

The bonefish is an inshore species, seldom frequenting water more than 10 to 12 feet deep. Much of the time bonefish will sweep over a flat to feed in water only 1 to 2 feet deep, foraging for food in water so shallow that their dorsal fins and the top half of their caudal fins are completely exposed. This proclivity for a shallow-water environment is one of the things that makes bonefish ideal fly-fishing targets.

Bonefish frequently are seen "tailing"—tipping down on their suckerlike noses in extremely shallow water to grub for shrimp, crabs, worms, etc., often exposing half or more of their bodies. Their bright silver scales flashing in the sun make them visible from great distances—an ideal situation for the fly-rodder. Tailing fish are not as alert as usual and are more likely to accept a sloppy cast.

Bonefish are easily spooked. When startled they will desert a flat instantly—sometimes sooner. Dropping a fly too close to a bonefish is a mistake; it will flush at the shadow of a passing sea gull on the bright sand or marl bottom, and putting a fly line over a bonefish is a mortal sin.

Flats bonefishing is ideally suited to wading, but fishing from small, shallow-draft skiffs (push-pole power) also is popular, and offers greater mobility.

Some places that today offer excellent bonefishing include the Florida Keys, the Bahama Islands, Belize and most other Central American countries, and Christmas Island in the Pacific.

The tarpon, or "silver king," is easily one of the greatest gamefish in the sea. Dedicated fly fishermen today are catching (and releasing) record numbers of 100-pound-class tarpon. Many a trophy-driven fly fisherman nowadays is vying to be the first angler to land a tarpon over 200 pounds on standard fly-fishing tackle. As of this writing no tarpon exceeding 200 pounds has been landed on fly-fishing gear.

The typical fly-fishing outfit for the silver king is a rod taking an 11-, 12-, or 13-weight line and a heavy, strongly built "saltwater" fly reel. Leader construction is very important, with the weakest section of a leader usually being a strand testing 12 or 15 pounds but attached to a 12- or 15-inch shock tippet of hard nylon testing 60 to 100 pounds.

The hot spot for big tarpon on a fly or bug at this writing is Florida's Homosassa River on the Gulf Coast. But there are many other productive areas, among them the Caribbean and Mexico's Yucatan Peninsula. Very large tarpon are reported along the coast of Angola on the southeast coast of Africa.

Most anglers agree that of all the gamefish in salt water, among the toughest are those of the jack family, found almost exclusively in the warmer seas of the world. Among its many different species are the notorious amberjack and the plentiful jack crevalle. The jack decorating this page is an Atlantic horse-eye jack, a true barroom brawler if ever there was one. When hooked, jacks give no quarter and ask none. Jacks are the bulldogs of the sea; like bluefish they pursue their prey relentlessly, gorging on baitfish, regurgitating, gorging again.

Jacks are not difficult to catch—they'll hit almost any fly or bug that moves in the water. But when one hits a lure and is hooked, *you* have a fight on your hands.

A typical St. Mary's River (Florida) striper is hoisted by outdoor writer Bob McNally of Jacksonville. Stripers—called rockfish in some areas—are plentiful in several Florida rivers, especially the St. Johns and St. Mary's.

Striped bass are found on all three American coasts with the heaviest concentration along the Atlantic and Pacific coasts. On the Atlantic side, stripers range from the St. Johns River northward to the Gulf of St. Lawrence. In the Gulf of Mexico their primary range is from western Florida to Louisiana. Stripers were stocked from the Atlantic to the Pacific in 1886, and they have thrived, ranging from the Columbia River in Washington to Los Angeles. The San Francisco Bay region is noted for its striped bass fishery, and fly fishing is the popular method of taking them.

Most of the striped bass population on the Atlantic coast is found from South Carolina to Massachusetts. At one time the Chesapeake Bay was a striper stronghold and was even considered the striped bass "nursery" for the entire Atlantic coast. Overfishing—both commercial and sport—has decimated Chesapeake striper stocks in recent years.

Maryland has imposed some stringent fishing regulations, and pollution—another reason for the striped bass decline—has been greatly reduced and water quality continues to improve. There is renewed hope that the Chesapeake's supply of stripers is recovering. A lifelong Chesapeake striper fisherman said recently, "There are more stripers in the bay than I've ever seen."

While things look promising for the Chesapeake's stripers, officials are not relaxing restrictive regulations. At this writing, two seasons have been imposed for Chesapeake striped bass fishing: the month of May for "trophy" stripers ranging 36 inches or larger, one per angler, and all of October and the first three weekends in November for fish 18 to 36 inches long, one striper per angler daily.

It should be noted that Chesapeake striped bass fishing regulations will undoubtedly be changed periodically depending upon the condition of the fishery.

Incidentally, famed fly fisherman Joe Brooks once caught a 29-pound striper in Coos Bay, Oregon. "That was the best fish-fight I ever had," said Brooks.

ler for a grasshopper, a dragonfly, a dam-selfly, a surfacing stonefly nymph, a sculpin (commonly called "muddler minnow"), a bullhead minnow, one of several daces, or a wounded minnow skittering over the surface—all depending on how the fly is fished.

The mighty Muddler was designed and first tied by Don Gapen, a tackle manufacturer's representative living in Orillia, Ontario. A fly tyer from boyhood days, Gapen in 1941 was running a fishing camp on the Nipigon River, the Ontario spot once world-famous for its large brook trout.

"In the days when I ran a fishing camp on the Nipigon, there were no roads in there," Don once told me. "And there were no dams on the river and no logging being done. So the fishing was superb. We thought nothing of catching 2½- and 3-pound brook trout—thick, deep-bodied, healthy fish with brilliant coloring—and in a normal day on the Nip we'd catch twenty big ones ranging from 2½ to 6 pounds. And maybe you won't believe this, but 8-pounders were *common*."

On July 14, 1951, Don Gapen caught a 10-pound, 4 ounce brookie from the Nipigon River, his largest, and it hit a Muddler Minnow fly he had tied.

In those early days on the Nipigon, most fishermen used bait-casting tackle and Dardevle spoons. But the best fish-catcher was a real minnow native to the river that the Indians called a "cocka-touche," and when they could get these minnows they preferred them to all other baits or lures.

"The cockatouche was really a muddler minnow, or sculpin," Gapen says. "A sort

of burrowing, secretive minnow. They don't swim in schools, but instead hide themselves under rocks.

"Because of their strange habits, sculpins were hard to get, and the Indians would go out at night with flashlights and poke under rocks for a couple hours to get a half-dozen cockatouche. Those minnows were really good. Open any trout caught and it would have some cockatouche in it."

Since the real minnows were hard to get, Gapen decided to tie an artificial fly to represent the sculpin. He experimented for a year, tying hundreds of flies, before he got the fly the way he wanted it. The fly was tied streamer-style, on a streamer hook, the body flat gold tinsel, the tail a section of turkey wing quill. The fly's winging was made up of sections of turkey quill and white impala, generally tied sparse. A generous bunch of deer hair went on top of the hook, and was tied tightly at the head to flare outward. Then the deer hair was trimmed and shaped at the fly's head to simulate the broad, flat head of a real sculpin.

The fly was an immediate success in the Nipigon area. One evening, from five o'clock to nine o'clock, when large army-worm moths were falling to the water, Don caught more than fifty brook trout on his Muddlers. "In that particular area we'd normally only get two or three trout," said Don, "and usually they'd be small ones. But that day, the time I first fished the Muddler, I released 5- and 6-pounders!"

One of the Indians working in Don's fishing camp, a fellow named John Ogema, had spotted a very large trout in an eddy of the Nipigon's Devil's Rapids. He couldn't catch it. One day, a special guest arrived in

Spuddler

Muddler Minnow

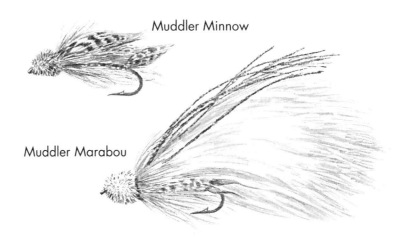
Muddler Marabou

The Muddler Minnow and
two popular variations.

Don's camp, a man Don wanted to be sure enjoyed himself. It turned out that the guest wanted a big trout badly. He hoped to win the annual *Field & Stream* fishing contest, Brook Trout Division. The man fished several days with only average luck.

One afternoon, standing on a bank overlooking the big trout's hole, John Ogema saw the brookie swoop out and literally inhale a string of six sculpins that happened by. Previously, the big trout had ignored single fish.

Seeing that, he rigged a leader with six of Don Gapen's Muddler Minnows, then went and got the special guest who wanted so badly to catch a large trout.

"John maneuvered the canoe just right," Gapen recalls, "and the special guest made two or three casts. On the fourth cast the trout came up and struck the fourth fly, and was hooked and landed by the fisherman—who was Charlie Mullins of Sioux City, Iowa.

"That fish had orange spots as big as oranges, and he weighed just a hair under 9 pounds," Don Gapen said. "Charlie Mullins went home a happy man, and who could blame him?"

Mullins' big brookie won the *Field & Stream* contest that year, and started the Muddler Minnow on its way to becoming one of the world's most popular flies.

Don Gapen's original Muddler Minnow pattern remains the one most anglers prefer today, but many Muddler variations have come along and been well accepted. All the variations are, of course, a basic Muddler design but with some alterations and substitutions of materials.

Dan Bailey, the late great pro fly tyer of Livingston, Montana, probably came up with the first important Muddler variation, called Don Bailey's Muddler Marabou. As the name suggests, it's heavy with marabou in the winging and, additionally, is tied with a much larger, broader head than standard Muddlers.

Another important variation of the Muddler is a big, sculpin-like fly called the Spuddler. Don Williams and Red Monical of Livingston developed this version, and it is deadly in the fall on outsized brown trout in western waters.

Don Gapen intended his original Muddler to be fished wet and retrieved in short minnow-like darts, in typical streamer fashion. However, a Muddler can be greased or oiled to float and then fished dry, with telling effects.

In trout fishing I like to grease a big-headed Muddler with a good silicone-base flotant, then cast it down and across stream and bring it back over the surface in short twitches. The floating Muddler puts out a little V wake as it skims across the top, making the fly look just like a wounded sculpin minnow or a scurrying grasshopper. In late summer, when hoppers fill the riverside meadows, greased-Muddler fishing is hard to beat.

A Muddler also can be fished at any depth under the surface—stroked along as a streamer fly to represent a minnow, or drifted along and bounced over the bottom, like a nymph.

THE MARSH HARE

The Marsh Hare is primarily a bass lure, though surely it would also take northern pike, pickerel, muskies, and walleyes. Neither bug nor fly, it is not unlike some other

A couple of McNally Bluegill Bugs at top; at bottom, a brace of Marsh Hare flies. The Marsh Hare, originally designed for tidewater bass fishing, also is deadly in freshwater lakes and streams.

flies that are tied with saddle hackles wrapped Palmer-style around the hook shank, but it is a long, thick-bodied fly with trailing hackle tips for a tail. Some tyers make them with wire weed guards, and with impala (calftail) tufts tied in to create some bulk at the fly's shoulders. However tied, what Marsh Hares do to largemouth bass at times is a caution.

The Marsh Hare was developed by the late Tom Loving, a real-estate man who lived on the Severn River in Maryland. In my college days I fished brackish areas of the Chesapeake Bay with Tom often, and always he struck me as knowing precisely when, and when not, to go bass fishing.

Tom designed the Marsh Hare solely for tidewater bass fishing, hence its name. The fly takes bass in strictly fresh lakes and rivers, but there's no denying it is somehow especially effective in brackish water. I've used them with fine results all along the East Coast, especially at Currituck and Albemarle sounds, as well as in the great salt-fresh bayous of Louisiana and Mississippi.

Until it's pretty wet, the Marsh Hare will float briefly when it hits the water, and it's good to let it rest motionless then. Its hackles will wave and flutter with no action imparted by the angler even while the fly floats. Many bass will slide up and suck the fly in right then.

After letting the Marsh Hare sit for a few moments, I twitch it lightly, which puts out little wavelets and a V wake, and there are not too many bass around that can resist *that* action. Following a few surface strips with the Marsh Hare, it should be pulled under and then fished back, much like a streamer fly. One difference, though,

in fishing a Marsh Hare as compared with a regular streamer fly is that you can pause frequently in bringing the Hare along underwater. It will only settle slowly, and if a bass has been trailing it he's likely to hit when he closes in and gets an eyeful of all those wiggling hackle tips.

Even without a wire weed-guard the Marsh Hare is reasonably weedless, which is another plus for using it in brackish-water bass fishing. Almost all brackish bass fishing is done in estuaries and marshland, and the banks are muskrat grasses, pencil reeds, and so on. You can cast a well-tied Marsh Hare right up on the grassy banks, jump it off (sometimes into the mouth of a waiting bass), and then fish it back.

THE MCNALLY MAGNUM

In 1952 I designed an oversize streamer fly called the McNally Magnum. It's not an especially unusual fly so far as design is concerned, but you won't find too many streamers that are larger, since these range from 5 to 7 inches—sometimes longer.

Using these flies in both fresh and salt water, I've taken just about every common gamefish that swims. They attract smallmouth black bass as quickly as Pacific sailfish. Some of the more interesting fish I've taken on Magnums include a 13-pound Arctic char (Tree River, Northwest Territories); 132-pound tarpon (Belize River, Belize); 116-pound Pacific sailfish (Pinas Bay, Panama); northern pike 18 to 26 pounds (Canadian lakes); 12-pound rainbow runner (Puntarenas, Costa Rica); 14-pound brown trout (Chimehuin River, Argentina); 18-pound coho salmon (Manistee River, Michigan); 24-pound lake trout

The McNally Magnum, which ranges from 5 to 7 inches in length, can be used effectively on many freshwater and saltwater gamefish.

(Nanjelini Lake, Manitoba), and a 22½-pound roosterfish (Bahia Pez Vela, Costa Rica).

Of all the different species of gamefish that will clobber these giant streamers, northern pike, muskies, and barracuda are foremost. I think those fish will hit a yellow-and-red Magnum before they'll take any other lure or bait. That old red-and-white striped spoon is supposed to be an extraordinary pike lure, and it is; yet I've cast a Magnum fly to one side of many a pike that was trailing a red-white spoon, and had the pike leave the spoon to hit the fly. And there have been few barracuda I've seen while fishing a flat that didn't smash a Magnum when I dragged it fast across their noses.

Magnums are tied on 1/0 to 5/0 hooks. The wings should be made of the longest saddle hackles available, preferably not under 5 inches in length. The body of the fly is thick chenille. At least six or seven saddle hackles should be in the wing, and they can be flared inward or outward. Either way is good. A heavy collar of hackles contrasting in color with the hackle winging is tied in Palmer-style just behind the fly's head.

I use Magnums in only two color combinations, but other colors might be as good or better. My favorite is red-and-yellow. The body chenille and the winging is yellow, while the thick collar is bright red. The other Magnum I fish has white winging and body, but a red collar.

On seeing Magnums for the first time many fly fishermen say they are too big to cast. Despite their great length, however, Magnums are not difficult to cast. They are not heavy, they are not as wind-resistant as are some other big saltwater flies, and they are not as hard to cast as bulky bucktails. The long saddle hackles of the Magnums do not absorb and hold water as do bucktail and marabou, and a false cast or two shakes most of the water out. Just be sure to slow down your casting rhythm when using ultra-large streamers. You've got to allow more time for your backcast to unfold, and then you must start the forward cast slowly.

Except possibly when fishing tarpon, a very fast retrieve should be used when working Magnums over most saltwater fish. With barracuda, you can't fish the fly fast enough. Dolphin also like a fast-moving fly, although they'll also often strike one that's practically motionless. Sailfish, both Pacific and Atlantic varieties, want a fast-moving fly. Most of the time tarpon prefer a moderate to slow retrieve.

On freshwater largemouth black bass you should experiment with the speed of the retrieve. First try fishing a Magnum fast, then slow, then mix up fast and slow, with pauses and quick jerks.

I went underwater once with scuba gear in the gin-clear water of Great Bahama Island, and had a friend on a dock make repeated casts with a Magnum over me. The big streamer would hit the water and nose down, bright yellow-red colors flashing, long hackles undulating. Then, when the line was tightened and a stripping retrieve started, the Magnum would lift up on a foot-long dart, dive again, rise . . . dive . . . rise . . . dive—like that. The fly actually moved through the water in saw-tooth fashion, with unusually lively, fish-attracting action.

Northern pike prefer a slowly moving Magnum. In wilderness lakes they'll frequently hit a Magnum as it flutters down. Fishing Eagle Lake in Ontario with George Strickler, once sports editor of the *Chicago Tribune*, I flipped a yellow Magnum out about 20 feet from the boat. The fly sank slowly as I stripped line from the reel to make a cast. Just before I started to lift the fly a big northern shot in fast and smacked it. He came to the fly and hit it when I was giving it no action whatever. Just the fluttering of the saddle hackles was enough to convince that pike that the fly was alive.

THE MCNALLY SMELT

Coho and Chinook salmon in the Great Lakes feed primarily on alewives, but they

The McNally Smelt streamer fly, shown dry at top, wet below, was designed for Great Lakes coho and Chinook salmon, but is effective on a number of saltwater and freshwater species.

also take large numbers of smelt, especially in the spring when smelt move into the shallows to spawn. Because I couldn't find a realistic fly pattern already established that would adequately represent a 4- to 6-inch-long silvery-sided smelt, I went to work at my fly-tying vise, and eventually turned out the McNally Smelt. The fly is smelt-size, smelt-shaped, and smelt color.

The McNally Smelt is tied on a regular-shank 1/0 saltwater hook (larger hooks can be used when desirable). Depending upon the availability of materials, the fly should be between 4 and 6 inches in length from hook-eye to tip of tail, which is the average size of smelt taken in the spring in the Great Lakes. The basic body materials in the fly are white bucktail, saddle hackles, and polar-bear hair (hard to get now, so white impala is substituted), and when tied in the proper proportions they give the fly exactly the correct silhouette—long and thin, flat-sided, but with smeltlike thickness at the shoulder. The basic color is white, as already shown, with a silvery sheen, dark edging along the top, and a broad silver stripe running lengthwise along the body.

A glob of white bucktail should be tied in at the hook bend. A couple of grizzly hackles go on either side of the fly, along with two strips of long, flat silver tinsel. A half-dozen strips of peacock herl go on top of the fly (to give the dark back of a real smelt), mallard breast feathers form "shoulders" on either side of the fly, and pearl lacquer goes on the finished fly's head. The Smelt is true to life right down to the silvery stripes along the side.

Various retrieves are effective with the Smelt fly. As a general rule it should be twitched along in foot-long hauls, first fast and then slow. Sometimes it is best to retrieve the fly swiftly, close to the surface; other times it is most productive if allowed to sink several feet, then worked back in 3-foot jerks. For coho salmon a slow, almost steady retrieve normally gets the most strikes, but at times—especially in river fishing—it is best to yank the streamer forward about a foot, then allow it to "rest" motionless, sinking for a few seconds, followed by another sharp yank, and so on.

The Smelt has proven to be an extraordinary coho and Chinook salmon fly, but it's effective on most other gamefishes as well.

CATHERWOOD SALTWATER STREAMERS

In recent years many professional and amateur fly tyers have been turning out more practical streamer fly patterns for saltwater fishing. But the man who deserves the credit for being the first to design realistic saltwater flies is Bill Catherwood, a pro tyer in Tewksbury, Massachusetts. I haven't been in touch with Catherwood for years—I've tried many times to reach him, always unsuccessfully—so I do not know if he is still tying or not. At any rate, in February 1968, I wrote a feature story on Bill's great and unusual flies for *Outdoor Life*, and that drew great attention not only to Bill's flies, which he called "Catherwood Originals," but also to the fact that until then fly tyers had done nothing innovative for years in the field of saltwater flies.

There are too many Catherwood saltwater patterns to describe each in detail, but all are large—5 to 8 inches long—and rather colorful. Most have long, flowing

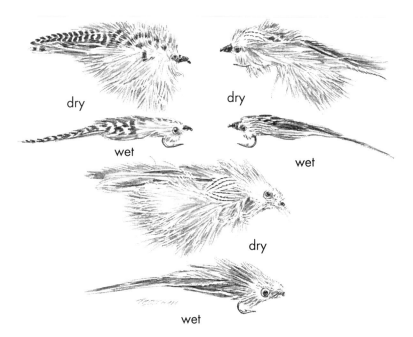

dry

dry

wet

wet

dry

wet

A selection of Catherwood streamers for saltwater game-fish. When dry, the streamers look plump and fuzzy; but when wet they try to imitate baitfish.

saddle hackles with lots of webbing, and some have big buck-hair heads. Marabou is in most of the flies, and some are tied with trailer hooks.

I first learned of Bill's flies in 1960. Bill had read stories I'd written on fly fishing, so he generously sent me two dozen of his big streamers to try. It wasn't long before I became convinced they are the best big-fish streamers ever developed. One afternoon, near the outlet of Lake Maracaibo, Venezuela, I hooked and released sixteen tarpon weighing 50 to 110 pounds. In three days of fishing, using Bill's Tinker Mackerel flies, I released eleven tarpon that weighed more than 100 pounds apiece. Manual Vieira of Wareham, Massachusetts, has caught bluefish up to 15 pounds on Bill's Tinkers, and many large striped bass, including a 36-pounder.

Each of Catherwood's flies is meant to represent a specific form of marine life—a sand eel, for example, or a capelin (a kind of smelt). One group of his streamers imitates small beakfishes, such as the balao (a favored natural bait for Atlantic sailfish), while another group represent various kinds of squids.

Some of Bill's streamer patterns—all originated and named by him—are the Herring, Capelin, White Squid, Mullet, Chub, Balao, Tinker Mackerel, Ginger Squid, Needlefish, Sand Eel, Pink Squid, and Marlinette.

SOME MCNALLY BUGS

Three special bugs I designed, and which I recommend you have for your bass-fishing kit, are the McNally Frog, Bullet Bug, and Bluegill Bug. They're okay, too, for other fish, such as northern pike.

The Frog is my all-round favorite bass bug. It's a popper, with its cork body mounted on a size 1/0 or 2/0 3X long hump-shank hook. I mount the hook at a downward angle. Its angle and length help guarantee hooking fish that strike.

Two green bucktail "legs" are fitted into the back end of the cork body, and they're what make the bug so attractive to bass. They kick and swim when you work the Frog along.

Pieces of wooden matchsticks are fitted into the front end of the cork body to make the Frog's "eyes." The body is painted

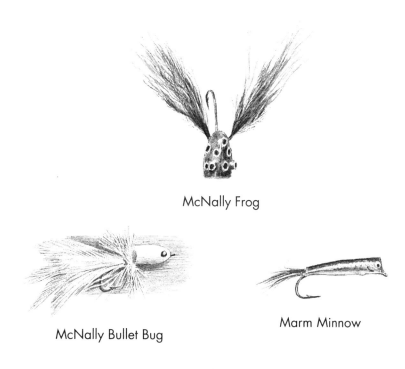

McNally Frog

McNally Bullet Bug

Marm Minnow

Excluding the Marm Minnow, a traditional pattern of the St. Johns river, these bugs were designed by the author to take various kinds of game-fish.

Powder Puff

green, with yellow and black spots dabbed on, and a natural-looking white belly added.

When the bucktail hair legs are mounted correctly in a Frog, they'll open and close as the bug is worked across the surface. Getting the legs working just right as you retrieve a Frog is a matter of feel. Each Frog bug is different. The legs of one will kick when you retrieve it at one speed, those of another Frog at a different speed.

The best way to fish this Frog popper is to cast to a likely spot, and let it rest motionless for a moment after it hits the water. Be alert, because many bass will hit it while it's sitting still. After a minute or two, "pop" the bug gently by raising the rod tip. That will make the legs jump. Now let the bug sit motionless again, while its legs flutter weakly. If there is no strike, work the bug along for a few feet, then pause again. Finally, pop the Frog steadily back, just fast enough to make its legs open and close.

The Bullet Bug originally was designed for striped bass. I was fishing the estuaries of Chesapeake Bay in Maryland and Virginia a great deal in those days, and wanted a bug that would imitate alewife minnows skipping over the top when pursued by stripers. Rockfish, as striped bass are called in the mid-Atlantic area, often drive schools of small alewives to the surface, and the 3-inch-long baitfish will shoot along the top, in and out of the water, as they strive desperately to escape.

I wanted a bug that would skip over the surface, and I felt it should be white, since alewives are silvery. It would have to cast well, too, because in striper fishing you frequently must reach out 80 feet or more, with little time for false casting, to hit a swirling fish.

The Bullet Bug was the result—4 inches long, flowing white saddle-hackles over the rear of the hook, and two feathers wound Palmer-style behind the 1½-inch bullet-shaped cork body. This bug is tied on a flat or ball-eye hook (rather than on a turned-down hook), because a flat-eye hook doesn't make a bug dive on the retrieve unless a sharp yank is given to force the bug to dive.

It was on Millington Pond on Maryland's Eastern Shore that I discovered how effective the Bullet Bug is on largemouth bass. Chuck Besche and I lucked into a bass feeding orgy. We came across pure mayhem in the shallows, where several large bass had trapped a big school of minnows. Shiner minnows were showering out of the water as the bass pounded them. Under such circumstances any lure should have worked, but we threw popping bugs into the mess without getting a strike. We switched quickly to silver-white Bullet Bugs and in the next ten minutes landed six bass 2 to 4½ pounds, and missed strikes from two or three others.

The Bullet Bug fishes the surface and a foot under as well. Fish it slowly and it will stay on top, sliding this way and that. Work it a little faster and it will dip under, then, when you pause, it will float back to the top. Retrieve it hard and fast and it will dive, and then can be fished back like a minnow darting along under the surface. All these retrieve methods can be mixed up—making the bug skip, hop, and bounce along the surface, then underwater for a few feet, twitching and darting, then back on top, jerking along like a wounded minnow.

I was a boy in Maryland, fishing Lake Roland one day, when I hooked a tiny bluegill 2 inches long. When I tossed it back it went flopping over the surface, lying over on its side, swimming like a flounder this way and that. It would dive a few inches under, lose its power, and surface again. Then it would go circling around crazily, all the while lying flat on its side. The bluegill flipflopped around like that for a while, and then I saw a dark shape come up under it. The bass was a good 5 pounds, and he eyed the bluegill coldly until the crippled fish convulsed and splashed water. The strike was instantaneous. One moment there lay the wounded bluegill, the next it was gone.

I remembered that incident for years until, one night tying flies and bugs with Harvey Schemm of Baltimore, I recollected the bluegill episode. He suggested tying a Bluegill Bug, and so I worked at it. I fooled with cork, balsa, cedar—all the usual bug body materials—and finally tried shaping a Bluegill Bug out of deer hair. It worked.

The Bluegill Bug is fashioned by tying all the deer hair possible on a hook, making it flare outward with the tying thread (this is how all deerhair bugs are made), then trimming it to shape with scissors. Natural brown deer hair is used for most of the Bluegill Bug, but every 1/4 inch or so along the hook greenish deer hair, with some yellow, is tied in. The brown gives the bug the basic body coloration of a bluegill, and the greenish hairs come out as stripes, with the yellow adding some natural bluegill coloring and further striping.

Trimming with very sharp scissors makes it easy to form the flat body shape of a bluegill, and even to trim in dorsal, pelvic, and anal fins. Long hairs are left flaring out at the hook bend to simulate a bluegill's caudal fin or tail. When the tightly packed deer hair is shaped like a bluegill, all that remains is to give the bug some eyes. This is easily done by applying lacquer generously to where the bug's eyes should be; when the lacquer coating is thick enough and dry, eyes can be dabbed on with yellow and red enamel.

Depending upon the size and weight of hook used and how the bug is tied, the Bluegill Bug will float on its side for some time. The more hair tied in and the lighter the hook, the better the bug floats. It can be retrieved like any fly-rod bug—with short twitches and hops, some steady pulls, long waits, then by drawing it steadily but slowly along. A couple of strong, straight pulls will take the Bluegill Bug underwater, and a lot of bass will hit it when it dives. When it's pulled beneath the surface you can keep the bug there by retrieving as you would a streamer fly.

Fly fishermen always are looking for a weedless surface lure that will hook bass. Some bugs made with light wire guarding the hook are weedproof, but many are bass-proof, too. Other bugs are made with heavy, stiff pieces of nylon monofilament tied in to protect the hook, but they frequently snag, and strikes often are missed.

To fish the weeds for bass, I use a big, bushy fly I make of deer hair. I call it the Powder Puff. It resembles a bivisible dry fly in overall structure, and is tied on a light-wire short-shank 2/0 hook. The Powder

Puff is made the same as any deer-hair bug—by laying bunches of hair over the hook and spreading them with a pull of tying thread. The hairs aren't trimmed, however, as would be done to shape the body of a hair mouse, frog, or crayfish. Instead, the hairs are left long and billowing in all directions, so they cover and protect the hook from snags and weeds. The scraggly hairs make the bug weedproof, but not bass-proof. When a bass hits a Powder Puff his jaws clamp down on soft hair, and so the hook goes home.

The Puff casts well, and on weedy water it's a dream to fish. It's a natural for places like the "hay fields" at Florida's famed Lake Okeechobee, the weed-filled bays and brackish sounds of the Carolinas, and for fishing along the muskrat grass in Back Bay, Virginia.

There's no trick to fishing a Powder Puff. Just throw one up there in the thick lily pads and weeds, where you know the bass are, then twitch it slowly along. It will ride high on the water, snake right over lily pads and logs, and waltz its way through tough reeds. Bass that see a Puff will hit it as though they hadn't had a meal in weeks.

One thing about the Powder Puff—it becomes waterlogged after repeated casting or after hooking and playing several fish. When waterlogged it won't float right and is difficult to cast. Just squeeze the excess water out of the deer hairs by pinching the bug between the folds of a handkerchief or, better, a wool or flannel shirt.

Finally, one really special bug every fly-rodder should have plenty of is the Marm Minnow. The Marm originated on Florida's St. Johns River. It is an old, proven bug,

used regularly by knowledgeable southern bass fishermen, but it's virtually unknown in the northern states.

The Marm Minnow is cork-bodied, or made of balsa, and is long and thin. It has a blunt nose, is built on a long-shank hook, and has just a tuft of hackle fibers tied in at the hook bend for a tail. It casts beautifully, with exceptional accuracy, and falls lightly to the water. It should be retrieved in short, quick twitches, then brought skipping and darting over the surface. The Marm represents a small minnow.

One trick I've used with it is fishing three on a single leader. I space the bugs about 6 inches apart, tying all but the point bug on dropper strands from the main leader. Naturally three bugs on a single leader are more difficult to cast than one, but the Marms are small, with little air resistance, and besides, fishing three or even more on a single leader can be worth the extra effort.

Fished as a group, the Marm bugs should be skipped quickly over the surface, with an erratic retrieve, because that way they best represent a darting, scooting pod of frightened minnows.

All the flies and bugs I've described can be readily made by most amateur fly tyers, and certainly by professionals. The Catherwood flies may be an exception, since there's no way I can describe them in detail, but some tyers will be able to turn out new and effective saltwater flies from what I've said about them.

The McNally Magnum, Smelt, Frog, and Bullet Bug can be ordered from pro tyer Jim Poulas, P.O. Box 8351, Hot Springs Village, Arkansas 71909.

12

How to Tie Flies

I T IS not difficult to turn out handsome, fish-catching flies. Granted, it may take some talent and years of experience to become a top-notch, recognized, *professional* fly tyer, but anyone with a yen to learn can become a reasonably accomplished fly tyer. Some people with special aptitude learn the art almost overnight. I have introduced many friends to fly tying, and all of them eventually succeeded in turning out attractive, fishable flies.

The important attractions of fly tying are having fun and shortening the time between the end of one fishing season and the beginning of the next. But by tying your own flies you can save a lot of money, too. A fly that might cost $1.25 at the local tackle shop can be made for 10 cents or less.

It's possible to get into the fly-tying game for $100, possibly less. A well-rounded outfit of tools and materials can be had for about $200.

To start, you'll need a few basic tools: vise, hackle-pliers, finely pointed scissors, razor blade, whip-finishing tool, and per-

haps a bobbin to hold your spool of thread when working.

The vise is your most important single piece of equipment, so buy a good one. A lever-and-cam–type vise is the most popular today. There are many good vises available; one of the best is the Thompson vise.

A beginner's basic materials include thread (size 6/0 nylon), head cement, hooks in various sizes, hackles (chicken neck feathers), saddle hackles (from a chicken's back), duck wing quills, mallard breast feathers, golden pheasant tippets, assortments of silk floss and chenille, various furs for bodies, silver and gold tinsel, and peacock herl from the "eyed" tail feathers of peacocks. These materials usually are stocked by better sports stores and hobby shops, and many tackle stores also carry fly-tying tools and materials. And if you hunt, or have friends who do, you can easily add to your stock of materials at little or no expense, since the hair or feathers from almost any kind of wildlife can be utilized by the fly tyer.

Rig a bright lamp on your fly-tying desk

or table, and place a large sheet of white cardboard or white paper where your vise will be. This will provide a white background, making the fly easier to see and your materials simpler to locate.

Large streamer flies, such as the McNally Smelt (illustrated in this chapter) are the easiest to tie, and by working on them first you'll acquire the fundamentals of fly tying. All the steps taken in tying a big McNally Smelt generally will apply in tying almost any fly pattern, whether it be a dry fly, wet fly, nymph, or whatever.

To tie a McNally Smelt you will need a size 2/0 hook, about 6 white saddle hackles 3 to 4 inches long, a couple of grizzly saddle hackles of the same length, white bucktail hair, silver tinsel, peacock herl, mallard breast feathers, and white nylon tying thread.

Mount your vise at a comfortable height, and clamp the hook in it. Although

---

FLY-TYING EQUIPMENT AND MATERIALS

Following is a brief list of the tools and materials needed to tie flies. Group I includes the essentials; Group II, secondary items; and Group III includes some of the fancy things you'll want as your experience grows.

GROUP I

Tools

vise
razor blades
wax
scissors
spring clothespin
bodkin
hackle pliers
whip-finishing tool
1 spool of "A" black thread
1 bottle of clear lacquer

Hooks

streamer #10 (long shank)
wet fly #12
dry fly #12

Body Materials

1 card each medium chenille: black, white, red, yellow

1 spool each color floss: black, white, red, yellow
1 each medium flat tinsel: silver, gold
1 peacock feather with eye
1 card of red yarn
1 each calf tails: black, white, red, yellow, brown
1 package each marabou feathers: white, yellow
1 gray squirrel tail
1 pair each matched duck quills: white, gray or slate

Hackle Feathers

1 package each saddle hackles: white, black, grizzly

GROUP II

Tools

scissors (curved blades)
thread bobbin

prewaxed thread is readily available, most tyers first wax the thread thoroughly to waterproof it. Start the tying thread behind the hook-eye, and wrap it tightly down the hook shank to the bend of the hook. The Smelt doesn't have a body, just the thread wrapped tightly over the hook shank.

With the tying thread at the bend of the hook, cut a good portion of white bucktail hair about 3 inches long, and hold it over the hook bend while you wrap tying thread over the bucktail to fasten it securely to the hook. Make several turns over the bucktail with the thread. A drop of head cement on the wrapped bucktail will help secure it in place.

Next wrap the tying thread forward to the hook-eye, then tie in the white saddle hackles and the barred grizzly hackles by wrapping the thread over the butts of the hackles, close to the hook-eye. Again, add a drop of head cement for added security.

black thread: sizes 3/0, 6/0
tongs
head cement and lacquer (various colors)

Hooks

streamer #6-8-12
wet fly #8-10-14
dry fly #14-16-18

Body Materials

chenille: additional colors and the essential four colors in fine and heavy sizes
floss: other colors
fine and large tinsels, flat: silver, gold
golden pheasant tippets, silver pheasant tippets
red fox, muskrat, and mink fur
peacock herl
assortment of yarn
polar bear hairs: red, white, yellow
marabou: assorted colors
fox squirrel tail, black squirrel tail
matched quills: black, red, yellow
mallard side feathers, teal side feathers
natural and dyed bucktails

Hackle Feathers

selected neck hackles

GROUP III

Tools

soft wax for dubbed bodies
wing-cutter
thread: various sizes and colors
small brush

Hooks

humped shank hooks for bass bugs

Body Materials

moose mane
deer hair
embossed, oval, and wire tinsels
spun fur: various colors
matched duck wings from which to make your own matched pair of quills

Hackle Feathers

complete necks: white, dark brown, ginger, black, badger, grizzly

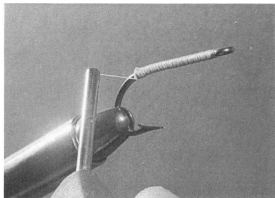

Saltwater type, 2/0 hook (with a flat or "ball" eye) is wrapped with heavy white nylon thread to start Smelt fly.

Tying flies is much more than a way to save money. It can be one of the most satisfying parts of fly fishing. Dedicated amateurs can turn out everything from simple chenille- or tinsel-bodied bucktails to true works of art. The stonefly nymph (third row from the bottom, second from left) looks real enough to crawl off the page.

With hook-shank thread-wrapped a generous amount of white bucktail hairs are tied in near bend of hook. Bucktail should be 3 to 4 inches long.

Now fasten a length of silver tinsel, about 3 to 4 inches long, to the fly with the tying thread, seeing that a strip of tinsel goes along either side of the fly. (This is to simulate the silvery side-stripes that smelt have.)

Several strands of peacock herl should be tied in to form the top, or back, of the fly—this representing the smelt's dark back. Finally, tie in two mallard duck breast feathers, one on either side of the fly, then finish forming the fly head by making sev-

eral turns behind the hook-eye with the tying thread, forming a neatly tapered head. Finish off with a whip-finish knot, using one of the popular whip-finishing tools, such as the Matarelli or the Thompson, according to the instructions packaged

Webby, soft saddle hackles are secured to hook shank with hackle butts tied in near hook-eye. Hackles should be 4 to 6 inches long.

Peacock herl is tied in to make back or top of fly, silver tinsel is tied in on either side of fly's body, and duck breast feathers form a "cheek" on either side of the fly.

with the tool. After knotting the thread and trimming any excess, coat the fly's head with ivory lacquer or clear fly-tying cement.

When you can tie large streamers so they won't come apart when you pull on a feather, and the flies are properly proportioned, you've mastered the fundamentals of fly tying, and are ready to move on to more complicated ties.

Beginners often are discouraged during early attempts to tie flies. It can't be stressed enough that starting—turning out that first dozen flies—is the hardest part.

The second fly the beginner ties, no matter what the pattern, is easier than the first, the third easier still, and so on. With practice anyone can learn to tie a fine streamer in less than ten minutes, a good dry in five minutes, and a wet fly in less than that.

Fly tying is a complex art, and space here is limited. The serious beginning fly tyer would be wise to arm himself with a fly-tying how-to book or two, along with some videos. I recommend *The Complete Book of Fly Tying*, by Eric Leiser, and *Mastering the Art of Fly Tying*, by Richard W. Talleur.

13

Wet-Fly Fishing for Trout

THE first trout I ever caught were 10- to 12-inch rainbows, hatchery types, planted in Maryland's Jones Falls by the state's game and fish commission. In those days the season opened on April 15, and when that magic morning arrived I always was on the stream flailing a Montgomery Ward bamboo rod long before the sparrows were up. My tackle was simple—a cheap, rickety single-action reel; a worn and cracked enameled level line; a heavy 5-foot gut leader; and a size 10 wet fly preceded by a small Colorado spinner. The spinner-fly combination was deadly, and by letting the current wash it beneath the undercut banks, under logs and into brush, I usually took a limit of ten trout home, with considerable pride.

I didn't learn how wet flies *should* be fished until I was fourteen years old. At this time we were living in Baltimore, but we had family in Maine, and it was our routine to visit them in Millinocket for a few weeks each summer.

One day a cousin, Paul Corrigan, took me to the West Branch of the Penobscot River, and it was there that I had my greatest thrill ever fishing a wet fly. I had started to rig my usual spinner and fly when Paul stopped me and tied a ready-made leader to my line, complete with a Parmachene Belle point fly and a Professor and a Grizzly King as droppers.

The West Branch is a boulder-strewn, chilly stream, but I waded into it "wet," up to my knees, and began casting. On the third toss across and downstream the line came briskly taut and a heavy jolt telegraphed down the rod and into my arm. That quick, a 20-inch, silvery fish was in the air, fully 5 feet over the water. It fell back and quickly came out again, skyrocketing to 3 or 4 feet. It raced upstream and whipped line off the reel, jumped again, then reversed its field and ran with the heavy current. Thirty yards downstream it leaped twice more, then settled into deep, dogged boring.

My angling experiences up to that time included taking bass on plugs, brook trout in New England waters, hatchery trout in Maryland streams, and of course panfish. I wasn't prepared for the gymnastics of oua-naniche, the landlocked salmon. I didn't even know a fish *could* jump that high! From that day on I became a dedicated three-fly wet-fly fisherman. It was some years later that I discovered dry flies, nymphs, and streamers.

Wet-fly fishing is one of the easiest methods for the beginner, possibly because no matter what the angler does a wet fly fishes all the time. On one Maine trip the old folks dispatched cousins Paul, Leo, and Ralph Corrigan and me to Trout Lake with the express assignment to catch a basket of brook trout for a family fish fry. Working from two canoes, Leo and Ralph fished worms while Paul and I stroked our three-fly wet rigs through the pellucid water. We pretty nearly filled a pack basket with brookies in less than an hour, and the wet flies easily outfished the garden hackle ten to one, probably because twitching them got the trout's attention. Also, Paul and I frequently took two and three trout on a single cast, and we never lost fishing time for having to bait up.

Much of the Madison River is riffle water, just one long, humpy run after another. It's tough to read that kind of water and to recognize the precise lies of trout. Guide Bobby D'Ambruoso and I were in the Varney Bridge area, and for some time I had been wading and shooting out a streamer while Bobby watched, walking behind and holding the boat. After a half hour without a strike he called for me to reel up. I did and went to the boat, where Bobby was tying a leader. He made up a 12-foot three-fly leader, and each fly was a size 8 Montana Mite—one black, one cream, and one brown. The Mite is a wingless wet fly, with hackle circling the head, and a hard, segmented, grublike body.

"Cast these down and across stream," Bobby instructed. "Hold your rod high and strip line in quick pulls so that the flies bounce and skim over the surface." I did as Bobby directed, casting across and downstream, fishing slowly, carefully, and moving along to cover all the water. On about the sixth cast a lively little rainbow hit one of the droppers and bounced 4 feet into the air. I released him and continued fishing—down and across, rod up high, strip . . . strip . . . strip—*splaaattt!* Now a good brown trout, about 3 pounds, was turning over in midair with the point fly firm in his jaw.

By the time we reached the takeout point I had enjoyed a trout-filled afternoon, with every fish hitting a wet Montana Mite.

I recall another day on the upper Madison, many years ago, floating with Dan Bailey, Bill Browning, Ed Zern, and Al McClane. We had stopped for a breather, but while the rest of us lounged on the bank Al walked into a riffle and started casting. He had a two-fly wet-fly setup, and on eleven casts he hooked and landed eleven trout. None was large, but they were trout.

I was on a mule-deer and elk hunt one October with outfitter Lee Wheeler of Hotchkiss, Colorado, and Lee shoved a fly rod at me and pointed to a nearby creek. "You're a fisherman," he growled. "Go get some trout."

The outfit Lee pushed on me was a beat-up old bamboo rod with a level line and a short 4-foot leader with one dropper

Here's a sea-run cutthroat from British Columbia's Babine River, fooled by a wet fly. Despite the guide's too-heavy grip, the trout was released unharmed.

wet fly and another wet on the leader end. I walked not too confidently out of camp to the little creek. It was clear as tap water, barely 10 feet across—all pocket water with an occasional narrow, shallow pool. But the little creek was quivering with hordes of small cutthroats 6 to 10 inches long.

Kneeling at the stream edge, I'd flip the brace of wets into a pocket and guide them along with the rod tip. Cutthroats would emerge suddenly from beneath roots and behind rocks to strike viciously at the sunken flies. Frequently I caught two fish on a single cast, and it wasn't long before I returned to camp with a limit of cutthroats enough for our dinner.

The tackle I had to use on that high Colorado mountain stream wasn't the best, but the wet flies were perfectly suitable for pocket dabbing, and I doubt if I'd have caught any more trout if I'd had sophisticated tackle and a wide selection of flies.

WET-FLY PATTERNS

There seems to be no logical explanation for the effectiveness of wet flies. The artificial nymphs we use look a great deal like real nymphs. Streamers when retrieved right do a reasonable job of imitating live minnows, and we know that trout take dry flies because they mistake them for floating insects. But wet flies?

I think trout hit wet flies believing them to be nymphs. Certainly many wet flies look more like nymph patterns than they do wet flies, especially the dark wet flies having soft hackles and no wings. Vernon Hidy coined the word "flymph" to describe such wet flies, and defined it as an "imitation of a nymph struggling toward the surface, or in the surface film, on its way to becoming a winged insect."

Trout also might take wet flies thinking they are drowned insects, small shrimp, various scuds, or a minnow. The gaudy

Author plays a modest Firehole River, Wyoming, brown trout hooked on a wet fly.

Parmachene Belle pattern is mistaken by trout for a tiny, brightly colored brook trout, some anglers believe, or a brook trout's fin. In any case, wet flies get trout, and as Ed Zern wrote, "A lot of trout fishermen persist in using wet flies, and somehow they catch a hell of a lot of trout." I think Eddie said it all right there.

There's a lot of history behind the wet fly. Joe Brooks called the wet fly the "father of flies" because Aelian wrote of them in the third century A.D. Dame Juliana Berners described wet flies and gave dressings for some in 1450, and in 1676 Charles Cotton listed sixty-five wet flies.

Wet flies may be tied in three different ways: with a wing and hackling, without a wing but with hackling, or with just a body and wing. The typical wet fly has a tail, a body, a folded-back double wing, and hackling. Wet flies are generally tied with soft hackling so that the fibers will undulate in the water, waving tantalizingly and perhaps suggesting the legs of an insect.

While most of the time we may want our wet flies to fish rather deep, there will be days when we want them to work at a level somewhere between the bottom and the surface. The depth at which the wet fly swims can be critical to success, so we should have wets tied sparsely on heavy hooks with lead-wrapped bodies; some tied sparsely with heavy hooks but no lead; some tied full, of buoyant material, yet on heavy hooks; and others tied with buoyant materials and on light wire hooks. With such a wet-fly assortment we can select flies to fish at any level. We will have flies that will sink very quickly, some that settle slowly, and some that will skim along just under the surface.

There are wet flies tied on short-shank, heavy double hooks so that they will settle quickly. An angler in London, whose name I can't recall, once sent me a box of beautifully tied double-hook wet flies. I've taken some excellent fish with them and still use them, especially when working fast water or deep runs.

The wet fly is a good early-spring fly because trout can see it readily even in high, discolored water. Generally the larger flies are the best choice in spring, and the brighter patterns—such as the Silver Doctor, Babcock, Royal Coachman, Colonel Fuller—seem to raise the most fish in heavy, turbid water. The Enco River, at Kip Farrington's Rainbow Fly Fishing Club in Chile, is a big, boiling ribbon of white water. It holds very large brown trout, and equally large rainbows that are strong and extremely active when hooked. On one trip to the Enco I was doing poorly with streamers and switched to a three-fly wet-fly rig. The flies were big (sizes 4 and 6), in March Brown pattern, Coachman, and Light Cahill. On the very first drift of the flies through a frothy rapids a 5-pound rainbow hit the point fly, the Light Cahill. That pleased me so much that I fished nothing but large wet flies the entire trip, and the wets took numbers of trout every day.

As the season progresses and streams drop and clear, the smaller wets (sizes 12, 14, 16), sparsely tied and of drab colors, seem to be most attractive to trout. At this time fur-bodied wet flies excel.

Unless the angler has a preconceived notion as to what wet flies the trout might prefer, he should start with flies of different sizes and patterns. With a three- or four-fly leader we would have bright flies and dull ones, each a different size, and some with wings and some without. Once we got into trout and noted a decided preference for a specific fly or two, we could replace the failing patterns with the winners. I met an angler one day on Washington's Quinault River who was fishing a leader with six Black Gnats. He said he had originally fished six different patterns but when the single Black Gnat caught all the cutthroats he changed entirely to Black Gnats. With that he occasionally caught two and three trout on a single cast.

Some wet-fly experts disdain fishing two, three, or more wet flies simultaneously. Multi-fly leaders can tangle, fishermen of the one-fly school reason, and, moreover, they feel they can better concentrate on a single fly and fish it more skillfully. Still other wet-fly experts adopt the multi-fly system, feeling each additional fly on the leader multiplies their chances for trout, and that multiple flies will trigger strikes from trout that become aroused on seeing a regular pod of bugs, or something, darting through the water. I sometimes fish a single wet fly, more often two, occasionally three, and rarely four or more. At times I mix nymphs with wet flies. Whenever we are trying to determine if the trout have a preference for a certain fly or flies, it is surely wise to fish a multi-fly leader.

Wet flies are among the oldest of all trout fly patterns. Many anglers fish two, three, four, or more wet flies on a single leader.

TACKLE FOR WET FLIES

Excluding the multi-fly leaders, no particular tackle variations are needed for wet-fly fishing. However, I prefer a long rod in this angling, and as light a fly line as I can handle with the selected rod. My first choice for most wet-fly work is a 9-foot graphite. It's more sensitive than bamboo, and I like to think that with it I can better feel my wets when they swing in the threads of current or skim the surface at the tail of a pool. The rod's length makes it easy, too, to lift a lot of line off the water when holding the rod high, and to bring the flies to the surface where they will skip and hop.

With the graphite I can easily go one line size lighter than the rod calls for and still cast well. It may be splitting straws

and assuredly it is no big thing, but I think the smaller the fly line the better, because the flies will work more naturally in the current. The larger the fly line in diameter, the more drag.

For the same reason—a more naturally drifting fly—long leaders should be used for most wet-fly fishing.

Depending upon the size and type of river, the method of wet-fly fishing, and other considerations, the wet-fly angler may want a high-floating line, a sinking-tip line, or a full-length sinking line. Which type is proper depends on the depth we want our flies to run. I most often use a sinking-tip double-taper line so that my flies will work 4 to 5 feet down, but under conditions of low, clear water I'll normally opt for a floater.

FISHING THE WET FLY

Some of the appeal of wet-fly fishing, and much of its effectiveness, lies in the great variety of methods of wet-fly presentation. Many different drifts and retrieves can be used to impart action to the wet fly.

Wet flies can be cast straight upstream, up and across stream, straight across, downstream and across, or straight downstream. Straight upriver casts will wash wet flies deep, but sometimes in casting up the flies come down much too fast and don't **fish** at all, just rushing by possible fish holds. Additionally, it is more difficult to hook fish on upstream casts because the fly line so often is not taut.

Wet flies are most effective when fished

The up-and-across cast (right) with a wet fly (or flies, if a multi-fly leader is used) is usually fished through the following phases. Every cast will not be fished exactly the same way, but this drawing and others that follow illustrate the different techniques of fishing flies in a stream.

(1) Flies are delivered with the lazy S cast.

(2) Line is mended, to prevent drag.

(3) Angler pays out line to maintain natural drift . . .

(4) . . . and as flies begin to sweep, pays out more line.

(5) Line is tightened to bring it into a "fish sweep."

(6) Rod is raised to lift line and start flies to surface.

(7) Flies are skimmed along the surface.

(8) Flies are retrieved by stripping line and working rod tip.

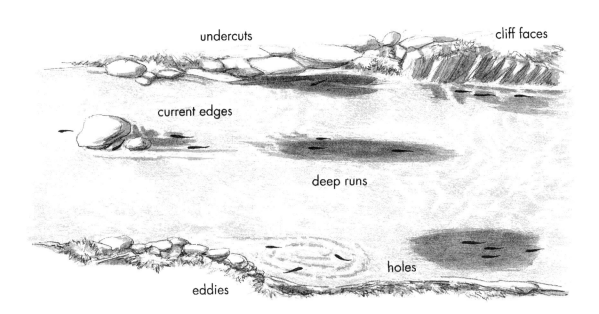

Places to fish wet flies in a trout stream. These are the spots where trout usually hold in the current, seeking either protection or food. The fly fisherman must learn how to read the water so he doesn't waste his time drifting his flies through fishless stretches.

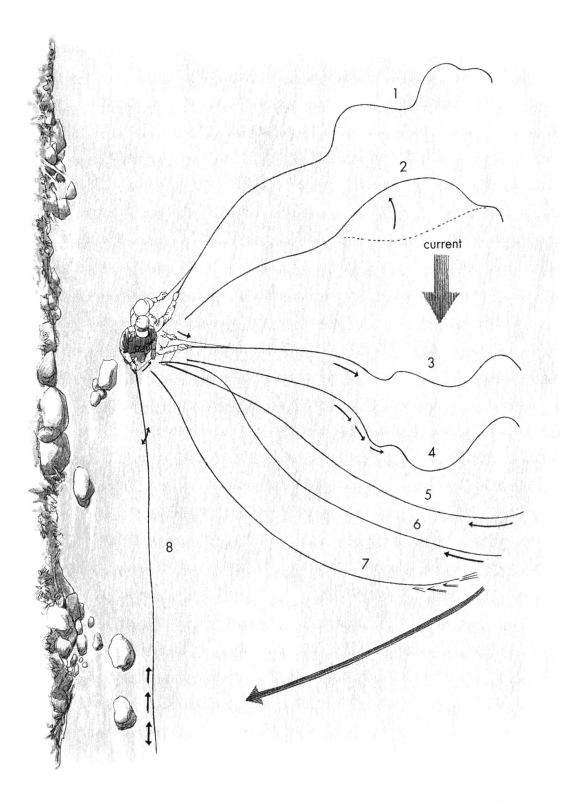

current

along the edges of currents, where they can pick up feeding trout. Drift them beside boulders, in and around brush, and to the many spots fish choose to rest in and escape sunlight. Deep runs and holes were made for wet flies. These, as well as eddies and pockets, are probed thoroughly with deep, long drifts of your fly. Rock or gravel bottoms, along cliff faces, under ledges—these are the places to scour repeatedly with a wet fly. The skilled wet-fly (or nymph) fisherman is expert at searching bottom crevices. Often several drifts are needed, particularly in heavy water, before that urgent strike signal is seen.

Casting up and across stream is a good technique because so much water can be covered this way, and diverse actions imparted to the flies. The flies should be sent out on a lazy S cast so there will be no initial drag and the flies will sink and drift naturally. Line should be mended as the

The down-and-across cast (right) is effective in situations where only a short drift is possible. It is a relaxing way to fish, as you are wading with the current and facing downstream all the time. If you are right handed, the ideal way to fish a wet fly downstream is with the bank on your left side, to avoid hangups in trees or brush along the bank.

(1) Flies are cast and fished dead . . .

(2) . . . until current tightens line and it starts to swing . . .

(3) Then flies are retrieved by stripping line and working rod tip.

current brings the flies down, and no action should be given the flies. At this point the flies will be drifting with the current much like real nymphs, or like real insects that fell to the stream and were washed under. When the flies come abreast of the angler or a little below, slack line can be payed out

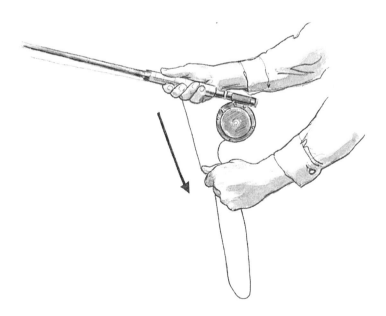

To retrieve flies by stripping line, encircle the line with the right first and second fingers and hold it against the rod grip. Grasp the rod with the left hand, near the grip, and relax right fingers' pressure. Bring in the fly in short jerks by pressing down on the line, releasing it, and grasping it again near the grip, until the fly has been brought close enough for a pickup and cast.

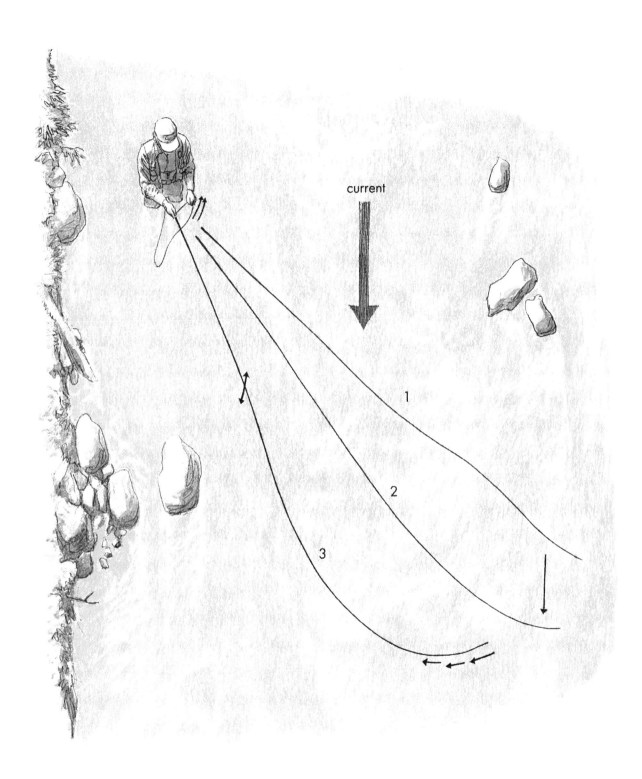

current

1

2

3

to continue the "natural" drift. No more slack, however, should be in the line than is necessary to provide a proper drift. If there is too much slack, striking fish can be missed.

When the flies have reached a point across and downstream and they begin to sweep around in the flow, more line can be released to keep the flies in that "honey" position a bit longer. This can be done one, two, three times. Trout will repeatedly whip out of cover and strike wet flies played in this manner.

Next the line can be tightened so that drag comes in and pulls the flies into a curving "fish sweep." Here the angler may or may not give some action to the flies by stripping line and twitching the rod tip. Either way is good, and this is the moment when most trout are taken on wet flies.

If no strike is forthcoming the rod can be raised high to lift the line up and start the flies swinging toward the surface, much like genuine nymphs rising from the stream floor and swimming for the top. Strikes are frequent at this time, too.

When the flies are at the surface, the dropper flies can be made to pop in and out of the water, or skim along with little V wakes as the point or tippet fly follows, swimming just inches under the surface. Often the angler will see a trout come from cover, trail the flies, then strike savagely when the droppers break the surface and start skipping along.

Once the flies are directly below the angler they should not be hurriedly brought up for another cast. Rather they should be allowed to fish there by raising and lowering the rod tip, which will cause the flies to dart against the current. This will give any trout nearby ample time to study the flies, and any trailing trout time to catch up.

When the angler is satisfied that the cast has been fished adequately he should retrieve the flies by stripping line steadily in short pulls, and working the rod tip. Occasionally a trout that was reluctant to hit at other points in the retrieve will strike one of the flies during the bring-back. With sufficient line retrieved the angler may cast again as before and repeat the entire procedure, or he may move a few yards downstream in order to work new water.

Casting down and across stream is another effective way to fish wet flies. The flies are fished "dead" for at least a part of the cast, then, as the current tightens the line and the flies swing, the angler activates the flies briskly by pulling the line and jiggling the rod tip. The down-and-across-stream cast, allowing the current to bow the line and pull the flies around and across the current, is a simple operation. The flies will fish by themselves, having action all their own, webby hackles "breathing" in the water as the fly line tightens and pulls the flies into that killing "fish sweep."

It's best to try to fish wet flies on as short a line as possible, since a short line gives better control and direction to the flies, and ensures hooking a greater percentage of the fish that strike. And we should fish wets slowly, thoroughly probing behind this rock, under that log, next to the brush pile, beneath the undercut bank, and through all of the riffled water. The skillful wet-fly fisherman, like the proficient nymphing specialist, is an efficiency expert—never moving on until satisfied that any trout present have had adequate time to eat his flies.

14

Dry-Fly Fishing for Trout

I T WAS warm and windless one evening in early June on Michigan's AuSable River near Grayling. Dusk was coming on, and the whippoorwills were singing. For two hours I had been working slowly upstream, drifting nymphs along the edges of sunken rocks and under brush piles. I had caught a few dozen trout—only normal fishing for that section of the AuSable—but none had exceeded 10 inches in length. I kept looking upstream, watching and waiting for the splashing rise of a surface-feeding trout. My companion, Fred Bear, the famed bowhunter who is equally skillful with a fly rod, was somewhere downstream, and he had promised that by dusk there would be a mayfly hatch and "dry-fly fishing you won't forget."

The shadows lengthened, and soon a noise like a soft, rising wind settled over the river. A cloud of insects engulfed the AuSable. The sound of struggling wings rose and fell, and soon the swarm was dropping to the surface as the female insects started laying their eggs. The air was so full of mayflies I stood spellbound

and watched the spectacle. Buzzing flies flew into my face, bumped against my rod, and spun to the surface. They covered my clothing. I could swing my hand through the air, close it, and catch a fistful of mayflies.

The half-dollar-size insects soon had every respectable trout in the stream off on a mayfly kick. I looked back over a stretch of water I had fished with nymphs, and saw at least a dozen large trout sucking and slurping at the surface. Smaller fish dimpled the roof of the river until it seemed like hailstones were pelting the stream.

I snipped off the nymph I had on and replaced it with a big No. 8 Irresistible dry fly. I didn't cast immediately, but waited until I saw the washtub roll of a good fish. Shortly a fine trout lifted from behind a half-submerged rock, and, in one long sweeping rise, picked the surface clean of a half-dozen mayflies. I needed three casts to get the fly floating just right along the rock. The Irresistible passed smoothly into the eddy behind the rock, and even in the failing light I could see that great trout's nose bulge out of the water to meet the fly. It took all the control I could manage to keep from striking and pulling the fly away prematurely. I tightened slowly but firmly, felt the weight of the fish, and was fast to the best brown I ever caught in the AuSable. It weighed a hair under 4 pounds.

MAYFLY HATCHES

That is the kind of action dry-fly fishermen everywhere can expect when mayflies swarm over good trout water. While mayfly hatches and nuptial flights are short-lived, probably no other flying-insect periods are more productive to the dry-fly fisherman. Actually, some mayfly types hatch almost daily on most trout streams. The big hatches, such as the one on the AuSable I described, occur less regularly but they can be as punctual as a government payday.

Dry-fly fishermen in many areas count the days to the "big Drake hatch" the way kids mark off the days before Christmas. In some sections anglers make friendly wagers as to the exact date each season that the big Ephemeroptera will first emerge. Some rod and gun clubs build their stag-party kitty by conducting a pool in which members draw dates of the probable appearance of his majesty, the mayfly.

Pennsylvania streams get a heavy mayfly hatch, usually around Memorial Day, which local anglers call the Green Drake hatch. In Michigan, some fishermen call the big mayflies "caddis flies"; some easterners call them "eel flies," and in Wisconsin I've heard them called "shad flies."

One day in late May I received a call from Al Miller in Oshkosh, Wisconsin. He said the big Green Bay mayfly hatch was on, and I should come up for some fast dry-fly action. The very next evening Al and I were on the Red River, above Greshen, Wisconsin. We were there well before dusk, and not much was going on. But just before dark, huge mayflies were spinning around at the tops of trees doing their nuptials—the males then falling dead, the females dipping to the stream surface and depositing their eggs. Trout started coming up everywhere, and we caught fish where earlier we would have sworn there were none.

By any name, in any area, mayflies are the most important fly for the serious dry-fly fisherman. Anyone who has witnessed the emergence of hordes of mayflies may wonder where so many millions of insects come from—and where they go as suddenly as they came. Mayflies belong to a large order of insects named Ephemerida, which means "lasting but a day." Here today and gone tomorrow, the mayfly usually enjoys but one day in the sun as an adult. In the nymphal or larval stage, they may live along the stream floor for as long as three years, but in the winged state they rarely live longer than a day or two.

The designation "mayflies" was given by the English, because in their country the bulk of Ephemerida hatch out in May. In the United States, however, mayflies may appear on streams throughout the spring and summer. I have even seen mayflies along U.S. streams in December, when snow blanketed the ground.

There are great variations in the habits and general characteristics of our mayflies, but on falling to the stream dead mayflies usually lie on the water with wings out-

What every fly fisherman loves to see—a big hatch of mayflies swarming over a stream stiff with trout. These flies are just emerging from their nymphal cases.

stretched, and at this time they are well represented by the spent-wing type of artificial dry fly. Of course some mayflies, even the dead ones, float along with wings upright. And freshly hatching mayflies, or those that are airborne but accidentally fall to the surface, normally float with wings erect—and they are best imitated by upright-wing dry flies. The perfect mayfly, the imago, is the insect beloved by fish and fishermen. They have sparkling, transparent wings, long, curved, delicate bodies, and forked tails that sometimes are 3 inches long.

DRY-FLY PATTERNS

There are so many mayflies in various sizes and colors that each angler should learn which is most common on the streams he fishes, then endeavor to find *suitably* representative artificials. Most important is that the mayfly artificial be of the correct size. At best, an artificial

With a heavy hatch of mayflies trout often lose their cool and rise with abandon. In this photo flies are both in the air and on the water, as a good trout smashes into a floating fly.

dry fly only *suggests* its natural counterpart to a trout, so we must remember that we cannot suggest a piano by offering an accordion. The important mayflies referred to as drakes are large. Their imitations should be tied on 3X or 4X long hooks, with the bodies curved nicely upward. Common colors for mayflies are pale yellow, cream, white, gray, green, and brown. Standard patterns that are popular as mayfly imitations include the Green Drake, Light and Dark Cahill, Hendrickson, Brown Drake, Irresistible, and Adams (best with three long boar hairs tied in as a tail).

Unquestionably, nothing stirs trout to surface feeding like hatching mayflies. But countless other flies at times can be nearly as important—the caddis, for example, and the stoneflies. And it isn't always necessary for natural flies to be on the water, and for

trout to be actively rising, to catch them on dry flies.

In fishing dry flies for trout the exact imitation of real flies is not only unnecessary but *impossible*. Some fly tyers, and some fishermen, like to think that certain ties so perfectly represent the real insect that trout can't resist the phony fly. Certainly trout feed very selectively at times, and the closer we match the hatch the better, but in the end it is approach and presentation that fool the brainy trout.

Scientists tell us that the eyes of fish have rods and cones very much like those in human eyes, and therefore a human underwater, with suitable protection for his eyes, should see objects about the same as fish do. I once donned a diving lung and went underwater on the Big Hole River to observe dry flies floated over me. The current was so strong that, despite the lead-weight belt around my waist, I couldn't hold a position underwater. I simply floated away and bobbed up at the tail of the pool. We solved the problem by going to a pool where there was a sharp bend in the river, and cottonwoods on the bank. I tied a rope to one cottonwood, and the other end around my waist. Then I went in, the flow washed me to the end of the 40-foot rope, and I was able to hang there in the current. All manner of dry flies floated over me, most riding the surface just inches from my face mask, and presumably I saw the artificials much as would a feeding trout.

What impressed me most was the indentation in the surface made by a floating fly. The fly proper, its specific materials, were impossible to identify. Size and form were important, and to some extent color. A bivisible, for example, didn't float the same nor look anything like an Adams. And the bright colors of a Royal Coachman were more striking than the dull brown of an Irresistible.

KEEPING DRIES AFLOAT

Since the manner in which a dry fly floats is what is most important, beginners should use patterns with good floatability. In my own fishing, unless I have specific reason to do otherwise, I invariably start dry work with a fly I know will float high and handsome, and will likely bob to the top again even if washed under. Two flies I use much of the time, but in varying sizes from a tiny 18 to a buggy 8, are the Rat-Faced McDougal and its near-twin, the Irresistible. Both have bodies of deer hair, which is hollow and buoyant and keeps the flies high on the surface. You have to make some pretty bad casting errors to drown one of these flies. Others that are especially good floaters are the bivisibles, the hair-wing patterns, and the spiders and variants.

Any dry fly, no matter the pattern or how well fished, will drag at some time and "drown," and then not float properly on following casts. A fly with a deer-hair body that has "drowned" or been clobbered by a fish can be fixed like new if you squeeze it in the fold of a wool or flannel shirt or a handkerchief. That takes the water out. Then, when you blow air on the fly hard, it will fluff up perfectly and once again float nicely. Executing short, fast false casts will shake off surplus water, and a couple such false casts ought to be made before each final delivery of a dry. After several fish are caught or a fly has been dragged down in rough water too many times, it isn't going to float right no matter what is done to it. Then it's time to change to another fly, and this is one reason skilled dry-fly men may carry several dozen flies in one size and one pattern.

Before putting out our first cast with a dry we will have applied a commercially prepared flotant to it, either the spray type, liquid, or grease. There are many kinds of good dry-fly flotants, most either Mucilin- or silicone-based. I use grease on certain flies, such as grasshoppers and the Muddler Minnow, but usually a silicone dip with other flies. In the course of a few hours' fishing you may have to dip, spray, or grease a fly several times.

The fly line has got to stay up, too, if you want your dries to float saucily. The line should be the lightest you can fish commensurate with the rod and other conditions, and it should be a double-taper, and in this instance (strict dry-fly fishing) it is better if none of the fine forward taper of the line has been cut back. The line should be thoroughly greased, and excess grease wiped off with a handkerchief or cloth so it will not pick up dirt or gum up rod guides. (Some fishermen feel it's not necessary to grease the modern synthetic plastic-coated fly lines, but for prolonged, hard dry-fly work I always grease my tapers. I wipe the first 30 feet of line with a felt pad rubbed with a silicone-base line dressing or a Mucilin flotant. Thus treated, my line will float high most of the day, even in bumpy water.) A fly line is most easily greased by stretching it out on a lawn or grassy bank (never over sand), or by fastening it at shoulder height between a couple of trees. Only grease the portion of line you expect to have on the water. In the course of a day's dry-fly fishing, when you take breaks, as for lunch, it's smart to strip the line off your reel and lay it in the sun to dry. And you should have a reel with quick-interchangeable spools so that if one line starts to sink, you can readily snap in a fresh, dry line.

Some fishermen grease their leaders, too. Others feel the leader should sink, and thus be less noticeable to wary trout than a floating leader that is curling in and out, denting the surface, showing an obvious connection of *something* to the floating fly. Some experts will argue that they never, but never, cast their leaders over trout anyway, so whether the leader sinks or floats is of no consequence. For whatever it's worth, I rarely grease a leader, preferring that at least the last several feet be underwater.

LEADERS AND RODS

The leader for dry-fly fishing ought always to be as long and fine as possible—something I recommend for almost all forms of fly fishing. The greater the distance between the fly and the line point the better, and the lighter the tippet the less likely trout are to be spooked by the leader, and the more likely the fly will drift easily and naturally with the current.

Speaking of fine tippets, Ben Hardesty, at the time a vice president of Shakespeare, gave me some tiny spools of the finest monofilament for test and diameter I ever saw. Shakespeare made the stuff, which it called "Wonderthread," for sewing-thread outlets. It was so fine and so strong for its diameter that doll manufacturers used it in making baby-doll eyelashes. The model number of the thread was SN40; perhaps you can find some at your local sewing-thread supplier.

A long rod is of great assistance to the dry-fly fisherman, and in this area the newer graphites are fine choices. They are much lighter for length and work with lighter lines than similar glass or bamboo sticks. With a long rod you can lift more line off the water than with a shorter rod, thus better avoiding line drag when a cast

A drag-free float with a dry fly can be achieved by casting a right curve up and across stream (right). The fly comes down ahead of the leader and line, which might otherwise spook the fish, and floats freely for sufficient time before the current causes drag. Working upstream allows the angler to approach trout from behind (they face into the current) and avoid being seen.

current

float

has been made over fast water to float the fly on calm water beyond. Mending line is easier, too, with a long rod, and larger mends can be made—which contributes to more natural floats.

CASTING AND FISHING

There are five basic methods of dry-fly fishing in streams: We can work and cast straight upstream, up-and-across stream, straight across, down-and-across, or straight downstream. The accepted practice is to work upstream, moving cautiously and keeping low so as not to scare fish, and to cast chiefly across-and-up. By moving upcurrent we approach fish from behind and therefore are less apt to be seen. By casting up-and-across we can better achieve drag-free floats and better put the fly and none of the leader or line over the fish, and from this position in the stream we can readily throw right curve casts—so the fly comes down well ahead of the leader and line to float perfectly by that rock, along the edge of that watercress bed, or down that thread of current channeling between the weeds.

It was my good fortune as a young man to fish Pennsylvania's Fishing Creek one day with the late John Alden Knight, famed author, originator of the Solunar Tables, and one of America's pioneer fly fishermen (he built the first flat-bodied nymph). We came to a long run with a big fallen log against the far bank. The base of the tree faced upstream, jutting about 5 feet out from the bank, with half the trunk sticking out in 4 feet of water. As we approached a good trout slurped at a floating fly in the V of water between the log end and the bank.

"That's a fine trout," said the Old Master. "He'll take your dry fly."

"I can't cast to him," I replied. "I can't cast over the log, and I can't move above to cast down."

"Watch," said Knight, as he moved a couple of yards upstream to position himself just across and below the end of the log. He put line in the air, measured the distance carefully on three false casts, then threw a 40-foot curve cast. The line straightened 10 feet over the water, the leader and part of the line jumped around

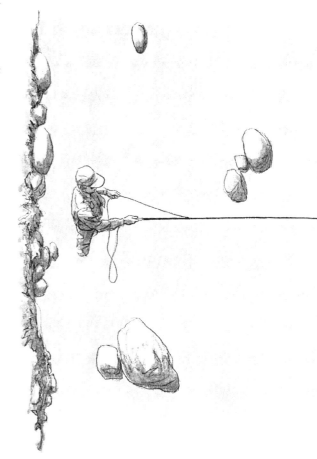

in a perfect right-hand curve, and the fly settled to the surface 5 feet above the log. The fly came down between the bank and the log end, and the trout took. The fish went right down, pulling the leader and line end with him, and when the line came up good and taut Knight put the pressure on and drew the fish from beneath the log. There were no underwater branches down at that end of the log, so Knight had planned the entire show. It was quite an exhibition of all-around trout-fishing skill.

In all of our upstream casting we must be careful to mend line as required, to gather in slack line apace with the speed of the current—thus avoiding drag that comes when the current bellies or tightens the line and pulls the fly along at a speed faster than the normal flow. Drag not only causes a dry fly to move unnaturally, but it can drown the fly. Either may result in a trout refusing to take.

In fishing dry flies we are trying to coax trout to the surface, and a fish near the surface can see an angler much more readily than one holding on bottom. The cautious angler moves slowly and carefully, tries to stay out of the stream as much as possible, avails himself of any cover (a tree, large rock, anything to help conceal him), and he keeps a low silhouette. I sit and kneel so much when fishing small, clear streams that normally I wear out the knees of my boots before anything else.

Moving into the best position before casting is another trait of the skilled dry-fly fisherman. There will be one best place to stand, for example, to deliver a cast to a rock 50 feet away that will result in the best possible drift of the fly. We come to recognize these things through experience more than the printed word, but what the

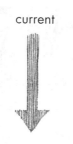

current

The across-stream cast is an effective presentation with the dry fly. Since the fly floats "broadside" into the trout's vision, the fish cannot see the leader or line. The lazy S cast helps in delaying drag.

angler does is so situate himself that the least amount of fly line or leader will be put over heavy current, or opposite currents, which will give the fly an improper float when the cast is put down.

Dry-fly fishing calls for more precise casting than other forms of fly fishing. We must be adept at making curve casts right and left to achieve precision in fly presentation; we must be "up" casters rather than "down" casters so that the extended fly line settles lightly to the surface; and we need to master the lazy S cast (see Chapter 8). The lazy S goes out in a series of snake-like curves, with the curves large or small depending on how the cast is made. Throwing a lazy S across current gives the fly a long, natural float because drag cannot set in and pull the fly badly until the current has washed out all the curves and started dragging the line. Sloppy line work destroys effective dry-fly fishing as much as does drag or drowning of the fly. Line slapping the water, or a bad pickup of the line—with the line sliding or splashing back—can put down every trout in a pool 100 feet long.

In shallow, clear water, especially smooth-flowing pools, the smaller flies generally account for the most trout. In dingy water, deep pools, or fast, broken runs, large patterns seem to draw the most strikes. Always work for trout rising close to you first, then extend your casts to cover the more distant fish. Taking the near fish first will usually leave the others undisturbed, but if you lay out a long line and hook one way out there the resulting scrap will have all the other trout diving for bedrock.

The straight-across-stream method of dry-fly fishing is a favorite technique, at times deadly. It is not, however, practiced by many dry-fly fishermen. I particularly like the across-stream method on the larger rivers, because you can make long casts this way without putting down fish. This is the "broadside float" system, the fly coming to the fish—which is facing upstream—on a sidewise drift. The trout sees the fly in perfect silhouette, and if the cast is right he sees none of the leader or line. A typical situation has the angler wading upstream, out a bit from the left bank, and casting straight across, using the lazy S throw. His fly comes down along the opposite bank, swinging in against the reeds, washing around a log, drifting by a ledge, curling along with the current edge near a hollow bank. Casting across stream, and fishing an Irresistible with the broadside float, I had one of my most memorable days of dry-fly fishing on the Firehole River in Yellowstone Park.

I was fishing a long, shallow stretch, with great cover and holding areas to cast to on the far bank. There were logs and downed trees, sticks jutting out from the grassy bank, little indentations in the bank—all kinds of interesting targets every fly fisherman enjoys casting to. Moreover, I was able to fish well at a distance of some 60 feet from the bank, and casting and tak-

Three ways to fish a dry fly down and across stream (right):

(1) Cast normally and pay out line to avoid drag.

(2) Cast a lazy S.

(3) Cast a curve to the right.

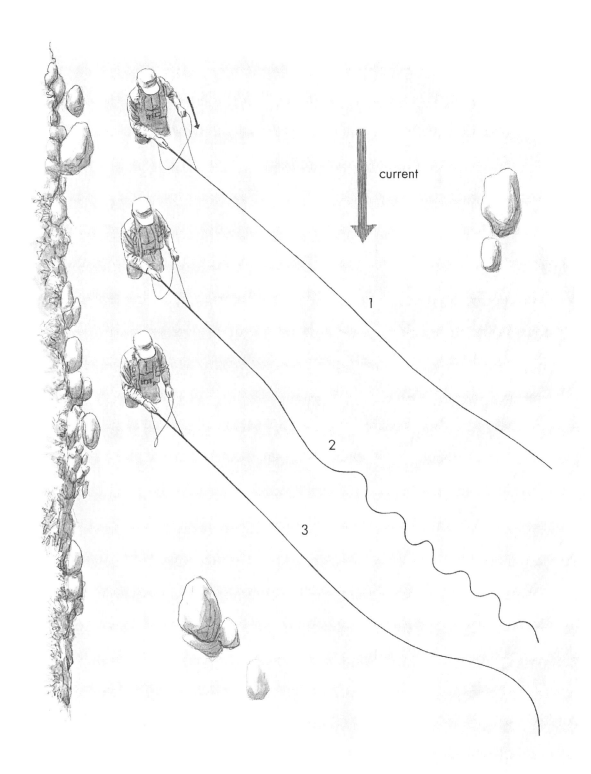

current

1

2

3

ing trout that far out repeatedly, cast after cast, on dry flies, is a special kind of fun. The Irresistible would bob gently along the far bank, and everywhere there should have been a trout there was. I took dozens of browns 14 to 22 inches.

This particular stretch of the Firehole is paralleled by a major road, and at one point I was in the river no more than 100 feet from the road. I was vaguely aware of passing autos as I fished contentedly on. A particularly wild 2-pound brown hit, jumped 3 feet into the air, then skidded and splashed all over the river, running line. He was well below me and swinging in when he jumped again, flashing ivory and gold in the sunlight. A car on the road screeched to a halt, and then came a crash. I looked up, and there were two cars crunched front to rear. The driver in the first car had seen my trout jumping and, excited and wanting to watch, he'd foolishly hit his brakes and the following car plowed into him. The guy in the second auto jumped out waving and yelling angrily. I just stood in the river, holding the trout up on a tight line, and watched. The two tourists cussed and yelled head to head, then started swinging. They had a real old-fashioned head-and-knuckles fistfight until other passing motorists stopped it. It may be unkind of me, but the truth is I guffawed almost out of my waders, thinking that the simple joyful scene of a fly fisherman in a lovely river jumping a trout could cause an accident and start a fight.

In fishing down-and-across stream we should make a straight cast, then pay out line to avoid drag, or make a straight lazy S cast, or do either and endeavor to drop the fly on a leader curving to the right and downstream. What cast should be used depends upon the current forms and the position of whatever the target is we've fired our fly at.

Fishing a dry fly straight downstream normally is not as effective as up-and-across fishing, but in some circumstances it may be the only way to present a dry fly to a fish, and other times it may be the best way. There'll be times on the stream when a promising spot can't be fished any way except by a downstream cast because the angler cannot position himself for any other kind of delivery. And sometimes we'll be hip-deep and fishing our way upstream when, suddenly, a large fish rises directly below us. We must get a cast to the trout instantly, so there is no time to work into a different position.

The lazy S cast is needed here, because the fly must alight in the current several feet above the trout, then drift down to it naturally. If the line is dropped to the surface far enough above the trout not to alarm it, there will be a good float—with the fly preceding the leader and line—and chances are excellent for a take. The parachute cast can be used in this same situation, or you can false-cast line to a point some 10 feet above the trout; then on the final cast, as the line starts to drop, pull back on the rod, keeping the tip high, bringing it to about the one-o'clock position. This will pull the cast up short, and

Sometimes it's necessary to cast a dry fly downstream in order to reach a particular lie (right). Again, a lazy S should be thrown in the line, the fly lighting above the trout's lie and floating downstream freely as the coils straighten.

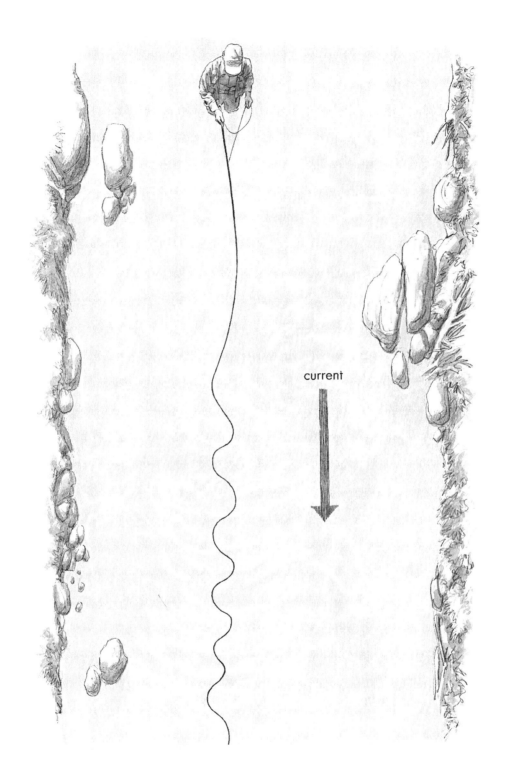

current

cause the line to fall softly to the surface 10 or more feet above the trout. By slowly lowering the rod tip, in keeping with the speed of the current, you can guide the fly down to the fish on a very natural float.

GIVING LIFE TO THE FLY

To be sure, we normally want our dry flies to float naturally, to drift at the right speed and in the right place according to the current. But deliberately activating a dry fly, fishing it with a skipping, skittering retrieve, can bring surprising results.

Sometimes when floating a typical small standard pattern, such as the great Quill Gordon, you will have the fly coming down perfectly with the current, perhaps now

edging slowly over a sunken boulder, but no trout comes up. A gentle lift of the rod tip, just enough to move the fly an inch or 2 or 3 inches across the flow, may convince a lurking trout that the fly is a live insect and bring him rushing up. We must never feel that the dry fly should *always* be fished on a natural float.

On any cast—upstream, across, or down—when the natural float is complete, it is an effective technique to give life to the fly by skimming it over the surface. You can twitch it along, in little hops and jumps, then let it drift naturally a few feet—making the fly look like some winged insect struggling and kicking, trying to get airborne. You can twitch it in long pulls, too, or you can make it skim swiftly right

Having cast a small dry fly across stream to a slick run, McNally skimmed the fly carefully and raised and hooked a nice trout.

The 1-pound cutthroat, played out, rolls on its side and is easily drawn in and gently released.

across the surface. This kind of dry-fly action often excites otherwise listless trout, and they'll chase after a skittering dry fly and hit it hard.

The hop, skip, jump technique of fishing a floating fly can be done with any tackle and with any fly pattern, but there are refinements. Use the longest rod you can, with the lightest possible line and the longest, finest leader. Certain flies lend themselves to skipping better than others. Among these are the big bushy-haired flies, the variants and spiders, and the bivisibles. The Rat-Faced McDougal, Irresistible, and Al Troth's great Elk Hair Caddis are excellent for this fishing. The McDougal is best because its wings are of clumps of deer

hair, which is hollow and buoyant, whereas the Irresistible wings are of grizzly hackle tips. The McDougal floats so high you can pull it swiftly across the surface in a smooth sweep, the fly creating a little V wake as it's pulled along, or you can make it jump into the air, fall back, then twitch it right across the surface. The big hairwing dry flies also are excellent for this kind of fishing. Their impala hairwinging and heavy hackling keep them floating well no matter how hard you jerk them around. The larger flies are best for skittering—10s and 12s, for example, and 8s, too.

Even in this system of dry-fly fishing, drag must be avoided, or at least minimized and controlled. It is one thing to make a fly

Skimming a greased grasshopper-type dry fly over New York's Beaverkill River brought a solid strike from this brown trout. Skimming, or imparting action to dry flies, often triggers good strikes.

crawl over the top, quite another to allow drag to pull it into the surface film and then under. It is best to make drag work for you, not against you; in fact, the ideal in skating flies is to activate the fly without using drag whenever possible.

Skipping a dry fly works best on comparatively flat water, not so well on fast water. In quiet pools we should not activate the fly too much. A gentle bobbing, spaced with an occasional quick, short hop, is most productive in pools. The lip of a pool, where the water pours over, is a good place for this method. Cast quartering downstream-and-across, placing the fly 15 to 20 feet above the pourover. Let the fly float naturally until the current grabs the line and bows it, then begin skipping the fly—making it dart and hop—so that it cuts along just above the pourover. This is a killing technique on the larger rivers at twilight when the big browns take feeding positions at the tail of pools.

When grasshoppers are in the meadows and blowing or falling into the rivers, the fly fisherman can enjoy a trout-catching orgy, especially on the larger western rivers where, in late summer, grasshoppers are abundant and trout feed on them greedily. Skimming a hopper imitation—a greased Muddler Minnow, for instance, or a Whitlock Hopper—at such times can be devastating to the trout.

The various kinds of artificial beetles available almost match the variety of genuine beetles, but most are built with hard backs and meant to be fished under the surface. However, the few that are tied to float fish well, and when skimmed along in the surface film will frequently pull reluctant trout off the bottom.

15

Nymph Fishing for Trout

THE finest trout fishermen in the world are those who are expert with nymphs. One of the patriarchs of American trout fishing, Edward Ringwood Hewitt (1866–1957), who wrote, among other books, a classic entitled *A Trout and Salmon Fisherman for 75 Years*, said that a skilled nymph fisherman can fish out a trout stream. I respectfully agree with the venerable Mr. Hewitt. Given time, with normal conditions of weather and water, I am convinced a masterful nymph fisherman can catch every trout in a stream. Nothing takes more trout than nymphs. And no form of trout fly fishing is more difficult to master—but once the angler has achieved total proficiency in the nymphing art, the rewards are great, not the least being that he probably never again will suffer fishless days. Nymphs take trout when all else fails—including bait.

We had come by helicopter to the Machichi River, in the polar-bear country of northern Hudson Bay. One afternoon I stood huddled against the arctic wind and watched as Patti McClane artfully cast a

big nymph across and downstream. When the nymph hit the water by the far bank she payed out a little slack so the current washed the fly down. Then she teased the nymph along in 6-inch jerks. Patti caught six sea-run brook trout, 3 to 6 pounds, on six successive casts. Granted, this was wild country with wild, unsophisticated fish, but the streamers and even spinning lures that Al and I fished didn't score like Patti's nymphs.

I received my first lesson in nymph fishing from John Daley on Big Hunting Creek one cold opening day in April. The stream had been freshly stocked with hatchery rainbows, and fishermen lined both sides of the creek. The pool above the Third Bridge had so many fishermen we thought we wouldn't be able to get a line in. Under such crowded conditions, either you stand next to someone and share the water or reel up and go home.

Despite the high, discolored water, trout were readily visible. There were hundreds in the pool, most clustered in little knots—sitting motionless on bottom in 4 to 6 feet of water, or finning listlessly about. Even the trout were cold. And since none of the fishermen were catching any, they were colder.

Finally John secured a big rock at the near end of the pool, and I climbed up beside him. In a bottom depression 15 feet upcurrent from us we could see a large pod of 8- to 12-inch rainbows. John roll cast so his nymph fell 10 feet above the trout. He held his rod high, keeping line off the water, and stripped to remove slack. Suddenly John struck swift and hard, and a very surprised rainbow was twisting and turning, fighting the hook, in the current. The crowd looked on as John played out and released the trout. Then, fishing the same nymph, the same way, in the same place, John took seventeen more rainbows, releasing every one. Frequently he had trout on successive casts; other times there'd be two or three casts before another hit. It was an impressive exhibition, and it boggled the minds of the other fishermen. They kept crowding in on us, trying to see John's fly and to study his technique, and since John never has had much rapport with what he calls "opening-day trout fishermen," he reeled up and we left.

Another time on Big Hunting Creek I came to a deep hole where good current washed along a rock wall on the opposite bank, and in the center of the hole, at a depth of about 5 feet, was a large patch of yellow-amber sand. The polarized glasses I wore cut the surface glare as I crept up to the hole. There, taking his leisure smack in the middle of the sand patch, was a 12-inch rainbow.

I slipped into position and rolled a nymph, weighted with a BB-size lead split shot on the leader 15 inches above the fly, on a cast that put the nymph into the water 10 feet above the trout. The lead took it to the bottom and the current washed it to the rainbow. He took. I set the hook, played him out, and landed and released him. The trout scooted around, dove to bottom, finned tiredly over to the sand patch, turned into the current—and again was in his original position. Thinking there might be other trout along that rock wall, I rolled the nymph upstream again. Down it came, drifting naturally with the current, and when it reached the trout I'd just released the fish moved a foot to one side to line up with the oncoming nymph. When I saw his mouth open I struck and had him again. The nymph had caught the same fish on two successive casts. I'd never experienced anything like that before, nor since.

Each spring, sportsmen conduct a kid's fishing jamboree, called the Brotherhood of the Jungle Cock, on trout streams in Maryland's Catoctin Hills. The idea is to teach the kids fly fishing and sportsmanship. We all were up at the lunching area on Fishing Creek, and I joined a group of adults and children munching hot dogs by a long, flat pool. Nobody had been catching many fish, except those very few of us using nymphs. One of the freshly stocked hatchery rainbows was fanning in a foot of water out in front of us, at the edge of current by a sunken rock. I called attention to the trout, and one of the Liberty Road Fish and Game Club members snickered and said: "Go catch him, McNally." I said I'd try.

Keeping low so as not to be seen by the trout, I moved upstream and to one side of the fish. The nymph fell lightly into the flow, sank, and with rod and line manipulation I eased it with the currents so that it bounced along a watery trail which led it straight to the trout. The rainbow lifted slightly, took, was hooked and landed. Those looking on who hadn't done well that day with their big streamers and dry flies were impressed, but such results are seldom surprising to the nymphing specialist.

In those days on the Catoctin Streams, John Daley and I would fish separate ways, one upstream, one down, chiefly because it is pocket and small-pool fishing and there's little room for more than one angler. Whoever had the downstream bit would hike down a mile or less, then turn and fish upstream with his nymphs. There was another reason for fishing different areas; it might be one portion of the stream had been heavily stocked, not so other areas. By fishing two different reaches we got a double check on the fish population. But we needed something other than scribbled notes to leave back at the car to signal our successes, or lack thereof. We decided that each time we caught a trout we'd pocket a pebble, then empty pockets when we reached the parked car left at the halfway point. Thus, if I counted out only five or six pebbles at the car, but saw a pile of twenty or thirty pebbles left by Daley, I'd go find him and determine why the variation in catch statistics. One day I went to the car and there was a pile of perhaps a dozen little pebbles—and one stone the size of a baseball. Ah! A big trout! Sure enough, John had a 2½-pounder, a fine brownie for Big Hunting Creek.

Big Hunting was flies-only fishing at the time, and two dedicated, shrewd wardens handled the patrolling. One was Glenn Butts and the other a wiry, sharp lit-tle guy named Kettels—I can't recall his first name. Some pretty slinking characters poached Big Hunting when they could, doing such sneaky things as attaching a piece of worm to the hook bend of a fly. On seeing a warden approach, they'd rip the meat off and continue casting. Suspicious, the warden would check the fly, only to find it okay.

Such hanky-panky worked sometimes, sometimes not. Kettels and Butts were no dummies and worked some cunning tricks themselves. They carried powerful binoculars. Concealing themselves in the shrouded hemlocks on the hills overlooking the stream, they'd watch a fisherman, and if he seemed to be catching more trout than the average they'd stalk closer. Those two green-uniformed officers could dippy-doo through the forest as unseen and as softly as a stalking mountain lion. Many times they would suddenly appear beside you on the stream edge, while you were concentrating on working your fly and your line was still in the water. *Brother!* If you had a worm, part of a minnow, or even a real nymph stuck on the fly hook you were going in front of the Thurmont magistrate and it was going to cost you at least $50.

I was catching trout regularly one afternoon, casting my weighted nymph upstream and letting it come down with the current—*just as we would if fishing a worm.* Each time I landed a trout I'd unhook it, then release it, then root around in the gravel for a suitable pebble to drop in the "pebble pocket" of my vest. Kneeling on a rock at the creek edge, I'd just hooked a trout and was swinging it toward me when—*Kaplumppp!*

Kettels was kneeling beside me right at

my shoulder. He startled me so I almost jumped out of my hip boots. "*Hoo boy!*" I said. "Where'd you come from?"

Kettels grinned, reached for my fly line, and said, "Here, let me help you with that fish." He brought the line in hand over hand, my little brown trout out there flipping around, and slid the fish up on the rock. The trout lay there panting, and stuck right in the point of his nose was my Hare's Ear Nymph.

Kettels wore the expression of a cat that had pounced on a rubber mouse.

"What the hell was that all about?" I demanded, still shaken and a little irritated.

"What you been pickin' up every time you catch a trout?" he demanded.

"Pebbles," I said, and explained why.

"Oh," Kettels said sheepishly, then related how he had been glassing me from the woods, noting especially how each time I landed a trout, and before resuming casting, I would finger around through the stones and gravel. "I thought," he said softly, "the way you were taking trout, and then digging around, that you were using real nymphs or some other bait."

My intent in presenting these historical accounts is to demonstrate the effectiveness of nymphs *properly fished*. I stress "properly fished" because there is much more to the nymphing art than merely casting a nymph out and working it back. Yet, with some instruction plus some experience on the stream, the average angler can become adept at taking trout on nymphs.

WHY NYMPHS CATCH TROUT

Because of their abundance, nymphs are the major food item for trout. Nymphs are available in great quantity to trout all year long, spring through winter, and fishery biologists estimate that nymphs compose 80 to 85 percent of a trout's diet. Sometimes I think it's more like 100 percent.

Hatching nymphs are more easily caught by trout than are flies floating on the surface. In streams with a lot of fast water, stonefly nymphs are almost always the trout's dominant food.

When a stream decides to feed its trout population, the first part of a hatch is the emergence of nymphs. Perhaps little life has stirred in the stream for days, and the trout are lethargic. But with the appearance of the first nymph, then another, and another, the little dace and larger chubs begin darting about, stabbing at the gravel, sucking up nymphs at the instant of appearance. Then the trout move, leaving cover and taking position in the currents as wriggling nymphs begin to speck the sunlit, clear

A stonefly nymph (also called a salmon fly) emerges from its husk to change into an adult insect. These flies are extremely important on our large western rivers in June.

Angler's fly wallet is stuffed with artificial nymphs. The one in hand is a stonefly imitation. Note the cases (on rock) of nymph husks shucked recently by live stoneflies. (Photo by Bill Browning, Montana Chamber of Commerce.)

water. The nymphs rise from their beds in the gravel and become caught up in the flow. They bounce over riffles, spin in currents, and lodge in eddies and pools. They fill the water with a creeping, squirming, halting abundance that rises and falls with each beat of the river.

Nymphs are the lifeblood of a trout stream. Thus artificial nymphs, rightly presented, will take trout from opening day to the final day of the season. They get fish when the water is high and when it is low. They produce in hot weather and cold. They get trout Maine to Maryland, Wisconsin to Washington. They consistently catch brook, brown, and rainbow trout—as well as goldens, aurora, cutthroat, steelhead, Dolly Varden, splake, tiger, Alpine, and sea-run trout—which is to name only some of the Salmonidae that are suckers for nymphs.

In the early season when most trout streams are high and turbid and the trout

are on bottom, a nymph gets them because a nymph can be rolled slowly over the gravel right next to a trout, making easy pickin's for the fish. Trout do not feed actively when water temperature is under forty to forty-five degrees, but they will readily take a slow-moving, easy-drifting nymph. And sometimes trout will gorge so heavily on nymphs through an afternoon that they ignore the heavy hatch that comes in the evening. Floating flies are all over the place (we have all seen this) yet not a trout comes up.

Many fishermen mistake the surface disturbances made by nymphing trout to be "rises," the swirls, rings, or even splashes trout will make when taking floating flies. Because usually no floating fly is seen by the angler, he assumes the trout are rising to flies too small to be readily seen. Sometimes there may even be flies on the water, but no matter what the fisherman does with dry flies he can't get a strike. When

Two signs that trout are feeding on nymphs. "Tailing" trout (left) break the surface with their caudal fins; they're feeding on bottom-dwelling nymphs in shallow water. "Bulging" trout (below) break the surface with their dorsal fins while taking nymphs just below the surface. Anglers often mistakenly interpret these surface disturbances as rises and use dry flies.

trout are just dimpling the surface, or "humping" or "bulging" the water and refusing all dry flies, they usually are catching nymphs just below the surface. Sometimes a surface-nymphing trout will show its entire back, and dorsal fin and tail, as it noses up, takes a nymph, then goes down again.

When trout hit the knots in your leader they usually are mistaking them for midge nymphs. If you see trout flashing underwater, sunlight reflecting silver from their sides, you can be sure they are nymphing. There will be times (happy ones when the angler recognizes what is going on) that "tailing" trout are seen. These are fish grubbing for nymphs on the bottom, in shallow water, and most often it occurs at the tail of pools. The feeding trout noses along, dislodging pebbles and sand and nymphs, and occasionally his caudal fin or tail splits the surface. Whenever the situation is baffling to the angler, he is wise indeed to sit down and watch the stream for a time, and to study the movements of the trout.

OUTFITS FOR NYMPH FISHING

Nymphs can be fished with almost any fly outfit. In fact, I have caught small-stream trout by fishing a nymph with a BB-size lead split shot, a 4-foot length of leader material, and a broomstick. (Honest!) In general, though, it is best to go as fine as we can with our gear, particularly linewise. It won't hurt to underline your rod by one size, because the finer fly line helps with gentler presentation, and provides less resistance to the current and less unwanted drag.

Long rods are preferred by many excellent nymph fishermen, even when fishing the narrowest streams. John Daley, for example, often used an 8½-foot rod on very small streams. With the longer rod, he was able to reach out to drift his nymph through likely pockets, keeping all or most of the fly line off the water, and just steer the nymph along with only part of the leader in the water. Fishing such a short line, you detect strikes easier and it is easier to strike quickly and set the hook when a trout takes.

It's a matter of choice, and long rods certainly have their place in nymph fishing, but I like a long rod only on the larger rivers. An overly long rod can be unwieldy in tight quarters on a small stream. I for one don't want to be fighting a 9-foot rod on a stream 10 feet wide. In some ways the

long-rod syndrome gets overdone. With a little 6-foot rod we can lift ample line off the water, and have the pleasure of casting some line even on the tiniest stream. I select my nymphing rod chiefly according to the size stream and the casting job to be done. I generally use rods ranging from a 6-foot-long, 1½-ounce stick to an 8-foot-long, 4-ounce rod (these are bamboo). But I also use a graphite rod measuring 9 feet 3 inches, which weighs a mere 2¾ ounces and takes a No. 5 line.

The 6-foot rod is used on the smaller mountain streams. I like a 7- or 7½-foot rod on medium streams, and the 8-foot rod on the larger rivers. The 9-3 graphite I'll use anywhere it handles well, and I especially like it on the western spring creeks, big rivers, and lakes.

The fly line used in nymphing should be double-tapered, because DT lines cast well, make proper presentation of the fly easier, and are smooth to handle in the currents. Floating lines are used a lot in nymphing, sometimes with weighted nymphs, sometimes with nonweighted ones. Sinking-tip lines are fine, and most nymphers use ones with a sinking tip about 6 feet long. Some fishermen cut back tips that are 6 feet long if they don't want to fish too deep. Full-length sinking lines have a place in nymphing, too, with line selection depending simply upon the level at which we want to work our nymphs. I'd caution against using a full-sinking line that will feel "heavy" in the water, because with such a line it is easy to lose the feel of your underwater nymph and therefore not fish it well. Generally a full-floating line, or a floater with a fine, short sinking point, is the best line for most nymphing situations. In any case, these lines handicap the angler the least in presenting his nymph, working the fly on a natural swim, and detecting strikes.

Many fly lines now are designed just for nymph fishing, having a foot or more of the line's forward end in some bright color, a color different from that of the rest of the line. Usually the line points are bright red or orange, the balance of the line white. The idea is that the angler can see the end of such a line even when floating out there on a long cast, and you have to see the line end to perceive the delicate pause in the drift of the line, or that telltale twitch of the last few inches of the line that indicate a trout has picked up the drifting nymph.

I always use a white or ivory line for nymph fishing because they are the easiest to see. I was instrumental, as a matter of fact, in getting the Cortland Line Company to make the first white (cream-white) lines in the late 1940s. Prior to that fly lines were all dark-colored, usually mahogany, green, and so on. With a white or ivory line, even in early morning or at dusk you'll be able to spot that little *tic* that signals a trout has sucked in the drifting fly.

When a sinking line touches a rock or scrapes bottom you can have difficulty detecting strikes. To my mind the ideal nymphing setup is a full-floating double-taper, used with a weighted nymph or with a single BB-size (or smaller) split-shot sinker on the leader 15 inches up from the fly.

Tapered leaders are needed in nymphing, just as for most other fly fishing, and the tippet should be as long and fine as possible. A light tippet is least visible to trout, and if it's long (3 to 4 feet) and of supple monofilament the nymph will swim far more naturally than if tied to a heavy, stiff tippet. In fishing the larger streams a leader about 9 feet, tapered to 4X, with the tippet about 3 feet long ought to be satisfactory. On the smaller streams a 7-foot leader should do, with a 4X tippet about 2 feet long.

NYMPH PATTERNS

There's no need to become overly concerned with nymph patterns. Some nymph flies are superior to others, but it would be hard to find a standard nymph that—properly used—wouldn't catch some trout. In general, the good standard nymph patterns are less than an inch long and are drab, slightly tapered, and flat. One artificial of this sort will represent a multitude of real nymphs. Fill your book with "attractor" nymphs—ones that in size, form, and color are fairly representative of many kinds of real nymphs—and leave those precise imitations to the fellows who are more concerned with entomology than with catching fish.

I knew a Chicago fly tyer who did such perfect nymph imitations that I felt he was *modeling* insects, not tying flies. His nymphs were so perfect they even had eyes. I fished them many times, and never caught any more trout with them than with ordinary nymph ties.

There are nymph patterns, however, that have tested well through the years. Several are named in Chapter 10.

If you want to get a good idea of the kinds of nymphs trout are feeding on most in your pet stream, one easy way is to open fish you catch and check their stomach contents. Some fishermen wash stomach

These four plump Wolf River (Wisconsin) brown trout hit attractor-type nymphs, and were saved for the fry pan to feed several hungry fishing-camp anglers. All other trout caught were released. (Photo by Bill Browning, Montana Chamber of Commerce.)

contents out in a basin of water, to free nymph husks and better identify them. Most fishermen have examined trout stomachs and noted they were full of 1/2-inch-long evergreen needles, usually little spears from hemlocks. Trout eat them thinking they are green caddis-fly larvae, which abound in many eastern streams.

When we want to examine the contents of trout stomachs without killing the fish, a "stomach pump" can be used. These are bulb-and-tube devices, available at the better tackle shops in good trout-fishing areas. The suction bulb is depressed, then the plastic tube inserted in the trout's mouth and down through its gullet. The bulb is released, and that sucks the contents out of the trout's belly. The fish can then be released unharmed.

An ordinary window screen, butterfly net, or something similar can be used to collect live nymph samples. The screen or net is lowered to the stream bottom in an area of good current, where the bottom is rock, sand, and gravel. Raking the bottom a few yards above the screen net, or dis-

lodging rocks and stones with the feet, will turn up any nymphs present and the current will wash them to the trap.

A still easier, though not as thorough, way to check a stream for nymphs is to turn over rocks and small stones in the shallows and look for little wrigglers, or for the tiny stone or stick cases of caddis larvae.

Some streams are no good for nymph fishing. Unless the water contains lots of real nymphs, don't expect to do much with artificials. Warm and muddy meadow streams rarely support many nymphs, because silt and high temperatures can kill them off. Nymphs are most plentiful in cold, sweetwater streams having rock, gravel, or sand bottoms. Almost any unpolluted mountain creek will have millions of nymphs.

FISHING THE NYMPH

One of the most effective ways to fish a nymph is with a floating line and a BB sinker up the leader, 12 or 15 inches from the nymph, and to work upstream. Casts are made up-and-across stream. The nymph should be dropped at current edges that will bring it down alongside sunken boulders, through foamy chutes, deep through the bottom of pools, close to brush piles, etc. We are making upstream casts and downstream drifts. Unless the nymph should wash into slow water, no action is given it. We merely allow the current to carry our fly along just as it would a real nymph, but one that is more or less helpless in the flow. As the line washes down, we mend the line and keep slack out, and at the first indication of a hit we set the hook fast and hard. When the nymph has swung abreast of us, we follow its drift with the rod tip, keeping the line as taut as possible at all times—watching the line end for any telltale pause or other movement that would be unnatural to the normal drift of the line. As the nymph bounces on down current and begins to swing below us, we can pay out a little line and extend the drift, perhaps to put the nymph by a sunken log or other good spot. As the nymph starts to swing we can give it a lively swimming action by stripping line in short pulls and twitching the rod tip. Most nymphs are fast swimmers, so quick little 6-inch jerks are called for. When the nymph is swinging below and crossing over in the current, rising gradually to the surface, we can lift it closer to the top by raising the rod tip. Such action is very natural to a real nymph swimming surfaceward, and many strikes come at this moment. Holding the nymph at the surface and causing it to skim over the top is a good technique. Once the line has straightened and the nymph is directly below, it can be fished back upstream in little twitches and hops, until picked up for another cast.

Start fishing a nymph shallow, casting a short line. Then, as the nymph moves with the current, take up slack and raise the rod tip. This will give you a very good pass at any trout that may be feeding on or near the surface. Gradually lengthen the casts to cover all of the water with shallow drifts. After that, go deep with your nymph until, finally, you dredge the bottom. Fish the stream floor thoroughly, not leaving any spot until you're certain trout there have had a chance to grab your nymph.

I'm convinced that these techniques are what make nymphing so deadly; the skilled nymph fisherman works with painstaking exactness, sweeping every crevice, crack, and corner of the streambed.

Instead of casting up-and-across stream, sometimes it's better to cast directly across stream, or down-and-across, and to give action to the nymph as soon as it hits the water.

Stream configuration or current conditions sometimes dictate fishing the nymph straight upstream. And straight-upstream casts often work well if fishing slow, deep water so long as there is no danger of spooking fish with the fly line. It's most difficult to detect strikes, however, when fishing the nymph directly upstream. The angler must strip line swiftly to remove as

Casting a nymph straight upstream (right) often produces strikes, especially in slow, deep water. Angler must strip line to take in slack as the fly floats toward him. Other methods of fishing a nymph are the same as for a wet fly, shown in Chapter 13.

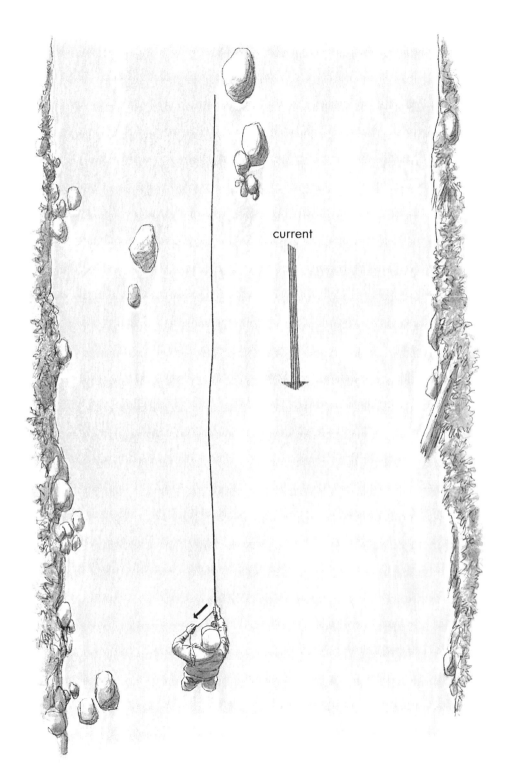

current

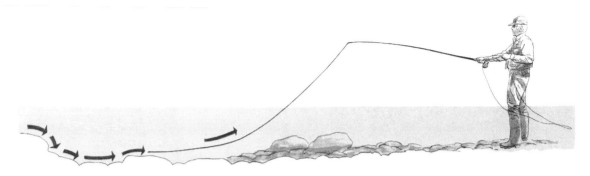

The upstream cast seen from the side. The nymph should sink on delivery and rise to the surface during retrieve, much like the natural itself during emergence.

much slack as possible, and be doubly alert for any sign that a trout has sucked in his nymph. Striking to set the hook in a taking fish must be instantaneous. Straight-upstream nymphing should be avoided if at all possible. Often the angler can reposition himself in the stream, approaching a spot from another angle, and thus avoid making straight upcurrent casts.

It takes skill to cast consistently so that the nymph will fish deep and tumble naturally with the stream, and at the same time to control your line so that you will sense even the gentlest take. The lazy S cast is useful in this, because it forms a series of small curves in the line which keep the nymph drifting at a natural speed with the current, yet you still have good control of the line. Upstream, such a cast allows the nymph to sink quickly because it delays drag on the line from the current, and that also allows the nymph to work more naturally than if there were drag in the line. When sent across stream, the lazy S accomplishes the same things. Tossed downstream, the lazy S is used to sink the nymph, because the fly will drift and sink naturally as the current straightens the curves.

SENSING THE STRIKE

Most beginners at nymph fishing have trouble identifying strikes. Herein lies the real art of nymph fishing. It takes a sort of practiced sixth sense to know when to set the hook. Often a drifting nymph will rub a boulder or scrape bottom, sending a light signal up the line that jangles your nerves, but with experience you'll learn to separate these from signals transmitted by trout. It is impossible to describe it in words, but there is a difference, usually, in the way a fly line pauses or jumps when the sunken nymph brushes a stone, as compared to the line-end action when a trout has halted the drifting nymph. With experience you'll come to recognize the differences. There will be times when you will strike and set the hook in a deep-down log, but there'll be times, too, when you'll think the nymph merely rubbed a boulder, when in fact a trout had it.

It's a lot more fun to fish nymphs without a split shot, but a tiny shot puts the fly down where the fish are, and it helps tell you when a trout has grabbed. The shot straightens a short line and makes a direct connection between you and the fish, so the slightest pause or twitch in the drifting line is noticed immediately.

Since a nymph-hooked trout is nailed before he has a chance to spit out the fly, he'll usually be neatly hooked in the upper lip. If the hook's in any other spot, the trout probably hooked himself, or else you were lucky and he still had the fly even though you struck too late. Speed in striking is especially important. Trout do not slam into nymphs as they do streamers and dry flies. Since a correctly fished nymph comes to a trout slowly with the current, he doesn't have to chase it, so his pickup is easy and deliberate. And if you don't strike immediately the fish ejects the nymph. Many times, wearing polarized glasses, I've seen trout inhale nymphs. They swim up to one and float with it for a few feet. Then, having made up their minds, they swim below and assume a feeding position. When the nymph arrives the trout simply opens his mouth.

Some anglers, especially those new to nymph fishing or with failing eyesight (or short attention spans), have trouble distinguishing these striking-fish signs, even when they know what to look for. Using light-colored lines, as discussed earlier, is a big help. I also said earlier that some lines are available today with brightly colored tips. We used to apply red paint to the first 6 or 10 inches of our white fly lines, and that's something you might want to try. Red fingernail polish can be used as well.

One trick you can use, if necessary, is

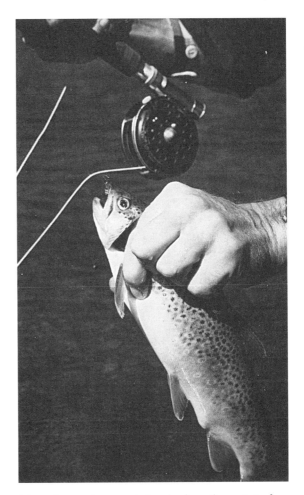

Nymph-caught trout is hooked on the point of the nose, a common characteristic which is the result of the fast strike needed when fishing nymphs.

tying a bit of white cloth or fly-tier's wool at the point where the line and leader meet. I knot it, forming a ball the size of a matchhead, and that little glob of white out there can be of real assistance in evening or night fishing. The knotted cloth should only be used as a last resort, though, because it interferes with casting.

There's the bearded trick of adding a dry fly to the leader when fishing a nymph. A large dry, preferably white or yellow, is used on a dropper strand of nylon, and the fisherman watches the floating fly, which presumably comes downcurrent with the sunken nymph on an identical float. The underwater drift of the sunken nymph ought to be reasonably similar to the surface float of the dry fly. When the dry fly twitches or bobs the angler strikes, on the assumption that this action is caused by a trout halting the submerged nymph. The shortcoming to this system is that the angler tends to forget he's fishing a nymph. He'll find himself casting to flat water, mending his line in a way not likely to sink the nymph, and in general he'll start thinking dry-fly fishing more than nymph fishing. The nymph fisherman *always* must project his mind to the nymph working down there along the rocks and gravel.

A recent innovation for nymphing is the strike indicator—brightly colored bits of foam or other high-floating material now available inexpensively at most quality tackle shops.

I stopped in a tackle shop the other day and bought five different kinds of strike indicators. One type, called the Pinch-On-Float (from Palsa Outdoor Products of Lincoln, Nebraska), consists of two aspirin-sized, blaze-orange foam stickers that you bend around the leader butt and press together. Another similar strike detector is the Roll On, by Umpqua Feather Merchants. These are tiny rectangular squares of sticky-back closed-cell orange foam that you roll onto your leader.

A few other strike indicators I picked up are a little more difficult to describe.

One is a blaze-orange cylinder about ¹⁄₂-inch long, with a hole through the center for stringing your leader; another is teardrop-shaped and bright red, with a hole in the center for the leader; another is a brilliant green pea-size ball, also with a hole for the leader.

Experience at nymph fishing will do more for you than all the paint marks, cloth strips, white lines, light lines with bright tips, dry flies, and strike indicators combined. That special sixth sense I mentioned before is really there; it just takes time to develop. It will grow so keen you'll respond to strikes when the light's so dim only a kind of trained hunch guides you. It's a tremendous satisfaction—feeling that hunch, suddenly flexing your rod tip, then seeing the river boil as your nymph stings a trout's jaw.

There will be times, certainly, when trout will hit your nymph as fast and hard as if they were striking a streamer. Such hits usually come when you are imparting action to the nymph, or when the nymph is rising and swinging in the current on a tight line.

MIDGE NYMPHS

One of the most difficult situations facing the trout angler is "smutting" fish. These are trout taking midge larvae in the surface film, and such feeding activity has been known to drive many an angler up the nearest hemlock or cottonwood.

To be effective, Midge Nymphs must be fished on the longest, finest leader practical for the conditions. Normally the tippet can be no heavier than 5X, and 6X and 7X are commonly used. Tippets should be very long (3 to 4 feet), since the longer tippet will stretch and absorb some of the jolt of the strike. There's no need to strike a trout taking a Midge Nymph, as the tiny hooks are very sharp and readily catch in the skin of a trout's jaw. Deliberate, fast striking will break fish off. Instead, a quick but gentle lifting of the rod tip is all that is needed—merely a tightening of the line.

There are a couple of ways to fish Midge Nymphs. They can be fished dead in the surface film (greasing all but the last 3 to 4 inches of the leader point is helpful here); they can be twitched gently along the surface, fished slow and easy or with occasional jumps just under the surface; or they can be allowed to sink a few feet, then drawn slowly to the top to simulate a real midge swimming up from the bottom.

16

Streamer Fishing for Trout

"N OW YOU will see the river," intoned Prince Carlos Radziwill as he spun the car around an abrupt curve and braked to a halt. We had been pounding the dusty road for hours on the 125-mile drive from San Carlos de Bariloche. Getting out of the car was a welcome pleasure. The hillside fell sharply away at our feet, where a dislodged pebble rolled down, trailing a streamer of dust, and finally plopped into the Rio Chimehuin. "It is beautiful. No?" said Carlos.

A few hundred yards below us, the clear, broad Chimehuin River rolled out of Lake Huechulafquen. Even at that distance I could count baseball-size stones on the bottom in 15 feet of water. The calm lake reflected soft indigo from a cloudless sky and, to the west, the cordillera of the Andes pushed up its purple peaks. The trout country of Patagonia, in Argentina, is desolate yet awesomely beautiful, not unlike much of the Rocky Mountain region of southwestern Montana. From its *boca* the Chimehuin gathers itself and pounds swiftly along hanging cliffs, around truck-

size boulders, through deep slick pools, and tumbles beneath a rickety bridge that carries the dirt road past the river and on toward the Chilean border. Beyond the bridge the Chimehuin swings sharply right, gathers momentum and white water as the stream gradient drops abruptly, and then plunges into a narrow, foamy, boulder-strewn canyon.

On the other side of the river, upstream from the bridge and near the *boca*, there is a campground, and this day there were four colorful tents set up, and pickup trucks and Land Rovers parked around. Women and children in the campground below were waving at us. "There," said Carlos, pointing to the camp, "is where we will live—and fish—for a month."

We drove into the camp and soon were sipping *maté* with our hosts as they prepared the evening's *ensada*, barbecued beef sides done crisp over wood coals. The *maté* had not made two turns around when a lone angler—still in his waders—was seen high atop the hill on the other side of the *boca*. He was waving and shouting excitedly, beckoning us to come up the hill. When Carlos and I reached Bebe Anchorena he pointed to the river below. My eyes popped like black olives set in a couple of boiled eggs.

There in the first deep pool of the Chimehuin, just below the fast water pouring out of the lake, was a school of huge brown trout. I had never before, nor have I since, seen anything like it. The smallest fish was perhaps 8 pounds, the largest 15 or 16. The trout obviously had just entered the river from the lake, because they hadn't been there when Carlos and I stopped for a look earlier. Our vantage point was so perfect, the water so clear, the trout so large that we observed them as clearly as if in an aquarium. The trout were *schooling* just as surely as a pack of bonefish. There were eleven fish. They lay tightly packed on the bottom gravel, covering an area of perhaps 10 square feet. Now and then the school would flit nervously about the pool, swimming quickly upriver, turning, swinging to the tail of the pool, then back to the deep depression by a submerged boulder. They'd rest there motionless for a time, then move to another station, rest, then back again. It was too much for me. "I'm going down and try them," I told Carlos and Bebe, and minutes later I was wading into the edge of the pool and putting line in the air.

I had a big, size 3/0 white bucktail streamer on, the Platinum Blonde. Because of light conditions I couldn't see the fish, but up on the hill Carlos and Bebe kept pointing and gesturing excitedly, indicating where I should cast. My heart was pounding when I put out the first cast. The big fly swung in the current and darted along as I stripped line. Any second I expected a long,

dark shadow to loom up under the fly, then for the water to explode as one of those huge browns hit the streamer. I felt prickly all over as I fished out the first cast. I looked up questioningly to Carlos and Bebe. They signaled I should make a longer cast, farther downstream. I did, and then cast again, and again. Not a strike, not a follow, nothing. Carlos and Bebe weren't signaling now and, even at that distance, they looked deflated. I waded out and walked to the head of the pool, then fished my way down and through it methodically, laying casts out that covered all of the water. Carlos and Bebe had left the hill and were back in camp by the time I hobbled up.

"What happened?" I asked. "Where did those trout go?"

"We don't know," Bebe replied. "The light changed just after you started fishing and we couldn't see into the pool. Then when we could see again the trout were gone. Perhaps they went on downriver or, more likely, back into the lake. They were big fish."

Bebe Anchorena knows big fish. He has taken many Argentine trout 15 to 20 pounds, and in 1961, at the Boca Chimehuin, got a brown of 24 pounds on a bucktail streamer.

While we caught fish every day, it was slow fishing for the Chimehuin, and nobody could come up with a big one. Then one evening I was fishing with Bebe down below the bridge, at the last pool before the canyon. Bebe left the river and climbed the bank, then stood on an outcropping of rock above me and watched as I fished.

The water was deep and very strong, so

Bob McNally prepares to land a brown trout that hit his streamer by the brush pile on the opposite bank of Minnesota's Straight River.

Streamers effectively draw trout out of very heavy cover.

I couldn't wade. The high bank behind me made normal casting impossible, but I could roll cast and get the Platinum Blonde out 30 to 40 feet. I was only 40 feet above where the Chimehuin broke over the rocks and fell off into the canyon. "Fish right at the lip of the pool," Bebe called down. "I've caught many trout there."

I rolled the fly out, let it swing down in the current, and then payed out a few yards of line, until the streamer was working around rocks right at the breakover. I had a powerful 9-foot glass rod and WF-9-F line, and the 3/0 streamer was knotted to an 8-pound-test leader tippet.

With my rod parallel and pointing at the opposite bank, the fly line almost straight downstream from me, I worked the fly by yanking the line and twitching the rod tip. "Hey!" Bebe suddenly hollered. "A trout came up, rolled under your fly, then went back down." I put another cast to the spot, worked the fly, and Bebe cried: "There he is . . . came up again. Looked about 6, 8 pounds."

Long shadows played over the pool as the sun disappeared behind the Cordillera, and I put out another cast. Leaning way out to better work the fly, I pumped the streamer up and down in the current. My rod tip snapped down abruptly with such force that the rod almost jumped out of my hand. What little slack line was in my left hand disappeared through the rod guides. I held onto the rod with both hands, dug my heels in, and leaned back on the rod. I knew I had to hold the fish right there, at the top of the canyon, at the very lip of the pool, or down into the chasm he'd go. I held the trout there long enough to appreciate his weight, even though much of the power I felt came from the heavy current the fish was in. It was over almost instantly. The leader popped and the fly line came back like a rubber band. "Damn!" I said, slapping the rod tip on the water. "Double damn! That was some trout."

"Yes, I saw the fish," Bebe said sadly, walking over. "It wasn't the first trout. This was another one. He came from out of a cave in the rocks to take the fly. He would have gone 20 pounds."

It was dusk now, so I just reeled the line in and Bebe and I limped into camp. I couldn't sleep that night, nor the next, for thinking of that big brown sulking down there in the rocks with my fly drooping from his jaw. I kept wondering how much he really weighed, and how long he was. Was he brightly colored or one of those black ones? How old? If I'd gotten him away from the falls and headed upstream, would I have caught him? How could I have played a fish that size successfully in the position I was in—backed against the bank, at the edge of deep water? What would I have done with that trout if I'd landed him? Killed him, just for photos? An American visiting Argentina doesn't have fish mounted.

A lot of questions went unanswered,

and of course still are. The memory of that Chimehuin brown is clearly with me today, and I'm sure it always will be. The incident was one of my most exciting fly-fishing adventures, or misadventures. And I'd never have had the experience had I not yanked a big bucktail streamer around the rocks at the top of the canyon in the Rio Chimehuin.

BIG FLIES, BIG TROUT

It is a well-established fact that streamer flies catch the largest trout. Of course, big trout are taken on nymphs and dry and wet flies, but day in and day out streamers will account for the greatest number of sizable trout.

To repeat a time-worn phrase, big trout want a big mouthful. It is axiomatic that a good-size trout eats far more 2- to 6-inch-long minnows (or smaller trout) than he does small floating flies or drifting nymphs. So the chances of taking big trout anywhere, any season of the year, under any conditions of weather and water are best with the angler fishing streamer flies. No other artificial fly better represents a real live minnow in the water than a streamer fly, no matter what type streamer it is.

On Wisconsin's lower Tomorrow River, Russ Gaede and I were netting the odd small trout on dry flies. Then just before dark, along a deep, brushy bank, minnows suddenly showered out like sparkling slivers of glass. We both put several casts over the spot but failed to raise the fish. Again minnows showered out, some popping up onto the mud bank, and this time we saw the swirl and broad back of a husky brown.

"*He* doesn't want a dry fly," said Russ, quickly tying on a No. 6 Dark Edson Tiger. On his first cast Russ's rod tipped down to the water as the big fish hit hard. It was a 4-pound, 7-ounce brown, the best I've ever seen from the Tomorrow.

That was a case of a large trout feeding on minnows and ignoring nicely floating dry flies. But I've seen it the other way around, too. Assuredly it is the exception and not the rule, but often I have seen a couple dozen trout sweeping the surface clean of floating insects as a major hatch occurred, yet falling all over a well-presented streamer fly.

A famous angling writer once broached the idea that trout take bucktail flies for mice. He wrote that a brown bucktail, allowed to drift broadside downstream with the current, is quickly gobbled by large trout that believe the bucktail to be a mouse, which they "relish." I don't know how many mice the average trout gets to see *in the water* in his lifetime, but I don't think too many mice fall into too many rivers. I think few trout ever get a chance to eat mice, let alone learn to "relish" them, and I suspect no trout ever hits a streamer fly because he thinks it's a mouse.

The Muddler Minnow, which can be fished in a number of ways, took this chunky brook trout for the author when it was fished under the surface in short twitches to resemble a darting minnow at a central Wisconsin lake.

WHEN TO USE A STREAMER

There are specific times when streamers are your best choice of fly (some mentioned in earlier chapters), but to reiterate briefly, streamers are good in spring when insect hatches are few and light, streams are high and roily, the water is cold, and trout are sluggish. Streamers imitate minnows, the prevalent food in spring; they are the easiest fly for trout to see in heavy, turbid water; and they can be fished slowly and tantalizingly, repeatedly in the same place, and so encourage an otherwise unwilling trout to strike.

Streamers are a good choice in very large rivers, or in deep water. On big water we must cover a lot of it, and fishing streamers is a good way to accomplish that. Fall is a favored time for streamer fishing. The big hatches of spring and summer are over, so trout now are starting to scratch bottom for their food more than they are tipping toward the surface. Too, the big trout start to move in the fall (in some watersheds there are major migrations), and the big spawners will go for streamers like nothing else.

Midsummer conditions do not negate

streamer fly fishing. Sudden storms can raise and cloud rivers, making streamers the most effective flies. Under normal summer conditions of low, clear water, a small (size 10 to 12) sparsely dressed streamer often will take trout when other fly types fail. Even when streams are in a low state, there are always heavy runs, deep holes, undercut banks, dark pools, and white-water boils where streamers prove uniquely productive. And by summer the spawn of the year has reached fry size and become important trout forage, and that's another sound reason for summer streamer fishing.

In any stream where minnows are abundant the streamer should be a first selection, particularly if no surface activity is observed. Many good trout rivers, especially in the Midwest, have poor insect hatches because their silted sand bottoms do not have the gravel required by some nymph forms. But they produce heavy crops of minnows, so the trout learn to chase tails and scales rather than winged insects.

STREAMER PATTERNS

Some specific fly patterns for trout are discussed in Chapter 10, but to that we should add that your kit should include a lot of bucktail patterns, and marabous. Marabous are very special, with their undulating action, and seem to encourage strikes from even the most lethargic, disinterested, well-fed trout. Bucktails have some special appeal to trout, too. The lively hair in a bucktail-winged fly flares out in the water, wiggles and waves when the fly settles, then closes and opens as the angler works the fly through the currents. Bucktails also put out a bubble stream, and

diffuse light in ways no other flies do, and these attract strikes from wary trout.

The size of the streamer used can be very important. In high, dirty water, use bigger flies; in clear, shallow water, use smaller, more sparsely tied patterns. A lightly dressed streamer on a small hook is far less likely to spook trout in thin, bright water than are bulky, heavy-hooked patterns. Streamers on heavy hooks, but sparsely dressed, sink deeper and faster than heavily dressed flies on light hooks. When you want a streamer to fish in inches-deep water, or to merely skim along inches under the surface, select a fly with buoyant material in the wing, such as bucktail, and tied on a small light-wire hook.

One of my favorite streamers for western fishing is a Muddler Minnow, on a regular-shank No. 12 hook. This is just a pinhead of a fly by western standards, and I could never tell you why, but I have taken untold numbers of 2- and 3-pound brown trout on it, and a few 4- to 5-pounders.

FISHING THE STREAMER

Next to fishing nymphs, I believe streamer fly fishing is the most difficult to master.

The angler must constantly have full control of his fly, and always must have it behave in the water as though it were a wounded minnow, or a strong, fast-swimming minnow, or a loafing minnow, or one fighting the currents, or one coasting on the currents. Unlike the dry fly, which will take fish when it is floating "dead" on the surface, a streamer must always appear to the fish as something *alive*, or nearly alive. If the streamer is not properly activated at all times by the angler, it becomes to the trout nothing more than a glob of feathers and fur drifting downstream; the fly is another little stick, a colorful leaf, a bit of flotsam—not something to be eaten. I have observed even veteran trout fishermen who were very careless in their streamer work, so much so that I was amazed whenever they caught a decent trout on a minnow-imitating fly.

There are times, naturally, when a streamer just dunked in the water draws a strike. Phyllis and I went to Catherine Creek one April, to see the spawning run of big rainbows out of the Finger Lakes in New York. Fishermen were shoulder to shoulder along the banks, so I didn't even put a rod together. The stream was low and clear, and you could see those broadsided, red-banded rainbows clearly. They were magnificent fish, but they could see the fishermen, too. Huge rainbows fell over one another rushing from one end of a pool to the other. When all the trout were flushed to the tail of a pool, all the fishermen would move down and throw in their assorted lures and bait, and the trout would jump out of their scales and race to the head of the pool. That action went back and forth. How those Finger Lakes trout ever got themselves emotionally together to engineer the spawning act I'll never know.

I was shaking my head at streamside, watching some trout zip up and then down, when a guy with a spinning outfit eased a 3-inch-long Flatfish into the water. He just payed out line, let the current wash the Flatfish down, then, when he had the plug shaking its paint off by submerged roots, he tightened up and held it there. I watched in total fascination as the Flatfish, right at my feet, wiggled and wobbled, shook and shivered, dipped and darted, all with no assistance whatever from the angler. The lure did its solo just under pressure of the current. As I stared a big rainbow swam out from the sunken roots, curved up behind the Flatfish, dropped down and circled, came up again, opened a huge mouth, and chomped on the Flatfish. I gasped. I *know* that fish was 10, 12 pounds. I didn't take my eyes from him. The strip of red on his side looked 3 inches wide. The big 'bow had the Flatfish in his lips, and any minute I expected a yell from the fisherman, a quick strike and tightened line, and then the trout bursting up and out, tearing little Catherine Creek apart. Instead, the 'bow shook its head and the Flatfish fell free.

In dismay and astonishment I looked upstream at the spin fisherman, 30 feet away. "You just had a big rainbow," I said, over a fluttering stomach. "A magnificent fish—why, he just came up and sucked your plug in, and you didn't do anything, you didn't strike. If you'd set the hook. . . ." The whole thing excited me.

"That right?" questioned the spin fisherman. "Didn't feel nuthin'." I looked at Phyllis, who'd been standing at my shoulder and had seen everything. She shrugged. We went upstream.

There is, or was, a small bridge, perhaps 30 feet long, crossing Catherine Creek just downstream from a town I can't remember. This day you could not have placed another fisherman on the bridge. On both upstream and downstream sides fishermen sat side by side, lines hanging in the water. Behind each row of sitting fishermen was a row of standing fishermen. I counted thirty-seven anglers on one side of the bridge.

Sitting in a key spot in the center of the bridge, downstream side, was a boy about twelve years of age. He held a big Hardy salmon reel in his left hand, fly line he'd stripped from the reel in his right hand, and swinging down below him in the current was a big orange bucktail streamer fly, on a leader no more than 2 feet long. The boy had no rod, just that expensive Hardy reel, old, cracked silk fly line, a doubtful leader, and a bucktail fly that looked better designed for northern pike than Finger Lakes rainbows. I hunched down by the kid.

"Hi! Nice reel you have there. How come no rod?"

"I found everything in Grampop's attic. Weren't no rod."

Now and then the youngster would give the line a twitch, which made the fly jump upstream a foot, but mostly the big bucktail just sat there, nosing into the current. Abruptly, five or six rainbows dashed into the pool, spooked upriver from downstream activity, and I thought I was dreaming when one of them looped up and plowed head on into the kid's orange bucktail fly. "Suicide," I thought. "Plain, obvious, everyday fish suicide." The boy yanked hard with his line hand, set the hook, dropped the reel and, as the rainbow went berserk and skidded across a half-dozen lines, started hauling on the line hand over hand. This was a new experience for me. I'd never before seen a youngster handlining from a bridge, on fly, a 5-pound rainbow. The trout tore the pool apart, but he couldn't beat a handline. The pressure was too much, and quickly the boy had the trout right below him, hanging in the current, with a dozen other fisher-

men's lines tangled on the kid's fly line. Everybody shouted to the young Ike Walton—more instruction than encouragement. The boy, now flushed with fisherman's passion, got the trout's head out of the water and started to handline him up. "*Pop!*" The crowd gasped when the leader snapped. I never saw a fish make a bigger splash falling, free, back into the water. I glanced at the boy. He mumbled something that sounded pretty raw, reeled in the bare line, and strode downcast off the bridge.

While the Flatfish incident serves only to show that fishermen must be alert to striking fish, the drama of the boy with the bucktail proves that at least once in a while even a motionless bucktail will catch trout. Of course to that Catherine Creek rainbow the fact that the boy's bucktail was *stationary* in the current indicated that the fly was something alive. Otherwise, it would have drifted on in the current. But we must always *work* a streamer fly, keep it moving in twitches and jerks, in short hauls and long pulls, and simulate as best we can the movements of a free-swimming minnow.

Action is imparted to a streamer fly in the water in three ways: by stripping in line with the left hand, by jiggling or twitching the rod tip, and by a combination of those methods. As a rule I fish a pool or run by starting at the head and fishing down. I make quartering casts across and downstream. With help from the current, I see to it that the line is taut as quickly as possible. I make an initial strip-in of line with my left hand right away, as soon as the fly hits the water, so the streamer darts ahead 6 inches to a foot. I do that with the idea that a trout nearby will see the streamer as a darting minnow—perhaps one that just

Dry flies and nymphs were first put over this 9-pound rainbow clearly visible in a small Ozarks mountain stream, but it refused everything, until the author tried a streamer. Despite the gill-plate grip, the fish was released unharmed. (Photo by Joan Salvato Wulff.)

dimpled and now is scooting downward. I let the fly drift with the current for just a few feet, then I make it hop across current—swimming toward me—by stripping line quickly in short yanks. I'll make another cast to the same area, this time fishing the fly faster by adding rod-tip action to the stripping of line. If I'm fairly certain there are trout there, I'll make a few more casts before moving downstream. I'll fish the streamer slow and deep, then fast along the top, and on another cast I'll try to break up the retrieve, fast then slow, short pulls then long, and so on.

We will comb all of the pool, moving slowly and cautiously so as not to raise mud, or grate on the gravel and frighten the trout. For the same reason, we will not wade any deeper than necessary and, in fact, do our fishing from the stream edge if possible. Casts will be made about 10 feet apart, as we search the water and prospect for trout. When we see promising holding water, such as a submerged boulder, a bottom depression, a deep current edge where trout will lie, or a hollow bank, we will cast to the spot repeatedly. We want to give trout every chance to see the fly.

Regarding casting to promising water, we should never drop our fly directly on the spot where we believe a fish may be. Rather, we cast several feet beyond and let the current and our rod-hand action bring the streamer past the fish's lie. Casts are made so that the fly line never falls over a trout.

Casting a streamer across and down-stream is the best way to present a minnow-imitating fly, and also is the best way to get action into the fly, because the current will help. On the casts across stream the current will tighten the line, bow it, and then sweep the fly around in an arcing curve. Fully eighty percent of the strikes on streamers come when the fly swings around down below the angler. Trout hit then so often that I call this the "fish sweep." When possible the angler should so station himself, and so cast, that his streamer will swing as described just above each likely looking lie.

Let's place our streamer fisherman on the face of an imaginary clock. We will use one-half the clock, splitting the clock face from twelve o'clock to six. The angler stands in the exact center of the clock, at the edge of the stream, on the right-hand bank, looking downstream. The river flows from twelve o'clock toward six. The angler makes a cross-current cast toward the three o'clock position, or perhaps three-thirty. By the time the fly has reached four o'clock the current has washed any slack out of the line, and of course the angler also has accomplished line control by a combination of line-hand and rod work. Soon the fly is sweeping into the five o'clock position, and with the current pulling it along plus the action imparted to the fly by the angler, now is the time to expect a strike. On our imaginary clock, the fly will have its fish-sweep action somewhere between four and five o'clock. When the streamer fisherman sees a sunken log, a boulder breaking the current, or other likely cover, he should position himself in casting so that the cover is in the four-to-five o'clock position; this way his fly will sweep into the spot and fish it properly.

After the fish sweep, when the fly is directly below the angler, he should strip it back upstream preparatory to delivering another cast. But in bringing the fly back, it should be fished, too. Handstripping will impart lively action to the streamer, and occasionally the fly can be allowed to drift back downstream a yard or so with the current, held in one spot momentarily, but given action by a series of quick, short lifts of the rod tip. This will make the streamer appear as a minnow struggling in the current, and such action often draws sudden hard strikes, frequently from trout that come a long way to the fly.

Throughout the retrieve we must be prepared for a strike. Though most trout will hit on the sweep, it is possible for a strike to occur at any time when fishing a streamer. For this reason we will retrieve line by stripping it over one or two of our rod-hand fingers. In all fly fishing, the fly line always should be under fingers of the rod hand so that on a strike we may close our fingers against the rod handle, thus securing the line between the fingers and the cork. This has the fish striking on a taut line, resulting in proper setting of the hook.

Additionally, in fishing a streamer the rod tip should be held low, close to the water, never above the parallel unless the rod is raised to mend or otherwise manipulate the fly line or leader. A low rod tip makes it possible to maintain complete control over the line, leader, and fly, and to strike quickly upward when a fish hits. Proper line and rod work is imperative if we are to hook a decent percentage of the trout that strike our streamers. It is easy to miss

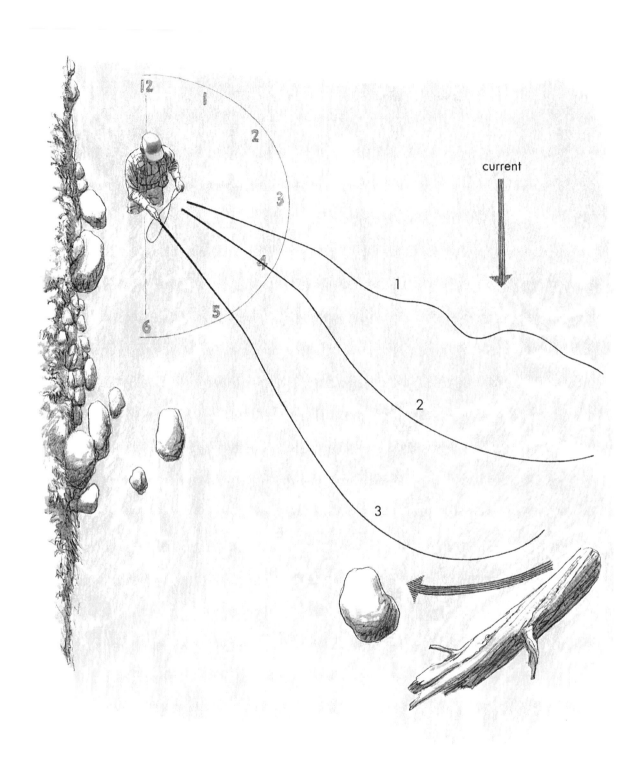

current

strikes when fishing streamers. Sometimes a miss is due to slack line, to the angler setting the hook too late, or to the angler not striking hard enough. Of course, sometimes the trout are to blame, with a fish not hitting the fly right, but most missed strikes are due to angler error.

Except when trout are actively feeding, as browns normally do at dusk, streamer fishing is a searching, probing game. So all areas should be fished slowly, carefully, presenting the fly time and again, working it cautiously in and around each likely trout den.

Fenwick Keyser and I were on Pennsylvania's Skoharie one June afternoon, and to say fishing was slow is an understatement. It was bright and hot and there were no hatches, but we were fishing dries and picking up an occasional 6- to 8-inch brown. In a stretch below a bridge I saw an old rusted steel drum on bottom. The drum had been there so long, resting on its side, open end into the current, that it had half filled with gravel and sand. I once took a 3-pound smallmouth bass from such an oil drum on the bottom of Indiana's Tippecanoe River, so I started floating my dry fly over and around the barrel.

The down-and-across cast (left) with a streamer can be visualized on a clock face.

(1) Angler casts across current toward three o'clock.

(2) At four o'clock the current has washed slack out of the line. The angler controls the line with left hand and rod work.

(3) Between four and five o'clock, the fly goes into a "fish sweep." When the line swings below the angler, he strips it in and delivers another cast.

After a dozen floats I switched to a white marabou streamer. I cast across and upstream from the barrel, letting the fly swing down and work across the opening. Nothing happened on the first pass, but on the second a chunky brown trout shot out of the barrel, did a rubbery turn around the marabou, then ducked quickly back into the drum.

"Hmph!" said Keyser.

I moved a little more upstream, so that on the next cast I could work the streamer more directly into the barrel opening. This time the fly swung down and fairly hung in the current right in front of the barrel. I twitched the rod tip and pumped line with my left hand, and the marabou danced a jig. The strike was so fast that neither Keyser nor I actually saw the fish hit. One moment there was the marabou fluttering crazily; the next instant the trout was turning over in the air.

"Hmph!" Keyser grunted. "Hmph!"

It was a brilliant, golden 2-pounder, which I promptly released. For all I know, that trout might still live in that barrel in the Skoharie.

In addition to the down-and-across method of fishing streamers, they can be cast straight upstream, or up and across, or straight downstream. The straight-upstream cast is used when more of a dead drift to the fly is thought desirable, and when you want the fly to wash deep. You must be careful on upstream casts to catch up to the streamer and strip slack out of the line as fast as possible, or you'll never hook any fish that picks up the fly. Up-and-across casts are usually made because there is specifically attractive cover, or a hole beneath a pourover or a waterfall that can't

While all types of flies occasionally take very large trout, streamer patterns normally account for the most large ones. This is a 22-inch brown trout from Montana's Yellowstone River, on a streamer, of course.

be fished any other way. You can let the streamer cast to such a spot, sink and work with the eddying currents, or you can strip line and bring the fly quickly back. The latter method most often gets strikes.

In general the straight-downstream cast with a streamer is the least productive, but under some situations of angler position, water depth, or the location of a certain trout hold, it is the only practical way to present the fly. On such casts the fly should be dropped well upstream of the exact spot to be fished, and then allowed to drift into the area by paying out slack line. As the fly drifts down, give it action by lightly pumping the rod tip, with some left-hand line pulls. One advantage to presenting a streamer in this fashion is that it comes to the trout directly; the leader and line are straight upstream and not likely to be detected by the fish.

Many times in streamer fishing a trout will chase after a fly, perhaps rising from beneath far roots or a sunken bank and, as the fly swings into the fish-catching four-to-

five o'clock zone, the fish will curve out of the water in a foot-high arching leap and fall upon the fly—usually missing it, but sometimes getting hooked. Rainbows hit this way often, but so do western browns. When such strikes are missed the trout usually can be taken readily on subsequent casts. There's no need to rest such an active fish. Cast again, carefully, try to keep leader and line away from the fish's area, work the fly slower than before, keep the line firmly tight, and be ready for a jolting hit. If the trout doesn't return on a second cast, or on several subsequent casts, leave him, mark the spot for a try later, and fish on.

Skidding a streamer fly across the surface, especially Muddler patterns, is a deadly technique. In late season when grasshoppers are in the border meadows and blown into streams, a greased Muddler is devastating. The same technique can be used with bucktail streamers and other somewhat buoyant patterns. Their winging should be well greased with a Mucilin or silicone flotant, and tying a riffling hitch (also called the Portland Creek Hitch; see Chapter 6) behind the fly head is further insurance that the streamer will fish the surface film.

Some fishermen tend to be sloppy in casting streamers, but an effort should be made to present these flies as delicately as we might a dry fly. Don't be a "down" caster with streamers; instead, throw the fly to ten o'clock, check the cast at nine o'clock, and let the line, leader, and fly settle flat to the surface.

Always fish the near water first, and in a good hole—one likely to contain several fish—try to remove the first few fish taken with as little disturbance as possible. At dusk trout can be anywhere in a pool, and they frequently drop to the tails of pools to feed before and after dark. Fish such areas carefully, and expect big trout. I was on the Yellowstone one evening with Charley Waterman, Joe Brooks, and Gurney Godfrey, and Joe and Gurney went to the head of a long, deep pool, while Charley led me down to the tail. I had a 3-inch-long streamer on, and Charley directed me to cast to the far bank, and work the fly right across the tail of the pool. Charley watched as I followed his instructions. On the second cast I had a jolting strike and a 24-inch brown flipped into the air. The fly fell

out. I cast again, and had a 3-pounder on, then lost it. Another cast, another large fish—lost. I checked the streamer hook, saw it was okay, and put it out there again. It was nearly full dark now, and a fish hit that yanked my rod tip right to the water. I landed that one, and killed it. That evening at our motel in Livingston I lay the trout lengthwise on a newspaper, and it was almost as long as the paper— a fine, heavily built 4-pounder. What made that evening's fishing interesting is that neither Gurney nor Joe found a decent trout at the head of the pool. The big ones just were not there or they would have caught them.

I know a fisherman who fishes two and three streamers on a leader, and this may be something you'll want to try. He uses a heavy fly on the point and lighter, smaller ones as droppers. The heavier point fly helps straighten the leader on the cast.

Avoid the tendency to cast too far in big rivers. The shorter the line, the better you can work the fly, and the more trout you will hook.

Streamers weighted with lead or copper wire on the hook shanks are useful, but so are the various types of sinking lines. Normally a sinking-tip line is adequate to get your streamer down to pay dirt, but there'll be times when heavy, full-sinking lines may be necessary.

17

Hooking, Playing, and Landing Fish with a Fly Rod

MOST experienced anglers and guides agree that fully eighty percent of fish hooked and lost are lost because of human error. Most of the time the fisherman doesn't set his hook, doesn't handle his tackle correctly, or otherwise plays the fish wrong. Of course, sometimes fish are lost because a mangrove root gets in a tarpon's way, a boat cuts across a fly line, or a bass tangles in pencil reeds.

SINKING THE HOOK

We can't hope to land any fish—bluegills to blue marlin—unless we set the hooks properly. Sinking the hook in a striking fish is partly your job, partly the job of your rod. You can't hook fish with a rod that has an action like wet spaghetti.

It takes a solid jerk to sink hooks past the barb. The larger the fish and the larger the hook, the stronger the yank needed. Use a rod with enough backbone that it will drive hooks into fish when you pull back and upward sharp and hard. This is

especially important with hard-to-hook species such as tarpon and muskies.

Often speed in striking is essential. Many skilled anglers set fly rod poppers so fast and hard that if a bass misses, the bug comes sailing back through the air. In fishing dry flies for trout, all we normally need do is tighten up and the barb goes home. But if you're bouncing dries on fast water and a trout takes, set the hook fast.

Some fish are slow, deliberate hitters, so your strike should be delayed. When an Atlantic salmon sucks in a dry fly you can get your barb in the corner of his mouth by letting him turn after the rise, and hook himself on a tight line.

On the other hand, the surest way to lose bonefish is to be anxious and set the hook when you see the fish clobber your fly. Bonefish have pebbly growths on the top of their tongues and the roof of their mouths, so if you try to sink your fly as soon as a bonefish grabs it, the hook point may hit these hard growths, and you will not hook the fish.

Author plays a fly-hooked dolphin at Pinas Bay, Panama. . . .

. . . and moments later gaffs the fish to be presented to the camp cook. Dolphin are delicious eating.

FIGHTING THE FISH

Most fishermen have little understanding of how to play, or fight, fish. They simply grunt, reel, and hope—turning what should be a well-controlled, exciting scrap into a tug-of-war.

A sportsman *fights* a fish. He doesn't bull it, but he doesn't baby it either. A hooked fish should be worked steadily, without putting undue strain on the tackle. Certainly a fish should be "played out" when we try to land it, but we shouldn't be so afraid of losing a fish that we don't give it something to pull against. In my own experience, I've found that I lose far fewer fish when I reach the stage where I *don't care* whether or not I land a hooked fish.

In fighting a decent fish, put the rod butt against your middle while you pump-and-reel. Pumping and reeling is standard technique for fighting strong fish. To pump a fish, lower the rod tip, reeling fast to keep a tight line, then pull up smoothly, repeating the process.

Drag

The average angler has very little understanding of fly reel drags and how to set them, and how to employ them in playing fish correctly. If we are messing with blue-gills in a farm pond, the drag is not important; but if we are messing with bonefish or tarpon on some distant flat, the drag is *damn* important.

Generally speaking, with fly reels we need a "striking drag" and a "playing drag." I'm talking, of course, of strong fish.

With a decent fish, let's say a tarpon, we want enough resistance against our reel's drag that the fish will be solidly hooked when he strikes. Then we want to reduce the drag so he will fight against sufficient tension but not pop the leader.

Fish that make long, fast, hard runs should be played on light drags once they are hooked. Line creates drag in the water, and naturally the more line out the more drag. Too, the heavier the line the greater the drag. A fly line sawing through the water, for example, creates immense drag, so when a fish has taken out a lot of your fly line you should reduce your reel's drag to almost zero.

There are times, naturally, when an angler is forced to screw down on his fly reel's drag to hold a fish up tight. If you've hooked a big bass in flooded timber there's nothing to do but tighten up, hang on, and hope.

Before the first cast is made, a fly reel's drag should be adjusted to provide the correct amount of resistance so that a striking fish can be hooked. Thereafter, throughout the fight the angler should make whatever alterations in drag are dictated according to conditions. In the course of playing a hooked fish many skilled anglers will adjust their fly reel's drag half-a-dozen times or so.

Saltwater fishermen know the importance of correct drag, because they often fight tough fish, but fly reel drag can be vitally important in freshwater fishing, too.

The fly-rodder who tightens a drag down too much—whether in saltwater or freshwater fishing—is going to break off one fish after another.

Grip

Always let your fly rod do the work. It's built for it. A fly rod works best when it is held nearly vertical. Never point your fly rod at a fish to play him from the reel.

Many fly fishermen have trouble with big fish because they have a single handhold on the rod. It's impossible to exert maximum pressure with a fly rod by using a one-hand hold. For run-of-the-pond freshwater fish this doesn't matter. But take your fly outfit to salty water, where fish come big and tough, and you'll learn quickly that freshwater rod-handling techniques don't work.

Most fly-rodders tying into strong fish—such as the various crevalle, amberjack, or Bermuda chub—grip the rod with two hands. This is the proper hold while a fish is running, but when you've got him coming your way, or when you want to exert pressure to turn him, lay one hand across the rod butt and push down, at the same time pulling up with the rod grip hand. This system for pumping with a fly rod isn't tiring, it doesn't require much strength, and your "push and pull" is on a short axis so that you get maximum leverage.

Slack

A fish that's hooked right will not escape in open water if you give him slack, but a fish getting slack near roots or stumps may break off. Always keep a tight line to have constant pressure on a hooked fish.

When fish leap, like this husky northern pike, the angler should lower the rod swiftly to put slack in the line so the fish won't fall on a taut leader.

Slack line should be given deliberately when fly-hooked fish jump. The reason for this is that a leaping fish, falling back on a tight leader, can break the leader or rip the hooks out.

When you start fishing, be sure there's nothing in the boat that may catch your line. Don't let ropes drag in the water. If you're anchored and hook a good fish, haul in the anchor. The fish may run around the anchor line.

LANDING THE FISH

Sighting a boat usually spooks a fish into a last-ditch run, so be ready for it. Let him go if he wants, being sure not to "horse" him. A "green" fish is hard to boat, and you'd probably injure it during handling—which is no good when you want to release it. If a hooked fish dives under the boat, let out line, move to the bow, and work the line around so that the boat no longer is between you and the fish.

A landing net isn't needed for most freshwater fish. When a fish is played out he'll come in on his side, so tired all you have to do is pick him out. Too many guides and fishermen chase after fish with their landing nets, making long sweeps—and get only misses. Startled by a flashing net, many a fish makes a last-ditch dash against the short, tight line and breaks off. The antics of some fishermen trying to net fish would be comical if they weren't so sad.

The correct way to net a fish is to play it out, then to lower the net into the water, hold it motionless, and lead the fish into the net *head first*. Handled properly, a hooked fish will actually swim into a net.

When preparing to land a fish, leave a little more than a rod's length of line out, and ease the fish to you. If he doesn't come easily you haven't worn him down. When he tires bring him toward you, and if it's a species with no sharp teeth you can put a thumb in his mouth and other fingers under his chin. Push down and in on his jaw, temporarily paralyzing the fish, swing him aboard, and then you can release him unharmed.

Northern pike, muskies, walleyes, and other toothy species can be landed easily by grasping them from above just behind the gill covers. Some fishermen grab northerns with a thumb-and-forefinger grip in the fish's eye-sockets. This hold isn't necessary, is not as good as a behind-the-gill plates grip, and should never be used if the fish is to be released, as it can damage his eyes.

A small hand gaff (with no barb) is useful in landing toothy fish such as muskies and barracuda. But never gaff a fish to be released anywhere in the body or top of the head. Such gaffing can kill a fish. Fish to be released should be gaffed only in the lower jaw.

Regardless of how skillfully we play fish, we're going to lose some. It's part of the game.

18

On the Stream

THE beginning trout fisherman often is a well-dressed, well-equipped, but totally confused angler. He's read a lot of the books and talked to a lot of trout fishermen, but has spent very little actual time on the stream. He's rigged his rod and pulled on his boots and he's ready and eager to go—but as he stands there, alone, looking at the stream, he has no idea whether to fish upstream or down, or to begin with dry flies or wets, streamers or nymphs.

The experienced trout fisherman may want to skim through or pass this chapter, but an attempt must be made here to get the beginning trout fisherman past the novice stage as quickly as possible—and on his way down the rough, long road to expert status.

SAFETY

There's one thing all beginning trout fishermen have in common: a quick and early plunge into the brook. No wading fisherman is going to fish many years without

going in over his boot tops, or without taking a tumble. And being up-dumped in trout water is not an activity peculiar to neophytes. It happens to the seasoned veteran as well.

I've fished trout streams and rivers all of my life, and other than the usual slight trips and stumbles I had never fallen in or had a really bad experience—until the summer of 1976. Prior to that the wettest I'd ever gotten was when I stepped into slow but shoulder-deep water on Argentina's Traful River. The water was so clear I thought it was only 3 or 4 feet deep, but when I stepped off the grassy bank I went in over my chest-high waders and right to my armpits.

The summer-of-'76 incident, on Montana's Beaverhead River, was considerably different, and it could have cost my life. I'll relate what happened there in some detail, in the hope that my experience—in the reading—will become yours, and encourage you to use the utmost caution *always* when wading.

I was alone, and having set up my rod

(an Orvis graphite, with Orvis CFO reel, total value about $300), I donned waders and a fishing vest. Like most stream fishermen I always strap a heavy belt around my waist, outside the chest-high waders. Such a belt makes wearing chest-highs more comfortable, but more important, a belt is a safety factor. Should you take a dunking, the belt will keep water from swiftly filling the waders and pulling you down.

The buckle on my belt broke, though, while I was trying to strap it on. I had no spare belt, so started upstream without one on. I casually noted that the Beaverhead seemed a foot or two higher than the previous day, when Al McClane, Jim Poulas, and I had fished there. I was mentally preoccupied, so didn't study the river as carefully as I should have.

I started crossing the river at a point where the three of us had crossed easily the day before. The current was extremely heavy, pulling powerfully against my legs, but I foolishly did not realize I was in a bad situation until I was ninety-five percent across the stream. I was chest-deep in the current, fully committed, and could not turn back.

With only about 6 feet to go to reach the brush-lined bank in front of me, I tried to fight off panic and to arouse confident strength. The pull of the river against my legs and lower torso was awesome. Deep and justifiable fear swept over me. I lifted my right foot to take a step forward. Instantly the current washed my right leg upward and tore my left leg from under me.

Flipped horizontally in the water by the surging current, I dropped the fly rod and fought with all my strength to reach the bank, trying to get close enough to seize overhanging limbs. Ice-cold water washed into my waders and the shock was intense. I cried out, involuntarily, and struggled furiously to keep my head up. The waders filled instantly and I was unable to lift or move my legs, which felt like lead.

The water was only about 5 feet deep, but I couldn't stand in the violent current and the waders were pulling me down. I'm not ashamed to admit that I felt terror.

The current rushed me downstream about 20 yards, then rolled me closer to the bank, where the Beaverhead turned slightly. I clawed frantically at overhanging limbs and brush, and left a brush-torn trail of broken limbs and snags—as though a tiger had clawed the bank. The force of the current held me horizontal at the surface, but the weight of my legs, so heavy that I couldn't move them, was pulling me under. Finally I gripped a couple of green boughs that didn't break, and held on as though my life depended upon it—which it probably did.

I started pulling and lifting myself from the river, rolling onto supporting limbs and brush that hung over an undercut bank, finally getting one leg onto the bank, and then the other. I lay heaving and panting on the bank, bringing up water I'd swallowed, and fought to regain some calmness. Half the Beaverhead River rolled out of my waders.

After a long rest with my clothes drying in the bright Montana sun, I hiked to my car, thoroughly shaken. I was minus an expensive fly outfit, but I couldn't have cared less about it.

I nearly drowned in the Beaverhead because of carelessness, and because my judgment of the river's current had been

A nice brace of brown trout from Maryland's Big Savage River, caught through careful stalking and saved for the fry pan.

less than sound. The river had, indeed, come up a couple of feet from the day before because they'd let irrigation water through from an upriver dam. If my mind had not been elsewhere when I started into the river I likely would have noticed the higher level and stronger currents—but I didn't.

I think the incident shows that no matter how much experience a fisherman has, he still can make mistakes—sometimes with serious consequences. Every season trout fishermen wearing waders drown. You can be the best wade fisherman alive, be young and strong and a top swimmer, but it all means nothing when river current rolls your feet from under you and your waders fill. A trout fisherman normally has not only his waders to fight, but also when dunked must usually free himself of a jacket or vest, perhaps a sweater, and the wader suspenders. All that must be accomplished while being bowled over and over in the current, in icy water, and while fighting shock under panic conditions.

I hope to impress upon you the importance when wading of always using the utmost caution, and of *being alert*. Never permit yourself to be lulled into a feeling of overconfidence. That is the first step toward what might prove to be tragedy.

An important safety rule to follow when wading with chest-high waders is to *always* wear a strong, wide belt. If ever again I'm forced to fish in chest-high waders without a belt, I will not wade deeper than my knees.

Many different kinds of special flotation belts are available, as are certain fishing vests that can be swiftly inflated by the wearer in the event he takes a plunge. They are good investments.

A wading staff—you could buy one of the fold-up kinds or make one yourself—is helpful in keeping your feet when negotiating strong current. Even in comparatively shallow, slow-moving water a staff is helpful when streambed rocks are as slippery as greased bowling balls.

Felt-soled boots, or ones with some sort of built-in cleats, are an aid in keeping your footing. Special chains, cleats, or cleated "shoes" that pull over boot feet also are good.

In swift water it is wise not to wade deeper than the knees; in slow water not deeper than the thighs. Approach all unfamiliar areas with utmost caution, feeling ahead with the wading staff, and take short steps, planting one foot firmly before lifting the other. Keep checking the water immediately in front of you, as well as making more complete observations of the general water situation around you. When in doubt, never hesitate about going on; simply turn around and *go back*. Don't take chances. An extra trout isn't worth it.

DECIDING HOW TO FISH A STREAM

The beginning trout fisherman, in planning to fish a specific stream, should get what information he can before going. Perhaps the local newspaper has an outdoor writer who is familiar with its trout fishing, or there's a tackle shop with knowledgeable clerks, or you might place a call to the area conservation officer. Best of all is to fish the stream with experienced anglers, and to learn from them.

What a trout fisherman, beginner or expert, should do on a specific stream, at a specific time, under specific conditions is something only experience can teach, but there are some time-tested basic rules that usually apply.

On opening day, streams usually are high, discolored, and cold. (Because of this many fishermen will give their attention to the smaller spring creeks.) Dry-fly fishing normally is out, since the water is too high and not clear enough and because water and air temperatures are still too cold to bring off hatches of natural insects.

Fishing a streamer fly is a good decision. A large streamer, about size 6, will be easiest for the trout to see in the dark, heavy water. And yellow is a good color under such conditions, so let's make it a size 6 Yellow Marabou. A weighted fly will be best, or we can add a BB-size split-shot lead sinker to the leader about 12 inches up from the fly. Trout in the early season, when streams are cold and turbid, lie close to bottom, so we want our fly to get down there, too. (A sinking fly line might be used to avoid lead shot.)

Fishing downstream, casting the Marabou across and downstream at about a forty-five-degree angle, is the way we'll start. We'll fish it this way because the current will keep our fly line taut, help to give the fly "action," and also make it easier to hook fish. On each cast there will be a point at which the line will be quite bowed in the current, and the flow will then sweep the fly cross-current and well downstream from the angler. This is the moment when most trout strike a streamer. Prior to that, when the fly hits the water the angler will "activate" it by stripping a little line and twitching the rod tip, making the fly dart along in 6- to 12-inch "swims." The attempt is to make the streamer look like a scurrying minnow.

When the fly line has straightened in the current and the streamer is directly below, it should be "fished" (jerked and twitched) upcurrent to where it can be conveniently picked up for another cast. The fisherman may change his position now, moving along downstream a few yards or so, before placing another cast. All of the water should be covered, every likely spot fished carefully. The streamer should be cast across stream to swing past that rock, close to that log, along that undercut bank—everywhere trout are likely to be holding. Trout always face into the current, and unless they are in midstream actively rising and feeding, they tend to position in or near cover.

After fishing through the first pool, deep hole, or long riffle, the angler moves on to the next. Perhaps midway through the second pool we "roll" a trout—that is, a trout sees the Marabou, chases it, catches up, then turns away and returns to its original lie. The trout, a rainbow, flashes crimson-chrome as it rolls at the fly—and only a blind man would not see it, only a dead man's heart not skip. We may fish farther on a bit, giving the located trout a "rest" before casting to it again, or we may elect

to cast back to the fish immediately. Assuming the latter is done, and no strike is forthcoming, we'll offer the trout something different—another streamer (since that's what got the trout's attention to begin with), but a different type and color. Let's say we tie on a Black Ghost, having white saddle-hackle winging, and then fish it repeatedly throughout the area where we feel the trout may be. We use different retrieves—fast then slow, short twitches then long, close to the surface then as deep as we can get. Nothing. Assuming this particular trout to be worth the effort, we may try another streamer pattern, and if that fails switch to a nymph. A couple of nymph patterns may be tried and, those also failing to raise the trout, we'll move on downstream, marking the fish mentally for another try later on.

Since it was a Yellow Marabou that first turned a fish for our questing angler, it's tied on again. More of the creek is pounded with a streamer until, at last, a 10-inch brown trout snaps at the Marabou and is impaled on the hook. Voila! Our hypothetical beginning angler's chest swells, and swells further as, sportsman that he is, he carefully releases the gold-specked little brown.

Fishing is resumed with added vigor, if not results. Shortly another angler is encountered, working his way *upstream*, and our hero naturally asks the inevitable question: "Any luck?" It turns out that the stranger, a typical and honest trout fisherman of experience, is more than willing to share the wealth. He shows our neophyte a 15-inch rainbow, and four browns 12 to 14 inches—all taken on weighted nymphs fished upstream. The expert explains that the high, discolored water has the trout right on bottom; that they won't come up very well to a fast-moving streamer, but will slide over quickly to suck in a slowly drifting nymph, which they can see well enough in the off-colored water.

More questions from our beginner, an examination of the nymph patterns that worked, a single demonstration of one cast-and-drift of a nymph by our expert, and our novice is off on an upstream nymphing binge.

He learns quickly that a nymph is best fished upstream because it then is washed deep by the current, and comes swinging down with the flow in a "natural" drift, as would a real nymph dislodged from the stream floor and caught in the curling currents. To end this imaginary first day on the stream, our beginner manages to pick up a few additional trout on his nymphs, and returns home an elated and well-hooked angler.

ADJUSTING YOUR TACTICS

Whatever the conditions, and no matter whether the fisherman be novice or expert, it is important to keep changing tactics on the stream until the winning method is found. In other words, if we start by fishing streamers downstream, and they fail, we can try working upstream with nymphs—letting them swing down with the current and bounce over the bottom. If that doesn't work we might try fishing wet flies downstream, perhaps with two or three patterns on the leader so that we give the fish a wider choice and, too, work more water with our flies on a single drift. Wet flies are best fished across-and-downstream for the same reasons streamers are—the current will bow the line, sweep the flies, etc.

In general, during the early season when streams are cold, high, and discolored we should fish larger flies in bright patterns, hoping they will be more quickly observed by the trout. We can fish streamers and wet flies down-and-across, or dredge bottom by casting nymphs upstream and letting them come down with the current.

After the spring thaw and runoff, when streams drop and clear, there still will be times when conditions include high and discolored water. These conditions may occur anytime through the season, following thunderstorms and flash floods, so we would return to the tactics used in early season.

Trout normally are sluggish and will not actively feed if water temperature is below forty to forty-five degrees. At such times the angler should fish as slowly and as thoroughly as possible, and fish his fly as slowly as he can while still maintaining lifelike action.

As the trout fisherman's season progresses according to the calendar, streams will drop and the water may become as clear as glass. The water temperature will rise, too, which will trigger hatches of natural insects, increase trout activity, and bring about frequent periods of brisk feeding. Streamer flies may still be used productively under conditions of low, clear water, but generally the smaller-size streamers are then most productive, and usually in periods of dim light (early morning, late evening, on dull days or during rainfall). Wet flies can be used, too, in the smaller, sparser sizes, and nymphs as well. What is

Here's how *not* to fish a low, clear trout stream. The fisherman is wading a small stream, spooking fish in front of him instead of casting from behind rocks, out of sight of the fish, or by kneeling or sitting on the bank.

most needed now are long, fine leaders, gentle approach to the stream, and careful, delicate presentation. Trout can see an approaching angler easily under conditions of low, clear water, and the trout that sees you is a trout you won't catch. Stomping along the stream bank is no good, either, or wading noisily and scuffing bottom—all of which will put trout down.

Low, clear water and bright days call for the utmost caution in trout fishing, and especially when fishing small streams. (Small-stream trout can be more easily frightened than those in large, heavy rivers.) When the water is low and air-

clear, the wise fisherman uses crouch, creep, and crawl tactics.

Insect hatches call for dry-fly fishing, but this doesn't mean dries will not take trout unless there is a hatch. They assuredly will. The ideal, however, is to approach the stream when insects fill the air, a hatch is in progress, and every trout worth his spots is lifting to the surface and gorging himself on floating flies.

If you see insects on the water, and trout rising, catch one of the real insects and look it over. Try to match it for size, general form, and color with something from your dry-fly box. The normal technique in dry-fly fishing is to work upstream, since this positions the angler behind the trout (which faces upcurrent, and rises to pick off insects floating down with the current). Fishing upstream makes it easier in dry-fly fishing to avoid drag on the fly line, which occurs when the current bows the line and sweeps a fly. While such action is desirable in fishing underwater patterns, it isn't in dry-fly work. Here we want the floating fly to react naturally to each twist and turn of the current, to as nearly as possible approximate the normal drift of a real fly fallen to the surface.

Another situation that often befuddles beginners is how to fish fast water, and how to fish slow. You needn't be so careful in approaching fast water, since trout will not be able to detect your presence as readily as when in shallow, clear, slow-moving pools. They also cannot see a fly as readily, so larger flies should be used, and they should be fished slowly, to give the trout ample time to see, chase, catch, and hit the fly.

In fishing slow water, just about the

opposite would be true. We must play the sneak thief, the wily fox, in slipping up to a thin, transparent pool. Long casts with a fine leader, soft presentation, smaller flies, and faster retrieves are called for. Trout are less likely to detect that a fly is fraudulent in the smaller sizes, and they don't have much time to look it over on a quick, jerky retrieve.

When fishing dry flies in heavy, fast water or foamy riffles, use large sizes and cast and float them repeatedly. Large deer-hair patterns, such as the Irresistible, size 6 to 10, or the Wulff flies, are good choices.

19

Techniques for Low-Water Trout

THE flat surface of the river reflected the summer sun like a mirror. And the water was so shallow and clear this bright August afternoon that I had the sensation of wading through air. I waddled heavily over to the bank, climbed out, and deposited myself in the shade of a hemlock. As I munched a sandwich and mused over the solitude one reaps along even popular trout streams in midsummer, a gent built like an ox came creeping around the bend and began peering cautiously into my pool.

For a long time he stood motionless, stiff as a statue; then he pussyfooted lightly along the shoulder of the river, all the while bent over, craned and stretching, staring into the shadows that blotted the deep side of the pool. Finally, kneeling *in the water,* he stripped line from his reel and looped out an easy, effortless cast. His technique lacked nothing. I had the feeling of watching a rogue elephant doing a ballet at a water hole.

I was so interested that I mentally projected my hand around his rod grip, and when the strike came I reacted by jerking

my hand upward and involuntarily flipped my sandwich into the bushes behind me. Ox's fish split the surface, skidding on his tail, then bolted downstream. Still kneeling, Ox played the trout until it could barely swim upright; then he swooped it close, eased the hook out, and watched it swim away.

Again the big guy's fly was in the air, driven by a wrist that had authoritative grace and power. Again the floating tip of his line twitched. And again a trout was racing the length of the pool, the fly line sawing the water. He released that one too, and after a few more probing casts moved on upstream. Before he disappeared around the next bend I saw him catch and release a third trout.

None of this would have been particularly unusual, except the gent I'd spied on was the only angler I saw that day with fish, and that stretch of Big Savage River above Avilton, Maryland, isn't known for producing many trout in August.

Nearly everyone catches fish during the first few weeks of trout season. We are all familiar with the opening-day crowd and the opening-week crowd, which still exist in many areas although some states now have year-round trout fishing. But as soon as stream levels drop and the water clears, some anglers find the fishing so difficult they figure the rivers are "fished out." A lot of trout fishermen, notably those in the east, actually quit trout fishing by the end of May and turn to bass or other fishing.

There is no need to forgo trout for warm-water species in midsummer. All that is really necessary is to sharpen your technique, to polish your good habits and shelve the bad. It's a fact that skilled trout fishermen eagerly await the sparkling days of June, when water conditions are generally good and hatches frequent, but they are as active and enthusiastic about their trout fishing in July, August, and September. The serious trout fisherman doesn't prefer spring fishing because streams are usually high and discolored, the water too cold, insects scarce, and fish are relatively inactive. But later on the streams drop and clear, the trout move, hatches occur daily, and that opening crowd of fishermen has disappeared.

Careful approach and long, fine leaders are needed to take wily brown trout in low, clear water.

KEEPING LOW, KEEPING QUIET

The reasons for the success of Mr. Ox that August day on the Savage were many. First, he "cased" each spot before he fished it— trying first of all to see fish in the water. A trout seen is normally a trout caught. If you can discover a holding trout before it discovers you, the presentation and drift or float of your fly is most likely to be perfect. In low, clear water trout are hypersensitive—totally attuned to the approach and presence of an angler, to the slap of a hard, bad cast, and to the improper, unnatural movements of a fly.

Ox did not blunder up to the pool, spooking fish ahead of him. Instead, he walked lightly, bending low, and fished from a kneeling position to avoid being seen by the trout. When streams are discolored in spring, or are high following thaws or rain, a careful approach may not be too vital to success, but when your pet stream is running clear as a martini, the fish will dive for cover if you walk boldly up the bank or wade clumsily along the edge. We should be mindful of how we approach promising water all season long, but careful approach is absolutely essential to success during conditions of low, clear water. Keep

Under conditions of low, ultraclear water in midsummer or early fall, often night fishing is the way to go.

well back from the stream when fishing the smaller creeks, and creep and crawl when you must to keep from scaring fish.

This is a good place to point out that one of the worst breaches of angling etiquette is for one fisherman to approach a stretch of water badly when it is being worked by another. For illustration, let's say you are fishing downstream on a small stream, and a couple of fishermen are walking upstream on the bank, close to the water's edge. If they are knowledgeable anglers, and sportsmen, they will leave the stream edge and circle around behind you—knowing that if they continued following the creek they'd spook trout you'd hoped to catch.

Many anglers hide behind trees, stumps, and boulders when fishing low, clear water, but while those are beneficial styles it is more important to keep low. A trout cannot see you very well if your nose is down on the gravel at streamside. And casting should be done from this low position, too. It does no good to creep up to a spot, then stand erect and start waving a rod around. The best way is to move into a casting position keeping as low as practical, to remain low while casting, and when possible to cast with the rod held horizontal to the water. I do not mean to overwork this low-and-out-of-sight business, but it is vitally important to your success. Stated simply, the trout that sees you is a trout you won't catch.

Obviously in low, clear water we will use a leader as long and fine in the tippet as we can comfortably control and handle, in keeping with the sizes and kinds of flies being used and the conformation of the stream.

The leader tippet should be considerably longer for this fishing, with a 4-foot tip not impractical. And while heavy butts are normally desired in leaders for most fly fishing, you may find it helpful to scale down the diameter of the strand connecting to the fly line. The fly line, too, should be as light as possible for situations of low, bright water and nervous fish.

Because a gentle presentation of the fly is so important, we should eliminate long casts as much as possible. It is better to work slowly into a good position than to cast a long line from far off. I know countless fly fishermen who can easily handle 60 to 70 feet of fly line, but when streams are down and translucent, they sneak around and take their fish on casts of less than 25 feet. For the average angler, a cast longer than that usually ends up hitting the water hard. Next to actually knowing you're there—by seeing you—nothing flushes a trout faster than the slap of a long line.

Another important reason for avoiding long casts is that following a short cast you can raise your rod tip quickly and keep most of the line and some of the leader off the water. This prevents drag and eliminates the need to mend line. Your fly will fish nicely and be much more of a temptation to low-water fish that are shy of line and leader. After every cast, try to lift as much of the line off the water as possible.

FLIES FOR LATE SEASON AND LOW WATER

One afternoon John Marsman, vice president of Heddon Tackle Company, and I stopped at a bridge over Blaine Spring Creek in Montana. It was September, the water was hardly a foot deep in the deep areas, and it was as translucent as fine crystal. Looking down on the upstream side of the bridge, we quickly spotted half a dozen trout holding in the little winding runs of current. One brown of about 15 inches was nosed in behind a rock; most of the other trout were lined up along the borders of watercress. Checking the downstream side, we saw more fish, each placed strategically in the flow. Once in a while a trout would come up and ring the surface.

"They're taking something," John observed. "I wonder what."

"Whatever it is, it's small," I said. "Why don't you go down and try them with a midge nymph?" Marsman ties about the finest nymphs I've ever seen by an ama-

teur. He went down and started in toward the stream. Fifty feet back from the water, on the upstream side of the bridge from where I watched everything, John stopped and lengthened his fine leader tip (6X), then wrapped on a size 20 Olive Midge Nymph. He moved to within 30 feet of the stream, then stopped and watched. He picked out the trout he wanted and moved closer, staying very low, and quartering a little upcurrent from the fish. The trout was fanning in the shadowy edge of a bed of watercress, which was washed lightly by the current, the water a foot deep. John dropped to his knees and crawled closer. Staying about 10 feet back from the water's edge, John stripped line from his reel and made some false casts upriver, more over the bank than over the water. When he had 15 feet of line out, counting his leader, he made a rolling, sideways presentation of the line that dropped the nymph some 10 feet above the trout and 5 feet beyond. John had cast so that his rod was low, and there was no casting motion the fish could see. Now he quickly lifted his rod tip and raised almost all the line from the water as the current swung the nymph down and around to the trout. When the fly was 2 feet from the fish John had all the line off the water and all but about a foot of the leader. The trout took with absolute confidence, no inspection, no hesitation whatever—just straight up and *glump!* It was as nice a piece of low, clear-water trout work as can be done.

The midge nymphs are like a secret weapon for late-season trouting in low, clear water. While many anglers will whip dry flies around simply because it is summer and there are bugs, some of the craftier types will wash weighted nymphs under rocks and brush where all the trout go to keep from getting sunstroke, and drift their midges in the surface film, as well.

It must be understood that the main, large hatches of flies normally are over in the spring and early summer. So seldom will there be anything more deadly for the period of low, clear water than a properly selected nymph.

At various times through the late summer and fall season, trout go on midging binges, taking midge flies or midge nymphs. Whichever, there is no way to catch them without offering a reasonable artificial counterpart of the natural fly.

There is a difference between the rise forms when trout are taking midge floaters or sunken midge nymphs. When a trout snaps a floating midge, a ring is formed on the surface which spreads into a series of concentric circles that melt away with the current. But trout taking midge nymphs work differently. There may be only a swelling bulge near the surface, the water humping up if the nymphs are in the surface film or close to it, or you may see the fish's sides flash silver as they turn left, then right, then left again, sipping in nymph after nymph.

Streams have four layers of water, two of which are of real importance to the trout fisherman. The bottom layer of water is the slowest-moving, due partly to the friction caused by the streambed. The second layer is the fastest, and the third layer, at the surface, is somewhat slower than the second. The fourth layer is the meniscus— the surface film mentioned earlier.

The fast-moving second layer is the level carrying most drowned insects and

When streams are running low and clear, twilight can be the most productive time of day.

washing nymphs. This is chiefly the area where your phony nymph will be most successful in low, clear water and when trout are feeding normally. Other times—and this is especially true of the late-season period— a small nymph allowed to float in the surface film is your best tactic. Dry flies with the hackles snipped off sometimes work nearly as well, right along with the midge nymphs.

Because of contact with the air, all water gets a surface film. This is what supports our dry flies. This is what enables insects to float long enough to deposit their eggs. This is what keeps a fly line up.

I can think of few other facets of fly fishing requiring more skill or providing more fun than floating nymphs in the surface film under conditions of low, clear water and bright sun. It is precision fishing. Normally you can't see your fly, so you must exercise that sixth sense (discussed in

Dry flies frequently are the most productive patterns when streams are low and clear.

Chapter 15) in striking your fish. Other times, of course, the trout will be seen readily—particularly if you're fishing a proper short line—as it comes to the top.

The Strawman Nymph is a good pattern for this type of fishing. I work it in short jerks to give the fly the quick, trembly twitchings of the natural insect in the pupal shuck coming up to hatch. Allow the nymph to settle, then rise, then drift 4 or 5 inches—then rise again, pulsating swiftly, in imitation of the fast-swimming caddis nymphs.

Minute flies in sizes 18 to 22, having mere wisps of hackle fibers at the hook-eye and bodies of raffia, peacock herl, stripped peacock, moose mane, or quill, and tied without tails, account for many low, clear-water trout when worked in the surface film.

Black Gnat Midge dry flies are something special for late-season fishing. At one time I had dozens of them made by the Lyon and Coulson tyers, but strong fish and chiseling friends gradually depleted the supply. I've nursed what remains and each season they put low-water fish on the line for me that refused other patterns.

Large spiders and variants excel as low, clear-water flies. When presented to skittery trout with care, and lightly activated on the water, surface-dancing spiders can break up every trout in a pool. The animated dry fly gets attention from midsummer trout that will ignore the same fly allowed to drift naturally.

Very small "midget" streamers sometimes do well in late-summer fishing. Ones with very fine hackle winging, tied on 3X long size 10 or 12 hooks, can draw a lot of trout from under the banks and up from the rocks. A friend of mine designed a couple of streamers he calls "Simple Brown" and "Simple Black." They have no body or tail, only hackle winging and some Palmer-style hackle at the hook-eye. They've proved to be superior low-water streamers.

20
Fishing Bass Bugs

I T IS a warm summer evening on Tit-willow Pond. The single water-skier the lake supports has long since headed for dock, and the kids who had been swimming off Walnut Point now are chowing down.

A lone angler slowly sculls a leaky skiff along one shore. Periodically he drops the paddle, picks up a fly rod, and deftly casts a popping bug to the brushy shore. He works carefully around tangled logs, beneath overhanging limbs, along pencil reeds, and into lily-pad pockets.

A bobwhite quail whistles from a honeysuckle patch, and a distant string of crows caw excitedly, flying to roost. A stinkpot turtle slides off a log and slips into the water as the fly-rodder's bug splats to the surface nearby. The angler lifts slack from the line and rests the bug momentarily. Tense as a heron ogling a minnow nibbling at one of its black, stilted legs, the fisherman raises the rod tip and pops the bug lightly. Eyes never leaving the floating cork, he twitches it again. There's a swirl, the bug disappears, the angler tightens line

swiftly, and a 3-pound bass comes up and out, standing on his fan-shaped tail, mouth agape, head shaking, the little cork bug flapping from his jaw.

The angler skillfully turns the bass when it attempts to dive under the log, and as skillfully lowers his rod and gives slack line when the bass jumps a second time. A faint smile crosses the man's face as he backpaddles the weathered skiff to more open water with one hand, still grasping the rod, controlling the line, and playing the fish with the other. Soon the bass is at the boat. Our angler reaches, lifts him out by the lower jaw, carefully removes the hook, and returns the fish unharmed to Titwillow Pond.

We can't be sure who's responsible for this particular brand of angling delight, but there is no denying that bass-bug fishing is close to the pinnacle of fly-rodding pleasure. It offers certain enjoyment and gratification not found in any other form of fly fishing.

The absolute origin of the fly-rod bug is lost in the yesterdays of time, but most angling historians credit a Tennessean, Ernest H. Peckinpaugh, of Chattanooga, with creating the first bass bug. Peckinpaugh, who died in 1947, engineered his first bugs around 1905. He built them on double hooks because he found it easier to secure the bug's cork bodies to double rather than single hooks.

Origins and old traditions aside, perhaps what is most important is that both largemouth and smallmouth black bass like nothing better than to tip back on their caudal fins and rise to the surface, sweeping it clean of insects, bugs, wounded minnows, mice, and so forth. Even though the greater part of a bass's menu consists of underwater life, he's happiest when feeding at the surface. So it is that more bass are taken on surface plugs, including fly-rod floating bugs, than on any other lure.

Surface lures seem especially designed for bass, particularly largemouths. Nothing raises the ire of shallow-water bass more than fussing, sputtering fly-rod bugs. I'm convinced there is no deadlier system for taking bass than fly fishing with popping or similar bugs *when the fish are in the shallows*. I've fished with many anglers who were devout spin casters and plug fishermen, but I've never known one who didn't take up bass-bug fishing after seeing poppers in action on days when the fish were shallow. Naturally no surface lure is very effective when bass are deep, but when they're close enough to the top to see a floating bug they'll go for it.

Unfortunately, most of the time bass are very deep, and really effective bugging is ruled out. But on most waters bass usually visit the shallows a couple of times a day; they're plentiful in the shallows during the

A nice bug-hooked bass rockets out of a southern Wisconsin pond. Fly-rod bugs are deadly on bass in shallow water.

spring spawning period; they move shallow for prolonged periods often in the fall; and in some places bass are shallow all the time simply because there is no deep water. So both largemouth and smallmouth bass are in water less than 12 feet deep enough of the time to make bugging very productive.

Probably it is the small size of bugs that makes them so appealing to bass. Bugs hit the water with a gentle, lifelike *splat* instead of the loud, fish-scaring *plunk* of most oversized, heavy plugs. A fly-rod bug acts *natural* on the water, much like a real locust or grasshopper. And because they are light, bugs behave realistically on the water.

A largemouth comes out of lily pads to close in on a popper.

Each time you twitch or pop a bug a stream of bubbles filters down into the water, then curves to the surface again. This bubble trail draws fish, too, causes them to investigate, and helps make them strike.

Many fishermen try bass bugging briefly, then give it up as a bad job because of casting difficulties. Fishing bass bugs is the most difficult form of fly casting. Because of the big wind-resistant bugs used, what amounts to a minor fault in ordinary fly casting becomes a major problem when bugging. Each error in casting form or timing is magnified when casting popping bugs.

So the would-be bass-bug fisherman must first take the time to develop his casting skills. It is not necessary to be a tournament caster to take bass on bugs, but more bass are taken at ranges of 40 to 60 feet than on casts dropping within 20 feet of the boat. And if you can't cast well, bugging will tire you quickly. Master the double-line haul (explained in Chapter 8), and you'll never feel fatigue no matter how long you fish bugs, no matter what the wind conditions or the distance of your casts. The inept caster, on the other hand, after only an hour or two of sawing his fly line through the air, will be completely bushed and have to quit bugging.

TACKLE FOR BASS-BUG FISHING

Most starting bass-bug fishermen underarm themselves, choosing equipment so poor that bugging is impossible with it. A fly outfit that is just right for small-stream trout fishing simply won't do for bass bugging. It is not necessary to fish with the biggest fly rod you can find, but you need a rod and matching line sufficiently powerful to handle bugs well. Rods 8 to 9½ feet long, weighing 4 to 6½ ounces, and taking WF-8-F or WF-9-F lines are preferred. For years I used an 8½-foot, 5-ounce bamboo rod with great satisfaction. Then I went to a 6-ounce bamboo stick 9½ feet long, but eventually decided it had far too much authority for bass fishing. I finally settled on a 9-foot, 5-ounce glass rod. It takes a short-bellied WF-9-F line, has a fast tip action that helps put line out quickly, and a slow power reserve in its butt section that makes casts of 100 feet possible with only one false cast or, if enough line is on the water, no false cast at all.

Another of my favorite bugging rods today is a 9-foot graphite taking a WF-9-F line. Not only is the graphite rod lighter than glass, but it has a smooth, pleasing action. I use an 8-foot glass rod often, too, in bugging. It takes a WF-8-F line. I use it chiefly for what I consider "light" bugging—that is, fishing small ponds or river fishing for smallmouths, or when using somewhat smaller bugs than usual. The lighter outfit will throw a bug a long way and handle any size bass, and it's fun to use.

Assuming you have the right rod and matching line (always use a floating, weight-forward line, since a weight-forward line casts bugs best), let's consider the reel and leaders.

A quality single-action reel should be used, and it ought to be large enough to readily accept your size 8 or 9 weight-forward line, as well as sufficient backing so that the fly line is not spooled in tight turns on the reel. Most important, the reel should be so designed that its spool can be quickly removed. Buy an extra spool, maybe even two, and mount them with extra lines. This way in the course of a day's bass bugging, when one line starts to sink you can snap that spool and line out of the reel and replace it with a second spool holding a fresh, dry line.

Most weight-forward, or three-diameter, lines cast bugs a little better if some of the forward taper of the line is cut back. Depending on the make of line, I usually cut from 1 to 2 feet off the front end. The last several feet of a weight-forward line is level, not tapered line. By cutting off some of that level section of line, you get the belly taper closer up front, and this casts and turns a bug over better.

I know some bass-bug fishermen who use level lines, rather than weight-forward lines, because level lines float better. Almost all of their casting, however, is at ranges under 40 feet. There's nothing wrong with using a level line if you can do a satisfactory job of casting bugs with it.

Regardless of the make or taper of fly line, keep it clean by wiping with flotant or cleaner provided by the manufacturer. Use a clean dry cloth to wipe off excess cleaner. An ungreased dirty line takes on more water than a clean one, and it will start sinking faster.

Leaders can be dispensed with quickly (Chapter 5). We must stress, though, that the leader has to be correctly tapered, with a good heavy butt and then properly graduated sections, or good casting with a heavy, wind-resistant bug will be difficult. Always use a tapered leader. Mine range from 9 to 15 feet, depending on the clarity of the water. Tapers are altered somewhat according to the size bug used and wind conditions. The tippet size, or test, will vary according to bug weight or its resistance in the air, wind, average size of the bass, or whether fishing reasonably open water or water infested with weeds, stumps, and snags.

BASS BUGS

Bass bugs can be complicated. Doubtless the ones in your box are all little bass killers, but not five percent of the commercial bugs available today are worth the space they take up in the local tackle shop. You're better off if you make your own.

Bug bodies are made of cork, balsa wood, cedar, Styrofoam, deer hair, or hollow plastic. The best bugs are made of cork, not balsa. Balsa is soft and will break from around the hook before you land many bass, and hooks turn more easily in balsa bodies than they do in cork. I described some of my favorite bugs and how to fish them in Chapter 11, and you may want to review that portion of the chapter. The bugs mentioned are the McNally Frog, Bullet Bug, Bluegill Bug, Powder Puff, and Marm Minnow.

The most important thing to look for in a bass bug is a quality hook. You shouldn't be able to straighten it by bending with your fingers. The shank should be extra long, and there should be good spacing, or "bite," between the hook bend and the bug body. If the hook isn't long enough, and lacks bite, a lot of bass that strike won't be hooked. Hook sizes 1/0 and 2/0 will serve for most bass bugging.

Some commercially made bugs have dished-out faces, or cupped faces. Such bugs pop very well, but because of the dished-out face they can be very difficult to pick up, especially on a long line. The dished-out face can catch the surface water and cause the bug to dive. A bug with a flat face, or one sloping slightly backward, picks up best, yet has good popping action when fished right.

The Heddon Tackle Company years ago made a plastic-bodied bug with long, flowing saddle hackles called the Wilder-Dilg Spook. The bug is no longer made, but it was a good one, so if you run into one try to con its owner out of it. Same for a hair frog designed by an old-time fly tyer, Joe Messinger. The Messinger Hair Frog was made of clipped deer hair and had two long hair legs that would kick as the bug was worked over the top.

The Muskie Hown is another deer-hair creation that takes a lot of bass. It looks somewhat like a moth, with two long hair wings, a thick, tapered body, and a bushy hair tail. The Deer Hair Mouse is a good bug, and quite a few types can be found in most tackle and fly shops. Just be sure any you buy have hooks with plenty of bite. Too many commercially made deer-hair bugs have hooks too short and too close to the body to provide decent hooking.

Except for some deer-hair bugs, or the "slider" varieties, a good bug ought to "pop" well. And it should pick up off the water easily on long casts, and not have too much hair or feathers. A lot of frilling may make a bug attractive to you, but normally it means little to a bass. Too much hackling creates excessive wind resistance and makes a bug difficult to cast.

I tend to use large bugs because I think

big bass want a big mouthful, and because the larger bugs tend to discourage bluegills and baby bass from hitting. I use the so-called saltwater or tarpon bugs a lot, especially the Skipping Bug, size 3/0, tied by pro fly tyer Bill Gallasch, 8705 Weldon Drive, Richmond, Virginia 23229.

A bug I use a great deal is a plain little popper I designed for hooking qualities, good popping, and castability. I call it simply the Standard Popper. I make them in all yellow, all white, all black, and all brown. The yellow bug, for example, has yellow saddle hackles extending about 1¹/₂ inches beyond the hook, usually tied so they splay outward in "breather" style. This way the hackles wiggle actively when the bug is worked. A couple of yellow hackles are wound Palmer-style just behind the cork body. The tapered cork body is about 1 inch long and ¹/₂ inch in diameter up front. The face slopes slightly backward, and a couple of big "eyes" are painted on either side of the bug. Hook sizes are 1/0 to 3/0, 3X long, and the hooks are mounted at a forty-five-degree angle downward to give top hooking qualities. The Standard Popper has no unnecessary frills or feathering to build up air resistance, so it can be cast far and accurately. You can drop this bug on a dragonfly's head way back there in the reeds.

Tom Loving invented the Gerbubble Bug, a zany-looking creation unknown to most fly-rodders. This bug is flat on the bottom and top, with hackles buried in slits in its sides. These side hackles add to the bug's air resistance, making it more difficult to cast than ordinary bugs, but they give it a fluttering appearance on the water. The thing looks almost alive even when sit-

This bass fell for a McNally Green Frog Popper, the author's favorite bug. The chin grip is recommended in handling bass to be released.

ting still. This is a bug that just can't be fished too slowly.

Color is comparatively unimportant in bass bugs, yet fishermen everywhere seem to prefer yellow, black, white, and brown, or combinations of those colors with red. Cork bugs with only a coat of clear lacquer often take as many fish as colored bugs.

FISHING THE BUG

How to work bugs is something learned only by experience. You can pop them too hard or too easy; some must be fished slowly, others fast. It's necessary to experiment until you find the best method for fishing each bug, and this can vary one day to the next, or what is right during a morning's fishing may be wrong that evening. Most important is to realize that you have put a dabble of cork and feathers out onto

The chin grip again. It temporarily paralyzes bass so they can be easily unhooked and released.

the water, and you must handle it in such a way as to make it look alive to a bass. In playing a bug, imagine there is always a bass lurking below it. Concentrate on animating that inanimate piece of cork, and if there are any bass around they'll do the rest.

In working a bug I attempt to project my mind to the bug, thinking of nothing else except making that cork and feathers come alive. It is this mental projection that gives the expert his heralded "touch." The concentration and feel a successful bug fisherman develops is difficult to explain, but it is real. Many casters dislike unnecessary conversation with an oarsman because it distracts them from what they're trying to do with a bug.

At the start of a day's fishing it is well to experiment with different actions, many of which can be tried on a single cast. The bug can be rested for a long time, then popped slowly, then quickly, then rested

again. You can make a cast and swoop the bug across the surface on a single, fast retrieve. It's important to break up your retrieve, making the bug wobble and waggle until it looks alive. When a bass hits during a particular kind of lure play, stay with that method as long as it continues to pay off.

In general, try to put your bugs down lightly by stopping your cast before the bug hits the water. This is done by halting the rod at the ten-o'clock position upon completion of the forward cast, then raising the tip up and back slightly as the line drops. The line will fall lightly to the water, and the bug will hit with a gentle *splat*. Remember that real bugs such as locusts, big beetles, moths, and grasshoppers are light and settle to the water without heavy splashes. Your bugs should settle lightly too, without any fish-scaring *thunk*.

Normally, bass hit best when a bug is allowed to rest motionless for some time after first striking the water. Think of a bug falling to the water and being momentarily stunned. After a few minutes it collects itself, realizes its predicament, and starts kicking furiously.

A bass usually swims off a few feet when an object falls to the surface nearby. If the object doesn't move the bass becomes curious and swims back, staring. It lurks below, watching and waiting for signs of life. When the object—in this case your bug—is twitched gently, the bass takes it for a struggling insect and comes roaring up.

Most fishermen allow a bug to sit perfectly still until all the rings caused by its falling to the water have subsided. When the surface is glass-calm again they twitch the lure—but not before. On the retrieve, bass most often are taken by working the bug lightly and slowly, with frequent pauses between twitches. Sometimes it's good just to tighten the fly line enough to make your bug nod its head a little— repeating this maneuver over and over.

Much of the time it's best for a bug to remain absolutely motionless just after striking the water. I wish to emphasize this because many fishermen just *think* their bugs are motionless. They do not deliberately twitch or pop the bug after it falls; hence they think it is still. I've observed that the average bug fisherman, however, makes his cast and then unconsciously moves the rod tip up—causing the bug to slide a foot or so across the surface. Most times the bug should be dead-still after striking the water, and this can be accomplished only by continuing to lower the rod on completion of the cast.

Many fishermen also take slack out of

the line carelessly, which also causes the bug to slide. After delivering a cast, take slack out of the line as quickly as possible but without moving the bug. Keep the rod tip low so that if a fish hits you can raise the rod sharply to set the hook. If a bass doesn't rise, raise the rod tip slightly but sharply enough to make the bug jump ahead and pop. Allow it to remain motionless again, then pop it again. Always be sure to strip in all slack line without moving the lure, so that you'll be prepared to strike a rising fish at any time.

Often, rocking a bug just a little is very effective. The popping, resting technique should be repeated constantly until the bug is near the boat. Some fishermen then strip line in steadily until the bug is close enough to roll it up for another cast. But often bass follow top-water baits, so it is better to just

Three excellent fly-rod bass bugs include the Bullet Bug (top left), Standard Popper (top right), and the Powder Puff (bottom). The Powder Puff is nearly 100 percent weedless.

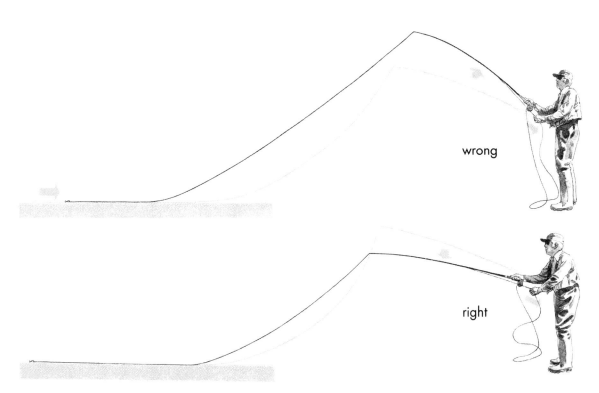

wrong

right

To be sure bug remains motionless when it alights on the water, do not raise the rod or strip line (top) at completion of cast. Instead, lower the rod tip when the bug lands and strip only enough line to remove slack (bottom).

pop them all the way in. This way a bug is working all the time, not just when it is against the bank in the shallows. Most bass taken on bugs are caught around shoreline cover, but many are hooked almost at the boat when bugs are fished all the way back on a full retrieve.

Sometimes, particularly in the fall, a very fast retrieve works well with popping bugs. On this kind of retrieve the bug is popped along steadily and fast. You make the water fly—but not so much that a bass thinks a water buffalo is swimming over him. The fast retrieve can be varied, too,

by popping the bug along steadily and fast for 3 or 4 feet, then resting it, then moving it again fast for several feet, then resting it again—this time waiting a long while before popping it again. Normally, when my bug is about halfway back to the boat—past the area where I believe the fish are—I work it straight in to the boat with steady twitches of the rod tip and stripping of the line.

It is not possible to overemphasize the necessity of keeping slack out of the fly line once your bug is on the water. If you have slack and a bass hits, chances are you won't hook him. Keep slack out of the line, and when a fish hits raise the rod tip as fast as you can, and with considerable authority, to drive the hook home. A swift, strong movement of the rod is absolutely necessary if you are to hook most of the bass that come to your bugs. I strike so hard and fast when a bass engulfs my popper that, if it's a small bass, I will likely skitter him right across the surface. Some anglers, even ones of experience, believe that a fisherman should delay setting the hook

when using surface lures. I've tried this method, but most of the bass merely spat out my bugs when I delayed setting the hook.

Bugs have a way of upsetting a bass's equilibrium. For example, you can often cast repeatedly to one spot and make a bass so mad he'll come rushing up to knock your bug silly. Whenever you find a submerged stump, log, or other cover that you think must surely harbor a bass, keep casting to it, and chances are if there's a bass

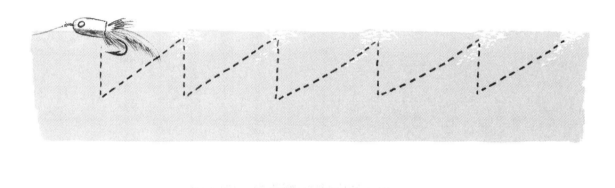

The sawtooth retrieve with the Bullet Bug (top) or Marm Minnow imitates an injured baitfish that can't stay down. On calm water the Marm Minnow can be stripped along the surface in

foot-long hauls to make a V wake like a struggling minnow (bottom). Both retrieves produce strikes.

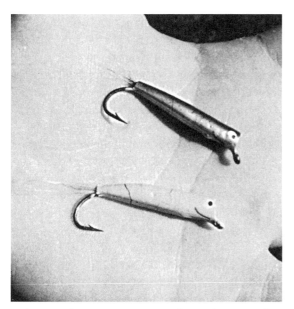

A brace of Marm Minnows. These do a good job of imitating live minnows and can be readily tied by amateur fly tyers.

there he'll eventually come up fighting mad. Sometimes it takes twenty, thirty, or even more casts to a spot before a bass is unnerved enough to strike. The important thing in making repeated casts to one place is to be certain only your popper and leader fall on the spot where you believe the bass to be. Never cast so far beyond a stump, for instance, that your fly line settles by the stump. There's nothing stupid about a bass, and if he's a big fellow he's got fourteen or fifteen seasons behind him. A bass can learn a lot about fishermen in fifteen years.

Too many bug fishermen work their poppers only by twitching the rod tip. But it's possible to make a bug really perform by working the fly line with the left hand. It's also possible to combine rod-tip work with left-hand action to make a bug struggle across the top in a very lifelike manner. Try casting a bug and allowing it to rest, then pop it by jerking the rod or line. Next make the bug swim rapidly over the surface for about a yard by pointing the rod at the bug and hauling quickly on the line. The bug will bounce and skitter over the top, much like a wounded minnow that's lost its marbles.

Making a bug splat when it hits the water is sometimes a killing technique. The Gerbubble Bug is great for this because it's flat on the bottom and makes a resounding splat when put down on the water properly. To make a bug splat, throw an open bow with your line instead of a tight loop, and as the forward cast straightens pull back hard on the line with your left hand, simultaneously raising the rod tip. This causes the leader to straighten quickly, pulling the bug backward and down so that it hits the water and goes *splat!* On such casts bass often strike the moment the bug hits the water.

The Gerbubble Bug is great around lily pads. Cast it directly onto a pad, putting an extra push into the rod so that the bug plunks down hard. Bass lurking beneath the pads will know something has landed nearby and frequently swim over to the pad waiting to see what happened. After a few moments, pull the Gerbubble Bug off the pad and it may drop right into the gaping mouth of a bass.

Fish your bugs slowly around lily pads, trying to make them act like some injured creature struggling to reach a pad and climb off the water to safety.

There are days when bass won't take regular bugs. Standard poppers are best when the water is glass-calm, but you frequently must fish under conditions of riffled water. Perhaps bass can't see a floater well when the surface is rippled by wind, or perhaps they don't like to rise under such conditions. On those days the Bullet Bug and Marm Minnow work wonders. Cast them out and sweep in line quickly so the bugs shoot across the surface. They'll dive under occasionally, where they act like feather minnows or big streamers. You can make them dart along under the surface for 3 or 4 feet, then let them rise slowly to the top. Bass hit them most often when they're floating dead toward the surface.

If you get the right cadence into your retrieve, you can make a Bullet Bug or Marm Minnow swim in sawtooth fashion just under the surface. They're fished like a minnow that's been injured and can't stay down. Cast, let the bug sit a moment, then yank it under. It will go down about 4 inches and move forward a foot, then float to the surface. Keep this up and the bug will move sawtooth-fashion, diving, darting, surfacing.

The Marm Minnow can give you a riot of fishing under conditions of calm water, too. Every fisherman has seen tiny minnows on the surface. Their noses break out of the surface film, and as the minnow darts along he leaves a V wake. When the water is table-top smooth these tiny V wakes can be seen great distances. The Marm Minnow, when worked properly, makes a V wake exactly like a minnow struggling over the surface. The bug should be fished with a high-floating line and stripped over the top by pulling line with foot-long hauls.

Bugs should be fished around logs, stumps, underwater obstructions, fallen trees, weed beds, lily pads, and so on. Pick out a likely spot, and try to make your first cast good. Generally, it's the first cast that produces. A good second cast, following a sloppy initial presentation, rarely produces adult bass.

Boat handling is important, too. Approach bassy spots carefully and with a minimum of boat disturbance. Do most of your casting sitting down, particularly if you are unable to toss a long line. Bass rising to a surface lure in clear water can readily spot a fisherman standing in a nearby boat.

Bass-bug fishing has its limitations, since it's most productive when the water is calm and bass are in the shallows. Thus bugging is no cure for all of your bass-fishing ills, but there are times when no other system will catch as many bass.

And bugging gets big bass, too. My best largemouth thus far on a fly rod weighed 11 pounds 1 ounce. He came out of an opening in lily pads in Florida's Withlacoochee River to inhale one of my Green Frog bugs. And that bass, incidentally, is the largest I've ever taken, anywhere—fishing *any* method!

21
Spinners and Porkrind for Bass

ONE afternoon, more summers ago than I care to remember, Tom Loving and I were fishing Middle River, a brackish-water estuary of Chesapeake Bay, not far from Baltimore. We were bugging for bass and had been taking fish with fair consistency until a stiff breeze came whipping in from the bay. As soon as the surface waters became rippled, we couldn't bring another bass up to our bugs.

Tom pulled his popper off and tied on a Mickey Finn streamer. I replaced my bass bug with a size 2/0 Yellow Marabou streamer. We went on then, moving the boat slowly, dropping our flies close to the thick weed edges, and tossing them far back to work through open pockets.

Many of the Chesapeake's brackish estuaries are full of duckwort, wild celery, and other aquatic greenery, and Middle River is no exception. As we rowed along, 50 to 60 feet out from the weeds, which reached to the surface, we could see the weed line beneath the surface, and it looked thick as a wall. Unlike many freshwater lakes, most Chesapeake estuarian

waters lack great depth and bottom structure. There are few deep hangouts for bass, no undercut rocky ledges, no sunken reefs, no wooded peninsulas jutting to water's edge and continuing far out into the depths.

So Middle River bass, like those in most tidewater tributaries, hang out in the weeds. Some go far back to escape the summer sun and hang around the pockets, while others back up just inside the weedy wall. The weeds provide them with cooling shade, and concealment from which they can strike bull minnows and other schooling baitfish.

Tom and I fished our streamers for close to half an hour, and all we got was a little 1-pounder that slapped my Yellow Marabou. I was dumb enough to stay with the Marabou, feeling if I had to fish something underwater it was as good a choice as any other fly or lure. Tom, however, grunted his annoyance over the sudden scarcity of bass and started digging into his tackle bag. I was only half aware that Tom had changed lures and was casting again, since I was busy concentrating on working my Marabou streamer.

Tom made three casts and hung a bass. A frisky little 2-pounder, the fish busted up and out right by the weeds, then jumped a couple more times close to the boat. On the near jump I noticed something whitish hanging from the bass's jaw, and figured Tom had switched to a white streamer of sorts. I paid no more attention until, only minutes later, Tom Loving had another bass. I cast farther and worked my fly harder, at the same time watching from the corner of my eye as Tom released that 3-pounder.

In the next twenty minutes Tom hooked, played, landed, and released *four more bass*. That was too much for me.

"What, pray tell, are you feeding these blankety-blank fish?" I demanded.

"Thought you'd never ask," Tom grinned, as he flipped his leader to my end of the boat. Tied to it was a nickel-plated No. 2 Indiana spinner. Attached to the spinner was an ordinary size 4 hook, and trailing from the hook was a 1½-inch length of narrow white porkrind.

"I'll be darned," I growled. "You're fishing bait!"

"I'm using a fly rod," Tom replied with a wide smile, "and I'm catching me some bass. You ain't!"

That was my first lesson in fishing a small spinner-and-hook tipped with porkrind for bass. Since then the spinner-and-strip combo has put a lot of bass in the air for me that I'm sure I would not have caught otherwise.

I greatly dislike fishing a spinner or any other hardware, such as small spoons, because I feel that it is not strict fly fishing.

When fly-rodding for bass I like, first of all, to take them on bugs; after that, I want them on streamers. But when legitimate bugs and flies fail, I now dig out the little spinners and the porkrind strips. In my experience if the spinner-and-strip system fails, the bass are very deep and other angling methods are called for.

Tom gave me one of his little spinners and a strip of narrow white porkrind, and soon I, too, was hooking bass. We'd poke slowly along the weed edge, casting our spinner-and-strips right alongside the greenery. The spinner rigs would hit the water with a soft *splat,* then the spinner would flash and flutter and the porkrind strip would wiggle and wobble as they sank along the edge of the weeds. The flashing spinner drew bass from away back, and while many of the fish we caught were small we had fast action all the rest of the day.

I had another memorable trip using spinner-and-strips on bass. This was to the Mississippi River sloughs near LaCrosse, Wisconsin. Most of the Mississippi is just a mudhole, but some of the backwater areas along the upper river are clean and clear and full of largemouths.

While my wife, Phyllis, ran the electric motor and kept our Ranger bass boat moving slowly through the lily pads, I fished with a spinner-and-strip, dropping it into open pockets and letting it glitter down. The water was very clear, so I used a smaller spinner than usual, size 0 (small ones work best in clear water, larger ones best in murky water). When we quit in mid-afternoon I had tallied thirty-seven bass, most 1 to 2½ pounds, but there were a couple of 3-pounders, and one 3½.

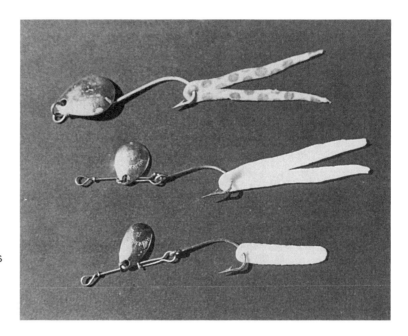

Certainly using porkrind strips behind spinners is not true fly fishing, but such set-ups often get bass when nothing else will.

All gamefish, incidentally, will hit a spinner and porkrind. Stream smallmouths love such a rig. Charlie Dorn, of Randallstown, Maryland, and I used to take eastern chain pickerel in the winter months on spinner-and-strips fishing Maryland's Bush and Seneca rivers. Joe Brooks and I once struck out completely while fishing Virginia's Chickahominy River (a gorgeous waterway) for shad, but when we got around to the spinner-and-strip routine we couldn't keep the white perch away. They hit on every cast!

Yellow perch also go hard for the spinner-and-porkrind combination, as do crappies. A good way to use the lure on crappies is with the "strip-cast" method of casting. Monofilament line is used instead of standard fly line. A half-dozen or so BB-size split-shot sinkers are attached to the mono—8- to 12-pound test—then 3 or 4

feet below the shot the spinner-hook-strip is tied on. Casts are made by pulling several yards of mono from the reel and allowing it to lie loosely at the feet. Then the lead shot, which gives weight for the cast, is raised to just below the rod tip. Now the fly rod is brought backward smoothly, then briskly forward—as when casting with a spinning or bait-casting rod—and when the rod reaches the ten-o'clock forward position, the left hand releases the monofilament line. The spinner-and-strip will sail out, much like a lure cast with a spinning outfit, then plunk to the water 50, 60, or even 100 feet away. The lead takes the spinner-and-rind down to crappie level in a hurry, and all you need to do then is twitch it along on a slow retrieve. If crappies are there, they'll hit.

In casting a spinner-and-strip with regular fly tackle, the smaller spinners should be used to make for easier casting. The

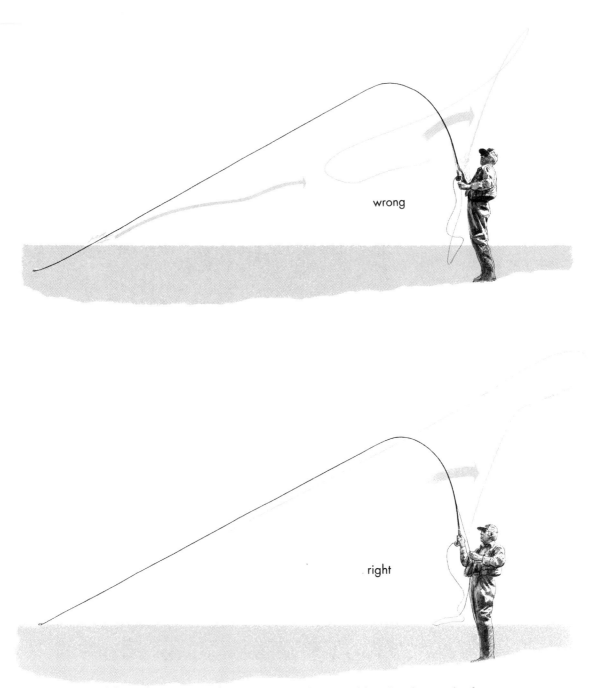

The wrong and the right way to pick up a spinner for the backcast. *Top:* Angler begins pickup while lure is still below surface. The line snaps back and lure hits him in the face. *Bottom:* Angler begins pickup with lure on surface. Backcast is clean and high.

larger the spinner, the greater the weight and air resistance, and therefore the more difficult it is to cast well. For the same reasons, porkrind strips should be kept on the small side. With the larger spinners, larger pieces of porkrind are used, and roll casting may be necessary, since it's easier to roll-cast a heavy lure for a short distance than it is to pick it up on a conventional cast.

The individual's casting skill, naturally, will have lots to do with his efficiency in fishing spinner-and-strips. Since spinners have a lot of air resistance, as well as heavy drag in the water, some special considerations are needed in casting. The normal overhead cast must be slowed down as much as possible, and no attempt should be made to lift a spinner out of the water for a pickup or backcast until the spinner is right on the surface. Any effort to lift a lure sooner may put it into your face or your lap instead of into the air behind you; moreover, such bad technique puts an undue strain on the rod. Since a spinner revolves faster and gives more resistance the quicker it is pulled through the water, raise it to the surface slowly just prior to the pickup.

The design or finish of spinner blades doesn't seem too important in this fishing. I prefer chrome or nickel-plated spinners, but have caught many bass using ones with copper, brass, gold, bronze, and even black enamel finishes. Nowadays spinners are available in many different enamel finishes—red, yellow, green, and ones with spots or stripes. You may want to experiment.

In very clear water a lot of gamefish will be spooked by large, brightly flashing blades. In clear water the smaller spinners in darker colors or finishes are usually most productive. With the Colorado type of spinner this would be sizes 4/0 and 3/0; with Indiana spinners, sizes 1 and 2; and with the Willowleaf variety, size W-2. In dirty water use bright, larger spinners.

There are several kinds of spinners, but the Colorado, Indiana, and Willowleaf are the most popular and most readily available. Stores normally stock the best selections in these types. The Colorado is the widest-type blade, the Indiana not so broad, and the Willowleaf kind is long and narrow, almost spear-shaped.

Colorado spinners are normally sold with treble hooks attached. I clip the trebles off and replace with a single size 4 or 6 hook, because porkrind strips foul on a treble hook, and trebles kill some of a strip's action. Colorado blades spin easily in the water, therefore they can be fished slowly. Indiana blades are my preference because they revolve steadily at slow speeds, and are designed so that a single hook can be quickly snapped on or off behind the spinner. Willowleafs can be a good choice for clear water because their narrow profile means less light reflection, but they must be retrieved fairly fast for their blades to spin. Colorado and Indiana blades will spin even when only sinking slowly.

I suppose double spinners might be used to advantage at times, but they would be considerably more difficult to cast, so a heavier outfit would be called for, as well as shorter casts.

Spinners not only have sparkle and flash in the water, but they also produce sound waves that attract gamefish, and with porkrind strips attached they have exceptional action. Black porkrind often may be substituted for white, with very good results. Porkrind strips are marketed in many different colors, and in addition to black other good colors are purple, blue, green, yellow, and red. I often use a "frog" strip (the porkrind is split)—the bottom is white, the top green with black spots.

Spinners can be fished with streamer flies, too, or with extra-large wet flies, once called "bass flies." Old-time bass flies aren't seen in tackle shops much any more, and you may have to tie your own or have some specially made. These big bass wet flies must be tied on flat or ball-eye hooks so they'll trail the spinner properly and not twist or interfere with the spinner blade. Bass flies are as big as a half-dollar, should be on size 1 or 1/0 hooks, and be bright patterns—like the Red Ibis, Yellow Sally, Professor, or McGinty.

My favorite spinner-and-strip rig is a 9-foot, 5-ounce glass fly rod with matching WF-9-F line, a 9-foot leader tapered to a 10-pound tippet, a size 4 short-shank hook, a size 3 Indiana spinner, and a 1½-inch-long narrow cut strip of ivory-white porkrind. I cut the porkrind in a taper, its head end (the part slipped over the hook) being about ⅝ inch wide. It's cut in a narrow

cone shape to the pointed end, and sometimes split so it has two "legs."

Ringed or ball-eye hooks always should be used when fishing spinners—rather than hooks with turned-up or turned-down eyes—because the flat eye of a ringed-eye hook allows a spinner blade to turn with no interference, and, more important, the hook will ride straight behind the spinner and connect better to the wire shaft for the spinner blade.

There's not much to fishing these spinner-porkrind rigs. All you need do is cast to where you figure there might be some bass, let the spinner-rind sink a bit, then start a slow retrieve. Lead the spinner so it flutters along likely cover—next to weeds, lily pads, stumps, logs. Don't be in a hurry. Give the spinner-and-porkrind time to fish through the good spots. The spinner will flash and sparkle and get the attention of bass, and when they close in they'll see that pearl-white strip of porkrind wiggling eel-like through the water. The revolving spinner blade apparently creates minute currents that roll around the porkrind strip, causing the rind to shiver and shake tantalizingly. No healthy bass can resist *that* kind of action!

22
Streamers and Nymphs for Bass

 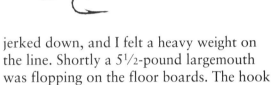

MANY fishermen never consider using streamers or nymphs for bass. That can be a big mistake, because bass go *hard* for both streamers and nymphs.

Once I was fishing Bull Valley Lake in northern Illinois with George Wold and Leo Pachner. Wold was rowing, Pachner was spinning in the bow, using small surface lures, and I was fly-rod bug-fishing from the stern. But after 1½ hours, neither Leo nor I had a strike on our surface lures.

"I'm gonna try a big streamer fly," I announced.

"Streamers don't take anything in this lake except bluegills," said George. "I've tried them lots of times, and the bass just don't go for them."

"Maybe the streamers you've used are too small," I replied, digging a 6-inch-long McNally Magnum out of my kit. We were paddling around through flooded timber, really bassy water. Leo was artfully dropping his spinning popper around flooded treetops, catching nothing. About my fourth cast there was a swirl behind the streamer, the water humped up, the rod tip

jerked down, and I felt a heavy weight on the line. Shortly a 5½-pound largemouth was flopping on the floor boards. The hook was removed gently and the fish released.

"That's the largest bass I've ever seen taken *anywhere* on a streamer fly," Wold said. "I never thought bass would be interested in a sunken fly."

"I've caught thousands of bass fly fishing," Pachner mumbled. "All on popping bugs. Never even thought to try streamers."

It's that way with most bass fishermen. When the average bass angler *does* try fly fishing, he invariably uses only poppers. Today—even though there has been rising interest in recent years in streamer bass fishing—the average bassman doesn't even own any streamers suitable for bass. All he has in his fly box is bugs. That can be a big mistake.

Much the same is true of nymph fishing for bass. Few fishermen ever give any thought to using artificial nymphs for bass, whether they be largemouths or smallmouths. In truth, however, fly fishing with

Proof bass go hard for streamers and nymphs. The three largest in this catch hit streamers; the smaller bass took a 3-inch-long hellgrammite nymph.

lakes will take nymphs greedily when everything's right.

STREAMER PATTERNS AND FISHING TECHNIQUES

Getting back to streamer fishing: There is an immense variety of streamer flies available suitable for bass fishing—flies made of marabou, bucktail, saddle hackles, impala, Mylar, and so on. Quality tackle shops stock plenty, as do large mail-order tackle houses. Most of them are very lifelike in the water, and most will do a number on bass.

Saltwater streamer flies work very well on bass. Tarpon streamers are excellent, but even small, size 1/0 short-shank bonefish flies will take bass. Bonefish bucktails are very effective on smallmouth bass in rivers and streams, but as a rule larger streamers are called for in fishing for largemouths in lakes. Don't be afraid to fish a 5-, 6-, or even a 7-inch long streamer for lake largemouths.

Big streamers with long, flowing saddle hackles for winging are a strong preference, but flies with bucktail winging also are very good. And don't overlook marabou streamers. A marabou streamer literally dances through the water, and it's got to be a pretty bullheaded bass that can resist a lively marabou streamer swimming within a few feet of his dome.

Streamers for bass needn't be gaudy, nor dressed with a lot of frills. Simple patterns will take as many fish as the intricate ones some fly tyers make in an effort to "model" some form of underwater life. A brown, yellow, white, or black bucktail, for example, will draw strikes from a lot of

large, buggy nymphs often can be as effective on both large and smallmouth bass as drifting a live hellgrammite past the nose of a hungry bass. Of course, it's true that stream smallmouths respond best to nymph fly fishing, but even largemouth bass in

Extra-large streamers designed for saltwater fishing take numbers of freshwater bass.

bass, and the same is true of saddle hackle streamers in those colors. A streamer's body in contrasting colors can be helpful, as can a "collar" tied in Palmer style in another bright or contrasting color.

Streamers—and nymphs, too—must be cast to the right places. For instance, if we figure there's a bass holed up by a stump, we shouldn't cast directly to the stump. Plopping a big streamer on a bass's nose may spook him right out of the county; instead, drop the fly 10 or 12 feet beyond the bass, lightly, then bring it by him.

The retrieve is every bit as important in fishing streamers and nymphs as is accurate casting. It does no good to place a fly in precisely the right spot, then have the fly sink dead in the water, finally hop forward (after the angler has recovered his slack line), twitch along half-heartedly for a few inches, sink dead again, then jump forward crazily, and so on. Real *live* action must be

imparted to a streamer. It must never be allowed to sit motionless in the water once the retrieve is begun. The accepted technique is to run the fly line beneath the first two fingers of the rod hand, pinching the line against the cork rod-handle, as the fly is stripped along. Stripping is done by bringing back 6 inches to a foot of line, in quick little twitches, so the fly simulates a darting, scurrying minnow. Speed-ups and pauses can be injected into the retrieve, but the basic pattern is "strip . . . strip . . . strip . . . strip . . . strip . . . strip . . . strip," and so on.

Bass are not easy to hook on streamers, so we must be very alert to the strike. At the first sign of a hit, strike back at the bass fast and hard. Try to break the rod. Keep hooks needle-sharp, and try to keep casts as short as practical. It is easier to sink a hook into a striking bass with a short line than it is with a long one.

Bucktail streamers are excellent choices for black-bass fishing. This Keel fly was designed to swim with the hook up, making it more snag-proof.

Really big saltwater flies like these two—nearly as long as a pencil—are not too big to use on bass.

Standard floating three-diameter fly lines generally are all that's needed in fishing streamers and nymphs for bass. Sometimes, though, sink-tip lines are a better choice, and occasionally even full-sinking lines are necessary to get flies down where the bass are.

NYMPH PATTERNS AND FISHING TECHNIQUES

In fishing nymphs for bass, especially if you're working on bigmouths, try to use large patterns, such as hellgrammites (larva of the dobson fly) or stonefly nymphs. In fishing lake-bass cast to likely spots, let the nymph settle a bit, then bring it back in short, quick little pulls—simulating the natural swimming rhythm of a real nymph.

Nymphs are at their best in rivers and streams holding smallmouths, because bronzebacks feed heavily on nymphs, which are abundant in that environment. Nymphs can be fished in many ways, but probably the most productive method in rivers and streams is to cast across and downstream, then let the fly swing in the current, and when the line is bowed by the current bring it back in foot-long hauls, to simulate a swimming nymph.

The pattern of nymph used on bass isn't important, but the fly ought to look bug-like and be of good size. Nothing much smaller than a size 6 will get the attention of bass. Hooks sizes 1 and 2 are best for bass nymphs, and of them all I like nymphs tied on No. 4 Sproat hooks best.

If you want to stick to standard patterns in your bass nymphs, then—in addition to dragonfly imitations—try the Gray (muskrat) Nymph, any of the various Stoneflies, Montana Nymph, and Zug Bug. The Zug Bug, a Paul Stroud creation, is a great bass nymph. The Big Hole Demon fly and the Wooly Worm are not nymphs, but they are similar and they get a lot of stream and lake bass.

WHERE TO FISH FOR BASS

The opportunities for good fly fishing for bass in the United States and Canada are legion. There are many lakes, rivers, and bays that provide exceptional fly-rodding just about all season long. Most of the Canadian smallmouth lakes, for example, are cold enough that the bass stay fairly shallow all summer. I think Rainy Lake, at Fort Frances, Ontario, is a fly fisherman's delight, and the smallmouths are big. The Winnipeg River is another super small-mouth spot, at Point du Bois, Manitoba, and so is the English River system in Ontario. Maine has many excellent fly-rodding smallmouth waters, such as Grand Lake and Schoodic Pond, and so does New Brunswick—with some of their lakes never seeing a bass fisherman from one season to the next.

There are many smallmouth rivers just right for streamer/nymph fly fishing. To name only some: Genesee (New York), Susquehanna (Maryland, Pennsylvania, New York), Delaware (New York), Potomac (Maryland), Rappahannock and James (Virginia), St. Croix (Wisconsin), Buffalo and Crooked Creek (Arkansas), the upper Mississippi (Minnesota), Musselshell River (Montana), lower Snake River (Wyoming), the Penobscot River (Maine—maybe the best smallmouth fishing in America), and the St. Lawrence River (New York, Quebec).

There are dozens of small lakes, called "ponds," on the Delmarva Peninsula (Delaware, Maryland, Virginia), that provide top-grade fly-rod bass-fishing all year long. The flooded woodland areas of the Santee-Cooper Lakes, in South Carolina, are hard to match for fly-rod bass opportunities.

There are isolated freshwater ponds near Nags Head, North Carolina, stiff with largemouth bass waiting for fly-rod lures. Our really top bass lakes, such as Toledo Bend (Texas, Louisiana) and Rodman Reservoir (Florida), have vast timber-studded areas perfect for streamer and nymph fishing.

Finally we have coastal estuaries—shallow brackish waters that are partly fresh, partly salt, and affected by the tides. Here are hundreds of square miles of generally shallow bass waters rarely fished—flooded marshes and sloughs with large populations of chunky, greenish-black bigmouths. Outstanding among the brackish-water areas are the upper estuaries of Chesapeake Bay (all of them), and Pamlico, Albemarle, and Currituck sounds in North Carolina. The Gulf States also provide extensive brackish-water fly fishing, especially around places such as Biloxi, Mississippi, and the Louisiana bayou country near the town of Thibodaux. Fishing streamers in water less than 4 feet deep, in bayous north of Thibodaux, I once landed 177 bass (actual count) in one day. Almost all of them were taken on streamers.

23
Dry Flies for Stream Smallmouths

WHEN I was a boy in high school in Towson, Maryland, the old "Ma and Pa" (Maryland–Pennsylvania) Railroad crossed the Gunpowder River via a high wooden trestle not far from Cromwell's Bridge. One afternoon in late summer Paul Murphy and I were hiking across the trestle (the Ma and Pa ran only twice weekly). Halfway out we sat down, sneakered feet dangling, and stared at the clear river 75 feet below.

The Gunpowder was low, and the pool beneath our feet was no more than 5 feet deep at most, 125 feet long, and 40 feet wide. A limestone ledge lay left of center in the pool, and strung out along its shade were seven smallmouth bass.

Bear in mind that the sight of seven smallmouth bass, *live ones,* hanging on their fins unmolested, was a stirring scene to a youth who spent his classroom study periods reading *Outdoor Life* camouflaged within the open pages of a notebook. To us in those days, seeing those bass was some kind of a find. Paul and I had been into bass fishing for years (plug casting with old

Pflueger Akron and Summit reels, and hard-braided Black-Oreno silk lines), and we fished regularly not only the Gunpowder River but also nearby Loch Raven Reservoir and Lake Roland. We caught bass once in a while, too, but seeing those smallmouths down there, looking like ducks waiting to be plucked, really turned us on.

After seeing those bass, Paul and I fished that part of the river regularly, using small topwater and underwater plugs, and while we may have taken a bass now and then I remember mostly failure. Each time we'd finish fishing the Trestle Pool we'd wade out of the river, climb the bank, and go out on the trestle. Sure enough, we would see bass we had not been able to interest in our plugs.

Some years later I attended a meeting of the Maryland State Game and Fish Protective Association, of which Joe Brooks, originally a Baltimorean, was a member. In the course of "fishing talk" I told Joe about the Gunpowder River bass, and he suggested trying for them with large dry flies.

At first chance I was at the Trestle Pool (alone, because Paul Murphy was somewhere else in the world), and using big, fluffy bivisibles and equally bulky salmon dry flies, I knocked those Gunpowder smallmouths stiff. That first try I took fifteen or twenty bass—nothing bigger than maybe 1½ pounds, but that's all the river *had*. The Gunpowder is not a trophy smallmouth stream. It provided me with much sporty and interesting fishing thereafter, however, and I've since used dry flies on stream smallmouth bass with great success in many areas.

Some places where I've used dries on river smallmouths with excellent results are Missouri's Gasconade, Current, and Pine rivers; Wisconsin's upper St. Croix River; Michigan's Nett River and St. Joseph; Indiana's Tippecanoe; Pennsylvania's Delaware and Pine; Maryland's Potomac, Patuxent, Antietam, Big Savage, and Deer Creek; and Arkansas' Crooked Creek and Buffalo River. That's naming just some of the places where I've had good smallmouth fishing with dry flies, and I hope it will encourage you to use dries for stream smallmouths when you come across the right conditions.

Wading a stream or small river for bronzebacks, and fishing for them with dry flies, is entirely different from any other kind of fishing. It has an atmosphere and special appeal all its own.

For one thing, in fishing stream smallmouths you normally are on water much larger than when fishing a typical trout stream. Your average cast may be 30 or 40 feet, frequently 50 or 60 feet, and occasionally you will want to throw a fly way out to a rock or a sunken log that may be 80 feet away. So stream smallmouth fishing gives you the opportunity for some distance work, and it's fun to feel your rod bending just right on the backcast, to watch the line unfolding in a fine, tight loop—then the big dry fly settling down lightly. And when you hook a bass on one of those long casts, well, that's a kick all its own. A smallmouth hooked 60 or 70 feet from the rod tip, in fast water, is good for six or eight jumps, sometimes more. And those jumps are going to be high and clean, 1 or 2 feet into the air, and some bronzebacks will go cartwheeling up 3 feet.

There are very few fly-fishing smallmouth specialists. Even on the better rivers, such as the Potomac, Susquehanna, and Genesee, we seldom encounter serious bass fly-rodders. The stream smallmouth fisherman usually has the water to himself, especially when fishing the smaller streams.

Becoming a stream smallmouth dry-fly fisherman can open a new world of angling, also. Usually the tiny feeder creeks of the larger bass rivers also hide smallmouths—sometimes fish of surprisingly large size. It's fun to explore and fish little tributaries that may not even be named, and occasionally you'll have the excitement of hitting a real smallmouth bonanza. Spring is the best time to fish the tributary creeks, because the smallmouths will enter the smallest streams to spawn. The Kankakee, for example, is one of Illinois' best-known smallmouth rivers. It produces a lot of good-size bass, but the top fishing in the valley is not in the big river but in untold numbers of nameless little Kankakee feeder streams, in late April and early May.

And dry-fly fishing can be a dirty trick to play on stream smallmouths. In late

This chunky little smallmouth hit a bushy deer-hair dry fly skimmed across Wisconsin's lower St. Croix River.

summer and early fall, when the rivers are very low and clear, a 1- to 2-pound smallmouth can be as angler-wise as a 6-pound brown trout in a Pennsylvania limestone stream. Toss a spinning lure or heavy plastic plug in front of a smallmouth under the conditions of low, clear water and you'll see the fish spook right out of its scales. Nothing disappears faster than a brainy smallmouth hit in the head with a plug in clear water.

But when you approach the scene properly, and present a bushy dry fly correctly, the bass that would only run from a plug, spoon, or spinner becomes a near setup. The long, fine leader is less visible to the fish than is casting line, and there is no fish-scaring *plunk* when your dry fly settles like goosedown to the surface. And, too, big dry flies appear lifelike to bass, no matter how low or clear the water, while the opposite is generally true of plugs and hardware.

TACKLE FOR DRY-FLY SMALLMOUTH BASS FISHING

In my opinion the ideal rod for dry-fly fishing in smallmouth streams is 8 or 8$\frac{1}{2}$ feet long, taking a WF-7-F line or WF-6-F. The lighter "bass" rods, with lighter three-diameter lines, are most practical for this fishing. The bigger rods with heavier lines used in typical bass-bug fishing are out of place on the smallmouth streams. After all, we're dry-fly fishing—not bugging.

I often use a 9½-foot graphite rod, weighing just 4 ounces, that handles a No. 6 line beautifully. I use a double-taper line with it more frequently than a three-diameter line, however. With this rod I can drop a dry fly just about anywhere I want it, and its extra length allows me to keep a lot of line off the water, and to better control the drift of the fly.

The torpedo-taper or three-diameter lines are best for most stream smallmouth dry-fly fishing, but occasionally conditions dictate the use of a standard double-taper. The double-taper line casts better (we're not talking about distance), creates less disturbance falling to the water, offers less drag, and generally assists you in better handling of the fly—for example, you can mend a double-taper easier than a three-diameter.

I cut the forward tips of three-diameter lines back a foot or so for bass bugging (see Chapter 20) because the lines then cast bugs better. But I don't do any trimming at all to a three-diameter line I intend to use in dry-fly smallmouth fishing. I want as long and as fine a forward taper as possible for fishing dries.

Leaders are no problem; just go as long and fine as possible. This for two reasons: First, the longer, lighter leader will catch more bass; and second, the finer the leader point the better action, or float, the fly will have. As a general rule I seldom use a leader shorter than 9 feet in stream smallmouth fishing, and the most common tippet used is 3X. *Always* use a tapered leader.

DRY FLIES FOR SMALLMOUTH BASS

All flies used in stream smallmouth fishing, *under most circumstances,* should be oversized. One evening at Schoodic Lake in Maine, however, I was amazed at the spectacle of hundreds of small bass rising to a midge hatch. And on Maryland's upper Potomac River, every year Gurney Godfrey, Joe Brooks, John Cheape, Harvey Schemm, and I used to have a picnic taking small bronzebacks on size 10 White Millers during the big hatches that came off in early summer. But to get the interest of bass with dries they've usually got to be of good size—like salmon dry flies, for example.

Pattern is of little if any importance most of the time. But the fly should be bulky and "meaty" if it is to interest a bass that is not actively rising to a natural hatch of insects. In this fishing your dry fly, it must be remembered, is just the *odd* bug coming down the pike. So the most productive flies are ones having fat, buglike bodies.

Under certain circumstances large mayfly imitations are called for. On summer evenings miles of the upper Mississippi River get incredible hatches of mayflies. The hatches are the largest I've ever seen anywhere. Spent mayflies coat the sidewalks of river towns so thickly that they must be shoveled into the streets. Pedestrians slip and cars skid on dead mayflies. This may sound like irresponsible exaggeration to those who've never witnessed a Mississippi mayfly hatch, but it is not. Some trout fishermen scoop up mayfly husks, fill shoeboxes with them, freeze them, and later thaw the dead flies and throw them into trout streams to create artificial hatches.

When these mayfly hatches come off, every fish in the Mississippi rises to the surface and gorges on half-dollar-size mayflies. Some of the largest smallmouths I've taken on dry flies were hooked during Mississippi mayfly hatches. We fish from anchored skiffs, casting to the current edges close to grassy banks, and float size 6 Isonychia Duns over the bass. The Isonychia is a superior mayfly imitation, and few smallmouths that see one will refuse it.

Any large bivisible is a good dry fly to put over a smallmouth. I use a lot of all-white ones, and brown, yellow, and black, which I tie on size 4, 6, and 8 Mustad hooks. The 6's are used most often.

The Muddler Minnow, when greased and skimmed over the surface, will drive a smallmouth frantic. Sizes 2, 4, and 6 do the job. Any of the grasshopper imitations (I know, the Muddler can be fished as a hopper), such as the Michigan Hopper, will take a lot of stream bass, but a hopper in the strictest sense probably is not a dry fly, nor is the Muddler.

All of the big hairwing flies (winging is of impala or calftail) are very good. The larger fanwings, such as the Fanwing Royal Coachman, will get fish but they're a little fancy to feed to bass. Two of my all-time favorite dries for stream smallmouths are the Irresistible and the Deer Hair, both in size 6. There's a slight difference in the flies; the Irresistible has grizzly hackle tips for wings, the Deer Hair only tufts of whitetail belly hairs.

Standard salmon patterns you can buy (or tie) and use successfully on stream bass include the Hairwing Rat-Faced McDougal, MacIntosh, Black Gnat (hair body), and Soldier Palmer. The Dr. Park Dry Fly is a big, fluffy, white fly that gets a lot of smallmouths, and the Colonel Monel is a good one, too.

FISHING THE BASS DRY FLY

In fishing dries for smallmouths it usually is more productive to "activate" the fly. The fish will frequently come up to a fly swinging along in a natural drift with the currents, but often when you fish the fly over a run or pool or next to a "feeding lane" on a natural drift and no bass takes, you can present the fly again, twitch it and skip it along as it comes down with the current—and catch bass that otherwise would not have hit.

A well-greased or well-oiled dry fly can be fished in at least four ways: on a "dead" or natural drift, by retrieving in short twitches (4- to 8-inch-long hops), by skimming over the surface ("sliding" the fly 3 to 4 feet), and by a combination of those actions. In presenting a fly to a likely spot I normally first try a natural float, fishing two or three casts that way; then I activate the fly on subsequent casts.

Repetitive casting can pay off with stream smallmouths. You must be careful not to make any sloppy casts in presenting the fly time and again to a promising fish-holding area, since a bad cast will surely turn away a reluctant fish, but often a bass will refuse (or perhaps fail to note) every float of a fly until the tenth or fifteenth toss.

Smallmouths have a habit of rising to a dry fly from the side, turning, and following the fly nose-first downstream. Many a smallmouth strike at a floating fly is a *downstream lunge*. The opposite, of course,

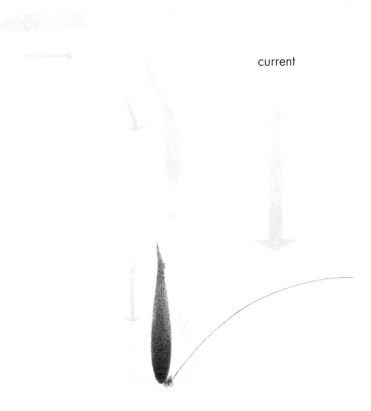

current

The smallmouth usually rises to a dry fly from the side and follows it downstream. When it lunges for the fly, both are moving downstream; the current tightens the leader and the fish often hooks itself.

is the rule in dry-fly fishing for trout, which come under the fly looking upstream, and then drift with the fly tail-first until they decide to take. The strike of a trout, then, is almost always an upcurrent rise.

The smallmouth's peculiarity of often hitting a dry fly while moving *with* the current is an aid to the angler, because if anything the fish's strike tends to tighten the leader and line, thus assisting in setting the hook. Smallmouths that hit a fly on a downriver strike invariably hook themselves solidly.

Casting across and downstream is a good way to fish dries for smallmouth bass. A sensible routine is to drop the fly lightly several feet above a likely spot, then pay out line and reach a bit with the rod so that the fly drifts naturally for a few feet. Then tighten up, gripping the line and lifting the rod tip, and as current bows the line and creates drag make the fly skip, jump, and hop over the surface. That kind of action unhinges many a brainy smallmouth.

The play of the current is important in locating stream bass, just as it is in trout fishing. The skilled angler learns to read the

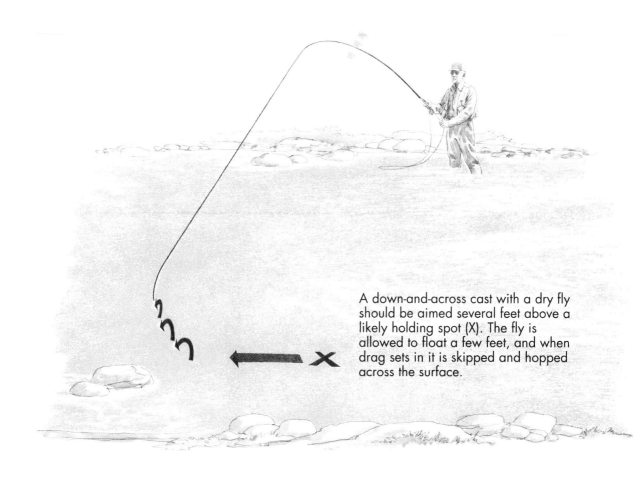

A down-and-across cast with a dry fly should be aimed several feet above a likely holding spot (X). The fly is allowed to float a few feet, and when drag sets in it is skipped and hopped across the surface.

current flow, and to note the edges, eddies, and runs that are likely to hold fish. When not actively feeding, bronzebacks will lie in areas having only moderate current, as beneath rock ledges, in pockets behind boulders, by a sunken log, or at the bottom of deep pools. When feeding deliberately they will move to the current edges, to the borders of fast water entering a pool or long run, or they will nose along rock and gravel bottom looking for crayfish and nymphs.

Smallmouths dislike mud and silted bottoms and "dead-water" pools, much preferring gravel, boulders, and rock-bottomed runs and pools. Mornings and evenings they often move to the head of pools to feed from stations near current. All the usual bass cover is worth fishing for stream small-mouths—boulders, weed lines, fallen trees, submerged brush heaps. In many instances smallmouths will lie up behind what appears to be totally insignificant "cover," such as a single pencil reed protruding no more than 6 to 8 inches out of the water, or a thin, bare tree limb dipping into the water. So the dry-fly angler should prospect each run, glide, and pool thoroughly, first noting the current flow, then the probable spots where bass might be holding.

River smallmouths do not school to the extent lake bass do, but nonetheless they are gregarious, and where there is one bronzeback there almost surely are two or three, or more. On many occasions I've taken two and three smallmouths on as many successive casts to the *same place*.

The smallmouth bass eats many more insects than does his largemouth cousin. While bronzebacks take their share of minnows, crayfish, and hellgrammites and other nymphs, they consume large quantities of airborne insects, including mayflies, dragonflies, bees, grasshoppers, locusts, ladybugs, and Japanese and other beetles— all of which are readily imitated by the dry-fly fisherman.

24

Fly Fishing for Northern Pike

ONCE a gent named David Jordan described northern pike as "mere machines for the assimilation of other organisms." Very true. About the only thing a pike won't eat is whatever eats him first.

Pike are among the fiercest, most-feared critters roaming fresh water. Like bass, they'll eat any kind of minnow, suckers, smaller pike, tadpoles, salamanders, worms, hellgrammites, crayfish, baby ducks and other birds, mice, even small muskrats. No doubt about it: The northern pike (old *Esox lucius*) is a glutton.

Most serious fishermen all over the country—even in the southern states where northern pike do not occur—at one time or another fish for northern pike. The pike is such a ravenous gamefish that sportsmen from about everywhere are willing to travel great distances to tangle with them on rod and reel. All fishermen in America's northern tier of states enjoy fishing for pike; all over lower Canada there are countless superb pike rivers and lakes, and fishermen come from all over the

world to fish Canada's pristine, wilderness pike lakes.

What baffles me, however, is why so few pike fishermen ever go after them with standard fly-rod gear—fly rods, fly reels, fly lines, leaders, and streamer flies and popping bugs!

Most pike fishermen use regular bass-type plug (bait) casting rods, reels and lines, or similar spinning outfits. Probably not ten percent of our fly fishermen ever try for big northern pike on flies and bugs. They think pike will "cut off," that they "can't be handled on a fly rod," and still believe that the only efficient tools for northerns are a metal spoon, a stiff casting rod, a heavy line, wire leader, and a multiplying reel. They never even *think* to try regular fly-rod tackle with big streamer flies or popping bugs. Yet there is no more productive way on earth to fish for northern pike (when they are in reasonably shallow water) than with regulation fly-rod tackle.

Fly-rodding for pike will cost you the occasional fish, of course, but then some northerns occasionally break things up regardless of the tackle used. One day Harvey Dryden hooked a 14-pound Middle Lake pike on a spoon. The fish broke off. An hour later I hooked the same pike on a fly, and recovered Dryden's spoon. No one can complain much about fish that cooperate like that.

How large are the pike likely to be that we take on fly rods? That depends, of course, on where we are fishing. If the lake we are fishing holds chiefly small or medium northerns, and very few lunkers, then we can't reasonably expect to hook a monster. On the other hand if we are fortunate enough to be fishing, say, a wilderness pike lake, we can readily expect to land a trophy on our fly rod. It has been my good fortune to have fished annually for more than 35 years many of the prime pike lakes in this country and all Canadian provinces, chiefly Manitoba and Saskatchewan. In that time I've lost count of the northerns landed weighing over 20 pounds.

The first big one, 18 pounds, was taken at First Cranberry Lake, in northern Manitoba, on a 7-inch-long, saddle-hackle, winged, red-yellow streamer fly in June 1959. The largest pike I ever landed on a fly, and had weighed, was 26 pounds. But I am confident I have hooked and lost on fly tackle pike weighing to 28 pounds and more. I once lost a northern that I saw plainly in 4 feet of water on Saskatchewan's Middle Lake, a broadening of the Fond-du-Lac River. The fish hit a giant streamer he had trailed right to the boat, was solidly hooked, streaked away for flooded alders some 70 feet from the boat, muscled his way into the dense brush, and snapped the leader like it was thread. I'm

sure that northern was close to 30 pounds. It was a scene and experience I've never forgotten, and never will.

FLIES AND BUGS FOR NORTHERN PIKE

For some reason unknown to me a northern pike completely loses his cool when suddenly confronted with a twitching, darting, scooting streamer fly, or a slowly worked fly-rod bug.

Experienced fishermen know that a well-tied, properly designed streamer is extremely lifelike in the water. But then, so is a quality spoon, and particularly so if it is carefully garnished with a strip of porkrind and then skillfully teased and wobbled through the reeds at the hands of a bait caster who knows what he's about. Yet given an immediate choice between a big streamer, a spoon-and-porkrind, that famous-brand red-and-white spoon, or any other good lure, a northern will, in my experience, strike the fly ten times out of ten.

I'm speaking, of course, only of times when northerns are in shallow water—when they're laying up in the muddy or sand-bottom bays, in weed- and lily pad–filled water less than 15 feet deep. If they're too deep, naturally they won't come to a fly. (I'm excluding ultradeep fly-fishing techniques.)

I have never experienced a shallow-water northern pike situation in which streamer flies did not outfish hardware cast by other fishermen to the same places. I recall one instance, however, when fly rod streamers were outfished dramatically by ordinary spoons. Wilf Organ and Cory Kilvert, of Manitoba's Tourism Branch, and I were fishing the mouth of a deep creek entering Reed Lake in northwestern Manitoba.

I was fly fishing. They were bait casting, using traditional chrome, and red-white spoons. Big pike were literally stacked in that creek mouth. While Wilf and Cory took a northern on nearly *every* cast, I didn't hook one. The fish were down 20 feet, hanging under a peat bank, and none ever saw my shallow-running fly.

But a pike lying in shallow water will charge a large streamer fly quicker than anything else. A streamer fly 5 to 7 inches long is deadlier on pike than any surface or underwater plug, any popping bug, or any spoon. On several occasions while fishing Canadian wilderness lakes, I've seen large streamer flies draw pike away from spoons they were trailing and about to hit. Most fishermen know of a pike's tendency to follow slowly—from a distance of a couple of feet to a couple of inches—a sparkling, wobbling spoon. Often—on seeing a pike stalking a companion's spoon—I've cast a big streamer to one side of the fish and had the pike turn away from the spoon and smash head-on into the fly. Friends and I have done that time after time, just to prove the effectiveness of ultralarge streamer flies on pike. Something about them breaks pike up!

Over many years of writing about taking northern pike on standard fly-fishing tackle, and with flies and bugs, I've received many letters from readers implying that while streamers may get pike in the wilderness waters of Canada, they won't score in "civilized" lakes—such as exist in the Midwest and West. If you believe that,

you may miss out on what is one of freshwater angling's biggest thrills—namely, taking large pike on flies and bugs.

In places where there are large northern pike (Idaho, Montana, South and North Dakota, Wisconsin, Minnesota, Wyoming, Canada, etc.) we are not going to get decent pike if we do not offer them a decent fly.

Any large streamer fly will prove to be highly effective on northern pike when the fish are in shallow, weedy bays. One of my favorites, however, is a fly I designed myself years ago.

It's called the McNally Magnum, averages 6 inches in length, and has a short chenille body and long, webby hackles for winging. It seems most effective on northerns in red-and-yellow, but it's also very productive in red-and-white. The fly is tied on size 1/0 to 3/0 hooks, saltwater types, and larger hooks aren't necessary since a pike's spade-like mouth will engulf the entire fly when the fish strikes.

These Magnum streamers, incidentally, are tied commercially in small quantities by professional fly tyer Jim Poulas, P.O. Box 8351, Hot Springs Village, Arkansas 71909; (501) 922-4615.

Bucktail streamers are very good in white and yellow, or in those two colors mixed with red. The double-wing type of bucktail, such as in the "Blonde" series of flies (Honey Blonde, Strawberry Blonde, etc.) are excellent pike flies, chiefly because of their long, full bodies. Streamers of polar bear hair and impala do well.

The size of the fly is most important. They should be no less than 4 inches long, and 6 inches is better if you're hoping for northerns 10 to 20 pounds or more.

Such large streamer flies have an up-and-down movement in the water, and ones with webby saddle-hackle winging are preferred because the feathers "breathe" in the water.

Northern pike hit most readily when plugs, spoons, flies, and bugs are fished *ultraslowly*. Seldom will a northern *chase* after anything. In spring he lives in a bay that is probably stiff with suckers as well as other pike, all in assorted sizes. *Esox lucius*, alias "water wolf," alias the northern pike, could care less whether he eats a sucker or another northern, so most of the time to get a meal all he need do is swim about briefly with his mouth open. He becomes indolent about food, and wants the easy meal. Streamers of saddle-hackle winging can be fished ultraslowly, and they have good action even when merely sinking in the water.

One June afternoon George Strickler, former sports editor of the *Chicago Tribune*, and I were fishing Eagle Lake at Vermilion Bay, Ontario. We reached a rocky point where the water dropped off to about 40 feet. Two small weedy bays fringed the point. Standing in the bow, I flipped a big, yellow-red McNally Magnum out about 15 feet, then began stripping enough line from the reel for a normal 60-foot cast. When I'd pulled all the line from the reel that I wanted and dropped it at my feet, I looked up and saw that the fly had sunk to about 10 feet. The fly's long hackles were waving and fluttering in the clear water.

As I started to take up slack to lift the fly, a giant pike suddenly appeared, opened his mouth, and inhaled the fly. My fly rod bowed as the fish dove for the rocks, then

it suddenly whipped back as the leader snapped.

"That was a BIG pike!" I said, turning to Strickler.

"I know," George grinned. "I didn't see the fish, but when you hooked him your mouth dropped open and you turned pink."

Here's a good example of the fun you can have, and the effectiveness of fly fishing for northern pike: In June 1960 I flew to Black Lake, a wilderness uranium-mining town near Stony Rapids, Saskatchewan. I caught dozens of large northerns on big streamers I'd made from *the hair of a wolf-skin rug*.

While flying into Black Lake's Camp Grayling, which then was operated by Walt Schaeffer, a side compartment door on the Cessna float plane opened and out tumbled my tackle bag full of reels, flies, and other gear. When I bemoaned my loss to Schaeffer, he said that a friend of mine, outdoor writer Jack Parry, was fishing at nearby Hatchet Lake.

The plane was dispatched to Hatchet and later returned with a fly reel and line, and some small streamers—on loan from Parry. The reel and line would be okay with one of my rods, but I knew the flies were too small for decent pike.

Seeing a huge wolf-skin rug on the lodge wall, and eyeing the long, ivory-cream hairs in the tail, I asked Schaeffer if I could snip enough hair for a half-dozen streamer flies. Schaeffer's wife, Bea, provided some red yarn and a spool of coarse black thread. Using a plier, I twisted the single trailing hooks off some spoons. I wrapped the red yarn over the hook shanks then tied on generous bunches of wolf hair

When the author lost tackle on a Canadian bush flight, these streamers were fashioned from the tail hairs of a wolf-skin rug. All they caught were pike.

as winging. The big, bushy flies ranged 4 to 5 inches in length.

Next morning Walt and I rowed into a quiet bay fringed with low, thick willows. Following us in another boat were a Cree Indian guide and Al Hill, a professional photographer from Regina, Saskatchewan.

Soon after entering the bay we saw the wake of a surface-cruising northern. The pike's tail, dorsal fin, and tip of his nose protruded. He looked like a small alligator lounging on the surface sunning himself.

Schaeffer paddled quietly forward and at 70 feet I cast one of the wolf-hair flies. The streamer settled 10 feet beyond the pike. The northern bolted forward, struck, was hooked, and—ten minutes later—was boated, weighed, and released. Schaeffer said the fish went 18 pounds, 6 ounces.

Moments later, as Al Hill made photos, a second large northern was seen cruising near alders. Hill was alerted, a cast was made, and as the pike hit the wolf-hair fly

Hill got a photo of the fish blowing a hole in the lake. That one weighed $17^3/_4$ pounds. So two casts with the makeshift wolf-hair flies had brought two good northerns to the boat, and suddenly the loss of my fly-fishing gear didn't seem so bad.

One day Schaeffer and I saw a northern lying just under the surface, looking like a floating log or an alligator. It was the biggest northern I ever saw, and Schaeffer and I both guessed he weighed 28 to 30 pounds. I cast my streamer to one side of the fish, and he ignored it. I cast again, and he ignored it. But on the third cast, as the fly stripped past him he turned, opened a spade-size mouth, clamped onto the fly, rolled over, burst into the willows, and broke off.

That particular Saskatchewan trip was the best pike fly fishing I ever had.

Some fishermen use weedless streamer flies on pike, and some also use spinners

In this vintage photo Walt Schaeffer looks on as a youthful Tom McNally fights a large northern to the boat. The fish hit a wolf-hair fly.

with their streamers. I dislike weedless hooks and prefer snagging a weed occasionally to the possibility of not hooking a striking fish. And spinners are an unnecessary addition since big streamers are, by themselves, attractive enough to pike.

The need for big flies on large pike can't be stressed enough. Big pike will take small flies—but mostly they ignore them. A northern better than 15 pounds has a maw like two clamped shovel blades, so the bigger the fly offered him the better. Bill Catherwood makes some very large streamers that are super for pike. His Catherwood Originals are fantastic fish-getters—5 to 8 inches long—but Bill has trouble filling orders.

Some of the big standard saltwater flies are very good on northerns, but some of the popular South Florida tarpon flies, even those effective on 100-pound silver

kings, are smallish for pike. That's the way it is.

To put this matter of fly size for pike another way: a 100-pound tarpon very likely will take a 3- or 4-inch-long streamer stripped across his path. A 20-pound northern pike *likely* will take the small 3- to 4-inch fly, but he *surely* will pop the streamer 6 to 8 inches long that is drawn across his nose.

Northern pike will hit fly-rod popping bugs, which can be a lot of fun, but in my opinion they do not take bugs as readily as large streamers. When northerns are in the back end of weedbeds, in water only 1 to 3 feet deep, a popping bug that is too large or popped too hard can spook the fish. Streamers are the thing to use in such shallows.

Popping bugs get good results along the outside fringe of weed and lily-pad beds,

McNally (left) and Schaeffer show two of the big northern pike that hit wolf-hair flies and were saved for the camp chef to steak-out and feed hungry fishermen.

where the water may be 8 or 10 feet deep. Poppers also are productive when fished around rocky points, where the water may drop off to 15 feet or so. A gurgling popping bug often will bring pike up when a streamer fly will not.

Long, thin-bodied poppers tied on 3X long-shank hooks, in hook sizes 1/0 to 3/0, are preferred for northerns. The bug's tail or "winging" can be of saddle-hackle feathers, polar bear hair, impala, or bucktail. Long white bucktail is excellent; enough should be tied in to give the bug good length and bulk.

RETRIEVING

How a streamer fly is retrieved, or how a popping bug is worked, is very important to a fly-rodder's success in fishing for northern pike. There are little niceties you can impart to the retrieve of your streamer that force a fish that was only trailing to tear suddenly at your fly like a mad dog.

There are no special or difficult refinements involved in retrieving big streamer flies through pike water. A slow retrieve generally is most productive, but it's possible to impart lively action to a magnum-size streamer without actually moving the fly very fast through the water. It's best to begin stripping a fly back slowly, in foot-long hauls, as soon as the fly hits the water. Sometimes it's good to allow a streamer to settle for a foot or so before starting it back. The fly can be brought slowly along, the retrieve speeded briefly, then stopped, then started again. When a watery wake caused by a trailing northern appears behind the fly, hurry the fly along for about

2 feet, then stop retrieving. Invariably the following pike will rush in and clobber the fly.

Never strip a fly in hurriedly simply for the sake of making another cast. Keep the fly in the water in "fishy" spots as long as possible, and make it flutter along slowly by jiggling the rod tip. Some pike will trail a lure right to the boat, so fish out every cast and don't lift the fly until you see it and know there's no pike behind it.

TACKLE

No one will get decent northern pike if they can't build decent leaders. We can get by with a variety of fly tackle on pike, but leaders *must be right.*

A common misbelief among many fishermen is that wire leaders are necessary when fishing for pike, especially with fly tackle. They are *not!* Heavy, hard-type nylon monofilament is more than adequate.

Leader design is very important, as it is in all fly fishing. Start with a 3-foot length of 45- to 50-pound-test stiff monofilament attached to the fly-line end with a nail knot. This serves as a permanent leader butt connection, with leaders being tied to it. In making up a typical leader for pike, try tying a 3-foot strand of stiff nylon, 35-pound test, to the 45- to 50-pound-test permanent leader butt knotted to the fly line. Going down from the 35-pound mono are a 2-foot section of 25-pound, 1½ feet of 15-pound, 1-foot of 10-pound, and then a 12-inch "shock" tippet of 20- to 60-pound-test nylon.

Some very large northern pike have been taken on nylon shock tippets of 20-pound test, but then some pike's teeth have sawed through tippets testing 45 pounds. Tippet size is relative to the average size of the pike we expect to catch. In waters where an 8-pound pike is a very good one there's no reason to use a tippet of more than 25-pound test. Where you might expect a 20-pound fish, it would be reckless to use a tippet testing under 40 pounds.

A 40-pound hard nylon leader tippet will usually do for most northern pike fly fishing, but occasionally in the Canadian wilderness lakes and some other areas it's possible to get into fish that too often chew up 40-pound strands, and one needs to up tippet strength to 60-pound test.

Big northerns will suck large streamer flies far back into their mouths, so a leader tippet frequently will be rubbing sandpaper-like lips, a tongue and pallet coated with tiny secondary teeth, and, of course, the fish's canine teeth. Although a pike's canine teeth are large and pointed, they are not the ones that do the most damage to leaders; the canine teeth are round, and therefore a leader tippet slipping between two of them is not likely to be cut. It's the secondary teeth that do the damage.

A pike's gill plates also can fray a leader, as can sharp edges on the fish's jaw hinges. A pike fisherman should check his leader frequently throughout its length, and immediately replace frayed sections. It's wise when catching pike with regularity to replace shock tippets periodically whether or not the tippet shows wear.

Northern pike certainly are not among the world's great gamefishes, especially compared with saltwater species, but a heavy pike in shallow, weed-filled water can be a tough one to handle. I've seen fly fishermen's leader knots pull out when they hooked good pike; I've seen knots at the fly come undone; and I've seen the knots connecting the leader butt to the fly line slip free under the pull exerted by a 15-pound pike trying to bore back into weeds. So—if you want big pike on flies or bugs—be sure of your knots.

It must be understood, however, that no matter how well knots are tied, or how heavy a leader tippet is, some pike are going to be lost anyway. So what? Even when bait casting or spinning with heavy nylon-coated wire leaders some northerns are lost.

The ideal fly rod for northern pike fishing is $8^1/_2$ to $9^1/_2$ feet long, weighs $4^1/_2$ to $5^1/_2$ ounces, and takes either a WF-8F or WF-9F line. Whether the rod has a slow action or a fast-tip action is a matter of preference. What's important is that you are able to cast large, wind-resistant flies and bugs with it properly—with no sweat and strain. Most of the time in fly fishing for pike I use a 9-foot graphite rod weighing 5 ounces. With it I can toss big flies or bugs around dawn-to-dark with no fatigue.

The reel for pike fly fishing is not particularly important, although, of course, a quality single-action reel is desirable. If the reel is of the proper size it will probably take about 200 yards of 18-pound test backing line, but likely none of us will ever hook a northern that will run out all the fly line and get into the backing line. Pike fight slowly and doggedly, darting here and there, splashing on the surface, sulking; seldom does even a large northern run more than 25 or 35 yards.

Nonetheless, it's wise (in any fly fishing) to have a quality reel. This doesn't mean you need to have a $300 diamond-studded, leather-backed mugawumps, but you should have a reel with good line capacity and a smooth, adjustable drag.

WHERE TO FISH

In early spring and again in fall pike frequent shallow, weedy, mud-bottomed bays. In hot weather they usually move to more open water, haunting shallow bars, reefs, rocky points, and islands. But easily the best fishing for the fly-rodder is when the fish are in the mahogany-colored water of weed-and-lily-pad bays. Always fish incoming creeks and streams, because pike often move out of lakes into such areas.

Pike often hang out in pools below waterfalls or rapids, provided the current isn't too strong, or if there are pockets, holes, or "edges" where the fish can avoid the heavy current. They prefer quiet water.

Pike occasionally go very deep, and some have been caught at depths exceeding 75 feet. They seem to go really deep, however, only when necessary to forage on deep-down ciscoes. Most of the time, throughout the year, northerns will be found in water less than 15 feet deep—which is another reason why pike are such excellent fly-rod fish. Deepwater fish are not readily taken on flies.

Excluding migrations during their spawning season, pike appear to be homebodies and do not move around much. But—for reasons best known to the pike—they can desert a spot overnight. Once Don Zienty and I found a shallow bay in Eagle Lake, Ontario, literally stiff with pike. We estimated we landed and released some 70 pike the first afternoon, all on flies. The very next morning the bay was empty of fish. Water temperature, time of year, food supply, and perhaps immediate weather conditions all seem to influence movements of northern pike.

As with so many freshwater species, early spring seems the best time to fish for northern pike. This is when the fish are in the weedy shallows, hanging on in the thin-water bays after their inshore spawning runs. Of course "spring" is relative, varying not according to the calendar but according to latitude. Pike will be in the shallows of Montana's Canyon Ferry Lake in March and April; in Idaho's Coeur d'Alene Lake they'll be in the border marshes in late April and May; but in the far northern lakes of Ontario, Quebec, Manitoba, Saskatchewan, and Alberta, June is the time. In a normal season the first two weeks of June are the best time for a northern pike fly-fishing sortie to anywhere in Canada's "big pike belt."

Some places that have provided extraordinary fly fishing for large northern pike include, in Manitoba—First Cranberry Lake, Reed Lake, Mitchell Lake, Winnipeg River, Cormorant Lake, Gods Lake, Simonhouse Lake, Grass River, Kississing Lake, and Nakomis Lake; in Saskatchewan—Black Lake, Middle Lake, Fond-du-Lac River, Cree Lake, Lake Athabasca, Hatchet Lake, Wollaston Lake, and Careen Lake; in Ontario—Eagle Lake, Peshu Lake, Lake-of-the-Woods, Rainy Lake, and Basswood Lake. Those are just some of Canada's good spots; there are, of course, many others as good or better.

To consistently catch trophy-size northern pike on flies and bugs it may be necessary to go into the northern wilds and fish "virgin" or near-virgin waters. But a great deal of good fly fishing for pike exists close to some large metropolitan areas, although the fish may average around 6 pounds or less, instead of running in the 12- to 15-pound class.

The fish-and-game departments and the tourism branches of the various Canadian provinces can provide additional information on their pike fishing areas, as can the fish-and-game departments in the United States.

25
Panfish on Flies and Bugs

THE most interesting day I ever had fishing for panfish was at Williston's Pond on Maryland's Eastern Shore. The Sho' ponds, as we called them, were notable for two things: green-backed, white-bellied largemouth bass, and slab-sided, orange-bellied pumpkinseed sunfish.

Cinematographer Dave Smith and I had been commissioned by the Cortland Line Company to do a film on bass-bug fishing. Most of what we needed was "in the can," as the movie types say, but some fill-in footage was necessary. It wasn't to be a day of heavy work, so I decided to make it a family outing, taking Phyllis along, as well as Bobby, who then was waist-high at age five. Dave got the important shooting done; then we charcoaled steaks and had baked potatoes and cold beer. Then I took Bob out in the old wooden skiff to fish for sunnies. I had my favorite small-stream trout rod along, a 6-foot Orvis Superfine bamboo stick weighing $2\frac{1}{2}$ ounces and taking a DT-5 line. I'd scull the boat along one willow-lined bank, 30 to 40 feet from shore, and, with Bobby nestled on the seat

between my legs, I'd cast a big bivisible dry fly into the shadows. Quick as I could I'd spool what little slack remained following a cast back onto the reel, then I'd reach over Bob's shoulders and give him the rod. By then a pumpkinseed would have inhaled the fly, and with the excitement that only a five-year-old enjoys, Bob would reel and the little bamboo stick would go into a deep bend as he fought the fish to the boat. Many times I watched with concern as my favorite mini-rod bent double, but while I encouraged Bob and tried to explain the niceties of rod handling, I was not about to interrupt his fishing. The rod, if need be, was expendable.

The pumpkinseeds cooperated perfectly. All I had to do was throw the fly up there under the trees, hand Bob the rod, and a fish was on. It was superb. No finer situation ever existed for a dad trying to show his son the excitement of angling. I don't know how many gold-sided sunnies Bob landed, but the floorboards were covered with them—all good fish, $\frac{1}{2}$ to $\frac{3}{4}$ pound.

We sat out in the backyard, Bob and I,

and cleaned and scaled those sunfish, and talked of the day's fishing. Then, when we had a couple dozen or so done, we took them into the kitchen and told Phyllis, "Look, Bob caught our dinner!" I'll never forget the look on Bob's face when he presented those fish to his mother. He absolutely beamed with pride. We seasoned and floured the fish and deep-fried them to a golden brown, and ate them the way kids go through popcorn at a picnic.

At this writing Bob McNally is age 41, but he still remembers that day of panfishing on Maryland's Eastern Shore, and of the pride in bringing the fish home, and of the scrumptious meal the family enjoyed.

Panfish overpopulate many waters—nation-wide—and ought to be fished for, and enjoyed, by more fly fishermen. In these days of catch-and-release for increasingly scarce gamefish, the chance to enjoy guilt-free fish-fries should not be overlooked.

PANFISH SPECIES

Ask the man battling a bluefin tuna off Cat Cay what were the first fish he ever caught. Ask the same of the man hooked to a 25-pound salmon in the River Mals in Norway. Ask, too, the guy in the bass boat wanging out a spinner-bait at Bull Shoals in Arkansas. And query the same of the gent who, so delicately, is delivering 60 feet of fly line carrying a size 22 midge to brainy browns in Armstrong Spring Creek, at Livingston, Montana.

To a man—or perhaps it would be more correct to say to a boy—they will chorus that they grew up catching bluegills, sunnies, and other panfish.

The panfish is important to the fly-rodder, young or old. It is the best fish for the beginner learning the basics of the fly fisherman's art, and it is a fish that all of us—no matter how many years, how many miles, how many rivers flow by—ought to take time out to occasionally fish for. A friend of mine has a shooting preserve and some small lakes about 40 miles from Chicago. Several times a summer I like to go there and walk the grassy banks, in the evenings, and fish small popping bugs for bluegills. Every bluegill taken is big enough to cover your hand, and they are strong, persistent little fighters on a light rod.

One thing favoring panfish angling is that the fish are everywhere. They are prolific breeders, and are abundant in just about all areas. You can find good panfish populations in city parks, farm ponds, streams, rivers, reservoirs, and natural lakes. They're even present in great numbers in brackish waters, and some panfish species are found in salt water.

What is a panfish? "Panfish" is a broad term that applies to a large group of small fish, including the bluegill and other sunfish, white bass, black and white crappie, yellow perch and white perch, rock bass, warmouth—and probably I've missed some. Some kind of sunfish is what most of us catch, and the bluegill is the undisputed king of the clan. They grow fairly large (though those 1 1/2- and 2-pound specimens we hear about are seldom seen), are widely distributed and populous, and take sunken or floating flies and bugs readily. Something else in the bluegill's favor is that, like the majority of panfish, he sits pretty well in a fry pan, too.

A lot of my boyhood was spent at rock

Bluegill

Green Sunfish

White Bass

Crappie

Yellow Perch

White Perch

Rock Bass

The most popular species of panfish.

quarries near Cockysville, Maryland. These were swimming holes—deep ones dropping down to 80 and 100 feet along sheer granite cliffs—but they had bass and bluegills in good supply. Excluding the odd fish, we couldn't catch the bass, which we could see plainly in the clear spring water, and which could plainly see us. Whenever I tired of swimming and jumping feet-first and screaming off the high cliffs, I'd grab the old metal GEP hollow jointed fly rod I had, sit myself in an inflated innertube, and hand-paddle across Lindsay's Quarry to a rocky corner swimmers avoided. With profound lack of skill, I banged a little bee-type wet fly to the cliff edge, executing some casts that easily went 15 feet. In some ways it was precarious fishing, because I had to keep both elbows hooked over the innertube, behind dangling down, knees up over the front of the tube, feet in the water, and all the time try to fly cast yet remain stable in the tube. It wasn't easy. With each rocking motion of casting the tube would spin, and while one minute I faced the rocky cliff in dropping the bee, the next I looked out across the vast expanse of quarry, while my little fly fished busily behind me.

Somehow I managed to hook and release a couple of small bluegills; then suddenly the rod doubled over and something *strong* hit the fly. Being a greenhorn fly fisherman I'd never felt anything like that. I hung onto the rod with both hands while the innertube skittered over the surface and started spinning crazily. Everything was out of control. I hollered for help to my brother-in-law, who was watching from a distant point. Holly had been a powerful tournament swimmer, and when he dove in his determination to reach the

kid in the tube in seconds was clear. Unfortunately, the bass came out of the water, that little yellow-black bee showing plainly in his jaw, and seeing that 3-pounder shook my roots. I bellowed again for help, and now could hear Holly's powerful strokes churning the water as he speedboated toward me.

The bass dug determinedly for the bottom. Not knowing enough to give line, I held on and was promptly up-dumped out of the innertube. Holly was at my side now and I held the rod high, in a death grip with both hands, while I tried to tread water and escape drowning. Holly was yelling and grabbing and giving advice while I kept swallowing water. Finally the bass couldn't take all the pressure, so he started full speed for the surface from 15 feet down. My nose and eyes were barely out of water when the bass burst out not 4 feet from my face. I don't know if you've ever experienced a 3-pound bass leaping wildly at eye level, and tailwalking into your face, but to a twelve-year-old it is disconcerting.

The bass ripped the bee out of his jaw and disappeared, diving for bottom. I gurgled and sputtered and panted and blew water. Holly laughed crazily and helped me back into the tube. Once ashore I hysterically reviewed the incident with all who listened, and over subsequent years the bass easily reached the 6-pound class. The event was, of course, an encounter with a largemouth black bass, but bluegills started it.

TACKLE AND FLIES FOR PANFISH

Regardless of which panfish species we fish for, the tackle for one usually will do for

The underwater camera catches a long-eared sunfish inhaling a minute popping bug. Small fly-rod bugs take a lot of panfish when fished slowly.

all. Light tackle is preferred, obviously, and although some anglers choose long, light, willowy fly rods, my preference is for short, light, willowy rods. I've never experienced a need for a panfishing rod more than 7½ feet long, and what I like most is a little bamboo job I can hold in my fingertips, which bends under the load of a No. 4 or 5 line, which goes just right with the lightest, smallest fly reel I can find and which, despite its diminutive size, will easily toss a little bluegill bug to 60 feet.

Graphite rods, being the lightest, certainly have an important place in the pan-fishing scheme. Some fishermen will go to 9-foot graphite rods, but such a pencil-thin stick should accept a No. 4 or 5 line, or even a No. 3, if it is to be a fun tool on panfish.

If bugging for panfish, a floating three-diameter line may be a reasonable selection, but usually the bugs used are small and light enough to be cast well with a double-taper. Sinking-tip lines and full-sinking lines can be helpful to the panfisher at times.

Lake Geneva in southeastern Wisconsin is a deep, clear, glacial lake heavy with

This nice string of rock bass from Wisconsin's Lake Geneva, all caught on sunken flies, will make a fine outdoor fish fry.

bass, walleyes, pike, and panfish. It has some of the chunkiest, red-eyed, always-hungry rock bass you can find. Trouble is that while Geneva is a cold lake, sunlight penetration is severe, so on summer afternoons the rock bass sink to the 15-foot level. Lake Geneva's banks are literally lined with old dock cribbings, sunken foundations of stone rubble and planking that start at the shore and go out to 10- to 20-foot depths. Rock bass, as their name indicates, like to hang around rocks and boulders, and I doubt if you can find a crib at Geneva without its contingent of rock bass.

We fish for them with full-sinking, high-density lines. We keep the boat close to shore and motor along softly with the electric, searching lakeward for the sunken cribs. Every 50 to 100 yards or so—

depending upon the extent of the estate property we're working off—we will find cribs. We hold up then and lay out our casts to cover the deepest crib. Small streamer flies, sizes 8 to 10, do the job, or wet flies, but large nymphs are best of all. Catches of twenty-five to fifty Geneva rock bass per angler are not unusual, and the fixin's for some of the finest fish fries I've enjoyed have been courtesy of Lake Geneva.

Easily some of the finest panfish for fly fishermen, in areas where the species occur, are yellow perch, white perch, white bass, and crappies. All will take a fly readily. The yellow perch is the only one of the four I've ever caught on a small floating bug, but I've read that the other three will take not only bugs but even dry flies. Come to think of it, maybe I've caught a crappie or two on a bug, but never one on a dry fly; the crappies I catch are almost always deep.

White perch go very hard for a fly. They are a setup for a small, sparsely tied streamer fly, and in the brackish areas where they are found I like to give them a shrimp imitation, like the Phillips Pink Shrimp, which was designed for bonefish.

The white bass is one of my favorite panfish. Many areas around the country, especially the Midwest and middle South, get very large springtime spawning runs of "stripers." The Mississippi River, particularly in the area called Lake Pepin, located below Red Wing, Minnesota, has more white bass per square inch of water than any place I've seen. Wisconsin's Wolf River gets an uncommonly extensive run of white bass each May from Lake Winnebago. I go out with Clayton Looker, at Fremont, when that run is on, and, fishing a two- or three-fly rig with bonefish flies, I've caught over a hundred white bass in an afternoon. Three fish on one cast is not unusual. What you do is throw your three-fly rig out there, twitch the flies along until a white bass hits one, then let him dart around, fighting the hook, dragging the other flies behind, until one after another white bass engulfs the two remaining flies. This may sound like big apples to someone who has never been into a full-blown white-bass run, but in truth it is about as difficult as slipping on Winnebago's ice in January.

White bass are well known for driving schools of shiner minnows to the surface, then piling into them in wild feeding orgies. At a lot of lakes fishermen drift around in their boats, scanning the distant surface with binoculars, watching and waiting for the first telltale splash of water for the first

Gordon Graves, of Kankakee, Illinois, shows the panfisherman's delight, a plump bluegill.

signs of minnows scurrying over the top, white bass in hot pursuit. The fly fisherman who comes across such surface-feeding "stripers" is lucky indeed. A fish on every cast is the rule, and they'll take about anything thrown to them. A white bucktail streamer fly is good, size 6 or 8, or a skittering bug, such as the Bullet Bug. A bug should be fished very fast at the edge of a school, made to skip along like a fleeing, frantic minnow, and the streamer fly also should be fished fast, in 2- to 3-foot jumps.

All of the panfish species can be taken by the fly fisherman all season long, but the fastest fishing usually is during spawning activities. Crappies, for example, can be

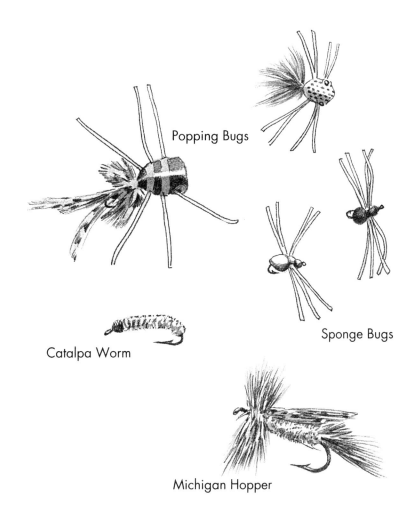

Popping Bugs

Catalpa Worm

Sponge Bugs

Michigan Hopper

Flies and bugs for panfish.

taken by the bucketful in early spring when they're spawning around brush piles 6 to 12 feet down. A streamer fly worked around the snags on a sinking line often will take one crappie after another. Try for them with marabous and bucktails, in white, yellow, and black. Patterns with silver tinsel bodies seem to be especially productive. After the spawning period you can expect crappies to be in deeper water, sometimes to 20 feet, but usually they'll stack up around sunken tree tops, brush,

bridge abutments, or other cover at depths of 10 to 15 feet. They like cool water and shade, and because they are school fish—like white bass and perch—where you catch one you can catch many more by careful, repeat casting.

Bluegills take a fly without hesitation when they are "bedding" in spring. Their nests or "beds" are easy to find, showing clearly as open sand pockets in shallow water along the banks, or on shallow reefs. Usually there'll be a cluster of bluegill beds in a single area, with a pair of fish on each. Drop a small bug or fly into or near a nest, and a bluegill will pick it up every time.

I attended a bass-bluegill tournament for fly fishermen once at Florida's Lake Okeechobee, fishing out of Buckhead Marina. Just about everybody got limits of fifty bluegills a day (released), fishing the beds. The rim canal at Okeechobee was spotted every couple of feet with big, circular beds, and using small cork bugs with rubber legs, we'd take one or more bluegills from every nest.

Small popping bugs with white, yellow, or black rubber legs are among the best panfish lures, especially for bluegills. The bugs shouldn't be popped hard, or fished fast. They should be worked gently, very slowly, for the bluegill is a slow, deliberate riser. The rubber legs of the bug provide enough action even when the bug rests motionless. Most strikes, in fact, come when the bug is sitting still. Throw a bug out there and let it sit. You'll see a bluegill swim in and stop, watching, a couple of feet below the bug. Then he moves up a foot, stops, watches some more. Now he may turn and drop out of sight, only to instantly reappear, this time closer to the bug. He's a foot away; now 3 inches. He backs off a bit, then *pop* . . . he has the bug and, hooked now, starts into that diving, broadside turn, then those frantic, swift little circles that put a bend in your rod and a grin on your face.

The sponge-rubber or sponge-plastic bug, both with thin rubber legs, is another top-rated panfish fly-rod lure. Some have cricket-shaped bodies, some spider-shaped, but they all are irresistible to bluegills and other panfish.

Grasshopper imitations, such as the Michigan Hopper and small greased Muddler Minnows take their share of panfish. As might be expected, nymphs are deadly. The fur-bodied patterns are good, but so are the flat hard-backs. A fly that will absolutely level the smartest, best-fed bluegill is a Squash Bug, with a thin sliver of white porkrind on the hook. The Squash Bug is a nymph type, with plump orange-wool body, gray turkey-quill back, and grizzly hackling. The addition to the hook bend of a $9^{1}/_{2}$-inch narrow strip of white porkrind is probably frosting on the cake, but the fly/rind combination is ice cream to bluegills.

Another fly good for all panfish, and bluegills in particular, is a green-bodied job meant to represent the catalpa worm. This is a worm found on the catalpa tree, which is common in many parts of the country, but mostly in the Mississippi Valley. Catalpa worms eat catalpa trees, or rather the leaves thereof, and panfish even things up by consuming whatever catalpa worms fall on the water. The worm is green, so we make our Catalpa Worm flies by winding heavy green chenille over a hook shank— going partly around the bend so that the fly has a curved, wormy look. The black tying thread is used to form a buggy black head.

26
Lake Fly Fishing

THERE is a great deal of difference in fly fishing on lakes, as opposed to rivers and streams, regardless of the species of fish sought. For one thing, there is no current, no flow to assist the angler in activating his fly. Most lakes the fly-rodder will fish are clear, and the fish are easily spooked. And lakes are normally deep, and deep water is never a boon to the fly fisherman. Moreover, the fish may be widely dispersed, or tightly grouped in limited areas—either situation adding to the fly fisherman's problems.

There are three basic ways to fish a lake: We can cast from the banks, wade the shallows, or cast from a boat. (Trolling will not be covered, since trolling a fly is not fly fishing.)

There are no special tackle requirements in fly-fishing lakes, but longer rods than usual are desirable, and the angler should have a good selection of sinking lines. Rods with good length make longer casts possible, and in lake fishing we often must probe a great deal of water. To the fly fisherman a lake often does not reveal the obvious fish lies we readily identify in stream fishing, so we must do a lot of blind casting and cover considerable water. A long rod also helps us hold more line off the water, which is desirable in lake dry-fly fishing, or if skimming a fly over the surface. The long rod is handier in bank fishing (longer roll casts, for example) and in working from a boat (easier to keep the fly line high, better in playing fish).

The bulk of the time in lake fishing we are swimming our tinsel and fur beneath the surface, and to do so with a standard floating line is generally a handicap. Floating lines can be used in conjunction with weighted flies, or by putting split-shot sinkers or lead wire on the leader, but these don't permit the angler to fish as well as he might with one of the various types of sinking lines available nowadays. Often a sinking-tip line will do; other times we'll want one that sinks half its length, on a slow fall; still again we may want the same line but in a quick-sinking style; and full-length, slow-sinking lines are useful, along with full-length, high-density, fast-sinking lines.

Does fly fishing work in lakes? George Wold, of Woodstock, Illinois, poses with a 27-pound Chinook salmon taken by the author on a giant streamer fly in Wisconsin's Green Bay, part of Lake Michigan.

Finally, for really deep work, a fast-sinking shooting-head line might be required, or it may be practical to go to a lead-core line. I'm not suggesting that the lake fisherman needs all these lines; only that fishing conditions vary lake to lake, season to season, and each of us must determine which fishing method (and therefore which kind of line) is most productive at a given time. Trial and error, which add up to experience, tell us the way to go.

Leaders are a vital consideration in much lake fishing. Unless the angler is pursuing largemouth bass in turbid waters, long and fine usually is the name of the game in lake fly fishing. I have fished alpine lakes, for example, where it was not possible to get a strike fishing a leader shorter than 15 feet. There have been instances when I've fished 20-foot leaders, and sometimes longer. There's no broken water in a lake to help conceal a fly line; seldom are we able to put our fly around a rock or behind a boulder, and thus keep the fly line out of the fish's vision; and most lakes the fly angler works are clear, some as clear as the alpine air. So long, fine leaders are needed to keep the fly line as far away from the trout as possible, and so keep the fish from detecting the fly line.

TROUT FISHING IN LAKES

The lake-trout species can be caught on the fly, as I'll get into in Chapter 29. But here we're talking about the same species you find in streams.

There's a high-country Montana lake I first heard about from a couple of fishermen in a fly shop in Ennis. "The lake's full of cutthroat trout," they said, "but nobody can catch 'em. Water's too clear, fish too spooky."

The very next day my son Bob and I went up there on our trail bikes and, as the fishermen said, the lake was jammed with cutthroats. They were wrong, though, about the trout being uncatchable.

I took one look at that flat, calm, crystalline lake and said to Bob, "Long, fine, and small." We fished size 18 and 22 dry flies (any pattern), on 6X tippets and 15-foot leaders, and caught trout all afternoon.

An interesting sidelight to that day's fishing was that at one end of the lake I directed Bob in his casting, so that he was able to put his fly right over trout. The lake is so clear you can see pebbles 20 feet down, and bottom at 60 feet. The trout, naturally, are readily visible. Most of the time walking the bank and casting out, we wouldn't cast until we threw to a specific cutthroat.

There's a high bank at the east end of the lake, but in fishing there the angler is so close to the water he can't see fish well, and the light is bad, too. But from the bank behind Bob I could see cruising fish easily. I'd call out, "Okay, Bob, there's a fish coming in from your right, 100 feet up the lake. Get ready." Bob would put some line on the water and get ready to cast. I'd say something like, "Okay, he's 30 feet offshore, still coming, and now only 50 feet down lake. Get some line in the air."

Bob would start false casting, holding 30 feet of line up (counting the leader), so he would be able to drop the fly precisely on target when I told him. Now the trout would be close and I'd start a countdown, like this: "He's coming on the same line, Bob. All right, he's 40 feet away, 30 feet straight out, now he's at 30 feet on your right, coming on, 20 feet, 15, 10 . . . cast!" Out would go the fly line, straight away, and settle down 30 feet in front of Bob.

The trout would spot the fly and speed up a little, closing in. Just for the fun of it I always gave a further countdown, saying, "He sees it. He's coming up. He's 8 feet away, 6, 4, 2 . . . *strike!*" There'd be a dimple, Bob would tighten up, and the trout would be on. The whole thing gave us some great laughs; it's little things like that that help make fly fishing the superb sport it is.

In all lake-trout fishing—for rainbows, cutthroats, brooks, and browns—if there are fish present and possibly actively feeding and you're not catching any, you can figure either the trout see you, or your leader is not long and fine enough, or they don't want the fly you are offering.

As a general rule, the smaller flies work best in lakes, especially high, clear lakes. Whenever you're having a tough time taking trout in some transparent lake, don't be afraid to build an extra-long leader, taper it down to 5X, 6X, or 7X, and fish patterns from size 16 to 22, 24, and even 26 if need be. Dries in sizes 16 and 18, fortunately, will normally do.

In lake fishing for trout the ideal situation is a hatch and rising fish. Sometimes we luck into both and taking a good mess for the fry pan isn't difficult. Other times we'll arrive at a lake and see trout dimpling here and there, obviously rising to the scattered fallen insects even though no genuine hatch is underway. Still other times trout in a lake will rise during a specific hatch, and so selective is their feeding that you can put every fly in your book in front of them without a strike.

The occasion of dimpling trout, with no major hatch underway, can be a good setup for the fly fisherman. This is fishing for "cruisers," trout that are aimlessly swimming the lake, a few feet below the surface, scanning the mirrored lake ceiling for the telltale revealing dent and dimple of a fallen insect. The trout rises then, takes, curves down, and continues his surface-searching cruise.

There's a large but shallow lake in the valley just down the road from our place in southwestern Montana. Our first five years there we never fished the lake, true to form of most trout fishermen, who, given a choice, prefer running water. Then one evening as Al McClane poached Rocky Mountain whitefish on the river at Frank Valgenti's house, the Valgentis told of the excellent dry-fly fishing in the lake.

"Morning's the time," said Frank, the father.

"Got to fish before there's any wind," said Frank, the son. "You can't spot rises unless it's calm."

"All kinds of 2-pound fish," said Vic, the brother, "and there are 3- and 4-pounders, and some lots bigger."

We were on the lake the following morning, fishing from three small aluminum car-top skiffs. Trout were dimpling here and there. When a fish showed we'd row his way, then try to figure the path of his swim. I was in a boat with Frank, Jr.

"When a trout rises," he informed me, "we try to figure the direction he's cruising. When he comes up a second time, and a third, we can readily tell his direction and speed, and so then know where to place our cast."

Trout were dimpling near and far, and now and then there'd be a good big swirl. Some of the fish working were of good size.

Al McClane got a dry in front of a 2-pound rainbow, landed it, and released.

"There's a good fish," Frank said excitedly, pointing an oar. Obliquely off the bow, at 40 feet, was a widening ring, its wavelets 2 inches high. "Watch now," said Frank, "for his next rise." It was quick coming. This time the trout dimpled closer, not 30 feet away, some 20 feet to the left of his initial rise. I flipped a No. 14 Irresistible into the air, made a quick false cast, and dropped the fly 10 feet ahead of the last dimple. I took up slack and waited. The little Irresistible floated jauntily out there, then there was a hump in the water, then a barely discernible oncoming ridge in the water, then a swirl and the leader tightened. I soon released a silver-bright 2 1/2-pound rainbow.

We caught more rainbows and nice brown trout that morning, but the fishing ended at nine o'clock when a stiff breeze swept down the valley. We had many more mornings, and evenings, too, of the same kind of fishing—always casting to cruisers, with long, fine leaders and small flies.

In lake fishing for trout, activating a dry fly repeatedly gets the interest of fish, and subsequently a strike, from trout that otherwise might have just swum on by your floater. Twitching or skimming a dry fly across the surface of a calm lake is a method of triggering many strikes that otherwise would not have been realized. It is well to remember that in addition to the carcasses of real insects, the surface of any lake at any time also has "junk"—a tiny leaf, a floating sliver of bark, weeds, perhaps duck breast feathers (our lake in Montana is coated with them), and other

Swimming a nymph over the surface of a good trout lake is one of the better ways to put fish in the net.

flotsam. So a trout must learn what he can eat and what not. It helps to show him that your fly is edible if, unlike the other stuff floating around, it *moves*. In my opinion, swimming a dry fly on a calm lake is a fly-fishing technique of major importance. It shouldn't be overdone, of course; we can't have our diminutive little dry out there tearing the lake up like a miniature speed-boat. Short, gentle twitches of the rod will do, with some reasonable pauses. The fly should be well greased or oiled so that it rides high when tugged over the surface.

Good patterns for this kind of lake dry-fly fishing include, in addition to the Irresistible, the Hairwing Royal Coach-man, McDougal, Western Bee, any of the bivisibles, and any of the skaters, spiders, and variants.

In stream fishing we normally float or drift our flies to trout, but in lake fishing, when there are no cruisers or risers, we must cast blind and hope to attract trout to our fly. Fishing terrestrials is one way to draw trout. With floating beetles, ants, grasshoppers, crickets, and the like we can make enough of a surface fuss to get the attention of trout a long way off. Good patterns for this kind of lake fishing are the Letort Cricket, Michigan Hopper, Joe's Hopper, Muddler Minnow, and any of many kinds of hair- or foam-bodied ants designed to float. Terrestrials should be cast out, allowed to sit, then gently eased across the top, with little twitches and jerks and long pauses, so that the fly appears to the trout as some land insect struggling over the surface and trying to regain its wings or the shore.

Because they are fishing lakes (open,

probably deep water), many trout fishermen believe they need large flies and need to create quite a stir to draw trout. That may be the case at times, but more often tiny flies and delicate casting and presentation take fish. Midge nymphs fished in the surface film, with no action whatever, many times will take any trout that swims near. There always are exceptions, as we try to point out constantly, but in lake-trout fishing the general rule is long and fine with the leader, and small with the fly.

I've fished many trout lakes where nothing scored as well as a nymph. This I've experienced even when a hatch was in progress and it seemed every trout between the top and the bottom was shooting to the surface and sucking in naturals. You can fish nymphs "blind"—that is, merely covering water and not casting to a specific rise—and catch plenty of trout. If you see a rise or a swirl or a hump in the water, each revealing the presence of a trout, all the better. Cast to it. You can drop your nymph right on the spot, or, better, go a few feet beyond where you feel the trout is, but be careful not to put the line too close.

A good technique in lake fishing for trout with nymphs is to cast and let the nymph sink a bit, carefully watching the line end for signs of a strike. If no strike, the nymph is twitched slowly back, and now and then allowed to settle. The retrieve can be broken up, slow and easy, then fast with long pulls—just as is done in fishing other fly-rod lures. Any of the standard nymph patterns may produce, but on given lakes at given times certain nymphs will far outfish others. It pays to ask around, and to personally test various patterns and techniques.

A great many trout will be taken in the surface film on nymphs, or just inches below, but at times we must go down several feet or even scour the bottom to enjoy any measure of success.

Thompson Lake fills a corner of Bear Basin, in Montana's Spanish Peaks, and when our party topped the divide and looked down on the lake, cutthroats were denting the surface wildly. We tried everything, but didn't really score until we lengthened our leaders to 20 feet, tapered to 5X, and fished a Red Mite (size 18) in the meniscus. Here were good fish, up to 22 inches, picking a fly the size of the half-moon in your little fingernail from the surface of a broad, deep lake. The next morning, however, the fish were deep and we had to sink weighted nymphs on sinking lines down among the boulders to catch them.

Trout in many of our western lakes feed heavily on daphnia, the red water flea, so tiny artificials suggesting this natural food account for many fish. Daphnia are so minute, however, that reasonable representation is impossible—and trout can feed on them merely by swimming around with their mouths open. But trout attuned to daphnia sometimes get all broken up when they spy a size 18 or size 20 nymph floating aimlessly in the surface film. The mite-type nymphs, with body material wrapped around the hook bend, outfish most other types.

Since it is possible to cover more water more quickly with streamer flies than with any other type, it sometimes is best to start lake fishing with streamers. It's a good system when you're confronted with the problem of locating fish. A weighted streamer used with a sinking line will put your fly down 15 to 20 feet or more, and often will produce fish when you're forced to fish transparent water under a bright sun.

There are numerous lakes where the only decent fly fishing is at night. Brown trout are notorious after-sundown prowlers, but other species as well do heavy nighttime feeding. One of the most unusual night-feeding situations I know of is at Great Bear Lake, in Canada's Northwest Territories, and it involves lake trout—big ones.

I had fished Great Bear a couple of times, and using streamer flies had landed lakers to 26 pounds, which is not particularly large for that lake. Then I read in an outdoor magazine that a fisherman had taken many Great Bear lakers on *dry flies*. Never having caught a lake trout on a dry fly, I returned to Great Bear the very next summer. Conditions seemed perfect if any lakers were to be taken on dry flies. The weather was ideal—sunny, windless days and flat, calm water. I surveyed the lake constantly, watching for signs of rising trout, but always nothing. I had a 9-foot rod rigged and ready, a size 12 Light Cahill on the leader, in case a trout dimpled the surface, but the only lake trout caught were by spinning or bait casting with deep-running lures, and occasionally by fishing a streamer fly. After five days I hadn't even cast a dry fly to a laker, and never once did I see a natural insect adrift on the surface.

We were standing around at the airstrip on departure day, waiting for the ancient PBY seaplane to arrive, and a couple of fishermen from Indiana came up and introduced themselves. Their names escape me now, but they'd been fishing out of Plummer's camp, while we'd been at Bill Haerr's Great Bear Lodge. We exchanged fishing notes, and I said I'd been disappointed in not catching some trout on dry flies, and that I'd come all the way to Great Bear for that purpose. The pair exchanged surprised glances, and then told how they'd each caught a couple dozen lake trout, up to 21 pounds, on dry flies. They did it by fishing from midnight to 3 or 4 A.M.

"It's been Midnight Sun fishing," they chorused. "We slept all day while everyone else was out there trolling deep. After midnight there has been a hatch of Light Cahills every night, and some enormous trout feed on them." They both fished from one boat, drifting with their Cree guide and casting only to visible rises. The guide would paddle softly in range when a trout surfaced, and they'd lay out their size 10 Light Cahills and take lake trout that were all over 8 pounds. I could just see the whole thing as they related their fishing to us: flat, calm lake . . . the Arctic tundra all around . . . that softly bright moonglow illuminating the surface . . . Light Cahill naturals spinning through the quiet air . . . then, over there, a swirling rise, a watery ring 15 feet across, the nose, then dorsal fin, then tail as a big lake trout sucked in a tiny Cahill. I was sorry to have missed that fishing.

WALLEYES ON STREAMERS

Many fishermen rightly believe the walleye to be a deep-going fish, and one that cannot often be taken on flies. But on their early-spring spawning runs out of lakes and into feeder rivers you can sometimes catch plenty on streamer flies. And at the cold northern lakes, even in early summer, fly fishermen frequently get good walleye fishing at the base of waterfalls or where cold spring creeks come into a lake. But night fly fishing gets walleyes with consistency in a lot of rivers and lakes. This is especially true of many northern Wisconsin waters. For the most part these are deep, cold, clear lakes. Sunlight penetration, and perhaps angler activity and boat traffic, put the walleyes very deep during the day, even when the water temperature is low. But after sundown when the baitfish confidently leave the shelter of shoreline weeds and brush and start to swarm over the sandy shallows in active schools, the walleyes move up and start to hunt in inches-deep water. Totogatic Flowage (also known as Nelson Lake), near Hayward, Wisconsin, has notable nighttime fly-fishing opportunities for walleyes. In recent years the fish haven't been running large, but they are plentiful, and a 3-inch-long streamer fly popped into the shallows anytime after midnight, and brought back in short, quick hops, can be expected to account for a fine string of 2- to 3-pound fish, with the occasional larger one.

FISHING DEEP FOR BASS

The bulk of the bass caught by fly-rodders in lakes are hooked on bugs and streamers, usually fished in conventional ways (see Chapters 20 and 22), but fishing bass bugs down deep is a seldom-used technique for lake bass fishing that should be discussed here.

Because of the excellent sinking lines available today, it is easy to fish bass bugs—which normally float—at depths of 25 or 30 feet, or more. The best lines for this are lead-core shooting heads, which go to the bottom like a rock and drag buoyant bugs with them. With a lead-core head you can fish a bass bug at depths of 15 to 30 feet without waiting forever for the line to sink and pull the bug down with it. But sinking lines other than lead-cores can be used effectively, too, since it rarely is necessary to get down much beyond 15 to 20 feet.

In fishing bugs underwater we need shorter, stronger-than-usual leaders. A long, light leader will cause the buoyant bug to stay too far off bottom. While the sinking line goes to the bottom, the bug will rise for the length of the leader—hence short leaders are needed. Leaders for this fishing might have a practical length range of from 4 to 8 feet, seldom longer or shorter; 5- and 6-foot lengths usually do nicely.

Because this is deep fishing, with less light penetration, fine leaders aren't necessary. I suggest going no lighter than 10-pound test in the tippet, with 12- and 15-pound sometimes practical. Heavy leaders are needed because, if the fly line is scraping bottom, the bug surely will occasionally hit snags, such as sunken tree limbs or submerged logs and stumps. With a strong leader you will often be able to tear the bug free.

A stout leader also is needed because several yards of a heavy, sunken fly line provide a lot of resistance when a bass strikes. Too light a leader will mean fish breaking off on the strike. I've also noticed that bass seem to really slam into a deep-swimming bug. While they may merely inhale a surface bug, just sucking it in, they

The author shows a light string of smallmouth bass kept for the shore lunch fry pan. Lake smallmouths are a fly-rodders delight when the fish are shallow.

hit bottom-hugging bugs fast and hard. Perhaps the reason for this is that the deep-fished bug is moving steadily, swimming along like a minnow or frog, and in a bass's mind more likely to escape than some injured bug jerking slowly along the surface. In any case, use shorter, stronger leaders in this down-under bass bugging or you'll defeat the purpose of fishing a sinking line and floating bug.

The major reasons for fishing bass bugs down deep, on or close to the lake bottom, is that they will suspend a few feet higher up than the line, and therefore be less likely to snag than would a streamer fly—and also because so many bugs are so true to nature, so effective in fooling big-domed bass. Bass get a lot of their food along lake bottoms—minnows, frogs, tadpoles, sala-

manders, crayfish, hellgrammites—and bugs designed to be fished on the surface do a remarkable job of imitating those life forms. And there's something about the buoyancy of a bug, fished deep, that gives it an unusual, lifelike action when it's drawn *through* the water, instead of *over* it.

The bass bug used for deep fishing ought to be selected with care, as much so as those used in surface fishing. Not all bugs are good for underwater work. The typical cork-bodied or balsa-bodied poppers, with flat faces, are not good selections for deep fishing. They offer more resistance in trailing a sinking fly line than do other kinds of bugs, and they are difficult to work through the water on the retrieve. The famed Gerbubble Bug is an example of a bug that is no good for deep fishing. We are not popping when fishing a bug 15 or 30 feet down. The McNally Bullet Bug is a good one for deep fishing because with its bullet-shaped, tapered body it noses through the water well. Moreover, its flowing saddle-hackle tail gives it a lot of action when it's stripped over the bottom of a lake.

Hair-bodied bugs are among the best for deep bass fishing. They have super buoyancy, which keeps them about leader length off the bottom, and they are very buggy and realistic in the water. Good hair bugs are made commercially that represent crayfish (a number-one choice for bottom fishing), mice, frogs, and big hairy moths. A deer-hair frog of the old Joe Messinger type is a superior bug fished down deep. So too are deer-hair mice and moths. How a mouse or moth happens to be swimming at a depth of 15 to 30 feet may be an intellectual curiosity to you and me, but the ques-

weed edges

lily pads

drop-offs

Here are some of the places to find fish in a lake. In general, they are places that provide fish with cover and food.

rocky points

boulders and logs

sandy bottoms

inlets

brush piles

shadowy ledges

tion doesn't seem to bother bass much. They hit the hair mice and moths anyway.

Be sure any deer-hair bugs you use in deep fishing have hooks with good bite and are needle-sharp. It's hard enough to hook a bass that hits a bug 50 feet from the rod tip and maybe 30 feet down without the added handicap of a dull hook or one without bite.

Following a cast to a promising spot, and allowing time for the sinking line to take your bug all the way down, you should lower your rod tip to the water. The low tip means none of the fly line is lifted out of the water, thus keeping the bug higher up from the bottom than it should be. The low tip makes it possible to work the bug better through the water, and a low tip allows a lot of room for striking with the rod when a bass hits the bug.

This bottom fishing with bugs designed for surface play doesn't have to be done at 15 to 30 feet or more. Sometimes when bass won't come to a topwater bug you'll find you can catch them on bugs fished just 6 or 10 feet down. It isn't always a deep, deep game. We must prospect when we go underwater to find the level at which our bugs produce. What's important is to realize that a hair frog, for instance, inching along over the bottom, can be a dirty trick to pull on a bass.

FINDING FISH IN LAKES

Where we do our fly fishing in lakes is as important as *how* we fish. In the absence of visibly rising fish, the angler must apply his efforts to *finding* fish, with a minimum of time spent in blind casting or working empty water. *All* the water of any given lake does not hold fish. Regardless of species, fully fifty percent of any lake will be empty of fish, and in some lakes the amount of barren water is considerably greater.

The situation regarding locating fish varies according to the species (we might expect largemouth bass in foot-deep water along shore at times, but not large lake trout), but overall we know that weed edges are good for bass and pike, sunken brush piles are likely places for crappies, sandy banks good for spawning bluegills. The fly fisherman always should work areas where streams or springs pour fresh, cold water into a lake, and areas where a lake overflows and pours out into a stream or sizable river are places with current—and therefore attractive to a variety of gamefish. Rocky points should get our attention, lily-pad flats and weedy bays, sunken boulders and deep-down log jams, islands, shadowy ledges, the tops of reefs, and anywhere the bottom suddenly drops off to sunless depths.

When Norm Barry operated Little Norway Camp at Eagle Lake, Ontario, we devised a system of lake-trout fishing we called "bartending." Eagle is studded with rocky reefs that push to the surface, usually with only 10 or 15 feet of rocky area showing out of water, and sometimes only the top of a boulder or two will reveal the presence of a reef. With two or three fishermen, plus Norm, in a boat, we'd go out and run from one reef top to another. A fisherman would be deposited on each reef, then Norm would find a reef for himself to fish. Standing on the top reef rocks, each angler would "fan" cast to cover all the water. First short casts would be made, circling the area, then longer casts. Fishermen using casting gear would work shallow-running baits first, then go to deep-running lures. I'd take two fly rods with me every time I stepped out onto a reef; one would have a floating three-diameter line, the other a fast-sinking shooting head. I'd start fishing with a popper for northern pike and smallmouth bass, then go to a streamer fly—fished with a floating line just under the surface. Finally I'd fish the sinking shooting head with streamers. Usually each fisherman would have about an hour to tend his particular "bar" before Norm and the boat arrived and we all moved to other reefs. Fly-fishing Eagle reefs as described, in one day I often caught smallmouth bass, walleyes, lake-whitefish, lake trout, and northern pike. But it was the lake trout that made our "bartending" notable. Fishing that way, we caught as many lakers at Eagle as other fishermen did trolling the customary spoons.

27

Fly Fishing Salt Water, Inshore

I T WAS more than fifty years ago, when I was a high-school student, that friends and I drove up to Joe Brooks' house in Islamorada, in the Florida Keys. Joe and his wife Mary had been living there only a few years, having moved down from Baltimore. We wanted Joe to take us bonefishing, but he had just started work on his book *Salt Water Fly Fishing,* and couldn't afford the time. Joe led us across the road and introduced us to Vic Barothy, the great pioneer fishing-camp operator who succumbed to cancer at Coral Gables, Florida, in the early seventies. Vic was running a fishing camp, so he took us to the wonderful, wild flats that existed then along North Key Largo, and I caught my first bonefish, a fine 8-pounder, on a fly. I was sixteen years old, and up to that time that was the greatest angling thrill I ever had. Vic and I became fast friends, and in subsequent years I fished with him often at camps he opened at Isle of Pines, Cuba, and on the Belize River and Turneffe Islands, in what then was British Honduras (Belize), in Central America.

The next day Brooks showed us a deep, coral-lined lagoon right beside U.S. 1 a bit outside Islamorada, saying it held 20- to 50-pound tarpon, and that if we fished it at night we might hook some. We were fishing the lagoon at dusk, and after an hour or so of casting big popping bugs and streamers, when it was full dark I caught a tarpon we figured weighed about 25 pounds. That first bonefish, and that first tarpon, hooked me for the rest of my life on saltwater fly fishing.

I'm often asked what my favorite kind of fly fishing is, and I always reply, "Brown-trout fishing with dry flies on western streams." But saltwater fly fishing offers so much excitement, so much variety, so many opportunities, and such strong fish, that it runs a close second.

The freshwater fly fisherman who has never hooked a saltwater fish on a fly cannot comprehend the difference between freshwater and saltwater gamefish. The power and speed of the important saltwater fish are incredible. There is simply no comparison between the fighting qualities of the saltwater species and the fresh. Some saltwater fish are plain strong when hooked, others are fast, still others jump like crazy—and then there are those species with all three traits. James Henshall (1844–1925), author of *The Book of the Black Bass,* was famous for saluting the bass with "I consider him, inch for inch and pound for pound, the gamest fish that swims." With fondest appreciation for both the black bass and Dr. Henshall, I suspect that bass aficionado Henshall never set a hook in a saltwater gamefish.

During the last ten years, many angling writers in discussing briny-water fly fishing have been prone to report the news that "saltwater fly fishing is coming of age," or, indeed, "saltwater fly fishing *has come* of age." Sonofagun! Well, if "coming of age" means that saltwater fly fishing is very popular, is practical, and is practiced in many areas (including abroad), then I submit that saltwater fly fishing has been of age for more than forty years. New England fly fishermen were taking striped bass on flies sixty years ago; the first bonefish on-fly was recorded, also, more than a half-century ago. And as a matter of fact, saltwater fly fishing in general is more than a century old.

It is true, of course, that many millions of fly-rodders are now fishing the salt, and that as the converts grow and publicity mounts we will have more and more salt-water fly-fishing fans. And that is as it should be, because for a fly fisherman to be near the salt and not swim his flies borders on tragedy.

Stand on the shore of any freshwater lake, say a midwestern lake, and think of the fish it holds that you might realistically catch on flies. Bass. Pike. Walleyes. Blue-gills. Crappies. About it? Stand on the sea-wall at, let's say, Lake Worth, where that salty lagoon hits the ocean at Palm Beach, Florida. What might we catch here on flies? Bluefish. Ladyfish. Jack crevalle. Spanish mackerel. King mackerel. Snook. Barracuda. Sea trout. Tarpon. Moonfish. Lookdowns. Gaff-topsail catfish. Pompano. And gray snappers.

The gray snapper, incidentally, is one of the most difficult fish to catch in salt water. They are cunning, and they have magnifying eyeballs. When hooked they are strong, game fish, and excellent on the table, too, but getting one to hit is something else.

On one Bermuda trip, Ries Tuttle (the retired outdoor editor of the Des Moines, Iowa, *Register-Tribune*), Joe Brooks, and I were at a swank hotel on the water. An open-air dance floor outside the dining room was built right to the water's edge. After dinner, Ries, Joe, and I strolled outside and, crossing the dance floor to the low wall at the waterside, we looked down. A bunch of gray snappers, 1 to 4 pounds, were hunched up in the clear water just below, attracted by a dance-floor light that threw a big yellow-bright circle on the water. The snappers hung in that circle of light, going around and around, feeding on glass minnows that also were being drawn by the light.

"Look at *them!*" I said. "Let's catch some."

"You can't," said Joe. "These fish are always here, they feed them bread and stuff, and they won't hit a fly. Too smart. I've tried many times."

While the orchestra played lovey stuff and the dancers waltzed on, I went to my room and rigged a fly rod. Wanting only to get strikes from the fish, and not caring if I hooked but lost them, I put on a 7X leader tippet, a mere 1-pound-test strand such as we'd offer cagy trout. I went on down, walking through the lobby and dining room carrying my fly rod and a box of flies, smiling back at the people who gaped at me. Out to the dance floor I went, excusing myself as I worked and threaded my way through couples lost in the sexy strains of the band. Once at the wall, looking down at the snappers, I got a workable length of line out, then picked it up and threw my backcast high in back of me—letting 30 feet of fly line sail over the dance floor over the heads of dozens of swaying, swooning dancers.

"*Cheez!*" said Joe. "For God's sake keep that line up."

"Hook one of those dolls and there'll be a fight," said Ries.

I kept the line up okay and got a pile of good casts to those fish—but never had a hit. They'd swim up to the fly, look it over, and turn away. I tried pattern after pattern, different sizes and colors, fast retrieves and no retrieves, everything, and couldn't get a strike. The snappers would come and look all right, but just wouldn't take even though they were feeding constantly on hogmouth fry and glass minnows that blundered in range. Joe took the rod and tried, with no luck. We finally quit, edged around the dancers, and went to our rooms. I'll always remember the fly line rolling out over the heads of those dancers, and the incredible wariness of the snappers.

Fortunately for us fly fishermen, most of the salty species we go for are much more cooperative. In fact, that's one of the good things about saltwater fly fishing: excluding the tough ones, such as gray snappers and permit, most of the saltwater fish that we do not spook, and that we get our flies to properly, will hit.

There are two kinds of saltwater fly fishing: inshore and offshore. Offshore fly fishing (Chapter 28) is the deep-ocean kind. Inshore fishing means angling in brackish waters, tidal estuaries, and salty bays and lagoons, as well as in the ocean proper but within reasonable distance of shore.

Inshore fly fishing attracts the greatest number of anglers. For one thing, the inshore brand is more generally available. It exists along every coast—in this country from Maine to Florida, to Texas, to Baja California, to Alaska. Inshore fly fishing can be done by casting from the banks, by wading, or by fishing from small boats. A great deal of this inshore "saltwater" fly fishing is even done in fresh water—in fresh or partly brackish lakes or canals where we have tarpon, snook, and other species that can thrive in water that is entirely or partly fresh. There are huge sharks, for example, and even sawfish in Lake Nicaragua in Central America, 125 miles from the Atlantic.

More species of fly-taking fish are generally available to the inshore angler, and inshore saltwater fishing also is less expensive than offshore sport. For the offshore variety, you've got to have a sportfisherman or similar boat of your own, or go on a charter cruiser with professional captain and mate.

There are probably fifty or more species of inshore fish spread from New England around Florida, into the Gulf and along the Pacific Coast that will take fly-rod lures,

Large popping bugs and giant streamers are preferred for most saltwater fly fishing.

but the ones most in demand are striped bass, bluefish, snook, tarpon, bonefish, permit, sea trout, the mackerels, channel bass (redfish, red drum), crevalle, ladyfish, and barracuda—not by any means in the order named. Among experienced saltwater fly-rodders the most desirable inshore fish are the scarce and hard-to-take permit, the speed-king bonefish, the wild-jumping tarpon, the shrewd snook, the powerful striped bass, and the bruising bluefish. It is interesting to note that each of the species just named, each of these great *saltwater* fish, could be caught in a foot of water against a grassy bank.

Until recent dredging and silting and shore-filling condominium construction, one of my favorite all-time salt fly-fishing grounds was the Loxahatchee River on central Florida's Atlantic side. Upriver not far from the U.S. 1 bridge is a shallow oys-

ter bar. It sweeps along the west bank, not 100 yards out from a gorgeous home where—almost every time I fished there—a couple of rambunctious boxer dogs loped about the yard. We'd fish the bar from a small boat, using either surface poppers or streamers, and *every time* in the winter season we would boat six to a dozen bluefish ranging from 2 to 5 pounds. Every time, that is, but one winter when I fished the lower Lox twice and never saw a bluefish. The point I'm making is that here we have an ocean fish which, when in the lower Loxahatchee, is swimming in as civilized waters as we might find.

TACKLE

Since rods, reels, lines, and leaders for all the varied forms of fly fishing, including saltwater, are discussed in detail in other chapters, I'll add only a few tackle notes here.

The saltwater fly rod naturally must be on the heavy side, measure about 9 feet, and take a line from No. 9, weight-for-ward, to No. 13. The rod must have pow-erful action to throw a long line into the teeth of wind sweeping across a flat, to cast heavy, large, wind-resistant flies and bugs, and to handle heavy, strong fish.

The reel is quite important. Most of all it must have sufficient line capacity (as explained in Chapter 3) and a proper drag for the kind of saltwater fishing you'll be doing. Saltwater reels are available with slip-drags, which means you can hold the reel handle even while the fish is running line. With other reels the handle must be released, and it revolves along with the spool as the fish takes line against the ten-sion of the preset drag. Which type reel is best is up to the individual angler. Some feel they may not release the handle quickly enough when a fish runs if using a reel without slip-drag, and break a fish off. Other anglers get in the habit of instanta-neously letting go of a handle when a good fish takes off. I use both types of reels, with equal satisfaction.

Many of the inshore saltwater fish are ideal fly-rod fish because they are active—always on the go, always hungry, always hunting, always ready to strike wildly at a well-presented streamer fly or surface-sput-tering bug. The problem in catching salt-water fish normally lies in finding them, then getting a proper cast off. Once located, once cast to, the majority of the saltwater inshore species are very likely to hit.

And these same fish, the ones we prize most, much of the time are in extremely shallow water—another factor making inshore saltwater species ideal fly-rod fish. True, any of them may occasionally be in very deep water, but even then they often will be roaming the surface and therefore be a proper fly-rod target. Bonefish and permit frequently will be found in ankle-deep water; tarpon will cruise as often in water 4 feet deep as in 40 feet; the barra-cuda is basically a deep-water reef fish, yet the fly fisherman will encounter hundreds on the bonefish flats in water 4 feet deep or less. The super-tough jack crevalle and the high-jumping ladyfish most often are found in water 10 to 40 feet deep—yet they'll come zooming up to powder a popper or smash a streamer. Saltwater gamefish are, broadly speaking, agreeable.

FLY-CASTING PROBLEMS IN SALT WATER

If there is a negative aspect to saltwater fly fishing it is the casting problems. To be suc-cessful, the saltwater angler *must* be an accomplished fly caster. Many saltwater fish will be hooked at 30 feet, but many more between 40 and 60 feet, and some even at 80 feet or farther. It isn't so much that the angler needs the ability to throw a long line, as it is that he must be able to get a good length of line out on target in a hurry. Saltwater fish almost always are moving, and there isn't much time for false casting. You must be able to cast success-fully in high winds, a condition that seems to plague the saltwater fly fisherman con-stantly. Unless we are inland fishing a pro-tected canal or lagoon for tarpon, snook, etc., we are almost surely out on a wind-swept bay, on a breezy flat, or some other open area where there's no protection from the wind.

Another casting problem is that the wind often will blow the loose fly line around the casting deck. You've made a 60-foot cast, let's say, then stripped the line in and set it in neat, loose coils at your feet. When a bonefish shows you're ready to flip some line up, make a single false cast, then shoot all that ready line right on target. Only just as a trophy bonefish nears, a gust of wind whips your slack line around and, when you make your shoot, a gob of line hits the first guide.

Still another casting problem is junk in the boat to catch on your fly line when you make an important cast. The best inshore saltwater fishing boats for fly fishermen have casting decks as slick as table tops— no exposed screw eyes, no open cleats, no anchor rope.

Before heading out in a boat, even with a pro guide, check to see that the casting area is as open and clean as possible. Some anglers carry netting, sheets of plastic, canvas, and so on which they lay over boat obstructions and weigh down so wind will not move the material. Some even use plastic garbage cans to drop loose shooting line into so it can't be blown around by the wind.

PERMIT

There are two distinct permit species: the Atlantic permit and the Pacific permit (palometa). The Atlantic permit ranges from Brazil to Massachusetts, the Pacific species from southern California to Ecuador.

While a permit, any permit, is generally regarded as an outstanding fly-rod catch, for practical purposes we really ought to scratch the species from our list. By comparison to other saltwater species, permit are scarce. Sure, there are areas where they may be considered relatively abundant, but the fact is there just aren't a whole bunch of permit around for you to shoot flies at. I have seen permit, singly and in schools, perhaps a hundred times. Of those encounters I've likely cast, or tried to cast, forty times. Of those forty attempts I'd guess the presentation and retrieve (no foul-up on grass, no strike from a baby 'cuda) were correct twenty times—and to date I've caught one permit on a fly, a little 12-pounder. Other anglers have had better luck, much better, even taking some giant permit, but most of us will have few suitable opportunities for permit, and when we do we'll get precious few strikes.

Permit inhabit the shallow flats, though they normally will not move as shallow as bonefish, and their feeding habits are similar to those of bonefish. They eat shrimp, crabs, and the like, but they have a remarkable disdain for the artificial fly. You can cast perfectly to an actively feeding permit, have him turn and follow your fly, nose almost to the hook, and chances are he'll refuse. Permit are warier and more easily spooked than bonefish, and even if you should hook one you are a long way from home. Most anglers claim permit are faster than bonefish, and with those broad-muscled, flat sides, they certainly are much stronger and have much greater endurance. A fight with a decent-size permit is something a fly fisherman never forgets.

Small flies are best, sizes 1/0, 2, or 4, bucktails, shrimp types, or marabous. A fly considered suitable for bonefish normally will interest, if we are lucky, a permit.

The best permit area in the Florida Keys is Content Key, and the Key West area also has a noticeable population. I've seen large permit in the Marquesas Keys, Mexico's Yucatán Peninsula is well known for them, and quite a few permit are seen on the flats along the barrier reef off Belize, in Central America.

BONEFISH

The worst mistake most fly-rodders (including me) make in bonefishing is going down to the Florida Keys, the Bahamas, Central America, or Mexico in the dead of winter. We want to escape northern cold, and so go south to fish for bonefish, but bones are sensitive to cold weather, and winter bonefishing most places isn't half as good as in the spring and summer months. In the Keys, the best fishing usually is in May and June. However, bonefish *can* be caught any month.

Of the millions of words that have been written about bonefishing, the line I like best was penned by Al McClane for the January 1975 issue of *Field & Stream*. He wrote: "Anybody who tells you bonefishing is easy has spent very little time on the flats." That pretty well tells it all.

By way of simple review, bonefish haunt the shallow flats, often tailing nose-down as they grub along for shrimp, crabs, worms, etc. When tailing, a bone's caudal fin protrudes out of the water—and sometimes so much of the fish is out that even the dorsal fin shows. The sight of a tailing bonefish, his caudal flashing like a mirror in the sun, never fails to give me the

Author shows a nice 10-pound bonefish taken at Chub Cay in the Bahamas.

shakes—and I've caught as many as forty-seven on a single tide, and more than 100 in a single day (at Cayman Brac).

Because of the shallow, clear water and usually bright sun, a bonefish can see an angler a long way off, and he'll flush even from a fly line extending in the air overhead. A scuffing, careless approach by a wading angler will drive every fish off a flat. A boat noise or badly handled push-pole will send a bonefish rocketing away.

Despite the fact that they are not easy, I consider the bonefish to be one of the "takingest" fish in salt water. By that I mean if the cast is right, if nothing happens to ruin the retrieve, if the fly is worked correctly, and if nothing beyond the angler's control flushes the bonefish, I believe the majority will hit the fly. Bonefish live in a constant state of panic, but when everything is right they will greedily pounce on a fly.

For the novice a major difficulty in bonefishing is spotting the fish. Polarized glasses are absolutely essential (they should be worn, in fact, for most fly fishing, including for freshwater trout), and a beaked cap that protrudes over the eyes and shields from the sun is a great help.

Some fishermen use flies much too large for bonefish. These fish have small, sucker-like mouths, and more hits will be had on flies in sizes 4 and 6, and short-shank 1/0 hooks. The best flies are small bucktail patterns, and one of my favorites is a blue-white size 4 bucktail, with the hair wing perhaps only 1¼ inches long. Marabous and shrimp flies also are great.

Casts should be well ahead of oncoming bonefish, the fly allowed to settle (if possible), then lifted from near the bottom as the fish approaches. I like to impart a sudden, quick hop to the fly to get the fish's attention, then slow the retrieve as the bonefish moves in. A trailing bonefish often can be induced to strike instantly if the angler halts the retrieve, lets the fly settle, then starts it moving again.

I had an interesting experience with bonefish one evening with Gil Drake at Deep Water Cay in the Bahamas. Gil is an excellent all-around fly fisherman, and as he poled us silently up onto a flat we could see the tails of bonefish silhouetted against the moonlit water, and the swirls, humps, and wakes they put up as they rooted innocently around the flat. This was the first time I'd ever been on bonefish after dark. "They'll hit better now," Gil advised, "than during the day." And he proved it, using a tiny, webby, hackled fly hardly larger than his thumbnail, a fly he designed and tied himself for bonefish. I watched Gil take one bonefish after another. It was a majestic scene—Gil silhouetted there against the pale, black-velvet sky, rod waving back and forth, the delivery, the strip, the tightening up, and then the swiftly rolling V wake as the hooked bonefish sprinted over the flat.

TARPON

His excellency the tarpon, the silver king himself, assuredly is the fly fisherman's nemesis. He is the one who presents us with just punishment, who exacts retribution for all those other fish we barb with our flies.

Action can be explosive when fishing the brackish-water canals in the upper Florida Keys. Here a baby tarpon, under 20 pounds, clobbers McNally's streamer fly.

El Sabalo is the supreme one. He is wonderfully exciting. Powerful. Strong. Enduring. Big. A leaper. Plentiful. And he loves to eat flies and popping bugs. Only trouble is, much of the time, after sucking in a streamer or inhaling a popper, he promptly leaps, shakes his head in disgust, and throws the lure back in the angler's face.

A tarpon's mouth was not designed for the ready acceptance of an angler's hooks. The inside of a silver king's mouth is like concrete, and it's been said that the fly fisherman who successfully hooks one out of ten large tarpon that strike is running a fair average.

One day in June I was on a natural fish trap on Buchanan Bank, on the Florida Bay side of Islamorada, a spot called the Pocket. The Pocket is an indentation along the bank. Big tarpon cruise down the bank, hit the abrupt pocket, and for a time swing around in there, as though momentarily confused that the perfect, straight configuration of the bank has changed. Offered a fly in the Pocket, the tarpon usually take it with a rush, though the actual strike is a mere soft inhaling of the fly.

The tarpon comes out in a scudding leap. Falling back, it jumped a second time, into the mangroves, and broke off.

With an Islamorada guide, I jumped eight large tarpon that day and landed none. Fly hooks were honed needle-sharp, I set on the strikes with the big rod I had as

A wide swirl marks the spot where a big tarpon inhales McNally's fly.

The tarpon comes out in a shallow leap as McNally hangs on.

The tarpon fights furiously at the boat . . .

. . . and puts a dangerous bend in the fly rod. Many tarpon fly-rod experts today are vying to boat the first 200-pound specimen.

hard as I could and often, and never had more success than to have one fish on for a 100-foot run, a towering leap, and then the fly coming back as though it were tied to a rubber band. Tarpon are like that. They are the toughest fish in the world to hook on a fly. Knowledgeable fly-rodders go out after giant tarpon and say they are "going to jump some tarpon," meaning they anticipate strikes and leaps, but not necessarily any fish brought to gaff.

But despite the structure of a tarpon's mouth—and the fact that his gill plates, scales, and thrashing tail all can fray or cut a leader—we successfully hook, play, and land enough tarpon to make fly fishing for them well worthwhile. Fishing tarpon, in fact, is my favorite saltwater fly fishing. Bonefishing is fine, but it doesn't have the shattering excitement offered by tarpon. The instant you strike a good-size tarpon (or a little one, for that matter) all hell breaks loose.

Since hooking tarpon that strike is the first problem, let's consider the techniques necessary to accomplish hookups. In the years I've fooled with tarpon and talked to tarpon fly-fishing experts, and fished with many of them, I've run into nothing but conflicting opinions. Perhaps the one thing all agree upon is that hooks should be as sharp as possible. Some feel the smaller hooks are more sure in getting a hold in a tarpon's bucket-size mouth; others claim the larger hooks do better. Most tarpon flies are tied on hooks from 1/0 to 5/0, but for the larger fish the argument normally is whether to use a 3/0, 4/0, or 5/0. I think the smaller hook is easier to set, and I use 3/0 most of the time. (We are talking here only about hooking characteristics and not the sinking rate of a fly.)

All tarpon fishermen agree that when a silver king draws a fly into his mouth the angler should attempt to set the hook several times. But they disagree on the method. Some tighten down on drags almost to the breaking point of the leader tippet, then when a fish takes the fly they point the rod at the tarpon, and just hold on—perhaps adding a few sharp, straight pull-backs with the rod. In other words, they avoid putting the rod to use on the strike, and will not even have a bend in the rod until such time as they think the tarpon is hooked. Other anglers follow the more traditional route, keeping the rod low, then rearing up and back, striking repeatedly and as firmly as possible with the rod to set the hook. I favor this technique.

Some of the real fly-fishing fun to be had with tarpon in the United States is on the canals in the Keys and elsewhere in southern Florida. The inland Tamiami Trail Canal, for example, has tarpon—which you can cast to from the bank—as do many other large canals in that part of Florida. But some of the best fun is in the tiny mangrove-lined canals in the Keys. Development, dredging, and like activity has ruined a lot of this fishing, but there still is some to be had if the angler looks for it.

One June my son Bob and Islamorada guide Hazen Jones were literally blown off the Gulf and ocean side of the Keys. Back on the dock we stood talking over what to do. "Let's go fish for some baby tarpon in the Key Largo canals," I said.

"I don't think there's much of that any

more," said Jones. "Too much development."

We went anyway, and calling on distant memories I found places I had fished years before; while they had changed—even to some dredging, sea-walling, etc.—we found tarpon to 20 pounds. They hit streamers fished in water not 4 feet deep, and when they felt the hook they came up and out, jumping right into the mangroves, falling back, snapping leaders, tearing hooks out, spraying water all around. We didn't land many, but it was riotous fishing—and a kind anyone can do.

Tarpon are indigenous to the Atlantic, in the warmer portions of both the western and eastern sides. But it is known that at least a few tarpon have bridged the Central American isthmus via the Panama Canal, and at least one tarpon has been caught in the Pacific. One day we may have recognizable populations of "Pacific" tarpon.

Snook are a truly excellent inshore saltwater species, viciously striking streamers and bugs. Guide LaMont Albertson looks on.

SNOOK

Snook are a fly fisherman's delight. For various reasons (severe winters, development) they are not as plentiful through central and lower Florida as years ago, but any fly-rodder who has a chance to fish them ought to do so. You can fish for snook as you would for largemouth black bass.

Snook are found throughout the American tropics, on both the Atlantic and Pacific sides. They lay up against the mangroves—and far back inside them, too—so you must get your popper or streamer in close to draw them out. But snook will be in the open water, too, and in such places night fishing for them can be the best routine. Most snook fishing is done inland, so it's protected fishing—it can be considered as much a freshwater variety of angling as a saltwater one.

BLUEFISH

The bluefish is a sure catch when you find him. These fish are so voracious, such ravenous killers, that they tear into baitfish, gorge themselves, regurgitate, then strike wildly into the baitfish again. If in the saltwater world there is a heartless killer, one who slashes and maims for the fun of it, it has to be the bluefish.

When I lived in Maryland I often went to Ocean City, the "white marlin capital of the world," for marlin fishing. But on all of those trips I managed to get in some fly-rodding for the little "tailor" blues (ones under 3 pounds) that often swelled through the ocean inlet into Sinepuxent Bay. Usually we'd fish from a skiff, but sometimes we'd get into blues by wading or casting from docks and jetties.

There is excellent bluefish angling around the offshore oil rigs in the Gulf of Mexico, and it's setup fishing for the fly-rodder. I usually go out with Captain Charles Sebastian, of Grand Isle, Louisiana, and as soon as we reach a rig "Cholley" throws some chum of cut fish or shrimp around the steel piers, and soon up come the bluefish—usually running 2 to 5 pounds but often much bigger. I fish a popping bug when the blues are up top, and I can't recall seeing one refuse yet.

Streamers and poppers should be fished very fast for bluefish, since, like many other saltwater species, they prefer a very fast-moving lure. Blues have severe dental work, and their choppers will go through a light leader like a razor. Some fly fishermen after blues use light wire, 4 to 6 inches long, for a tippet, but I prefer a shock tippet of heavy nylon, 20- to 60-pound test (hard material), depending upon the size of the average fish.

Bluefish have an extensive range, being found, in fact, in most of the world's warmer seas. Our Atlantic coast has extensive bluefish populations, with large schools along the Florida coast in winter that move progressively northward in spring and summer as the water warms. Chesapeake Bay gets a lot of bluefish, and by late summer–early fall blues are spread throughout New England waters.

LADYFISH

The ladyfish is an aerial gymnast, an acrobat that will jump as high as your head when you're sitting in a boat. Much of the time they are in 10 or 20 feet of water, but they'll come up quickly to a fast-moving saltwater popping bug.

Ladyfish are small, the average weighing about 1 to 2 pounds, but their great length makes them appear much larger, and since they are strong, super-fast, high-jumping fish, the fly-rodder who has just played out a little 2-pounder will swear the fish will go 6 pounds on the scale.

Ladyfish occur in the warmer reaches of the Atlantic, Pacific, and Indian oceans. They are really thick in southern Florida and the Caribbean.

SEA TROUT

The spotted sea trout is popular with many fly fishermen, chiefly because it is abundant, and they frequent shallow estuaries and grassy flats easy for the fly-rodder to work. They take small streamers and poppers, but one of the better ways to fish them is to snake a shrimp fly slowly through the bottom grass, using a sinking-tip or sinking line. Fly patterns that will not readily catch on weeds, such as the Keel Flies, ought to be used.

Sea trout are one of the most popular saltwater gamefishes in the southern United States, which is its major range. They occur, however, as far north as New York. Trout are really important to Florida fishermen, and while they're found throughout the Gulf of Mexico, wade fishing for spotted sea trout brings out angling armies on

Spotted sea trout take small flies and bugs readily and are excellent table fare.

the sandy coastal flats of Texas and Louisiana.

STRIPED BASS

The striped bass is a favorite with fly fishermen on both the Atlantic and Pacific coasts, where they are found year-round. (There are migrations, however, seasonal in character; from south to north as the water warms in spring-summer, and north to south as the water cools in fall.) There are "stripers" in the upper Gulf of Mexico, in limited numbers from northwestern Florida to Louisiana.

Striped bass take popping bugs and large streamer flies with walloping strikes, hitting about as hard as any fish in the salt. They run to good size, too, with 10- and 20-pounders not uncommon, and there are areas with 50-pounders. Finally, stripers are strong and fight well, and are delicious table fish.

You can get stripers casting from grassy banks. I remember an island in the middle of Chesapeake Bay, out from Solomons, Maryland, that was no more than a couple of acres in size, but its edges dropped right straight down to 5 and 10 feet of water, and there was very deep water nearby. Blue crabs, shrimp, and minnows all worked around the little island, and so did big striped bass. There was one handicap: The island was uninhabited, owned by the government, and it was a bomb and machine-gun target range for planes from the naval base at Solomons Island. The island was off limits to fishermen and boaters.

It was such a good fly-rod striper spot, however, that we couldn't help fishing it. A Baltimore dentist, Dr. Robert Smith, had a fast motorboat, one with twin Packards that could rip around Chesapeake Bay like it was a bass pond. There was good reason for the fast boat. Doc Smith, George Phillips of Alexandria, Pennsylvania, and I would run out to the island, jump ashore, spread out, and fish quickly. Those days the Navy had bombing and machine-gun practice almost daily. A circle of whitewashed rocks in the center of the island was the bombing target, and for the machine-gun strafing they'd built a bull's-eye canvas target with heavy wood framing that was as big as the side of a house.

We'd usually get in a half-hour or so of fishing, generally taking a couple of nice stripers, when a pair of fighter planes would come out from the Navy base. They'd swoop right in over our heads, the pilots giving us hand signals to get the hell off the island. We'd wave to the pilots, pretending we didn't know they wanted us out, and they'd roar over us lower and lower. We knew from experience that we had about another half-hour of fishing before the planes radioed the base and called for a PT boat. Once the planes left we kept an eye on the western horizon, watching for the PT boat to show in the distance. Pretty soon here it would come, so we'd run for Smith's speedboat, throw rods and stripers in, kick the Packards over, and go tearing northward up Chesapeake Bay. Whenever the PT boat reached the island we were never there.

Of course we had no business fooling around a gunnery-practice island, and such behavior isn't recommended. But those were big striped bass around that island, and sometimes the temptations facing fly fishermen can be too much.

28

Fly Fishing Salt Water, Offshore

THERE is great sport to be had in fishing the open sea with a fly rod, and it holds large numbers of fish that are fair game to the fly fisherman. Many so-called "fly catches" that are brought to docks are illegitimate, however, because the boat was moving and the fly therefore actually was trolled—and under the strict rules of competitive fly fishing and sportsmanship, the fish must be taken on a *cast* fly.

But there are plenty of true fly fishermen out there every day, in increasing numbers, banging away with giant poppers and streamers and recording some extraordinary catches. Just about *everybody* who fly fishes the ocean much, especially the Pacific, has by now taken at least one sailfish on a fly. I landed my first in August 1963 off Pinas Bay, Panama—after breaking a rod on one there during a trip a few months earlier. Sailfish, both Pacific and Atlantic varieties, can provide high excitement when hooked on a fly rod. Striped marlin have been landed on fly gear (up to 178 pounds, by Dr. Webster Robinson, in

Baha California), black marlin have been caught on flies legitimately, and quite a few fly fishermen who take their ocean sport seriously are planning to do in some giant blue marlin.

But for most offshore fishermen the fly game comes down primarily to Pacific sailfish, dolphin, rainbow runners, various crevalle, barracuda, amberjack (one of the toughest fish in the sea), cobia, king mackerel, albacore, bonito, Pacific and Atlantic yellowtail, the tunas, sharks (inshore, too), and assorted other species such as Bermuda chub. (The Bermuda chub is the strongest fish I have ever felt on a fly rod. I've asked famous saltwater fishermen such as Vic Dunaway—who for years was angling editor of the *Miami Herald* and is currently editor of *Florida Sportsman* magazine—what they thought was the strongest fish in the sea, and almost all named the Allison tuna. But they also said, to a man, that they had not caught Bermuda chubs. On the other hand, I haven't caught an Allison.)

Tom McNally fights a Pacific sailfish off Pinas Bay, Panama, with a fly rod. Fish was 116 pounds, one of the very first billfish ever taken on fly gear.

OFFSHORE TACKLE

You can get by with a fairly light fly rod, say a 9-footer taking a No. 9 weight-forward line, for some ocean fishing (I've caught piles of dolphin on such outfits), but overall sea fishing requires a really stout stick. Most briny-water anglers want 9- or 9½-foot rods taking lines from No. 10 to No. 13. Their fish-fighting "actions" are so heavy that large lines are needed to work the rods on a cast. Rods with real beef are necessary to lift a sailfish or amberjack, for example, that's played out and lying on its side at the boat, but is 6 or 8 feet down.

In our deep-sea work the fly reel becomes even more important than it is in inshore fishing, where it's important enough. Line capacity is the big thing here, plus faultless drag.

Two other new reels that should get your attention for ocean as well as inshore fishing are the Billy Pate fly reel and the Orvis D-XR anti-reverse saltwater reel.

These are a couple of beauties—good line capacities, super drags, strong construction. George Hommel, a great fly fisherman, former Keys guide, and bossman of World Wide Sportsman, Inc., in Islamorada, the sole distributors of the Pate reel, said the Pate has spool and reel casing in one-piece design, both hand-machined. The Pate takes a full-length heavy fly line, plus 250 yards of 30-pound-test backing. The Orvis reel is a slick, clean model with one of the smoothest, finest drags I've seen in a heavy-duty fly reel. With a full-length WF-11 line, it will take 400 yards of 30-pound backing.

Since heavy offshore saltwater fly fishing has become so popular, there are many quality heavy-duty saltwater fly reels being marketed—too numerous to mention them all. However, some the serious fly-rodder may want to look into include the Los Roques reel (Hunter's Angling Supplies, Box 300, New Boston, New Hampshire 03070); Peerless Reel (Peerless Reel Company, Nashua, New Hampshire 03063);

STH Reel (STH Reels USA, Inc., P.O. Box 816, Marathon, Florida 33050); Bogdan Reels (S. E. Bogdan Company, Nashua, New Hampshire 03061); Thomas & Thomas Individualist Reel, Model 361115 (Thomas & Thomas Company, Turners Falls, Massachusetts 01376); Marryat Reel (through Fritz von Schlegell, Coret Ltd., Zurich, Switzerland).

All of these heavy-duty saltwater fly reels are expensive—figure anywhere from $300 to $450 and more—but they are worth it.

GETTING THE BIG FISH IN CASTING DISTANCE

There are some minor variations in methods used to get sailfish and marlin to strike a fly or a big, wide-faced popping bug. But all involve trolling teasers and getting the fish excited and to within easy casting range of the stern. Some fly fishermen get pretty elaborate in making up teasers, cutting belly strips from fish such as bonito, then sewing them up so that they look—in the water—just like a real fish. But the times I've been on sailfish, working with a fly rod, we simply cut long V-shaped strips out of the bellies of bonito I caught by trolling a fly, then tied them to heavy line (pointed end of the strip first) and trolled them behind. The 6- to 12-inch-long strips flipped and flopped over the surface, attractively splashing and putting out nice wakes, and the sails came for them fast. We can simplify or complicate any of our fishing, I suppose, and in the end it comes down to how an individual feels about a specific factor.

Ashore, a Panamanian boat captain and McNally recover the huge magnum streamer fly the sailfish struck.

Anyway, sailfish are brought close with one or more teasers, and when their bills are out and the fish are slashing at the teasers, the teasers are handlined quickly aboard. (Teasers also are sometimes put out on rods.) When the teasers are removed and those excited fish are whipping around back there looking for the bait, you can put a big streamer fly or bug to them and usually they'll hit.

Once we had Pacific sailfish slashing right at the transom, so close that I reached down and momentarily held the bill of a free-swimming sailfish.

DOLPHIN

Dolphin are spectacular offshore fish for the fly-rod angler. They'll take a streamer fly or bug with little hesitation, and where you find one dolphin there'll be more, since they're school fish—particularly the smaller ones. Dolphin hang around flotsam, Sargasso weed—anything on top—and when floating objects are seen fishermen should go to them and cast. One day off Puntaremas, Costa Rica, outdoor writers Lew Klewer of Ohio and Eldy Johnston of Pennsylvania and I were aboard an old, slow-moving workboat trolling for sails and dolphin. I was on the forward part of the cabin roof with a fly rod after we'd boated a couple of sailfish, while Lew and Eldy continued trolling from the stern. Soon we came to a huge floating balsa log, which must have been 40 feet long and 8 feet in diameter. Since I was forward, I had a chance to cast to the log before the trolled lures were near it. I tossed a red-yellow 3/0 McNally Magnum streamer alongside the log, stripped it once, and suddenly the water was full of dolphin. One grabbed the fly and, because the boat was moving forward at a fair clip, the fish and fly line swung around toward the stern. All the other dolphin followed, and when the fly line and my hooked fish were straight back the others saw the trolled lures and piled into them. After that we made several passes along the log, and did the same thing each run.

Dolphin are the jumping-jacks of the open sea. Soon as one feels the hook he is up and out, going straight up and coming straight down, or else skidding across the surface on his tail for a dozen yards. They

Dolphin are among the fly-takingest fish in the seas. Find some flotsam, cast a fly or bug to it, and almost for sure the fly-rodder will have a dolphin on.

"light up," too, when coming to the lure and when hooked—flashing their brightest colors in yellow, blue, gold, and green. No fish in the ocean is prettier than an excited dolphin.

The dolphin commonly taken on fly gear range from 5 to 10 pounds, but many

larger than 20 pounds have been boated on regulation fly tackle. I had one in Costa Rica played out and lying on its side when the fly fell out. All of us judged that it was over 40 pounds. That's a large dolphin, but getting it on a fly outfit would have been no big thing, since there is the entire ocean in which to play the fish. Despite the fact that these are spectacular fighters, so long as the angler has sufficient line on his reel, landing even the largest dolphin poses no special problem.

BARRACUDA

The barracuda, while encountered often on the flats and other shallow inshore areas, runs to generally larger sizes on the ocean reefs. Here is some wild kind of fish. They'll hit big streamers and poppers, but you've got to retrieve as fast as humanly possible. You just can't move a fly-bug fast enough to suit a 'cuda. Yard-long strips of line, just as fast as you can do it, is what it takes to get strikes. And it takes wire shock tippets to hold barracuda after they're hooked, since their dentures are like slivers of chipped glass.

On the strike a giant barracuda makes a leap that is truly a spectacle, not to be believed until seen. At times they'll go 10 feet straight into the air, but more often the leap is an out-of-water run, with the fish sailing through the air for 20 to 25 feet. They are among the most astonishing fish in the warm southern seas.

KING MACKEREL

Another ocean fish that wants a very fast retrieve—and for that reason can be diffi-cult to get to strike a streamer—is the king mackerel, or kingfish. They've got a mouthful of choppers, too, and so again wire shock tippets of about 12 inches are needed.

Kingfish, like the great barracuda, are magnificent leapers. I remember a day I spent off Palm Beach, Florida, testing some new monofilament lines with a bunch of DuPont executives. I had a couple of kings in the 20-pound class hit streamers which, on the strike, bolted straight up into the air for 20 feet. I think the fish saw the fly from 50 feet down, and with that much head start they just surged through the surface when they struck. Kingfish on the surface can be really exciting on fly tackle.

AMBERJACK

The greater amberjack, like all the jack family, is a brute on a fly rod, or on any other tackle—including the heaviest. They don't jump, but they can pull like a bull.

Amberjacks like structure—coral reefs, sunken wrecks, buoys—and they tend to hang deep. The best way to get them is to attract them to the surface by lowering smaller hooked fish into the water. The frantic actions of the hooked fish bring the jacks up, and then they can be cast a large fly or popping bug. The fish get so excited they hit anything that falls on the water.

Once I went out to Cosgrove Light, near Key West, Florida, aboard a Navy recreational boat called the *King Ping*. We tied up to the light, and Captain Gainey Maxwell told me to take a fly rod up to the bow and work a small streamer around the light's big steel piers. I did, and instantly blue runners were all over the place snap-

The author hoists a 24-pound roosterfish that hit a sailfish-type popping bug off Costa Rica's Pacific Coast. The fly reel is the seaworthy Billy Pate.

Joan Wulff lands a jack crevalle in the Florida Keys. (Photo by Joan Wulff)

ping at the fly. I caught several, each about 2 pounds, and took them back to the stern. Gainey put a hook in the back of one and lowered it down. The little runner darted around down there at about 10 feet, then suddenly reversed his field and rushed to the surface, came right out, and went skipping and splashing all around as Gainey held him close to the stern. In a minute we saw what had so scared the runner. Huge black hulks, bomb-shaped and 4 to 6 feet long, were coming up from the bottom rocks. They came right to the stern and started slashing at the runner. Gainey kept pulling the blue runner away, and all that did was infuriate the amberjacks. These fish have what anglers call a "feeding line," a dark slash that runs at an angle along the side of the head, on either cheek. The more excited an amberjack gets, the blacker grows the line. The lines on those fish were as dark as charcoal.

I plopped a 6-inch-long streamer down and a jack took it instantly. What power! I held on with all I had, using a stout No. 9 outfit, but I couldn't stop his run for the bottom. He made the rocks and cut the leader. I lost five in a row that way, then hooked one that didn't dive. He ran along the top, straight away, and I was hooked to that one for thirty-nine minutes. He finally went to the bottom, found some coral, and cut the leader.

Those Cosgrove amberjacks were all 20 to 40 pounds, which is enough amberjack for me on a fly rod anytime. However, some of our leading saltwater fly fishermen—such as Al Pflueger and Lee Cuddy, both of Miami—have landed some giant amberjacks on flies.

The method of bringing bottom fish up to fly range by holding live hooked fish over the side is used on other species besides amberjack, and with equally good results. Sharks, of course, are always drawn by such commotion.

FISHING DEEP OR BRINGING THEM UP

The improved sinking lines now available to fly fishermen are bringing some changes, too, in deep ocean fishing. Lead-core lines are being used a lot, and in places fishermen now are sinking their lines way down to get bottom-hugging tarpon and various reef species.

Chumming also is practiced to get fish up for the fly fishermen. One unusual chumming system is used in Bermuda to get the bottom-hugging Bermuda chubs up. Captain Bobby Rae and top angler Pete Pereinchief, both of Hamilton, Bermuda, took me out one day and brought chubs up through 80 feet of water by using dead hogmouth fry, a saltwater minnow. You couldn't just throw the fry out, because the tide would take it away, running it off near the surface. So Rae had a bucket of wet sand, and he'd take a few fry and ball them up in a baseball-size glob of wet sand. Then he'd toss the ball overboard. It'd go down like a rock, the sand gradually washing off the fry, but not before the little fish were close to bottom. The water around Bermuda is so clear, because there are no rivers, that you can see bottom in 100 feet of water when the light is right and the bottom is the proper color. After several balls of sand with hogmouth fry in them were sent down we began to see chubs moving out of the coral and snatching up the fry. Rae gradually got fish to within 10 feet of the surface, where we hooked them on small bonefish flies that we cast and allowed to sink with no action—just the way the dead fry went down.

29
Special Fish Species

IN THE world of fly fishing there are some very special species of gamefish— Atlantic salmon, for example, and American grayling (formerly called Arctic grayling, Michigan grayling, Montana grayling, etc., until scientists with the American Fisheries Society determined that the grayling had no subspecies and was, in fact, one fish). Then there are steelhead, the silvery, red-striped migratory rainbow; Arctic char, the wonder fish of the North; the lake or common whitefish that flashes olive, gold, and chrome in taking your fly; the hickory and white (American) shad, silvery bullets that school inland from the sea to spawn; lake trout, old Mr. Deep, who despite his nickname often is shallow enough to be taken readily on flies; muskies, the Scarce One; and, finally, Mr. Wonderful, the landlocked salmon.

ATLANTIC SALMON

Of all the special species named, the Atlantic salmon is generally acclaimed to be the Great One. The Leaper. The King.

I've done quite a bit of salmon fishing in scattered areas, but about all I've learned for sure is that I don't know much about catching salmon. Oh, river to river I usually get my share, but I have seen an awful lot of salmon in the water that I couldn't catch.

Salmon are moody. Unpredictable. Today they do this, tomorrow that. Sometimes they are ridiculously easy to catch, to the point that angling for them is poor sport. Other times they will have the finest rods in the land scratching up the cabin wall, for days and weeks at a time.

Rainfall and water levels seem to have the greatest influence on the salmon's behavior. A sudden rise in a river's level often triggers a period of excellent fishing, so much so that as a rule when fishing is poor the veterans are heard chanting for rain. The presence of salmon, naturally, is also an important ingredient to angling success. Runs inland from the sea are *pretty much* by the calendar—which means not always. Some runs may be earlier than usual, some later than usual, and it is the unhappy lot of most of us to generally arrive in camp at precisely the wrong time.

Then there is the problem of salmon not eating. A fish that does not eat is a fish that will be very difficult to catch on-fly (or on anything else). The experts (many self-appointed) are still arguing the point, but it is generally agreed by the most knowledgeable anglers and scientists that Atlantic salmon do no actual feeding while on their inland spawning migrations. It is believed that they take a sunken or floating fly through some conditioned reflex triggered by the presence of the fly.

Which brings us to salmon flies, an area unique in all the world of fly fishing.

However they evolved, salmon flies are totally different from, say, the typical trout pattern. Here we have a group of brilliant, generally gaudy flies all to themselves. Very drab patterns, all-black for example, very definitely take fish, however, and should never be ignored by the would-be salmon angler. I have taken several salmon on the Muddler Minnow, fished "dead" as a dry fly, skimmed over the surface, and also allowed to drift broadside underwater.

Each area, each river, indeed each beat on a river seems to develop specific salmon patterns that are continually successful. Size of the fly is vitally important, as is presentation. In low, clear water the smaller sizes are generally selected; in high, turbid, or off-colored water very large flies may be used. Everyone knows salmon take both wet and dry flies, but really good dry-fly water (most is on this continent) is hard to come by.

Most anglers never activate a salmon fly, as is commonly done in trout fishing. Rather, the fly is drifted to the fish's lie, preferably in a broadside manner to give the salmon a full side view of the fly. Often dozens of repetitive casts are needed, each executed precisely the same as the previous, to finally bring an Atlantic up in a slow, rolling take.

Excluding those areas offering public fishing (and there is now a major turn-around from private leases to public water in the Canadian Maritime Provinces), fishing for Atlantic salmon is normally the most expensive angling we can pursue. I once fished Norway's famed Malangsfoss Pool and the rate was $1,000 per rod per day, and that was years ago.

A pleased Tom McNally steps from Norway's Driva River with a 21-pound Atlantic salmon. Much of Norway's salmon fishing has since dwindled due to overnetting.

Incidentally, Norway at one time offered some of the world's best Atlantic salmon fishing. Years ago I had great action fishing Norway's Driva, Reisa, and the River Mals, but now I'm told those once-fabulous rivers are almost devoid of salmon. Ocean netting of salmon migrating to spawn as they gather at river mouths is the major reason for the decline. "Excluding the Alta River," says Jim Chapralis, who runs the Pan Angling sportsmen's travel service, "few good salmon fishing reports are coming out of Norway." However, Norway still has some rivers offering good salmon fishing.

Anyone interested in fishing Atlantics in Norway, or anywhere else, would be wise to contact Chapralis at Pan Angling Ltd., Suite 303, 180 N. Michigan Ave., Chicago, Illinois 60601; (312) 263-0328. He specializes in arranging exotic fishing-hunting trips for sportsmen anywhere in the world. I recommend him highly.

Because Atlantic salmon fishing is lordly, it is a pleasure eagerly sought by kings and queens, princes and lords, barons and duchesses, industrialists and businessmen, and even you and me. Atlantic salmon fishing is costly for good reason. First, there isn't much of it. And for what there is, the demand is great. And the world is full of people who can pay the price.

Yet there is enough good, open, public salmon water spilling around to make the chase of Atlantics a possibility for just about any serious fly fisherman. Anyone who cares enough about catching some salmon will find a way to do so.

I was only 26 years old when I first fished New Brunswick salmon streams. Charley Dorn and I traveled 3,000 miles and fished for a month, and the trip cost each of us only $88. Granted, this was in the 1940s, when a dollar was a dollar, but we did the trip inexpensively chiefly because we never ate in restaurants and never stayed at motels—sleeping in our car and doing campfire cooking instead.

So there *are* ways any of us can fish for Atlantic salmon, and especially so now and into the future. Whereas once it was fashionable to kill salmon, nowadays most anglers release the fish they catch. Greater efforts are being made toward the conservation of salmon in the sea, and the commercial netting of salmon is being curtailed in nearly all salmon areas. A five-year moratorium on all commercial netting of salmon now is in effect in Newfoundland, and some Canadian provinces, such as New Brunswick, are imposing strict salmon fishing regulations.

On New Brunswick's famed Miramichi all salmon over 25 inches in length must be released, and anglers may keep only two fish under 25 inches a day, with no more than six in possession. Today, thanks to the lifting of all commercial nets at the mouth of the Miramichi, that river's salmon schools are making a decided comeback.

Alex Mills, a leader in the New Brunswick Outfitters Association and the New Brunswick Council of the Atlantic Salmon Federation, an international non-profit organization that has fought to control the commercial salmon fishery industry for more than 40 years, said: "Things are looking up. The salmon are back in big numbers again."

Commercial salmon netters in Labrador are going to be offered a governmental "buy out," and any who do not accept

Phyllis McNally admires a grilse (young salmon) she caught from the Channel Pool on New Brunswick's Miramichi River. On this particular trip Mrs. McNally outfished husband Tom three to one.

money in exchange for their licenses will be forced to fish under a very strict quota system.

By greatly reducing the commercial catch of Atlantics *generally,* salmon experts believe there will be 100,000 to 120,000 more mature salmon returning to spawn annually in their natal rivers, rather than ending up in fish markets around the world.

But Dave Clark, president of the Atlantic Salmon Federation, said "The fight to conserve this great gamefish is certainly not over, but the U.S. and Canada now can work together to put pressure on Greenland, which has the only major Atlantic salmon fishery left."

Slowly and at considerable cost, the Atlantic salmon sport fishery in the northeastern corner of the United States is being restored. Maine, for example, is reducing pollution in its Atlantic salmon rivers and striving to bring Atlantics back in numbers to its coastal rivers.

The best results have been on the Penobscot River, Maine's largest salmon river, where in 1990 1,045 angler-caught salmon were registered. In the Penobscot, Atlantics up to 15 pounds are not uncommon. Since the 1960s, the Penobscot River has received millions of smolt, parr, and fry stock, and as a result it has become the most productive of all of Maine's salmon rivers.

There is a viable and improving salmon fishery in Maine—with many more salmon rivers than I've mentioned—and it's fishing open to all for the price of a license and salmon tags.

The newest Atlantic salmon fishing area is Russia's Kola Peninsula, where last season the angling was described as spectacular. "Several anglers reported they caught 70, 80, or more salmon in a week," reports Jim Chapralis. "As the season progressed, catches dwindled somewhat, but fishermen still were taking 20 to 30 salmon in a week."

AMERICAN GRAYLING

The American grayling is ice cream and cake for the dry-fly fisherman. Few fish take flies more readily, but that doesn't mean they are pushovers. Grayling, like

American grayling—often called "sailfish of the North"—is one of the exotic species available to fly fishermen in the far North.

trout, feed very heavily on natural insects, especially in floating form, but they also hit nymphs readily. Grayling are in the clearest, cleanest water, though, so casts and presentations must be proper.

Before excessive logging and other environmental changes we had grayling in Michigan rivers, and also in Minnesota waters, but those species have long disappeared, and attempts to reintroduce the fish have failed. Our grayling now are found in the better far western rivers (the upper Big Hole River, for one), and the clean, high lakes. There is one lake in Montana, up in the mountains over Melrose, called Agnes

Lake, that has *too many* grayling. They are stunted, but if all you want is to add grayling to your list of fly-caught fish, that's the place to go. With small dry flies, casting from the banks, it's possible there to land fifty 8- to 10-inch American grayling in an afternoon.

One of the first things we hear about American grayling is that they smell strongly of wild thyme. That may be, but if so there's something wrong with my olfactory glands, because I've sniffed grayling at assorted spots from northern Wyoming to Saskatchewan, and have never detected any odor other than a fishy one. Friends who also sniffed agreed—no thyme.

Regardless of what grayling smell like, they surely go for flies. On the Blackbirch River (sometimes identified as the Clearwater) in far northern Saskatchewan, I have seen pods of grayling holding on bottom near strong currents in 15 feet of clear water. Yet they would come to the surface for a size 16 Black Gnat dry fly. That is most interesting fishing. There rides your little Black Gnat, bobbing gently around in the surface swirls, and then, in a moment, lifting from the bottom comes a purplish-black shape—nearly 20 inches long—which curves in a circular sweep beneath your fly, then sucks it in with an almost inaudible *slup*.

The fact that we can so often see a grayling before it strikes the fly is cause for many anglers to miss hooking grayling in streams. In current a grayling frequently will rise to the fly, let it pass him, then follow it 5 or 10 feet downstream before taking. I've stood by fishermen many times and watched as they put out a dry fly, had a grayling rise to it, then—as the fly swept on past the fish 3 feet or so—they'd pick the fly up for another cast, believing the grayling had ignored the first float. Actually in such cases if the fly had been left on the water, the grayling very likely would have performed true to character, tailed the fly, and sucked it down.

American grayling are slow, studied, deliberate takers. They like to move in close, coast along with the drifting fly, take a long hard look, and then take. Quite a few fishermen will report that the grayling has a tender mouth because they will strike to set the hook the instant they see the rise and splash at the fly; when the fly comes sailing back and they have "felt" the fish, they immediately assume they simply tore the hook out of the grayling's mouth. Not so. A grayling actually has a rubbery, tough, suckerlike mouth. Much of the time it is difficult to remove the small barbs from their lips. So what happens when our angler thinks he has torn the fly out of a grayling's mouth is that he struck too soon, and the hook never was far enough inside the fish's mouth to grab a proper hold.

The way to hook grayling on dry flies with consistency is to let the fish have it for a moment, then simply lift the rod tip and tighten up, and he'll be there.

Some of the most interesting grayling fishing is in the northern lakes, particularly in the twilight hours when the fish rise to hatching insects. You cast to actual rises, and it can be exciting to sit in a boat and see a 10-foot-wide swirl perhaps 60 feet away, as a nice grayling takes a natural. You get your fly out there, take slack out of the line, watch the little black fly sitting nicely motionless on the surface; then the water opens nearby and out comes a fish's

head, then it disappears (with the fly) to be followed by a broad, fanlike dorsal fin; and when *it* disappears, the deeply forked tail shows and then it, too, is gone. You tighten up, and now feel the strength of the fish, which makes a surface run, splashes wildly, then sounds, then circles, then comes out in a half-leap, its sweeping, sail-like dorsal fin showing clearly.

At Great Bear Lake, in the Northwest Territories on the edge of the Arctic Circle, is some of the finest dry-fly lake fishing for grayling to be found anywhere. Where Bear River flows out of the lake, the outgoing current builds up like a strong ebbing tide perhaps 100 yards from the rocks where the river proper starts to form. Grayling fill the area by the thousands. At any time you can beach the boat, walk along the gravelly bank, and look out to see fifty or more rings as grayling after grayling come to the top. We cast from shore there, dropping our flies just upcurrent from the swirls, rings, and soft splashes made by the actively feeding fish. At Great Bear's outlet, a capable fly fisherman normally can take a few dozen grayling, good-size ones to 3 pounds or a bit more, in a couple of hours of pleasant casting.

As is to be expected, the good grayling fishing on this continent is out in the boondocks—chiefly at wilderness fly-in camps in Alaska, Manitoba, Saskatchewan, Alberta, and the Northwest Territories; and there's some grayling fishing in British Columbia.

The Fond-du-Lac River, near Stony Rapids, Saskatchewan, has some extraordinary grayling fishing. The Fond-du-Lac is big, heavy, powerful water, and it is fished from edge rocks or an anchored boat. On one Fond-du-Lac visit I was in an aluminum skiff with Walt Schaeffer, who was running Camp Grayling on nearby Black Lake. We anchored near some large boulders where the river rolled down in deep, curling eddies. "There are always grayling here," Schaeffer announced. With that he curled up on a boat seat and soon was snoring.

I floated several dry flies around the boulders and along the natural current threads where feeding fish would search for floating insects. I never had a rise, and after several casts I looked down and started searching bottom. Over light gravel, about 12 feet under the boat, I saw the dark, shadowy forms of several grayling. They were holding in pocket water at the edge of strong current, just resting, turning, swinging this way and that, circling, now and then a fish moving out into the main flow, then returning. I replaced the dry fly with a weighted size 10 Leadwing Coachman Nymph. From the stern I rolled a cast upcurrent, with the line and rod tip just passing Schaeffer's head, which rested on a boat cushion by the gunwale. Down went the fly, and the fly line straightened and came swaying down with the current as I recovered all slack by stripping line in quickly with my left hand. The line and nymph, now down deep, came swinging in right by the boat. I could see all those grayling beneath us suddenly darting around excitedly, then there came that tell-tale pause in the fly line's float. I struck, and had a 3-pound grayling. I killed that grayling and eleven others, because our mission was to get a dozen grayling for dinner and there were seven guests in camp. I'd take a grayling from under our boat on just about every other drift of the nymph,

and drop it flopping to the bottom of the metal boat, up near Schaeffer, but he never stirred through all the action.

The usual flies, both in patterns and sizes, that work for trout will catch American grayling. The grayling normally is not choosy, although there are times when you surely will catch many dozens more using the right fly than if using the wrong one. Small flies seem to get the most attention from grayling—sizes 14, 16, and 18 in dries, and 10, 12, and 14 in nymphs. Wet flies will get grayling, as will streamers in small sizes (8).

STEELHEAD

The steelhead trout is chiefly a West Coast resident, although we have rivers in the Midwest containing piles of "steelhead." I'm a little perplexed over what truly is, and what truly is not, a steelhead. Some of my confusion is based on the fact that our fishery biologists periodically change their prior opinions of certain fish species, or strains.

At one time by definition a steelhead was a rainbow trout that migrated from the sea up inland rivers to spawn (specifically along the northern Pacific coast; there are no steelhead on the Atlantic side). But we had rainbows, and still do, leaving Lake Michigan and Lake Superior, that mounted the feeder rivers to spawn, and the boys called them steelhead. That had to be a misnomer, however, since the fish did not run inland from salt water. To make that situation more complex, consider that on several occasions the Michigan Department of Natural Resources brought true steelhead young from Oregon and Washington

Bob McNally and guide with an 18-pound steelhead fresh in from the sea on British Columbia's Babine River. This steelhead and all others taken on the trip were released.

and planted them in the Great Lakes. Those were genuine steelhead to begin with, and apparently they prospered and at spawning time left the big lakes for the rivers to spawn. Were they not steelhead because they came inland from fresh water instead of salt? Does a Pacific Ocean steelhead become a mere rainbow if immersed in Lake Michigan?

I suppose some of the confusion over what's a steelhead and what is not has been cleared up with the current definition of a steelhead being, simply, a migratory rainbow. In other words, the anadromous Pacific fish, *migrating inland* to spawn, assuredly are steelhead, and the Great Lakes rainbow, *migrating inland* to spawn, also is a steelhead. The species do look alike, with bright, pink cheeks and sidebars, and both are exquisite gamefish on a fly rod.

I've been lucky enough on a few occasions to hook steelhead in Lake Michigan on a fly, casting blind (no visible fish), and have them jump 6 to 8 feet straight up into the air. A scene like that, on the flat, open expanse of a huge inland lake, is enough to give one goose bumps.

Steelhead fresh in from the sea are, however, much stronger and much faster, and are better-leaping fish than the inland variety. Sea fish always are the strongest, with the greatest endurance.

There are countless excellent steelhead streams in the Midwest, with some of the best being the Big Huron River, which flows into Lake Superior on the upper peninsula of Michigan; Betsie River; Big and Little Manistee; Pere Marquette; and the St. Joseph. The St. Joseph River must have the most civilized steelhead fishing anywhere in the world. It flows into Lake

Michigan at the towns of St. Joseph-Benton Harbor, and is within a day's driving distance or much less of nearly thirty million people. It is 2½ hours from Chicago, and produces many steelhead bettering 20 pounds.

Much of the St. Joe, however, is not the kind of water serious fly fishermen prefer, and its structure is not particularly conducive to really profitable fly fishing. The river often is crowded with flatfish trollers and spawn-sack fishermen, and frequently is high and muddy. But as a result of extensive stocking programs started in the sixties and continued into the nineties, the St. Joseph River on a continental basis just might contain more steelhead than any other river. While there are many steelhead streams I much prefer to fish, annually we manage to get several steelies out of the St. Joe on flies, exceeding 10 pounds, with the odd fish to 15 or better.

Broadly speaking, the most pleasant steelhead fly fishing on the Pacific streams is in the fall, though the most productive, fishwise, is probably in the winter. There are, however, steelhead in all the major rivers all year long. As with Atlantic salmon, the river conditions and weather generally are important to success. A river high and roiled by rains may be full of fish, but the fly-rodder's chances of doing very well under such conditions are slim. I once spent a week at a steelhead camp on the Babine River in British Columbia, with the river high and discolored. There were twenty fly fishermen in camp, all well experienced, but only five fish taken.

The feeling among most anglers is that the steelhead spends most of his time resting his belly on bottom, so sinking lines are considered a must, along with weighted flies or heavy-hooked flies that will go down and stay down. It was the steelhead clan, in fact, who developed the shooting-head lines and much of our deep fly-fishing techniques. The veteran steelheader knows better than anyone how to scrape a fly over the gravel.

Because steelhead so often react best to a deep-sunk fly, the slightly up-and-across cast is preferred by a lot of veteran steelheaders. This permits the current to wash the fly deep, as the angler continually mends his line, and by the time the fly is at a forty-five-degree angle down-and-across stream, the fly ought to be bumping its nose on bottom when the angler begins a slow, darting retrieve.

Other typical methods of presenting a fly to steelhead are the straight-across-stream cast, then mending line and fishing out the cast much as described in fishing out the up-and-across cast. Yet another way to put flies to steelhead is on a down-and-across stream cast, either mending and/or throwing slack into the line to make the fly sink and slow its presentation, or letting the line swing naturally with the current, bowing and tightening and sweeping the fly across likely steelhead lies.

But while it has been traditional and certainly effective to work flies deep-down for steelhead, some western fishermen in recent seasons have devised some interesting methods that take steelhead almost on the surface.

One day in fall, 1977, guide Ed Curnow hooked sixteen steelhead in the Clearwater River, running 10 to 21 pounds, while fishing a Muddler Minnow tied on with a Portland Creek Hitch and used with a floating line.

"Four of those fish actually came to the surface to take the Muddler," Ed told me, "and believe me it is a fantastic way to take steelhead. Fishing this way I've had steelhead come roaring in from 20 to 30 feet to the fly—pushing up wakes and looking like alligators rushing a coot."

The system of skimming a Muddler for steelhead doesn't work on all rivers, Curnow advises. It's best on rivers having "active summer-run fish," such as Washington's Kalama and Cowlitz rivers, and other tributaries of the upper Columbia River.

Steelhead come into a river in waves, much like Atlantic salmon, so being there at the right time is a big part of the game. And they select certain lies, much as salmon do, so knowing the best runs and holds on a steelhead river can be more important than the ability to cast skillfully and work a fly.

The fly-rodder who has never done any West Coast steelhead fishing is certainly wise to contact a good, reputable guide; and also to go into a well-recommended camp or make previous contact with local expert fishermen, local outdoor writers, conservation officers, or others who can perhaps accompany him for some actual fishing. If you go into a commercial camp, try to learn all you can about the fishing there before putting down hard cash on a reservation.

At one British Columbia river I spent a week in a camp at a cost of $1,000, and had pretty miserable fishing. There are two camps on the river. Each morning powerboats from each of the camps race upriver and down, depositing anglers at the best pools. It's a constant race between guides from either camp to get their anglers on the best spots first. Once a fisherman is deposited on a special pool he has to fish it all day, unless he changes to another spot with a fisherman from his own camp; but that is seldom done. If his camp boat picks him up and the angler returns to camp or goes to another pool, guides from the opposing camp usually rush one of their anglers in—and the pool is locked up for the day. At $1,000 a week, that isn't my brand of fishing.

ARCTIC CHAR

Like the grayling, the Arctic char is a fish many fly anglers seldom if ever encounter. The char is even more remotely located than the grayling, and much more costly to pursue. The Arctic char, though, is one of the most gorgeous fish the fly fisherman may take, in spawning colors far more brilliant than the most handsome brook trout, and they grow to great sizes, being taken on-fly well over 20 pounds.

There are landlocked char, but with the camps now available for Arctic-char fishing the one most likely taken will be the sea-run char, the larger of the two. Arctic char apparently are scattered all over the top of the world, but for most anglers the opportunities to catch char coincide with trips to the camps now operating on Great Bear Lake, in Canada's Northwest Territories. These camps specialize in fishing for Great Bear's giant lake trout, but they also offer fly-out side trips some 200 miles farther north to the Coppermine and Tree rivers, which flow into Coronation Gulf on the

Author with an 18-pound Arctic char from the Northwest Territories' Tree River.

ing out of Great Bear. You put your confidence in the bush pilot, who himself has no intentions of risking being forced down or stranded somewhere in Eskimo land. Anyway, at least one Great Bear fishing camp has established an "out" camp on the Coppermine, and perhaps by the time this is in print there will be other special char outposts.

Char that are fresh in from the sea are silvery, with whitish spots and greenish backs. Those that have been in the river for a time, however, look more like the colorful brook trout, complete to the black-edged white pectoral, pelvic, and anal fins. A mature char in fresh water for a time is a crimson fish of blinding colors. When a 10- or 12-pound male Arctic char leaps clear of the stream and rolls in the air, his colors flashing against the barren, brown, treeless tundra, the absurdity of the contrast is so great the angler wonders if it is not all a dream.

On my initial visit to the Coppermine River we were met at the river mouth by a party of Eskimos (it was August and they all had colds), who ferried us in whale boats to pools far upriver. All the other fishermen were equipped with heavy bait-casting gear, and several had surf-type spinning tackle—the same equipment they'd been using for lake trolling back at Great Bear. They scattered around the lower pools, began banging out hand-size spoons, and soon were beaching Arctic char. It was one of the most incongruous and *revolting* angling scenes I ever witnessed.

With their powerful sea tackle and 25- and 30-pound-test lines they'd hook a char and instantly have it flopping at their feet. The beauty of the fish struck me intensely:

lower part of the Arctic Ocean. Weather always is a determining factor in whether or not one gets to fly from Great Bear to the Coppermine or the Tree, or, if once there, one gets to fly out on schedule. This is wild, barren country, and it is adventure not exactly set up for the kiddies. Being forced down by fog or snow in a float plane en route from Great Bear to one of the char rivers could be serious, and being stranded by weather for any length of time on one of the rivers also could be no picnic. But pilot skill, proper equipment, and weather reports make it worth anyone's while to take a crack at the char rivers fly-

Crimson, orange, black, white, blue, vermilion, yellow, green, and crimson spots circled in white. They were the most brilliant fish, excluding tropical varieties, I'd ever seen. Yet, instead of admiring a landed char, one after another of the fishermen would simply boot a hooked fish up onto the bank, where it would flop its life out in the mud. One instant a char was on the bank all orange and gold, then the next moment it was a black, mud-coated thing a mother carp wouldn't claim.

I left the lower pools to the spin fishermen and walked away from the river, making a wide sweep to cut back in again far upstream. I had no idea whether there were char in this area or not, but I had no intention of hanging around the lower pools and witnessing further char carnage. *The guys down there had no appreciation whatever for the quality fish they were banking.*

When I was about half a mile upriver I went down to a pool, looked it over, and started casting at the top. I kept looking for signs of fish but saw none. Using a Magnum red-yellow streamer on a 1/0 hook, I worked slowly downstream, casting over and across, bringing the fly back in short, 6-inch pulls. On about my sixth cast I saw a fish flash deep under the fly. Another half-dozen or so casts and another fish rolled beneath the fly. The water was around 6 feet deep and I was using a floating No. 9 line, so my fly was running at about 2 feet. When I saw a third char switch ends deep under the fly I stripped in quickly and changed to a full fast-sinking line. I tied on the same streamer and went back to the top of the pool. This time I took three fish, one about 8 pounds,

another around 10, and the best a bright male I guessed at 18.

In my estimation Arctic char are not the world's greatest gamefish, at least not when they've been in fresh water for very long and are far inland. But they're strong, make excellent runs in good current, and can execute some beautiful leaps. They are much like giant brook trout, and there's not much wrong with that.

WHITEFISH

The whitefish, like the American grayling, is one of the fly-takingest fish I know. Yet many fly fishermen will be on a lake or river and have whitefish popping up all around them, ignoring the whitefish while they try for some other species—brook trout, for example, or northern pike—even though they may not be doing well with the fish they're trying for. It seems a lot of fly fishermen just aren't very aware of whitefish, and of the great sport and great eating they can provide.

There are several species and subspecies of whitefish in the northern United States, Canada, and elsewhere in northern latitudes, but only two are of any importance to the angler: the lake or common whitefish, and the mountain whitefish, also called the Rocky Mountain whitefish. In the western states a lot of fishermen make trips deliberately to catch mountain whitefish in the dead of winter, when snow is banked high along the frozen edges of the rivers. They use fly rods, but most fish real nymphs as bait. They want the whitefish in winter because they claim the flesh is firmer and sweeter. I haven't eaten mountain whitefish that were caught in winter, but

I've eaten many taken in summer, and I enjoy them poached or fried every bit as much as trout. Poached on the river bank by a cook who knows what he is about (such as the late A. J. McClane), and served with a horseradish sauce, whitefish are a gourmet's delight.

Mountain and lake whitefish are pretty much lookalikes. The mountain whitefish has a rounder body than the lake, and doesn't grow as large. I've seen mountain whitefish of almost 6 pounds, but that is a monster, with the great majority well under 2 pounds. Lake whitefish are commonly 3 to 4 pounds and will go to 6 to 8 pounds frequently in some waters, and lake whitefish of 20 pounds have been reported.

The whitefish looks a lot like a sucker with a bonefish's head, and it's greenish-dark on the back, fading to a lighter brown, then ivory, then white on the belly. The overall shape, particularly in the mountain whitefish, is not unlike a bonefish's.

The mountain whitefish, while taking flies readily, sometimes can be as choosy as the most selective brown trout, and, even when rising to your fly, can be very difficult to hook consistently, rise for rise.

The mountain whitefish has a tiny, round, rubbery mouth, and very small flies are needed, from about size 14 to 20 in dries, and in nymphs it's best to go no larger than size 10. Methods of fishing for mountain whitefish in streams are cousin to trout techniques, except that in fishing dry flies you delay your strike on the rise, just lifting the rod firmly but deliberately. Mountain whitefish can be very leader-shy, and at times long and fine—as in trout fishing—is the only way to attract rises.

McNally calls the lake or common whitefish a fly fisherman's delight because they take flies so readily, especially dry flies.

The common or lake whitefish is a great sportfish, and happily very abundant in many northern lakes, especially Canadian lakes and some rivers. The lake whitefish is a deepwater fish as a rule, but in the evenings, or on cloudy days, they will roam close to the surface snatching up floating flies.

Dry-fly fishing for rising lake whitefish is the surest way of taking them, but on many Canadian lakes I've caught dozens of whitefish on weighted nymphs, fished 8 to 10 feet down, when no whitefish were rising. Even on bright days and when there are no hatches, sometimes the fish will be no deeper than that—hanging around rocky points, rocky islands, and reefs. If you work such areas with weighted nymphs, or small streamers on a sinking line, you often can locate whitefish that are willing to hit even though there is no sign of whitefish activity anywhere on the lake.

It is almost routine for rising whitefish to show at dusk on many Canadian lakes, places such as Reindeer, Cree, Athabaska, Lac La Ronge, Gods Lake, Lake Winnipeg, Lake of the Woods, Eagle Lake, and many more. At the typical Canadian fly-in wilderness fishing camp, in the period between the start of the cocktail hour and the end of dinner, some great fly fishing has been missed out on the lake.

Lake whitefish are school fish, and when you see one rise you can bet there are dozens more around. They come up in soft, head-to-tail rises. The fish's whole head will come out of water as he pushes up to take a floating fly with his underslung mouth. Then the back and dorsal fins show, and finally the tail.

Casting is important, in that you want to put the fly in the path of the fish; and since we're normally fishing a calm, clear lake, we can't lay the fly line too close to the fish. The best system is to determine the line a cruising whitefish is taking by noting the pattern in a series of two or three rises, then casting some 10 to 15 feet ahead of the last rise, on the fish's course. It's necessary to hold very steady after delivering a cast, not lifting or pulling the line, and to be patient enough to wait long moments for the oncoming whitefish to note the floating fly and take. It's a nerve-wracking business, and many anxious fishermen after waiting for a riser to reach their fly strike too hard and fast, out of

excitement, and either snap the fly away from the fish or break the leader tip.

SHAD

Both the American (white) shad and hickory shad have been likened by addicted fly fishermen to the bonefish, for their speedy though short runs (the shad, that is), and to the tarpon, for their leaping ability. Here is a truly fine gamefish for the fly angler, since it is taken in rivers or shallow streams. (White shad seldom are caught in small feeder streams, usually preferring the deeper water and stronger currents of the larger rivers. Hickory shad will ascend the shallow tributary streams.)

The trouble with shad is that they are available only in the spring, when, since they are anadromous fish, they come inland from the sea to spawn. "Spring," however, varies according to the area, since on the Atlantic side, for example, we have shad from the St. Johns River in Florida north along the coast to the Bay of Fundy. In the St. Johns the run is "on" in February, while in Maryland it is underway in April, and in Connecticut June is the time. Hickory shad, on the Atlantic coast where they occur along with American shad, always precede the American shad on spawning runs.

American shad were introduced from the East Coast to the West Coast in the late 1800s, and they've taken hold and give some great fishing over a wide stretch of the Pacific shore. Why hickory shad have not been introduced there is an interesting question. At any rate, hickories are found only on the Atlantic side.

In many ways the hickory is the better fly-rod fish, primarily because they are in very shallow streams, while the American is in heavy water. In Maryland, for instance, hickory shad and American shad mount the Susquehanna River, at the head of Chesapeake Bay. But while the American stays in the deep, dangerous, brawling Susque-

hanna proper, where most of the fishing is done from shore or boat, the hickory invades the shallow feeder streams—Octoraro and Deer creeks, where wading is easy. In streams such as Octoraro and Deer creeks, fly fishing for hickory shad approaches, in style and method, fly fishing for Atlantic salmon. In fact, anglers in the area refer to the hickory as the "poor man's salmon."

Shad are school fish, and like steelhead use the same areas of a stream or river season to season, depending upon water levels. A knowledgeable hickory fisherman will move from one lie to another, skipping a great deal of water in between, knowing from experience that a depression on the far side of one pool always has fish—if they are in the stream—while another long, good-looking pool never holds fish.

In the smaller streams, if they are running clear, which normally isn't the case in spring, you can spot shad schools. The fish are bright silver, looking like miniature tarpon, and may be seen as dark shadows over the bottom or as a flash of mirror brilliance as a fish turns suddenly and its chromed side catches and reflects the sun.

Again like steelhead, and to some extent Atlantic salmon, shad tend to hug bottom. In the days when I fished the East Coast shad streams frequently, sinking fly-lines were not available, and we used weighted flies or fished flies with a single BB-size lead split-shot sinker. Generally, shad will not rise to a fly. It has to be presented to them at their level, or very close, and most likely the fish take out of annoyance more than anything else.

Casting across and downstream, trying to make the fly have its "fish sweep" in the

Angler shows a hickory shad on Maryland's Deer Creek, a Susquehanna River tributary. Shad runs on the East Coast have diminished greatly, but authorities are working to restore the annual springtime migrations.

exact area it is believed shad are holding without imparting any other motion to the fly, is the standard technique among the experts. An attempt is made to have the fly presented to the shad broadside, and then to swing across in front of the fish, but as slowly as possible.

Shad flies are of special design. There are certain patterns that have long been proven, such as the so-called Connecticut River Shad Fly, which has silver tinsel over the hook shank and a short, upright "wing" of clipped red impala. That fly, and many other shad flies, is fished with a single red bead slipped onto the leader before the fly is tied on. The bead settles down against the hook eye, and apparently adds to the attraction of the fly.

Shad, both the hickory and the American but perhaps more so the smaller hickory, are superior little gamefish. A hickory shad seldom exceeds 3 pounds, more often is 2 pounds or under, but when hooked will go 2 feet out of the water a half-dozen times or so. The American shad, averaging 4 to 6 pounds, is in heavier water and is a larger and stronger fish anyway, and will jump and run and bore, and give any fly angler considerable pleasure.

I grew up fishing for shad on Chesapeake estuaries such as the Susquehanna River, Potomac, Patuxent, Wicomico, Northeast, Choptank, and other rivers. Virginia rivers, like the Chickahominy, which is a Chesapeake feeder, and others, had excellent shad spawning runs. So did Delaware rivers feeding Delaware Bay.

Then suddenly it all ended.

Due primarily to pollution and commercial overfishing, shad runs in the Chesapeake drainage and elsewhere along the East Coast all but disappeared. From the late 1800s to the mid-1900s white shad were the Chesapeake's top commercial fish, but by 1980 so few white shad returned to spawn in the Chesapeake that Maryland declared a moratorium on them. At this writing possession of shad in Maryland is illegal.

Another factor that affected East Coast shad runs was damming. Dams across Maryland's major shad spawning rivers, such as the Susquehanna, resulted in the loss of hundreds of miles of spawning and nursery habitat over the years. On the Susquehanna alone, with four dams, experts claim more than 400 miles of shad spawning areas were lost.

Maryland has undertaken an aggressive campaign to restore the American shad, and it appears to be paying off. Two new $12,000,000 fish lifts have been installed on Maryland's Conowingo Dam on the Susquehanna River—which should have been done thirty years ago. The lifts make it possible to capture spawning shad, which then are transported upriver in tank trucks so the fish are able to spawn as far north as Binghamton, New York. These extraordinary lifts, plus hatchery restoration and Maryland's closed season on shad fishing, have resulted in a continuing recovery.

LAKE TROUT

Lake trout are not often "in range" of the fly fisherman, but when they are shallow they can be caught readily on flies. The laker is a deepwater fish of the north, and in most lakes seldom is in water under 25 to 30 feet deep.

Lead-core line is one way to go after lake trout, and a fast-sinking shooting head is another. But there are lakes in northern Canada where trout are shallow right through the summer, even on the brightest days. The water is so cold at some of the far-north lakes and rivers that lake trout often can be taken in water only 5 feet deep.

Lake trout are no great shakes in the fighting department, and never jump. But they are the largest strictly freshwater fish the angler has real opportunity to catch (muskies are scarce and difficult), and a laker of 6 to 8 pounds will put a pretty good bend in a fly rod. A lake trout in the 10-pound class is a lot of fun, and when you get up to the 15- to 20-pound category you have a fish you will have to play for a while, and one that is going to get well into your backing.

One summer my son Bob and I went to an outpost camp Tom Ruminski built on the Wolverine River in northern Manitoba. The shoreline currents in the Wolverine are lined with American grayling that seem to be rising all the time, but farther out, in the deeper runs (6 to 8 feet), there are lake trout weighing up to 30 pounds, with most weighing 10 to 15. Using streamer flies on floating lines (we had no sinking types with us), we'd cast up and across current and let the line wash deep. When the fly was below us we'd strip it back in 6-inch pulls, and fishing that way we took dozens of Wolverine trout. With the strong river current, even the 10-pound fish gave good action, running well downstream and getting into our backing line. Bob took one lake trout out of the Wolverine that weighed 24 pounds. We had to follow the fish in the boat downriver for half a mile, and it took Bob thirty-eight minutes to wear him down.

Without current going for them, lake trout usually make a short run when hooked and then sound. Away down there they roll and turn, and you'll see the belly of a hooked lake trout as much as his back. Lots of times they'll roll up in your leader, and you'll bring a fish in that has literally tied itself up. For this reason, and because lakers have small but sharp teeth, heavy leaders are called for. When into big lake trout I go no lighter than 15 pounds in the tippet, and then use a shock section of 20- to 30-pound hard nylon.

Lake trout will hit a variety of streamer flies, either feather-wing or bucktail types. Extra-large flies are not needed, because a 30-pound laker in clear water will see and come for a 3-inch-long fly just as quickly as he will to a much larger streamer.

Streamers should be fished slowly for lake trout. Like northern pike, lakers won't go chasing after a fast-moving fly. Strip your streamer along in 6-inch pulls, occasionally halting the retrieve and allowing the fly to settle a bit, then start it up again. A lot of strikes will come right then. Lake trout will follow a fly some distance at times before deciding to hit, so don't pick up the fly too soon, and always look to see if there's a trailing fish before lifting the streamer out for another cast.

Lake trout in the northern lakes are not particularly shy. Sometimes they'll strike right at the boat, or at your feet.

Once I went to Mitchell Lake, Manitoba, on assignment for an outdoor magazine to get a story on fly fishing for lake trout. Earl Kennedy, a fine photographer in Winnipeg, had the photo assignment.

We'd gone ashore for lunch, and while the Indians were filleting walleyes I walked to the point and started casting with a 3-inch-long red-yellow Phillips Bead-Head fly. After a few casts a lake trout of about 6 pounds showed behind the fly. I stripped it along and the trout followed, not a foot behind the colorful fly. I had the fish right at my feet, and we practically stared each other in the eye. Whenever the trout got too close to the streamer I'd pull it away. The laker would stay right there, swimming this way and that, as though he was wondering what had happened to the fly. I called for Earl to come with his cameras. When Earl was all set I put the fly out again, and once again had the lake trout trailing right behind the fly. I toyed with that trout for fifteen minutes, as Earl shot a great series of photos of a lake trout, mouth open wide, closing in on a streamer fly.

MUSKIES

A long time ago (1968, in fact) I wrote the following lead in a story for *Outdoor Life*:

"Take one weedy bay in a Canadian lake, a sunny day in June, a fly rod and some magnum-size streamer flies, add a couple of needle-nosed characters named *Esox masquinongy*, and you have the ingredients for a picnic with muskies."

Today, nearly twenty-five years later, I wouldn't change a word in that lead.

If muskie fishing is something special, then fly fishing for muskies must be the pinnacle of the angling art. Imagine a fisherman trying to land a muskie that may weigh 10, 20, 30, 40, or more pounds with a rod weighing a mere 3 to 5 ounces and measuring a willowy 8 to 9 feet. The cast-

Most fly fishermen feel muskies are not practical fly fishing targets, but ones like this will chew up fly-rod bugs and streamers.

ing rods used by most muskie fishermen weigh a pound or more, and have stiff, powerful actions. Most muskie plug casters use line testing no less than 20 pounds, and many use lines of 30- or 35-pound test. But the weakest section of the serious fly-rodder's leader won't test more than 12 pounds.

Small wonder that catching muskies on a fly rod is almost unheard of. There are several reasons for this. For one thing, muskies are very difficult for most fishermen to catch by *any* method. And compared to other species of fish muskies are anything but plentiful. If memory serves, a Wisconsin study concluded that four acres of "good" water is required to support one adult muskie. Another reason so few muskies are taken on fly gear is that not many fishermen ever try with fly tackle. Finally, because muskies usually are in deep water (contrary to what most fishermen believe), they often are at depths impractical for fly fishing.

Most fishermen who have not experienced fly fishing for muskies feel it cannot be done, or at best that it is an impractical method for muskies. Some fishermen even believe a large muskie cannot be whipped on a fly rod.

Nothing could be farther from the truth.

Not only is it possible to catch muskies on flies, bugs, and fly rods, using strictly standard gear, but it is eminently practical. If fly fishermen take giant tarpon and billfish such as sailfish and marlin on standard fly tackle, why in heaven's name is fly fishing for muskies impractical?

Despite all the problems inherent in muskie fishing, they *can be* taken by fly fishing. In some ways, a muskie in shallow water can be a set-up for a skilled and knowledgeable fly fisherman. The chief reason is that the fisherman can offer a muskie flies and bugs the fish probably has never seen before.

A fly angler's lures fall gently and softly, with none of the fish-scaring *pluuuuuukk* that comes when the usual oversized muskie bait hits the water.

For some reason muskies completely lose their cool when suddenly confronted with a twitching, darting, scooting streamer fly. A large, properly designed streamer fly is extremely lifelike in the water, and a muskie lying in shallow water is more likely to charge a streamer fly, in my opinion, than any other lure.

I think a streamer fly 5 to 7 inches long is deadlier on muskies than any surface or underwater plug, or any spoon—including that famous red-and-white striped spoon, the Eppinger Dardevel.

Big streamer flies have an up-and-down movement in the water, and streamers with webby saddle-hackle winging "breathe" in the water—waving and pulsating to excite muskies like nothing else.

Remember, however, that muskies, like pike, hit best when flies or bugs are fished slowly. Streamers with saddle-hackle winging can be fished ultraslowly. They have good action even when merely sinking in the water.

Although in my estimation fly-rod bugs run second best to streamers in the muskie-catching department, don't ignore bugs. The first muskie I ever had on a fly rod went after a yellow popping bug, with which I was trying to get some largemouth bass.

Outdoor writer Buck Rogers and I were on Long Lake, near Phillips, Wisconsin. Buck was in the stern of the boat using bait-casting tackle. I was bugging from the bow with an 8-foot "bass-action" rod. I had cast into a pocket in some lily pads, allowed the bug to rest motionless for a moment, then gave it a good pop. *Blaaammm!* Water sprayed for yards when the muskie hit. I reared back to set the hook four or five times . . . hard. Then, convinced the fish was hooked, I settled back to play him. He jumped a couple of times, then was at the boat, apparently played out. It wasn't a big muskie, maybe 8 to 10 pounds.

Long Lake water is gin-clear, and Buck and I could see the muskie lying "dead" 10 feet down to one side of the boat. I put pressure on to bring the fish up. I'll never forget what I saw next. The muskie opened his mouth, out floated the yellow bug, and while the muskie righted himself and sank out of sight, the yellow popper floated slowly to the surface.

One of our finest muskie fishermen is Len Hartman, a part-time guide and full-time muskie fisherman from Ogdensburg, New York, on the St. Lawrence River. The St. Lawrence produced Arthur Lawton's world-record muskie, which weighed 69 pounds, 15 ounces. (In 1961, Hartman got a St. Lawrence muskie two pounds smaller).

"A good-size muskie on any tackle is exciting," said Hartman, "but I'll never forget one I took on a fly rod. My wife Betty and I were slowly cruising St. Lawrence shallows when we spotted two muskies. The larger one was in mere inches of water. I cast, darted the fly across in front of him, and *wham,* the water flew. The muskie headed for deep water, jumped once, went down, then came up again, shaking furiously three feet in the air. That was something to see! Half an hour later we had him at the boat."

That fly-caught muskie weighed 31 pounds, 10 ounces. As far as I know, that's the largest muskie ever taken on a fly rod.

Preferred fly tackle for muskies is a 9-foot, heavy-action rod taking a WF-9 line, and a quality single-action reel. The leader should be no less than 9 feet, tapered down to 12 pounds. A 12-inch "shock" tippet of hard nylon testing 40 or 60 pounds should be used.

Many fishermen believe the teeth of muskies are too numerous and sharp not to fray through or cut a fly-fishing leader. Muskies do have large, sharp teeth, but they are pointed and rounded like a needle. A fly-fishing leader can't be cut by sliding around a muskie's canine teeth. What cuts or frays a leader when fishing for muskies—as when fishing for northern pike—are the fish's small teeth that coat the tongue and palate. When proper shock tippets are used very few muskies will cut through a leader.

When using poppers on muskies, don't use ordinary freshwater-type bass bugs; use large saltwater-type bugs made with large, strong hooks. If fishing streamers, use the largest you can find. Elephants like peanuts, but muskies like a mouthful—so feed them big flies. A good streamer for muskies should be no less than 3 inches long, and preferably 5 to 6.

For whatever reason, muskies often will be in one bay on a lake but not in another. As a rule they seem to prefer weed-filled slack-water bays with silt bottom. Muskies like to back into weeds, facing open, sunlit pockets which they watch patiently for passing forage fish or a swimming frog. While to the angler one bay may look as "fishy" as another, muskies might be thick in one and avoid a second. Only another muskie knows why.

Anyway, when next on muskie water, spurn the spoon and favor the fly.

LANDLOCKED SALMON

One of the greatest angling experiences of my lifetime came on the Rio Traful near Bariloche, Argentina.

The Traful River is about the most beautiful stream I've ever seen. It rolls out of Traful Lake, which is stiff with big brook trout and absolutely air-clear. You can count marble-size pebbles on the bottom in 15 feet of water. The river is so clear that when I waddled up to its bank in my chest-high waders and looked down at the water, I thought it was only about 2 feet deep; so I stepped in. *Kaplash!* Instantly I was standing in chin-deep water. My waders filled, of course, but fortunately I was right at the bank so it was easy to turn around and crawl out.

I can't recall the name of the owner of the *estancia* (ranch) whose section of the Traful I fished, but then-president Dwight Eisenhower had come in by helicopter two weeks previously, and with companions had fished hard.

"The fishing is very poor," my host reported, "The Eisenhower party caught no salmon. There hasn't been a salmon taken in almost a month. The river is just too clear."

The muskie, like the northern pike, is an excellent fly-rod fish. This is a 24-pounder taken on a magnum streamer from a northeast Wisconsin lake in late fall, when muskies are very active.

After drying out from my dunking, I stood on the shoulder of the Traful with my host, watching landlocks fanning in the current as clearly as we would watch fish in an aquarium.

As all fly-rodders know, under such conditions the first thing you think is "long and fine." So I tied a 9-foot leader tapered down to 7X on my line, and waded out a couple feet into casting position of a landlocked we could see readily about 50 feet out. I'd put a Muddler Minnow on, and dropped the fly 10 feet above the fish and that much past.

I twitched the fly past the salmon and he hit instantly, and just as quickly snapped the 7X tippet. My host gasped and said, "That's the first salmon I've seen hit in nearly a month."

"The fishermen probably haven't been fishing leaders fine enough," I said, "for this ultraclear water. But obviously a 7X tippet is far too light to hold these fish."

I dropped down to a 4X tippet, which was light enough to get strikes, and hooked and landed landlocks steadily. It was some of the finest fishing I ever enjoyed in my life. E. L. "Buck" Rogers, the outdoor writer mentioned earlier, witnessed it all. At the time he didn't fly fish, but he sure was wishing he did.

The landlocked salmon, which the Indians called *ouananiche* and fishery biologists call *Salmo salar Sebago,* is one of the most glamorous and hard-fighting fish native to this continent. One of the things endearing landlocked salmon to the angler is its enthusiasm for flies. Streamers, nymphs, wet flies, dry flies—put one in front of a landlocked and chances are excellent he'll take it.

While landlocked salmon will take a variety of flies, the ones most often used are streamers, especially streamers imitating smelt—the landlocks primary forage fish. As with other flies, there are countless variations in landlocked streamer flies, but in general they all have a common trait: they are tied long and thin to imitate a smelt's silhouette. Some popular landlocked patterns include the Gray Ghost,

Black Ghost, Nine-Three, Colonel Bates, Supervisor, Magog Smelt, Parmachene Belle, Mickey Finn, and Edson Tiger. There are some comparatively "new" patterns that have become very popular with landlocked fishermen. They include the Pearl Flash, Joe's Smelt, Flag's Smelt, and the Spectrum Smelt.

While landlocked salmon are incredible gamefish, they are not often in the big-fish category. The world's record landlocked (taken from Maine's Sebago Lake in 1907) weighed $22\frac{1}{2}$ pounds; however, the majority come in at about $2\frac{1}{2}$ pounds. Occasionally landlocks of 9 to 10 pounds are taken, and I've just learned that a fly fisherman on the Rio Traful hooked, landed, and *released* a landlocked whose weight was estimated at between 19 and 20 pounds. That is a giant landlocked—and he's still there.

The problem with landlocked salmon—and the reason so few fly fishermen have been into them—is limited distribution. Originally landlocks occurred in Canada's Maritime Provinces, much of New England, Lake Ontario, and a few lakes in New York's Adirondacks. New Hampshire has some landlocked fishing, but easily the most abundant salmon fishing is in Maine.

Some of Maine's best-known salmon waters include the West Branch of the Penobscot, Kennebago Stream, Sebago Lake, East Grand Lake, Chesuncook Lake, and Millinocket Lake, to list only a few.

If ever you get a chance to fish for Sir Ouananiche, don't pass it by.

To Fight Another Day

IN SOUTHWESTERN Montana, where his majesty the trout reigns supreme, it is fashionable to sport bumper stickers that read:

RELEASE TROUT, EAT CATFISH.

Good idea. For one thing, catfish are a hell of a lot better eating than trout; for another, trout are too valuable as gamefish to end their days in a fry pan. The same is true of most of our gamefish—including largemouth and smallmouth bass, pike, muskies, grayling, char, and countless salt-water fish such as sailfish, marlin, bone-fish, tarpon, kingfish . . . *ad infinitum.*

There's nothing wrong with an occa-sional trout fry, but the combined pressures of overfishing, acid rain, clearcutting, and medieval irrigation practices mean that, for responsible anglers, the days of stringers and freezers bulging with trout and other gamefish are a thing of the past. We must learn to conserve our gamefish stocks by carefully releasing those we catch.

Eating the catch has long been a part of fishing, and we need not deny ourselves. I have a friend in a northeastern state who says flat out that he'd rather eat a white perch than a trout any day. Many catfish, white and yellow perch, bluegills, crappies, and other panfish are better table fare than many higher-prestige gamefish anyway. More important, these appropriately named panfish inhabit many waters in such numbers that they exceed the environ-ment's ability to feed them, resulting in stunted growth and even fish kills. In many areas, keeping and eating *pan*fish is often the best way to improve *game*fishing. Per-haps this suggests a new bumper sticker:

RELEASE GAMEFISH, EAT PANFISH.

But if gamefish are to live to fight another day, they must be released prop-erly. I recently viewed a home video on fly fishing for tarpon in Venezuela in which American anglers were catching and releas-ing "baby" tarpon of 5 to 20 pounds. Fine—except the guides, with no instruc-tion from the anglers, were grabbing the fish in the gill rakers and then tossing them overboard. I doubt if any of those tarpon survived. Fish to be released *must be handled properly*.

First off, never play a hooked fish to exhaustion. Bring it to hand as soon as possible, without horsing the fish in and half breaking his back. A fish that is exhausted and released is very likely to succumb.

Fish without a mouthful of needlelike teeth, such as bass and small trout, are easy to release; all we need do is wet our hands (so as not to break the mucous membrane protecting their bodies), and slip them back into the water. A good way to hold them without squeezing the body is to grasp them by the lower jaw, with the thumb on the jaw and the index finger under the jaw, then push in and up and lift them from the water. A twist of the fly should release it if you're using barbless hooks; if not, you may need a pair of forceps to work the hook loose.

Larger fish with a mouthful of teeth require different tactics. Gaffs, of course, are very useful in landing many species of fish, especially saltwater species. But gaff them only in the lower jaw. Gaffing in the upper jaw can kill a fish.

A lot of fishermen, especially pike and muskie fishermen, prefer nets. If a fish is to be killed, netting is okay. Not so, however, if the fish is to be released. Netting can break the protective mucous membrane fish have on their scales, and a fungus infection may result that can injure or kill them.

For those who insist on netting, there's a right way to do it. Draw the played-out fish close to the boat; lower the bag and hoop of the net completely underwater; hold the net absolutely still so as not to frighten the fish into a last-minute dash; bring the fish to the net head-first, never tail-first; then simply lift the net upward, with the fish safely in the bag.

If a netted fish is to be released, keep the net and the netted fish in the water while carefully removing the hooks, then turn the bag of the net so the fish can swim out and away.

Learn and practice the technique of catch-and-release. Releasing valuable gamefish—to be fished for and caught again another day—will ensure a fishing future for generations to come.

- Play fish as rapidly as possible; do not play to total exhaustion.
- Keep fish in the water as much as possible when handling and removing the hook.
- Lifting fish from the water strains them. If you must, lift the fish horizontally with hands beneath the belly to support the weight. *Don't squeeze the fish or put your fingers in its gills.*
- Remove hooks gently; use barbless hooks (or bend down the barb).
- If the fish is deeply hooked, cut the line; don't pull the hook out.
- Never grab northern pike, muskies, or any other fish to be released by the eye sockets.
- Don't toss fish back into the water, despite what you've seen on Saturday-morning fishing shows.
- Release fish in quiet water.
- Release a fish only after it regains its equilibrium. If necessary, gently hold the fish facing upstream and move it slowly back and forth so water flows over the gills. A submerged fish is ready to be released when its gill plates are pumping smoothly and it's waggling its fins.

Index

WOULD YOU ENJOY. . .

- ☐ **An evening sharing fishing stories**
- ☐ **Speaking up for the concerns of anglers and conservationists. . .**
- ☐ **Conducting stream improvement projects. . .**
- ☐ **Contributing to public education through conservation workshops and seminars . . .**
- ☐ **Access to more and better fishing. . .**

Then join TROUT UNLIMITED today! TU means clean water and better fishing for everyone. As a TU member your will receive a subscription to TROUT magazine; membership in your local TU chapter, a personal membership card, decal, car rental and hotel discounts and MORE!
PLEASE ENTER MY ONE YEAR MEMBERSHIP IN TROUT UNLIMITED. I CARE ENOUGH ABOUT THE SPORT I LOVE TO JOIN TU.

NAME _____

ADDRESS _____

_____

CITY/STATE/ZIP _____

○ Family $30   ○ Sponsor $50   ○ Regular $25
○ Check enclosed.
○ Charge my: ○ MasterCard   ○ VISA

Acct # _____

Exp. Date _____ Signature _____

Mail to: TROUT UNLIMITED
800 Follin Lane, SE, Suite 250, Vienna, VA 22180-4959
Contributions over $12.00 are tax deductible.